A TRANSLATOR'S HANDBOOK

ON THE

BOOK OF AMOS

HELPS FOR TRANSLATORS SERIES

TECHNICAL HELPS:

Old Testament Quotations in the New Testament
Section Headings for the New Testament
Short Bible Reference System
New Testament Index
Orthography Studies
Bible Translations for Popular Use
*The Theory and Practice of Translation
Bible Index
Fauna and Flora of the Bible
Short Index to the Bible
Manuscript Preparation
Marginal Notes for the Old Testament
Marginal Notes for the New Testament

HANDBOOKS:

A Translator's Handbook on Ruth
A Translator's Handbook on the Book of Amos
A Translator's Handbook on the Book of Jonah
A Translator's Handbook on the Gospel of Mark
*A Translator's Handbook on the Gospel of Luke
A Translator's Handbook on the Gospel of John
A Translator's Handbook on the Acts of the Apostles
A Translator's Handbook on Paul's Letter to the Romans
A Translator's Handbook on Paul's Letter to the Galatians
A Translator's Handbook on Paul's Letter to the Philippians
A Translator's Handbook on Paul's Letters to the Colossians and to Philemon
A Translator's Handbook on Paul's Letters to the Thessalonians
A Translator's Handbook on the First Letter from Peter
A Translator's Handbook on the Letters of John

GUIDES:

A Translator's Guide to the Gospel of Matthew

HELPS FOR TRANSLATORS

A TRANSLATOR'S HANDBOOK

on

THE BOOK OF AMOS

by

JAN DE WAARD
and
WILLIAM A. SMALLEY

UNITED BIBLE SOCIETIES

PRINTED IN THE UNITED STATES OF AMERICA

Books in the series of Helps for Translators
that are marked with an asterisk (*) may
best be ordered from

United Bible Societies
D-7000 Stuttgart 1
Postfach 755
West Germany

All other books in the series may best be
ordered from

American Bible Society
1865 Broadway
New York, N.Y. 10023

ISBN 0-8267-0128-0

ABS-1980-1,500,2,500-CM-08577

PREFACE

A Translator's Handbook on Amos continues the process of experimentation and development to be found in some of the earlier handbooks of this series. There are, therefore, several important changes from previous handbooks to be found here as an attempt is made to find the best ways of helping translators with their task.

1. The use of the Revised Standard Version (representing to some degree the literal structures of the original Hebrew) and the Today's English Version (representing one kind of more meaningful dynamic equivalence translation into English) continues from the handbooks on Thessalonians and Galatians, but in an expanded form. In the present work the Revised Standard Version is not only printed alongside the Today's English Version at the beginning of each section to be discussed but is also referred to regularly in the discussion. Quotations from the Revised Standard Version are indicated by broken underlining, while those from the Today's English Version are shown by solid underlining. Quotations from other translations, included as examples of interpretations, problems, or possible solutions, are enclosed in "quotation marks," as are other suggestions for possible ways in which the translation might be worded.

2. Normally the translation provided by the Revised Standard Version is close enough in its structure to the Hebrew (that is, literal enough) to stand for the Hebrew for purposes of discussing translation problems. When it is not, additional indications of the Hebrew meaning are given in "double quotation marks" (in the Notes 'single quotation marks' are used). The discussion of translation problems is then based on the Hebrew represented in these ways.

3. Recent handbooks have been giving increasing attention to the implications of larger discourse structures, that is, larger thought units, sequencing of ideas, logical relationships between sentences and paragraphs. This tendency has been greatly extended here. The Appendix, for example, explains in some detail the most relevant major features of the structure of Amos as we see it; the reasons for our understanding the structure in this way are also explained there. Translators working with this handbook are frequently referred to the Appendix to find the basis for recommendations made to them. The Appendix, however, is more technical than the body of the handbook, and translators may follow the recommendations of the handbook without trying to read the Appendix. In the introductory chapter on Translating Amos there are suggestions for translating the effect of the discourse structure.

4. The introductory chapter also deals with the problem of translating poetry, since this is the first handbook on a part of the Bible written largely in Hebrew poetic form. In addition, it discusses other larger issues like translating the geography of Amos (including a map) and translating the social relationships in Amos.

5. The divisions of the handbook, as seen in the Table of Contents, correspond to sections in the structure of Amos, not to traditional chapter divisions. The basis for these sections may be seen in Appendix, Figures 3,5.

[v]

We would like to express our appreciation to the following individuals who have helped in the preparation of the manuscript: Leigh R. Kambhu, Lucy Rowe, Jane A. Smalley, and Tine A. de Waard.

Jan de Waard
William A. Smalley

March 1977

CONTENTS

MODERN TRANSLATIONS CITED

BJ   La Bible de Jérusalem. Nouvelle édition entièrement revue et augmentée. Paris: Les éditions du Cerf, 1973.

Dhorme   Edouard Dhorme, Les douze petits prophètes, in: La Bible, L'Ancien Testament II. Paris: Editions Gallimard, 1959.

JB   The Jerusalem Bible. Garden City, New York: Doubleday, 1966.

Mft   James Moffatt, A New Translation of the Bible. Revised and Final Edition. London: Hodder and Stoughton, 1935.

NAB   The New American Bible. New York: P. J. Kenedy and Sons, 1970.

NEB   The New English Bible. Oxford and Cambridge: University Press, 1970.

RSV   The Holy Bible: Revised Standard Version. London: Thomas Nelson and Sons Ltd., 1953.

S-G   J. M. Powis Smith and Edgar J. Goodspeed, The Complete Bible: An American Translation. Chicago: The University of Chicago Press, 1951.

TEV   Good News Bible (Today's English Version). New York: American Bible Society, 1976.

TOB   Traduction oecuménique de la Bible: Ancien Testament. Edition intégrale. Paris: Les éditions du Cerf and Les Bergers et les Mages, 1975.

TT   The Translators' Old Testament: The Book of Amos. London: The British and Foreign Bible Society, 1975.

Zür   Die Heilige Schrift des alten und neuen Testaments. Zürich: Verlag der Zwingli-Bibel, 1947.

TRANSLATING AMOS

Very little is known about the prophet Amos himself. For example, nothing is known about the dates of his birth and death, the age at which he began his prophetic activity, or even the length of time that activity continued. Amos does inform us that he did not belong to the Northern Kingdom of Israel to which he preached his messages; he came from the town of Tekoa in the mountains of Judah, twenty kilometers south of Jerusalem. It is clear that Amos' prophetic ministry took place in the time of Jeroboam II, who ruled over Israel from 787/6- - 747/6 BC (7.10-11). The earthquake mentioned in 1.1 has been confirmed by archaeological evidence and has generally been dated 760 BC.[1] For what else may be known of the work and social position of Amos, see the discussions at 1.1 and 7.14.

Amos' time was one of peace, prosperity, and the expansion of Israel's territory. Previously, in the last part of the ninth century, Syria had made attacks on Israel, but these stopped after the Assyrian king Adadnirari III captured the Syrian capital of Damascus in 800. So Syria had been powerless for at least twenty years, and Israel enjoyed a period of stability. However, the stability of Amos' world was also breaking down. Because of shifts in world power, Assyria was now being forced to lessen its pressure on Syria. So Amos lived in the shadow of new border incidents like the one referred to in 1.3.

The prosperity of Amos' time can be seen in his mention of commercial activities (8.5), flourishing agriculture (5.11), and new developments in the fields of architecture (3.15) and music (6.5). However, it was also a time of social and economic injustice, when rich people became increasingly richer, and poor people became poorer. Amos mentions practices like selling honest people into slavery simply because they could not pay their debts (2.6), taking advantage of the poor (8.4), and taking bribes (5.12).

Amos states that it was the Lord who ordered him to go and prophesy to the Lord's people Israel (7.15). This means that the message he delivered was the message of the Lord. Amos shows the Lord acting in the history of the times and dealing with the sins of the people. He usually expresses the Lord's acts by verbs, not by nouns, so that what the Lord does and will do is told clearly. Theological vocabulary is carefully avoided.

The Lord speaks to people through the prophet: he first speaks to Amos, or shows him something through a vision. But even when the Lord uses a vision, the picture itself is not as important as the Lord's words which accompany it. The primary message which Amos receives and passes along can be summarized in a few words: the Lord will come to judge because Israel has sinned.

Amos describes Israel's future as disaster. Catastrophes like war (6.14), the death of the king (7.11), the captivity of the people (7.11), are announced. Only occasionally is a call to repentance given as a condition for a more hopeful future (5.14-15). Israel's dark future will result from what is actually happening in Amos' time when people do not even know how to be honest (3.10).

[1]

In particular, it is the high society of Israel which will suffer the punishment Amos announces. It feels political and social security which is falsely strengthened by relying on the performance of religious activities rather than by doing the will of the Lord (4.5).

Amos rarely mentions Israel's past. When he does so, it is to remind Israel of the Lord's loving care in saving the nation from Egypt. But this, too, becomes a basis for accusation, since Israel's history illustrates Israel's refusal to become God's people.

Everything Amos says about other nations only serves to clarify the Lord's message to Israel. What the Lord has done in the past to Israel's enemies (2.9), he will now do to Israel itself. Israel will in no way be more privileged than other nations (9.7), and the Lord himself will use unnamed nations to punish Israel (3.11). In fact, the messages against the other nations (1.3--3.16) make it clear that no distinctions can be made between Judah/Israel and their neighbors.

2. Translating the overall structure of Amos

The collection of prophetic messages (and other material) in Amos is not always organized with a smooth, logical flow from one passage to the next. In fact, a careful reading of the Hebrew (or of most translations) from beginning to end will show that some parts go together very well while others do not seem to belong logically where they are at all.

For example, why does the meeting between Amaziah and Amos (7.10-17) come between two visions which seem as though they should be together (7.7-9 and 8.1-3)? Or why does the statement that the Lord will not utterly destroy the house of Jacob (9.8c) come between two passages which say he will destroy it (9.7-8b, 9-10)? Or why does The Lord is his name come two thirds of the way down the piece of hymn describing the power of the Lord in 5.8-9 instead of coming at the end of the description where it seems to belong, and where it is found in other similar passages (4.13 and 9.5-6)? And, for that matter, why are these pieces of very similar hymns scattered through the book the way they are?

The footnotes in this Handbook occasionally refer to the large amount of discussion by scholars who have worked on problems like these. In specific cases we have suggested translational decisions based on the best judgment of such scholars. On the other hand, our suggestions are also frequently influenced by what we see as an overall structure to the book of Amos. Many of these seeming inconsistencies in the book fit into a larger design.

2.1 The structure of Amos

The general plan of the book, and some of the details which have influenced our suggestions to translators, are discussed in the Appendix to this Handbook, and we suggest the translator who is interested in that more technical background read it as part of this discussion. We will not go into detail in this chapter, but just say that messages or groups of messages in Amos are balanced off against each other in various ways, so that messages at corresponding places in the design are sometimes related to each other more than they are to messages right next to them. This can be seen in the Appendix, Section 1.1, Figure 3, where section A is balanced by A', B by B', etc.

But Figure 5 in the Appendix shows more of the story. There is evidence that the book has three parts, and that each of these parts also has a balanced structure within itself; these shorter balanced groups are there in addition to the larger balance shown in Figure 3. The basis for understanding Amos in this way is discussed in connection with those figures, and once the reader has seen all this, the book makes much more sense as a whole.

Many translators may find that the best policy is not to try to show their readers the more complicated ways in which the different parts of the book fit together, but to translate in traditional fashion. Others, however, may want to try to help the modern reader at least have a chance to see something of how the parts of the book of Amos fit together, so that the reader may possibly feel the message more strongly and understand the relationship between the ideas more clearly. We suggest some ways of trying to do this in the sections which follow. Perhaps some of these suggestions can be used only in translations for well-educated readers, but others may also be useful in situations where readers have more limited background. The translator will have to decide for himself.

2.2 Translating with a balanced structure

For one thing, when the passages which show balance are not very long, and not very far apart, it is sometimes possible to translate them and then print them on the page in such a way that a kind of balance similar to that of the Hebrew is seen in the translation. This should only be done if it would be effective in the language of the translation (see Translating Amos, Section 5). Using 5.4-6 and 5.14-16 as examples, we do not make any attempt to reproduce the Hebrew balanced structure as such, but do try to create one of similar effect, and to give some hint of it in the way the translation is organized on the page. Any translator who is interested in this sort of thing should study the Hebrew balanced structure as shown in Appendix, Section 3.5 to see how it compares.

(5.4-6)

The Lord says to the people of Israel,
"Come to me, and you will live.
    Do not try to find me at Bethel;
    Do not go to Gilgal;
    Do not go to Beersheba to worship.
    No, Gilgal's people are doomed to exile,
    And Bethel will come to nothing.
Come to the Lord, and you will live."
    "If you do not," said Amos,
The Lord will sweep down like a fire on the people of Israel.
The fire will burn up the people of Bethel,
And no one will be able to put it out."

      *   *   *   *   *

(5.14-15)

Come back to doing what is right, not what is evil,
so that you may live.

[3]

> Then the Lord God Almighty
>> really will be with you,
>> as you claim he is.
> Hate what is evil, love what is right,
> and see that justice prevails in the courts.
>> Perhaps the Lord God Almighty
>> will be merciful
>> to the people of Israel who are still left alive.

The above examples have the wording of the TEV as much as possible. In the discussion of these passages later on in the handbook other wordings will be suggested, and some of them would strengthen the balanced pattern. The examples have a small number of changes from the TEV, where it hides a relationship which we want to show. For example, TEV has come (5.4), go (5.6), and make it your aim (5.14), where Hebrew has seek. There are good reasons for not using the same word in the TEV, but because we want to show the balanced relationships we use various expressions which all include the words "come to."

Then again, in the example above the first part of verse 6 is included as part of what the Lord says in verses 4-5 rather than as part of what Amos says in verse 6 because the balanced structure in the Hebrew indicates this relationship. In similar fashion, we have translated "people of Israel" instead of people of this nation (Hebrew: house of Joseph) to keep the parallel with people of Israel in verse 6. We have changed the order in verse 5 back to the Hebrew order so that Bethel balances against Bethel, Gilgal against Gilgal, with Beersheba between them. Come to me, and you will live is balanced by "Come to the Lord, and you will live," providing a frame before and after the lines with the place names.

In 5.14-15 "come to," so that you may live, and "people of Israel" all pick up from the earlier passage. The meaning of the passage as a whole balances 5.4-6 in the contrast which it presents to it. Within 5.14-15 itself, right...evil balances evil...right, the Lord God Almighty is repeated in balanced position, will be merciful balances will be with you (in this context a very similar meaning).

We believe that this kind of arrangement of the translation can sometimes be done in a way that is not forced or artificial for English and some other languages, especially if the translation is in an oratorical style, which would be very appropriate to the prophets.

2.3 Use of paragraphs and connections

Once the translator has seen the organization of a particular passage and the way in which the parts relate to each other, sometimes he can make this clear in his translation by the way he divides up the material into paragraphs. He can also help by relating those paragraphs (and the sentences within them) to each other, using connecting words, differences in the order of words, etc. Amos 2.6b-16, for example, is an important passage which has a very complicated organization, as explained in the Appendix, Section 3.1 (see also the discussion of the text under 2.9-12). The most difficult problem is the way in which verses 9-11 come into the passage, breaking into the list of Israel's sins, and the fact that these verses have a balanced structure, with the events sometimes mentioned in

[4]

a different order from that in which they happened.

RSV and TEV have paragraph divisions only at verse 9. Few modern English translations have more than that; yet the English restructuring below uses paragraphing and different kinds of connections to try to make the relationship of the parts of the passage clearer. We start with verse 8 because paragraphs are not needed earlier.

8"...You drink up the wine you take from people in payment of fines. Yes, you do it in my house--the temple of your God.

9-- "But I was the one who defeated the Amorites who stood in your way, my people! They stood tall as cedar trees and and strong as oaks, but I withered their fruit and rotted their roots. 10Before that I rescued you out of Egypt, and for forty years I took care of you in the barren desert until I gave you this land--this rich land of the Amorites--to be your own.

11"Then I chose some of your sons to be prophets, to speak my message, and I called some of your young men to be Nazirites, to serve me.

"You know this is true, Israel, don't you? It is I--it is the Lord who is reminding you!--

12"But you, you made the Nazirites break their vows to me, and you ordered the prophets not to speak my message.

13"So, then, I will crush you to the ground, and you will groan with weakness, as a cart groans when it is overloaded with grain..."

1. In verse 9, in addition to the paragraph break, the dash helps to show that there is a major break in the thought, and the closing dash in verse 11 shows the end of that break. It is as though this part were in parentheses, except that the passage is extremely important and parentheses might indicate that it was of less importance.

2. "I was the one" (verse 9) not only translates the emphatic Hebrew, but also helps to contrast this paragraph with the previous one emphasizing Israel's sins.

3. "Before that" (verse 10) takes care of the fact that the rescue from Egypt came before the conquering of the Amorites. In some languages the translation will have to change the order of these two verses.

4. A new paragraph is made at the beginning of verse 11 because the action changes and because now the passage is setting up a contrast again between the Lord's helpful acts and Israel's disobedient ones. It is easier to see the balance between verses 11a and 12 where both are separate paragraphs.

5. The last part of verse 11 is made a separate paragraph because it does not fit the flow of the passage. It is as though the Lord is interrupting himself and asking for confirmation from Israel.

6. Verse 12 is not only made a new paragraph, but the contrasting pronoun "you" is repeated to help strengthen the relationship back to the end of verse 8, and the sharp change from verse 11.

7. Verse 13 begins the announcement of punishment and needs a paragraph because of that change alone. "So, then" relates the punishment to the discussion which has gone before.

Translators in other languages should follow the paragraphing systems of their own languages, not of English, of course. But it is very likely that in many cases translations of this passage, and others like it, can be made clearer by giving attention to the way in which paragraphs and their connections show up in the organization of the passage.

2.4 Headings and cross references

For the longer passages and the more distant relationships between them, however, the only way we know to help the reader see how they fit together is to use section headings and cross references to show the organization. Again, this is not something which all translators should try to do. It may be difficult to do effectively, and there would be no point to doing it for translations prepared for readers of very limited education. But for serious readers with some education, section headings prepared in this way might be of considerable help in seeing just what the book of Amos is saying and how it is built up.

Here follows one possibility of this kind, based on Appendix, Figure 5. This is only an example. Headings which accomplished the same purpose would have to be prepared according to what is clear and appropriate in each language. Suggestions are made in different places where section headings are discussed in the handbook.

```
      ISRAEL'S GUILT; THE PROPHET'S RESPONSIBILITY          1.1
      A   Introduction: the prophet
      B   The power of God to punish                          2
          (Also 5.8-9; 9.5-6)
              [Text printed in different type]
      C   Israel's special guilt among the nations            3
          (Also 8.4--9.4)
              Syria
              Philistia                                        6
              Tyre                                             9
              Edom                                            11
              Ammon                                          1.13
              Moab                                            2.1
              Judah                                            4
              Israel                                           6
              Basis for Israel's guilt                        3.1
      D   The prophet's role and commission                   3
          (Also 7.1--8.3)
              Role: witness to disaster
              Commission: to witness against Samaria          9
      C'  Israel doesn't learn God's lessons                 4.4
          (Also 5.18--6.14)
      B'  The power of God to create                         13
          (Also 5.8-9; 9.5-6)
              [Text printed in different type]
      A'  Conclusion: Lament for Israel                      5.1
          (Also 5.16-17)
```

These suggestions for the organization of section headings differ from the usual practice in Bible Society publications in four ways. 1) There are three levels of heading, whereas TEV has only two in Amos, and normally one elsewhere. (Jerusalem Bible sometimes uses three levels.) 2) Capital letters before the headings are used to help show the balancing passage within each of the three major sections. 3) Cross references (like those for the gospel parallels) are used to show the balancing passages in other major sections. 4) The wording of the headings is chosen to help point up the similarity between balancing passages. In addition, the introduction to the translated book would need to have some explanation of the meaning of the capital letters and the cross references.

But even if the translator feels that he should use a simpler, more conventional set of section headings for the book, he should still keep in mind the overall structure of Amos as he translates. Understanding how the parts fit together helps to see the overall meaning more clearly, which certainly helps to build the background for translating with greater understanding and skill.

3. Translating the geography of Amos

One of the problems which makes some translations of the Bible difficult to understand is that direction of movement (words like "come," "go," "climb," "descend," etc.) is not translated naturally. Amos refers to many places (see following map) and makes frequent reference to movement to them or away from them, from one place to another. In this section we would like to give the translator a little help which may make it possible for him to translate such movement more meaningfully.

For many languages, the place in which the message is spoken or written is the viewpoint place. Amos certainly travelled extensively, and it is hard to know exactly where his prophetic activities took place. Probably he stayed in Samaria and Bethel for some time and delivered some of his messages there. But he may have also visited Gilgal and other places. However, the translator should imagine the messages as spoken in Bethel. The choice is somewhat arbitrary, but has some justification, and for many languages the translation will be clearer if a specific place is kept in mind.

In languages where the place of speaking or writing is the viewpoint place, the choice of words like "come" and "go," and the use of expressions like "went up" and "went down," should be based not on what the Hebrew or English has, but on the relationship to that viewpoint place. For the translation to be natural, the translator must always keep in mind how the different places are related to Bethel on the map.

But in some other languages the question of viewpoint place is more complicated. Some messages are spoken or written as though the viewpoint place was not the place of speaking, but the place which is important in the message. In that case, the viewpoint place in translation will shift from time to time, as in the first two chapters of Amos, for example. In some languages these two different kinds of viewpoint place may each be used at different times.

On the map the different place names mentioned in Amos are in all directions from Bethel. Also, there are other features of the geography which are important for motion in some languages. The direction of flow in the Jordan River is southward, so north is upstream and south is downstream. For those languages where this is important, for example, Amaziah sent a message "up" to Jeroboam in 7.10.

The mountains are important for some languages where "up" and "down" is a matter of relative height on the mountain. In general, what is near the Jordan and the lakes is down, as is what is near the sea. Within the mountains it may be harder to know. Samaria is higher than Bethel so, again, for languages like this Amaziah's message went "up" to Jeroboam.

In some languages the important distinction is between going toward or away from the water. Here again, the map may be of help in translating meaningfully.

4. Translating the language of social relationships in Amos

In some languages it makes a great deal of difference what the social relationship is between people who are talking to each other. Titles, pronouns, and even words for many things may be different according to such relationships. In such languages, for example, Amaziah (the head priest) is likely to speak to Amos as an inferior (7.12-13). But he might or might

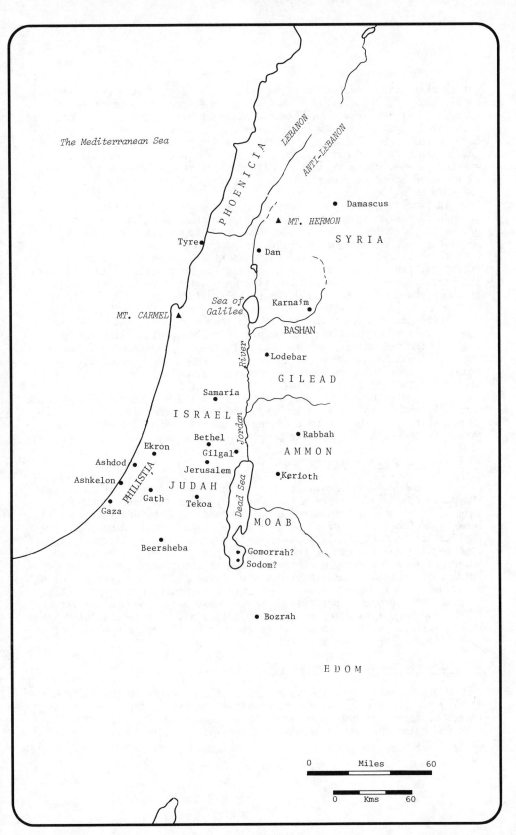

The Mediterranean Sea

PHOENICIA

LEBANON

ANTI-LEBANON

● Damascus

▲ MT. HERMON

SYRIA

Tyre ●

● Dan

Sea of Galilee

Karnaim ●

MT. CARMEL ▲

BASHAN

River

● Lodebar

GILEAD

Samaria ●

ISRAEL

Jordan

Bethel ●

Ekron ●

Gilgal ●

● Rabbah

AMMON

Ashdod ●

Jerusalem ●

PHILISTIA

JUDAH

Ashkelon ●

● Kerioth

Gath ●

Tekoa ●

Gaza ●

Dead Sea

Beersheba ●

MOAB

Gomorrah? ●

● Sodom?

● Bozrah

EDOM

| 0 | Miles | 60 |

| 0 | Kms | 60 |

not speak to King Jeroboam as a superior, depending on the rules in the particular language (7.10-11). But would Amos speak to Amaziah as a superior, particularly when he was denouncing him in the name of the Lord (7.14-17)? In languages where it makes a difference, every translator will have to think about that very carefully and try to imagine Amos actually talking in a real situation. The fact that the words of Amos and those of the Lord are so closely identified in much of the book might mean that Amos should speak, at least at times, to the leaders of Israel as though the Lord were speaking.

In some languages every name of a person must have a title with it. In such cases the translator should think carefully about what title to give each person mentioned in the book, and should consider what this means for the pronouns and other words which should be used for people with those titles. Amos himself may present a problem because of his sheep-owning background which may not be considered an important status in some languages. However, it is his position as a person speaking for God which is important in this book, and the title and language should be based on that.

There are also many changes in the tone of what is said. Amos some-times speaks disrespectfully to people of higher status (like Amaziah, and like the wealthy leaders in 5.11-12). The language should be in keep-ing with the tone of the message. In some languages it is possible to sound disrespectful even when the speaker uses all of the pronouns and titles for talking to a superior.

In translating such social relationships the translator should think carefully about just what is implied, and imagine the situation as vividly as possible. Then the language of the translation should be made appro-priate to the situation and the people in it.

5. Translating the poetry of Amos

This Handbook is the first one in the series to deal with a book of the Bible which is written in the poetic style of the Hebrew prophets. This style makes the translator's task considerably harder than in earlier books. The fundamental principles of translation do not change, but their application is more complicated.[2] The translator must still convey the true meaning and purpose of the Hebrew in the best way for his own lan-guage. So in translating a poetic passage he should not try to copy every-thing that makes up Hebrew poetic style. Actually, he may even decide not to translate into poetry at all, but into good prose. But if it is best to translate into good poetry, the poetry must be in the poetic patterns of the language into which he is translating, not of the original Hebrew; and if into prose, the prose must be that of his language without purpose-less relics of Hebrew poetic style.

5.1 Things to know about Hebrew poetry

Hebrew parallelism. The word "parallelism" refers to the fact that usually two or more lines, one right after the other, say very similar things or different things in a very similar way. On a small scale it is like the balancing we discussed for longer passages in Amos (Translating Amos, Section 2).

Clear examples of this parallelism can be seen constantly in Amos. In the following examples the parallel parts are lined up to show the relationship:

(6.4-6, RSV)

```
Woe to those who lie                upon        beds of ivory,
and                 stretch themselves upon their couches,

and eat lambs  from the flock,
and      calves from the midst of the stall;

who sing idle songs to the sound of the harp,...
who drink     wine  in bowls,...
```

(4.4, RSV)

```
Come to Bethel, and                 transgress;
      to Gilgal, and multiply transgression;

bring your sacrifices every morning,
      your tithes      every three days;...
```

(5.21-22, RSV)

```
I hate, I despise     your feasts,
and I take no delight in your solemn assemblies.

Even though you offer me your burnt offerings
and                                cereal offerings,
and                          the  peace offerings.

I will not accept them,
I will not look upon.
```

Such parallelism is an extremely common Hebrew poetic device, and without it there is no poetry from the Hebrew point of view. Parallelism in some degree occurs in all language, both in prose and in poetry, and will certainly be found in translation. However, the important point to remember here is that such parallelism should come into a translation where it contributes to effective communication in the language of the translation and should not be carried over only because it is in the Hebrew or an English translation of the Hebrew. This means that quite often when something is said twice in the Hebrew in this way, it will be said only once in a good translation, or if it is said only once in Hebrew it may need to be said more than once in translation. It also means that by comparing the parallel lines of the Hebrew, the translator can sometimes get a better idea of the main point which the original writer was driving at.[3] In English, for example, it is more common in some oratorical styles (such as might well be used in translating Amos).

Hebrew picture language. Picture language is technically called "imagery." It expresses an idea by drawing a picture with words. There are some outstanding examples in Amos:

[11]

(1.2, TEV)
     The Lord roars from Mount Zion;
          his voice thunders from Jerusalem.
(3.12, TEV)
     The Lord says, "As a shepherd recovers only two legs or an
ear of a sheep that a lion has eaten, so only a few of Samaria's
people..."
(5.24, TEV)
     Let justice flow like a stream, and righteousness like a
river that never goes dry.

     Picture language, of course, is to be found in all languages and in
prose as well as in poetry. However, the particular types of pictures
which are suitable in one language may not all necessarily be used in
another. And poetry tends to have quite a bit more picture language than
prose does. This means that the translator has to adapt the pictures of
the original and decide in every instance whether the original purpose
can best be kept in his translation by the same pictures, different
pictures, or no pictures at all.
     For example, here is a strong Hebrew picture:
(1.3, RSV)
     ...they have threshed Gilead
          with threshing sledges of iron.
The translators of the TEV, however, felt that this picture language would
not be understood if translated literally into English because it is based
on Mideastern agricultural work not known to modern English readers. The
TEV therefore translates instead:
     They treated the people of Gilead
          with savage cruelty.
This expresses the same meaning but not the same picture, and the emotional force is not as strong because the picture is not as strong.
     However, it would be possible to translate this passage into picture
language in English as well:
     They treated the people of Gilead with savage cruelty, as
          though they drove their oxen over them, pulling great beams
          with iron spikes to rip up their flesh.
With such a translation much of the horror of the Hebrew picture could be
kept. However, the translation is "wordy," without the precise, brief
power of the original. Perhaps a further improvement would be:
     ...pulling great hooks to rip up their flesh.
     Meter. Hebrew poetry has a regular rhythm or beat, with a limited
number of stressed or loud syllables per line (often three). We cannot
illustrate meter from the Hebrew because if anyone does not know Hebrew
he will not feel the meter anyhow. So we take an English illustration
instead, a verse from a familiar hymn, just to show what meter is in
English. The stressed (strong, loud) syllables are underlined.
     Oh, worship the king, all glorious above,
     And gratefully sing his wonderful love;
     Our Shield and Defender, the Ancient of Days,
     Pavillioned in spleandor and girded with praise.
                              Sir Robert Grant

[12]

We can show this more clearly by representing each underlined syllable above with x and the other syllables with o. And when we do that we find that there are some pauses which have the beat of an o. They are represented by ():

```
o x o o x () o x o o x ()
o x o o x () o x o o x ()
o x o o x o  o x o o x ()
o x o o x o  o x o o x ()
```

Each line has the same pattern except that the first two lines have () in the middle whereas the last two have o. The parentheses (), in fact, seem to be an alternative for o at the end of the first half of a line. All English styles have a difference between x type syllables and o type syllables, but in meter the different syllables are arranged to create a pattern, of which the above is only one of many possibilities.

In some languages meter is not related to stressed or loud syllables at all, but to patterns of long and short vowels. The principle of patterning is the same, however. The long and short vowels create a pattern which is repeated in the poem.

Meter does not show up in most English translations. If there should be meter in the English translation, it is not Hebrew meter, but English. The TEV does not normally have meter, even in the sections which are written to look like poetry, but if the translator is translating into poetry and if poetry in his language uses meter, he will want to use the patterns which are required.

Arousal of emotion. The characteristics of Hebrew poetry which we have been discussing so far are ones by which the author built up some of his poetic affects. We should go on, however, to something deeper, to the qualities which are necessary to a great deal of poetry in most languages and which must be reproduced in the translation. They are part of the basic purpose and meaning of the poetry.

The first of these is strong feeling. Amos is full of strong feeling, feeling of indignation, of terrible horror against injustice. And the feelings change from passage to passage. There is bitterness against the treatment of the poor, and there are hymns of praise to God, with the ending full of hope and promise. No translation is adequate if the reader does not feel the changes and intensity of the moods throughout the book. To achieve strong feeling in the translation, the translator must, of course, write forcefully and effectively in his own language. Notice that the emotional effects must often come from the way in which the translation is expressed, not by simply trying to carry over the way the original writer did it in Hebrew.

An attempt to provide an example of what we are talking about can be seen below. The TEV (in prose, and already heavily rewritten from the Hebrew poetic form) is on the left; another suggested writing on the right:

Listen to this, you that trample on the needy and try to destroy the poor of the country. You say to yourselves, "We can hardly wait for the holy days to	Listen, you merchants who trample the needy and destroy the poor. You can't wait for the holy days to be over to sell your grain, or for the Sabbath to end so you can start business

be over so that we can sell
our grain. When will the
Sabbath end, so that we can
start selling again? Then
we can overcharge, use false
measures, and fix the scales
to cheat our customers. We
can sell worthless wheat at
a high price. We'll find a
poor man who can't pay his
debts, not even the price
of a pair of sandals, and
buy him as a slave."

again. You overcharge; you
use false measures, and fix
your scales to cheat your customers. You even take what you
sweep from the floor of the
wheat bin and sell it to the
hungry at a high price. Then
you go out and look for a poor
man, who cannot pay his debts,
and make him your slave because he
owes the money for his cheap
sandals.

(8.4-6, TEV)

There are many obvious changes from the TEV to the restructuring on
the right, but the major one is that the quotation is taken out. In this
passage the rich merchants are being accused of all kinds of selfish and
cruel acts against the poor, and it seems to us that for English the quotation with its questions weakens the accusation. It seems stronger with
the direct "you...you...you..." The emotion of the last lines is also in-
creased by the more specific picture language: "to make him your slave
because he still owes the price of his cheap sandals." The use of specific
terms like "merchants" and "the hungry" also helps, as does the shorter,
more direct sentence structure.

Not all readers in any language necessarily react in the same way,
and what is effective in one language is not necessarily effective in
another, so it would often be wise for a translator to test different
possibilities on a variety of readers to see what seems more forceful to
most.

Making the reader think without saying something directly. Another
very important characteristic of Hebrew poetry is making the reader think
or feel something without saying it directly. This is often done through
the use of picture language, but also by drawing the reader to make his
own interpretation of what is being said. This quality is also to be
found in poetry and prose of many other languages, and is very important
for the translation.

Here is a good example:

How terrible it will be for you who long for the day of the
Lord! What good will that day do you? For you it will be a day
of darkness and not of light. It will be like a man who runs
from a lion and meets a bear! Or like a man who comes home and
puts his hand on the wall--only to be bitten by a snake! The
day of the Lord will bring darkness and not light; it will be
a day of gloom, without any brightness. (5.18-20, TEV)

In this passage we are not told what will happen on "the day of the Lord,"
but we are left with the strong feeling that it will mean disaster, that
it will be worse than the situation from which we are escaping. It makes
us think about the dangers without stating them directly.

By no means can all passages of indirect statement be translated indirectly. The knowledge of the modern reader is very different from that
of the original reader, and he would in many cases not understand, or
would misinterpret what the original writer was driving at. In Amos 7.7-8,

for example, the TEV has made the indirect language of the Hebrew clearer:

TEV

He asked me, "Amos, what do you see?"
  "A plumb line," I answered.
Then he said, "I am using it to show that my people
  are like a wall that is out of line."

RSV

"Behold, I am setting a plumb line in the midst of my
  people Israel."

The TEV is doubtless correct in thinking that the Hebrew figure is not clear enough for its readers and needs to be made more explicit. However, the meaning is stated so directly that the quality of making the reader think for himself is destroyed, too. Perhaps something of this quality could be kept, and the passage still be made clear, by translating:
  I am checking my people with it.
or, I am using it to see how straight my people are.
or, I'm measuring my people against it.
A translation must be clear, but for it to be without any of this kind of indirect statement would mean a serious weakening of its effectiveness.

Subject matter of Hebrew poetry. The last thing to keep in mind with regard to Hebrew poetry is the wide range of different purposes for which poetry was used. These included songs and hymns, curses and blessings, judgments of God and announcements that punishment was coming.

Some other languages have just as many subjects for which poetry is very natural. In still other languages it is not so. In English, for example, especially in modern times, poetry is used for love and worship and humor, but not for history, preaching, teaching, blessing, etc. When Hebrew poetry contains subject matter which is not suitable to poetry in any language it will often need to be translated as prose. This is what has been done throughout most of the book of Amos in the TEV. Prophetic judgments are not appropriate to modern English poetry. In many other languages, of course, they most certainly are.

5.2 Things to think about in the poetry of a language.

Before a translator can make an intelligent decision about how to translate the poetry of the Bible, he must stop and think about the poetry of his own language from several points of view. He needs to do this both to decide whether or not he is going to translate into poetry at all, and then if it is to be poetry, in order to decide what kind of poetry he wants to use. In doing this he should consult with literary specialists in his own language if there are such people, or with people who are known to be effective poets and writers or storytellers.

Subject matter. Here are some questions the translator can ask himself and literary specialists: What do people write poems about in this language? Are all subjects equally suitable for poetry? How about religion? Suffering? Love? Hatred? History? Law? Moral qualities? Other Biblical themes?

[15]

Of course, it may well be that within the culture of which this language is an expression, various types of Biblical subject matter simply do not exist at all. But the translator still needs to think about the poetry that does exist in order to help decide whether or not these new subjects would be appropriate within poetic tradition.

The situations in which poetry is used. Or, to look at it from another point of view, what do poets try to accomplish with their poetry in this language? Is poetry only associated with music? Only with entertainment? And for the book of Amos, particularly, are pronouncements of God's judgment appropriately expressed in poetic form?

Users of Poetry. Then there are questions about who uses poetry in this language. Is it only older people? Only the young? Are there certain kinds of poetry which are restricted to particular groups of people? For example, do older people like classical poetic forms but younger people like a free verse modeled after European patterns? The translator must decide whether or not the poetry which he might create in translation is suitable to the particular audience of the translation.

Poetic forms. The translator needs to think also about the different forms of poetry as they exist in his language. Some languages have only a very limited variety of poetic forms and others an enormous range. Are some poetic varieties associated only with particular subjects or a particular class of people? Do some forms require a greater degree of skill for the poet, and are they more likely to require changing the meaning in order to be able to keep within the requirements of the poetic rules? The more difficult the kind of poem, of course, the less likely it is that it can be successfully used in translation. Forms which are limited to a fixed number of lines are particularly unsuitable for the purposes of translation; for example, the sonnet in English allows only fourteen lines of fixed length. It would be a rare poem in Hebrew which could be suitably translated into a sonnet. In the same way, poetic forms with complicated rhyming or rhythm patterns and many rules become very difficult to manage in translation.

The poet. If poetry is to be translated into poetry, who can do it? Very often it will have to be someone different from the person who translates the prose passages, because writing poetry is often a special skill. Can people who have this skill be included in the translation team? Can they be trained to understand the principles of good translation such that their poetic gifts can be used, as they understand that the meaning of the text must be kept? To be successful, the translation of poetry must be done by a skillful person. Such a person has to be sought out, and the search may be difficult.

The basic decision: prose or poetry. With these various considerations in mind the translator will have to decide whether all or some of the Hebrew poetry should be translated into poetry or prose in his language, and also what particular forms and styles would be best. All of the various different types of poetic literature in the Bible should be thought about, and a decision made for each one in light of the styles and uses of poetry in the language.

5.3 How to proceed when translating Hebrew poetry into prose.

If the translator decides to translate certain passages of Hebrew poetry or all of the Hebrew poetry into prose, he may think that this solves all his problems, and that he may continue in the same way that he has been translating other parts of the Bible. It is not as simple as that, however, because he will probably have to make changes which are not required in translating the prose passages of the Bible. He may find that he has to work extra hard because the Hebrew poetic elements do not fit too well into a prose framework. We notice this in English translations of the parallelism of Hebrew poetry. A certain amount of parallelism is quite acceptable in English prose and may considerably strengthen its force. However, the amount of parallelism which exists in the Hebrew, if carried over fully into English prose, makes the prose extremely heavy, repetitive and uninteresting to read. This means that some of the parallel lines have to be reduced so that something is said only once. For example:
> In all the squares there shall be wailing,
>   and in all the streets they shall say, "Alas! Alas!" (5.16, RSV)
This has been translated in the TEV simply by:
> There will be wailing and cries of sorrow in the city streets.
At this point the TEV is translating into prose, and the simpler structure is preferable. This does not mean that it would be preferable in all cases in all other languages, of course. Notice that the meaning has not been changed, but the repetition has been reduced.

In translating from Hebrew poetry into the prose of any language the translation principles have not changed; the application is a little bit more complicated. The translator still wants to give the same meaning as the original. He wants to have the same emphasis, to keep the same mood or feeling, as far as is possible in prose; he wants to have the same ability to make people think, and in every way to accomplish the same purpose, even though the style is different.

In the case of Amos, the TEV will be of help in translating the Hebrew poetry into prose because that is what the TEV has done, except for a few passages which it considered suitable for poetry in English. However, here as in all other cases, the translator should not translate the TEV literally. He should make his own judgment as to what is the best way to put the meaning in his own language. This handbook will help to explain the meaning and to give ideas of ways in which it can be expressed in various languages. The original forms of parallelism (as seen in the RSV) may give ideas concerning ways of expressing this meaning in vivid fashion in translation. Sometimes the forms of the language of translation will be more like those of Hebrew than English is.

And when the draft is done, as in all translating, the translator should go over his prose translation again carefully to make sure that it really sounds like good, free-flowing and forceful prose in his language, and that it has the strong emotion of Amos. The translator will often find after he has put it aside for a while that he wants to do further improving.

The final improvements will sometimes be very small ones, but they will lend smoothness, clarity and emotion. Look, for example, at the following rewriting of the first three verses of Chapter 2 of the TEV Amos.

[17]

The changes are very slight, but the total effect is smoother and clearer:

The Lord says, "The people of Moab have sinned again and again, and for this I will certainly punish them. They dishonored the bones of the king of Edom by burning them to ashes. I will send fire on the land of Moab and burn down the fortresses of Kerioth. The people of Moab will die in the noise of battle, while soldiers are shouting and trumpets are sounding. I will kill the ruler of Moab and all the leaders of the land."

(2.1-3, TEV)

Listen to what the Lord says: "The people of Moab have sinned again and again. They have even dishonored the dead king of Edom by burning his bones to make lime! "So, I will punish the people of Moab. I'll send war, like a fire, on their whole country, and burn down their great fortress of Kerioth. People will die in the noise of battle, with the soldiers shouting and trumpets sounding their defeat. I will kill the ruler of Moab also, and all the leaders of the land."

That is what the Lord says!

Some of these changes would be necessary whether the original was poetry or not. However, in the process of translating from poetry into prose the result can often be more uneven than in translating from prose because the amount of rewriting required is much greater. But whatever the reason, final improvements to create a good, smooth prose form are essential.

Here are some of the changes that were made from the TEV in the above rewriting:

1. The addition of "Listen to what." This makes the Lord's saying more immediate, more directed to the listener and less like the recording of an abstract quotation.

2. "They have even." This unites the example of sinning with the general statement about the sinning and implies the very great repulsiveness of this action with the word "even."

3. "To make lime." The justification for this is to be found in the discussion of the text under 2.1.

4. "So I will punish the people of Moab." The order of I will punish is changed so that it does not divide the discussion of sinning and so that it comes directly with the description of the punishment to the sinning; "people of Moab" is required by the new paragraph.

5. "War, like a fire." See the discussion under 2.2.

6. "Great." The word helps to show how great is the disaster that is to come to Moab, and helps to smooth the passage.

7. "With...their defeat." These words help to show the changes from the confusion to the outcome. As the text stands in the TEV, the soldiers shouting and trumpets sounding almost sound like victory for Moab rather than for the enemy. The rewriting keeps the point of view completely on the side of the people of Moab and smooths the presentation.

8. "Also." This serves to tie in the sentence with what has gone before.

[18]

9. "That is what the Lord says!" (RSV: s̲a̲y̲s̲ t̲h̲e̲ L̲o̲r̲d̲.) TEV does not translate, probably because it may have seemed overly repetitive. The rewriting uses it to emphasize the point and carry back to "Listen to what the Lord says:" at the beginning.

5.4 How to proceed when translating poetry into poetry

As we said before, to translate a poem by a poem, the translation must have the qualities of a good poem in its own language. It must contain the ideas and the purpose of the original, but it cannot also carry over all of the details of the original poetic structure. If some of the Hebrew poetic devices create the same effect in the language of the translation, that may make it easier, but such help will not usually be very great. The translation should, as much as possible, have the same meaning, the same emphasis, the same feeling as in the original. It should have the same ability to provoke the reader to thought. However, the words, the images, the parallelism, the turns of language will often have to be different.

When translating the poetry of Amos into the poetry of his own language, the translator should be very cautious about the TEV. The TEV has usually translated as prose, for reasons we have already discussed. In other cases it takes the visual form of poetry with lines of different lengths beginning with capital letters, but it is not true English poetry. Some of these problems are discussed as we come to them in the text. Alongside the TEV, the RSV can help the translator see what some of the poetic characteristics of the original were, although they do not all come through in any translation, by any means. The literal translation and the structure of some passages analyzed in the Appendix may also help to give a better sense of what the author may have been trying to do with the poetic structure than the TEV sometimes gives.

The first step in translating into the poetry of any language is to make a simple translation of the ideas of the original into meaningful prose, without being too concerned with the poetic form. As that is done, the translator should keep track of the kinds of images used, the kinds of emotion that he wants to reproduce. This step is necessary in order to make sure that the meaning is preserved. After that, the same translator, or someone else who is more skilled in poetic style, can take this prose translation and restructure it into the poetic form of the language.

We suggest this procedure because it is easier for a poet to work within his own language as he tries to sense the feelings and rhythms that will make a suitable poem. In our experience, the translation is more successful if the two steps are done one after the other in this way, although the person rewriting a poem should keep referring back to the original so that he does not begin to miss the meaning. Then his work should be checked by someone else skillful in the original to make more sure that he has not distorted it.

He who translates a biblical verse according to its form (i.e. literally), such person is a liar (misrepresenting the sense), and he who adds to it, such person is a blasphemer.

Rabbi Yehudah

Tosephta Megilla 4.41

1.1 INTRODUCTION: THE PROPHET

Revised Standard Version	Today's English Version
1 The words of Amos, who was among the shepherds of Tekoa, which he saw concerning Israel in the days of Uzziah king of Judah and in the days of Jeroboam the son of Joash, king of Israel, two years^a before the earthquake.	1 These are the words of Amos, a shepherd from the town of Tekoa. Two years before the earthquake, when Uzziah was king of Judah and Jeroboam son of Jehoash was king of Israel, God revealed to Amos all these things about Israel.

^{a}Or *during two years*

This short section forms the title and serves as an introduction to the book of Amos. It has information about the prophet: his name, his social position, the time and place where he lived, why he did what is written here. However, in many languages it will not be understood as a title unless special care is taken in the translation. One way of doing this is to use special type and print the verse in a block under the modern book title:

> AMOS
> 1 These are the words of Amos,
> a shepherd from the town of Tekoa.
> Two years before the earthquake,
> when Uzziah was king of Judah, and
> Jeroboam son of Jehoash was king of
> Israel, God revealed to Amos all
> these things about Israel.

Section heading. Bible de Jérusalem (BJ) uses "Title" before verse 1; Smith-Goodspeed in taking verses 1 and 2 together uses the heading "Title and Purpose of the Book." New English Bible (NEB) prints the words of Amos in capitals. Today's English Version (TEV) omits any section heading.

What the translator should do depends in good part on what he decides about trying to show the balanced structure of the book of Amos in the section headings (see Translating Amos, Section 2.4). If he wants to stay with a simple, traditional set of headings, the best solution is probably not to have any heading here. If he decides to do something along the line of what is suggested in Translating Amos, and to reflect what he can of the balanced structure of the book, then he needs to consider both a heading for the first part of the book (1.1--5.3) and one for this single verse.

For a title to the longer part, in Translating Amos we suggest "Israel's Guilt; The Prophet's Responsibility." This can be translated in such a way as "Israel Has Sinned; The Prophet Must Proclaim/Announce God's Message." For verse 1 the heading could be simply "Title" or "Introduction," or it could be something like "Introduction: The Prophet" or "Introduction: The One Who Spoke God's Message."

[21]

1.1

In Hebrew this verse is a rather difficult sentence with three parts, as is clearly seen in the RSV: (1) words of Amos, (2) who was among the shepherds of Tekoa, (3) which he saw concerning Israel in the days of Uzziah king of Judah and in the days of Jeroboam the son of Joash, king of Israel, two years before the earthquake. The problem is how (3) relates to (1). One possibility can be expressed like this: "words of Amos, who was among the shepherds of Tekoa, and who had visions..." Depending on the needs of the language of the translation, such a meaning can be expressed in slightly different ways: "These are the words of Amos, who...; these are the visions which he had"; or "This is the book of the words of Amos, who...; this is the book of the visions which he had..." The translator may use this meaning,[1] which certainly shows the two major kinds of message in the book,[2] although it is not the meaning most scholars prefer. The possibility which most scholars seem to prefer, however, is "the words of Amos...which he received" (Smith-Goodspeed),[3] as many languages would express it. This implies "which he received from God." This meaning is the base of the TEV: These are the words of Amos...God revealed to Amos all these things... Or: "This is the book of the words Amos spoke... God gave him these messages about Israel..."

Amos. This is the only person in the Old Testament who has this name.[4] It should be translated as an ordinary name and the spelling adapted to the sounds of the language of the translation. (See Translators Handbook on Ruth 1.2) In doing this the translator should be careful not to use the same spelling as for the different name Amoz in Isaiah 1.1.

Amos' father is not mentioned, which may be a problem in some languages, but this does not mean anything about Amos' social position.[5] In languages where names should have titles with them, the title for Amos should be based on his role as prophet rather than shepherd (Translating Amos, Section 4). A title suitable for someone who delivered God's message and spoke it with authority should be used. However, Amos was not a priest or any other kind of official religious leader, and his title should not imply that he was.

In some languages the first introduction of a major person must be indicated by an expression such as "There was a prophet Amos" or "Have Amos," as it is expressed in some parts of the world. The translator will have to decide whether this introduction is more natural here in verse 1, or (if verse 1 is treated as a title) if it should be in verse 2: "Have prophet Amos, who said":

Who was among the shepherds of Tekoa,/a shepherd from the town of Tekoa. This simply means that Amos was "formerly one of the shepherds from the town of Tekoa." It does not mean that there were many shepherds living together, as RSV can imply. The TEV (compare New American Bible [NAB] and NEB) may also be misleading as it does not show that this was no longer true.[6] Moffatt (Mft) correctly translates: "who belonged to the shepherds of Tekoa."

Shepherd. The Hebrew word translated here is used only one other time in the Old Testament (2Kgs 3.4) where it is used of Mesha, the king of Moab, and where it has the meaning of "sheep-breeder." Sheep breeding must have been a rather profitable business as it enabled King Mesha to send the wool of a hundred thousand lambs and a hundred thousand rams to the king of Israel each year. Texts from related cultures[7] also seem to indicate that these sheep-breeders were well-to-do, and Amos was probably one of the important men of Tekoa. He was surely more than a simple shepherd:[8] "one of the sheep-farmers" (NEB).[9]

For languages which do not have vocabulary referring to stock raising, it may be possible to use some sort of descriptive phrase (such as "owner of sheep" or even "owner of many sheep") to show the importance of Amos' social position. Where people consider sheep to be dirty despised animals, it is even more important that the translation show Amos as the one profiting from owning the sheep rather than caring directly for them, if this is possible. Sheep are known in most parts of the world, although in some places they are called by such names as "cotton deer" or "woolly goat." Where a specific name for sheep is lacking it may be possible to use a descriptive phrase like "an animal which produces wool."

Of Tekoa/from the town of Tekoa. Tekoa was the town Amos considered his home, even though his ministry was in Bethel. Different languages express the idea of the home town in different ways: "born in the town/village of Tekoa," "his (father's) town/village was Tekoa," etc. In translation it will often be necessary to include the word "town/village." [10]

Which he saw concerning Israel/God revealed to Amos all these things about Israel. TEV has changed the order of this phrase. Each translation should use whatever order is smooth and clear. Possible translations have already been discussed, but there are some other problems for the translator if the meaning chosen by the TEV is followed.

Reveal. The meaning may be expressed by "made known" or "showed."

These things, in the TEV, are the messages of the book. In some languages the expression for "this" or "these" does not point forward to what follows in the text so cannot be used here. Other restructurings can take care of this problem: "This book contains (or: in this book are written) the words of Amos,...God gave Amos these words to say about Israel..." Note that now "this book" points outside the text to the book itself, and "these words" points back to "words of Amos." In other languages something like "the words continuing/going on from here" would be best.

Israel. Since this term has several meanings in the Bible, the translator should make sure that in the translation here it clearly means the kingdom which divided off from David's and Solomon's kingdom after Solomon died (1 Kgs 12.16-20; 2 Chr 10.1-19). It may be helpful in some translations to say "the country (or kingdom) of Israel."

Two years before the earthquake...king of Israel. See Translating Amos, Section 1. In Hebrew the time of the earthquake is mentioned last, the time of the rulers first. The order is reversed in the TEV because for English and many other languages the Hebrew order can be misleading. It can sound like the kings ruled two years before the earthquake rather than that Amos received the message then. Also, Two years before the earthquake is a more specific time than the longer period when the kings ruled. In each language the translator will have to decide what makes the clearest and most natural order.

All of these time periods are mentioned in a way which sounds as though the reader should know all about them, something which may not be true of modern readers. On the other hand, translations in some languages (especially languages without words like the) are likely to sound as though the reader should be learning about this time information for the first time, as though the English were "...two years before an earthquake, when a certain Uzziah was king of a country called Judah, and someone called Jeroboam...was king of another country called Israel." Such a translation is misleading. All languages have ways of indicating "the one you know about" either grammatically or with special words. Sometimes it is with the use of equivalents for "this" or "that": "two years before that earthquake...when that Uzziah...and that Jeroboam..." The reader may not actually know about the earthquake or the kings, but the wording should express to him the idea that he is not being told about them but that they are the setting for the rest of what is being said.

In many languages the two kings should have titles with their names (Translating Amos, Section 4).

Earthquake. Most languages will have a term for earthquake. This earthquake, however, must have been a particularly violent one because it was used for dating in a region where earthquakes are common. The translator may have to say: "two years before the great/violent earthquake." When there is no equivalent noun in the receptor language, the event can be described in a short phrase "two years before the earth/ground shook violently."

1.2   THE POWER OF GOD TO PUNISH

RSV

2 And he said:
    "The LORD roars from Zion,
       and utters his voice from
          Jerusalem;
    the pastures of the shepherds
          mourn,
       and the top of Carmel withers."

TEV

2 Amos said,
    "The LORD roars from Mount Zion;
       his voice thunders from
          Jerusalem.
    The pastures dry up,
       and the grass on Mount Carmel
          turns brown."

Amos' message to Israel begins with a strongly poetic statement on God's power to punish through destruction, a theme which is repeated from time to time and balanced against the idea of God's power to create (see Appendix, Section 1.1). It gives an introduction to the contents of the book.

Section heading. If the translator is not trying to show the structure of the book by use of section headings (see Translating Amos, Section 2.4), then probably there should not be a heading here. If he is, he can use something like "The Power of God to Punish" or "God Is Able To Destroy." Whatever is chosen, it should be something which can also be used in connection with 5.8 and 9.5-6, and which will contrast well with what is used in 4.13.

1.2

And he said:/Amos said. Since this expression introduces a brief message which is like a summary of the message of the book, it might be helpful in some languages to say "Here is what Amos' message was," "What Amos said was." In some other languages Amos said should be left untranslated, as it is included in the meaning of the first verse.

In some languages the end of a quotation must be indicated grammatically or by an expression like "he said." In other cases, like in English, the translator must decide where he will put a quotation mark to indicate the end of a quotation. So each saying in Amos will have to be studied carefully in light of the rules of the language and of the fact that in the book there are two or more levels of speaking, with Amos reciting the words of the Lord. In only two places (1.1; 7.10-12) is Amos himself not speaking.

TEV is somewhat misleading here. The TEV translation sounds as though Amos' words carry only through verse 2 and that another speaker (the Lord) replaces him in verse 3. TEV use of quotation marks is even more definite. According to them Amos stops talking at the end of verse 2, and does not speak again in the book except for a few remarks in chapters 7 and 8.

This confusion can be reduced by eliminating the quotation marks from verse 2, just as they are absent from some other section of hymn in the TEV (4.13; 5.8-9; 9.5-6). The same effect could be obtained, of course, even more directly by adding them to the beginning of each paragraph (verses 3,6, etc., all the way through the book), but that would be difficult for readers and make it hard to translate the quotations

[25]

inside quotations which would result when Amos in turn quotes the Lord.
Also, except for some brief sections in chapter 7, the whole book would
be in quotation marks. Taking the quotation marks out of verse 2 would
be a much easier solution.

The Hebrew poetry of Amos begins here, and except for Amos said
this verse is written in a style which is even more poetic than most of
the book of Amos, the style of a hymn.[1] On the characteristics of Hebrew
poetry and how to translate it, see Translating Amos, Section 5. If at
all possible, the translator should try to use an equivalent poetic
structure in the language of the translation.

What happens in the first half of this poem causes what happens in
the second half. That is, the drying up, the withering, is the result
of the Lord's roaring and thundering.[2] This must be clear in translation.
Compare Smith-Goodspeed: "So that"; Mft: "When...then..."

"The Lord roars from Zion, and utters his voice from Jerusalem:/
"The Lord roars from Mount Zion; his voice thunders from Jerusalem.
Along with the regular patterns of rhythm and sentence structure there
is unity in the use of very different pictures here. The Hebrew word for
roar is also used of thunder in the Old Testament (Jer 25.30; Job 37.3-4).

What these pictures mean is not absolutely clear, but the basis of
the comparison is probably God's anger and the threat of disaster or
punishment. Then when he speaks he has the power to destroy and is even
about to do so. This is certainly the general theme of Amos and comes
again in similar pieces of hymn in 5.9 and 9.5.

In translation, use of this picture language may or may not be a
problem. Everything depends on the possible meanings which equivalent
words in the receptor language may have, and on the poetic use of that
language. In many languages the sounds of some animals can also sometimes be applied to men (the translator should, of course, make sure
when that can be done and what it means). Such sounds can sometimes even
be applied to nature.[3] For example, in English the verb roar frequently
refers to a loud sound produced by a lion, a person in rage, or a water-
fall. It causes no problem to use it also for thunder. By using it TEV
keeps the relationship with thunder as in the Hebrew.

However, such an easy solution cannot always be found. Sometimes
roaring and thunder will give the wrong meaning like that of going crazy,
or no meaning at all. Sometimes the Hebrew picture cannot be expressed
as it is. If only animals, or even only a lion, can make the sound, a
comparison has to be expressed: "The Lord roars from Zion like a lion
roars when it is about to destroy its prey" or "The Lord speaks from
Zion like a lion roars when it is going to destroy its prey." In such a
case the link with thunder in the Hebrew may be weakened.

In places where lions are completely unknown, it may be useful to
keep a certain unity by combining the words roar and thunder:[4] "When
the Eternal thunders out of Sion, loudly from Jerusalem" (Mft). However,
in many languages a sentence such as his voice thunders from Jerusalem
is not easily translatable either. Very often a voice or a person cannot
"thunder," and "the Lord causes the thunder" hardly means the same thing.
So the translator must say something like: "and from Jerusalem he raises
his voice (calls out/shouts)" (compare NAB); "he calls out in anger from
Jerusalem, so that his voice is like a clap of thunder." As this is a
present reality, and a general statement, tenses which reflect that meaning should be used.

The Lord. See Translators Handbook on Ruth, 1.6.

Zion. Zion was originally the name of the fortress of the Jebusites (from whom the Israelites conquered the area of Jerusalem), located on the eastern mountain of Jerusalem. Later it became the name of the whole eastern mountain and of the whole city. In this passage it is another name for Jerusalem, and the translation should not sound like they are two different places.

The pastures of the shepherds mourn, (Hebrew: the habitations of the shepherds dry up)/The pastures dry up. As the Hebrew term for "habitations" is a very general one used of animals, men, and God, the of the shepherds is necessary to narrow down the meaning in the original text. However, this information is already included in the specific term pastures in the TEV. When a specific word such as pastures exists in the receptor language, the translator should follow the example of the TEV. Otherwise, a descriptive phrase could be used such as "the places/grounds dry up where men feed (lead/watch over/care for) the sheep." Older English translations say the pastures of the shepherds mourn (see also Smith-Goodspeed). Dry up is correct and should be followed.[5]

Where the meaning will not be clear from the picture alone, you may translate something like "when he speaks (he can command) the pastures (to) dry up" or "because of his anger he causes the pastures to dry up."

And the top of Carmel withers."/and the grass on Mount Carmel turns brown." It may be best to indicate that Carmel is a mountain, as in TEV.[6] The mountain ridge of Carmel was one of the most fertile parts of Palestine, abundant in woods, flowers and vineyards. But those facts are unknown to many present-day readers, and so the point may have to be made clear. TEV does this by mentioning grass. Any expression for rich vegetation would do. In keeping with the contrast as well as with the poetry of the text, this grass turns brown. Perhaps at this point TEV is not an easy model for translators, since in many languages colors are not easily used to express events. It may, therefore, be necessary to make a statement such as "and the woods (trees) on Mount Carmel's top wither."

1.3--3.2 ISRAEL'S SPECIAL GUILT AMONG THE NATIONS

Here begins the first long section of Amos, in fact, the longest
one. It is clearly separate from the verses which precede. In Hebrew
there is no word to connect verse 3 with what goes before. Furthermore,
in verse 2 Amos was speaking about the Lord whereas in verse 3 the Lord
himself speaks. The theme of God's judgment on Israel's neighbors begins
in verse 3.[1]

This section of Amos has a series of eight very similar messages
from the Lord plus a conclusion. In each message a different nation is
mentioned, its sins are vividly pictured, and a promise of punishment is
made. The first seven of these messages are about Israel's neighbors and,
in some cases, traditional enemies. Then the eighth, longer than any of
the others, is about Israel itself. So the first seven messages are pre-
liminary, setting a mood, establishing a rhythm in which the listener-in,
Israel, hears stirring but often reassuring words that foreign people are
going to be punished. But then, suddenly and dramatically, the eighth
message comes to Israel itself. God's own people are doing things as evil
or worse, and God will punish them also!

This section of Amos is a powerful passage because of its dramatic
use of language. With some thought and care the translator should be
able to prepare a powerful, moving translation as well. The strength of
the Hebrew comes from its picture language and from the rhythmical repetition as each accusation is made. The similar wording from message to
message helps to emphasize how the message to Israel is both similar and
different.

In general, each of the eight messages in this section has the same
six parts in the same order, although some of the messages leave out one
or more parts. Furthermore, some of the parts are worded nearly the same
in nearly all of the messages. Here is a list of the parts, and a literal
translation of the Hebrew in the cases where the wording is the same or
nearly the same in each message:

(1) The source of the message: "thus the Lord said."

(2) The general reason for God's punishment: "for three transgressions of...and for four, I will not revoke it."

(3) The specific illustration of the people's crimes: because they/
he...

(4) The standard punishment (not included for Israel): "but I will
send/kindle a fire into/on/in...and it shall devour the palaces..." This
is expanded with further detail about the battle in which the fire will
come in the cases of Ammon and Moab.

(5) Additional particular punishment (not included for Tyre, Edom,
Judah).

(6) The source of the message repeated (not included for Tyre, Edom,
or Judah): "said (the Lord) Jahweh."

Parts 5 and 6 are simply missing for Tyre, Edom, and Judah, and
part 4 is missing for Israel. Part 6 is not separately translated in the
TEV, but is included in part 1.

The translator should work on this section of Amos as a whole, and
before he finishes, all of these messages about the different nations
should contribute to the total effect. Each message should reinforce the

others and lead to the climax, which is the message to Israel. The whole section should be read aloud repeatedly after it is translated to make sure of the smooth, free-flowing rhythm and effect. The translation should have a tone of strong denunciation. The mood is dignified anger.

This overall tone, rhythm, and climax in the passage is more important in translation than is poetry as such. The section is poetry in Hebrew, but it is a different kind of poetry from verse 2. The question of whether or not to translate in poetry was discussed in Translating Amos, Section 5. If poetry is appropriate for accusation and promise of punishment[2] in the language of the translation, it should be used. And if poetry is used it should, of course, be in the poetic patterns of that language, not of Hebrew. If prose is used, it should carry the emotional tone of accusation just the same. Note the restructuring of 2.1-3 suggested to help increase the force of the English in those verses, in Translating Amos, Section 5.3.

In languages where God and kings or chiefs speak in a different style from ordinary people, special care must be taken to get naturalness in these messages where Amos, an ordinary person, is quoting God (Translating Amos, Section 4). The translator must decide what level is suitable, and this can be complicated by the fact that in some of these languages the form used by kings or God may not always be clear to ordinary people. In some cases the level will change back and forth in the translation. In 1.3, The Lord says is Amos speaking, but the remainder of the verse is Amos speaking God's words.

Section headings. When the translator is not trying to show the structure of the book through section headings he may follow the TEV, which separates off the judgment on Israel (2.6-16), or he may have one main heading for the whole section, although it is rather long. Alternative wordings for the TEV section headings which may be easier to translate in some languages include: "God Judges/Will Punish the Sins of Israel's Neighbors" or "God Judges/Will Punish the Nations," and "God Judges/Will Punish Israel's Sins." A heading for the whole section might be "The Sins of Israel and Her Neighbors" (NEB). In either case, it may be well to follow the TEV and indicate each separate message with a separate heading (the name of the nation) as well.

Where the translator is trying to show the structure of the book, it is important to have one main heading for the whole long section, something which is similar to the headings of 4.4-12, 5.18--6.14, and 8.4--9.4. We have used "Israel's Special Guilt Among the Nations," which could be translated something like "Israel Is the Most Guilty of All the Nations," or "Israel Has Sinned More Than All Other People."

Then the smaller sections within this section can each have its heading consisting of the name of the nation (see Translating Amos, Section 2.4). The heading for 3.1-2 will be discussed when that section is reached.

1.3-5

RSV   TEV

GOD'S JUDGMENT ON ISRAEL'S NEIGHBORS

Syria

3 Thus says the LORD:
"For three transgressions of
    Damascus,
  and for four, I will not
    revoke the punish-
    ment,^{b}
because they have threshed
  Gilead with threshing
  sledges of iron.
4 So I will send a fire upon
    the house of Hazael,
  and it shall devour the
    strongholds of Ben-hadad.
5 I will break the bar of Damascus,
  and cut off the inhabitants
    from the Valley of Aven,^{c}
and him that holds the scepter
    from Beth-eden;
  and the people of Syria shall
    go into exile to Kir,"
                says the LORD.

3 The LORD says. "The people of
Damascus have sinned again and
again, and for this I will certainly punish them. They treated the
people of Gilead with savage cruelty. 4 So I will send fire upon the
palace built by King Hazael and I
will burn down the fortresses of
King Benhadad. 5 I will smash the
city gates of Damascus and remove
the inhabitants of Aven Valley and
the ruler of Betheden. The people
of Syria will be taken away as
prisoners to the land of Kir."

^{b}Heb *cause it to return*

^{c}Or *On*

The message about Syria includes all of the six parts listed above.
The discussion of the passage below is numbered according to these
different parts.

1.3

(1) Thus says the Lord: (Hebrew: thus the Lord said)/The Lord says.
In some languages it may be useful to keep the Hebrew past tense in
translation in order to show the difference between the actual speech of
Amos and an earlier experience in which Amos received God's message.[3] On
the other hand, the message is a timeless warning with present and future
meaning. The translation should reflect this fact, as is done with the
use of the present tense in many English translations.
    The expression "thus the Lord said" or others similar to it is used
in the prophetic books of the Old Testament to declare God's authority
for the message. The translation should not be as flat as the Lord says.
The expression is not a simple introduction to a quotation. The words
should have the sound of authority in the translation: "Listen to what
the Lord says," "Here is the word of the Lord" (compare NEB: "These are
the words of the Lord"), "This is what the Lord has to say."

The expression used here should be something which will sound well when repeated many times in the Old Testament. Part of the strong tone of the prophetic books depends on the frequent repetition of this expression and others very much like it. The expression does not have to be repeated in the translation every time it occurs in the Hebrew, of course, but to have to leave it out because it is a weak expression and sounds weak and repetitive is much less valuable than to have the repetition itself make the message more urgent and powerful.

(2) "For three transgressions of Damascus, and for four,/"The people of Damascus have sinned again and again. As is clear from verses 4 and 5, Damascus stands for both the rulers and the inhabitants of the city of Damascus, and they can be taken together in a general way as The people of Damascus or "the people of the city of Damascus." The city of Damascus itself stands for the people and rulers of the whole country of Syria (verse 5). Syria is the heading in TEV for that reason. Damascus and Syria should not sound like different places in the translation. If the confusion of Damascus and Syria is a problem, one solution is to use "Syria" for "Damascus" right from the beginning except for verse 5, where its relationship to Syria should be clear in context. Another solution would be to translate "Damascus in Syria" or "Damascus, the capital of "Syria," etc., in verse 3.

It should be clear, furthermore, that Damascus is a city well-known to the people of Israel. The translation should not sound like "a city called Damascus" but like "the city of Damascus (that you know about)." This kind of difference was discussed under 1.1.

Transgressions are things that people do, and so are usually better translated with a verb: have sinned. In Amos the Hebrew noun here translated transgressions is used only for sins against people.[4] The word or expression in the translation should be one with the strong meaning of "to commit a horrible crime." Neither a weak word such as "to make a mistake" nor a highly specialized theological one such as "to disobey God" is adequate here. The difficult problems in translating words for "sin" are discussed in other Translators Handbooks.[5]

In for three transgressions...and for four the numbers should not be taken either symbolically or literally.[6] The progression from three to four expresses a climax or increasing intensity.[7] In languages where numbers have only a literal value, a literal translation of this sequence would give rise to a wrong meaning. On the other hand, some attempts at idiomatic translation such as "many"[8] are also misleading. Only translations such as "the people of Damascus have committed crime upon crime" (compare Mft) or have sinned again and again are adequate in English. Translators should look for something to give this meaning of piling sin upon sin.

I will not revoke the punishment (Hebrew: cause it to return or reverse/revoke it)/I will certainly punish them. "It" refers either to the punishment announced immediately afterwards (RSV) or to the word of God (NAB: "I will not revoke my word").[9] However, the word of God is a word of judgment in the context of these messages. Also, in many languages a negative statement as in the Hebrew is weak or does not have the positive meaning the Hebrew has here. That is why TEV has I will certainly punish them.

The punishment is the result of the sin, and the clause I will certainly punish them is connected as the result of what precedes (sinned
again and again) and what follows (They treated...). Furthermore, the
kind of punishment is shown in verse 4. In some languages such moving
back and forth between reason and result may not be fully natural or
clear. In such cases the order of I will certainly punish them and They
treated... may have to be changed, or some other restructuring employed.
Then I will certainly punish them may have to be introduced with a word
equivalent to "so."

Some languages do not use quotations in which I means the person
quoted (the Lord), not the immediate speaker (Amos). In such cases the
use of I here might even mean whoever is reading in the local situation.
In that case, the quotation often cannot be a direct one but must be
something like "The Lord's message is that...he will punish"; or the
language may have other ways of making the meaning clear. In some cases
a noun would be used even though the Lord is speaking of himself: "The
Lord will certainly punish them." This problem, if it exists, will carry
through the whole book and need regular attention.

The shift in style which will be necessary in some languages when
God begins to speak has already been mentioned (1.3--3.2). In some languages God should also use words or grammar which show that he is speaking disrespectfully of the people of Damascus. In many languages, some
pronouns are respectful and some pronouns are disrespectful. In that
case it might be best to translate as "the people of the city of Damascus,
they have sinned again and again," with the word for "they" one which
indicates the speaker's disapproval.

(3) Because they have threshed Gilead with threshing sledges of
iron./They treated the people of Gilead with savage cruelty. Gilead
probably stands for the people of Gilead or "the inhabitants of the
country of Gilead."10

Threshing sledges of iron were flat wooden platforms which were
studded with iron knives11 and pulled by animals across the harvested
grain to cut up the straw and separate the grain from the stalks:
"threshing-sledges spiked with iron" (NEB). As there is no direct evidence from elsewhere of doing this to people, the expression can best be
taken as picture language, to show cruelty by the picture of the violence with which grain is threshed. The picture should often be translated as a comparison: "because they destroyed the people of Gilead
like someone threshes grain with iron chariots." For other possibilities see Translating Amos, Section 5.

1.4

(4) So reflects the fact that verse 4 is a result of the terrible
deeds of verse 3. Making the last part of verse 3 connected with verse 4
is also possible: "Because they threshed Gilead with sledges of iron, I
will send fire..." (NAB; compare Jerusalem Bible [JB]). Whatever is done
to express this relationship should fit in with the same relationship
also shown between the parts of verse 3, as already discussed.

Send a fire/send fire refers to the burning which goes along with
defeat by a foreign army, in this case by the Lord. The battle of which
the fire is a part is mentioned directly in the punishment of Ammon (1.14)

and Moab (2.2). Sometimes fire has been translated "fires of war" (Mft).
Send is picture language for "make/cause (fire) to burn."
    The house of Hazael,/the palace built by King Hazael. Because of the
parallel between Hazael and Benhadad, this Hebrew expression could mean
"the royal family of Hazael," which in turn could be taken as "the kingdom of Syria." In the same way the fortresses of King Benhadad could mean
the town of Damascus.[12]
    On the other hand, it may be better to take house literally, as the
exact parallel word in the next line is a Hebrew word translated fortresses. Also, the expression I will send fire occurs in all the other
messages of this section except the one against Israel, and the fire always burns a building. A translation "on the house (palace) of King
Hazael" is therefore better.
    Make sure that the palace built by King Hazael and the fortresses
of King Benhadad do not sound like different places. In languages where
parallelism or the grammatical construction does not make it clear that
they are the same, some additional restructuring may do it: "the royal
palace of Syria, with its fortresses defended by King Benhadad" or "the
royal palace...among the fortresses..." or "the royal palace..., that is,
the fortresses of King Benhadad."
    Devour/burn down. The Hebrew idiom of "fire that eats (up) some-
thing" occurs frequently and can be carried over naturally into many languages. In other cases, the translation will have to have another picture
or translate the meaning burn.
    Strongholds/fortresses translates one of the most important parts
of the meaning of the Hebrew word (NAB: "castles").[13] Unfortunately, such
buildings are not known in many parts of the world so this meaning cannot
always be made clear in translation. Sometimes a more general word has to
be used in this context, and the nearest equivalent which is present in
some languages may be the word for "chief's compound" or "chief's house."

1.5

    (5) I will break the bar of Damascus,/I will smash the city gates of
Damascus. The bar was made of bronze or iron, fixed in the doorpost to
block the gate from opening. It formed part of the defense of the city
gate, and to break it meant that the gate was broken in (compare Mft: "I
shatter the defences of Damascus").
    Translation is difficult in those cultures where there are no city
walls or city gates. The translator may even have to use a slightly longer descriptive phrase and say, for example, "The bar which bolts the
doors of the mouth/opening/entrance in the walls/fences around the city
of Damascus." The verb used should show the violence of the action necessary to break through a city gate. I will smash expresses this violence
very well in English.
    And cut off the inhabitants (Hebrew: the ruler) from the Valley of
Aven (Hebrew: Biqat-Aven), and him that holds the scepter from Beth-eden;
/and remove the inhabitants of Aven Valley and the ruler of Betheden. The
Hebrew for "ruler" has been translated inhabitants (see also NAB, NEB),
but as the meaning "ruler" is a possible one, it is better because of the
parallel with "him that holds the scepter."[14] If the meaning "ruler" is
used and if the parallel is not needed for the style of the translation,

the repetition can be combined. This may sound more natural in some languages, and the translator will not have to look for often non-existing
words with similar meanings.

Cut off/remove. Remove may be weak for an English translation. Compare "wipe out" (NEB), "cut down" (Jerusalem Bible [JB]). In context the
meaning would seem to be that of harsh destruction or captivity.

Aven Valley...Betheden. There are many problems with the two names
of places in this verse. Different suggestions about their location have
been given (see commentaries). For translation the problem is that the
names in Hebrew have two purposes: they are names for areas in the normal
meaning of place names, but they are also moral descriptions of those
areas. "Biqat-Aven" sounds in Hebrew like "valley of iniquity," and
Betheden sounds like "house of pleasure."[15] The translator has to decide
which names or parts of names he will translate and which he will handle
as ordinary names.

The normal practice in English has been to translate Valley in the
first name and to treat the rest as names. However, this is probably
wrong. The name itself may be "Valley" and "Aven" may be a description.
If so, the place was "The Plain" (as it was called) between Lebanon and
Anti-Lebanon (see map in Translating Amos, Section 3), which is characterized as "Plain of Iniquity."

As much remains uncertain, it seems wiser to follow the French practice of treating both completely as names: "Biqat-Aven" and Betheden.
Then the additional meaning of the name can be given in a footnote.

And the people of Syria shall go into exile/The people of Syria will
be taken away as prisoners. The TEV uses less technical language than
"exile" (compare NAB, NEB, Mft), a word lacking in many languages. The
Hebrew means go into exile, but since this action was obviously not
voluntary TEV has restructured: will be taken away as prisoners. In many
languages the person or people who do the action will have to be indicated: "one/others will take them away/cause them to leave their country as
prisoners." The term used for prisoners, of course, should not mean
people locked up in jail, but rather people taken from their homes as
captives.

To Kir/to the land of Kir. Hebrew simply has Kir, but it is necessary in translation to show that this is a land. According to 9.7, the
Syrians came originally from Kir. Their return to the same region implies
that their whole history is reduced to nothing. The exact location of
this land of Kir is uncertain.

(6) Says the Lord (Hebrew: the Lord has said). TEV does not repeat
this last part of Amos' message, which gives its source once more, as in
verse 3. It has considered this repetition unnecessary, perhaps awkward,
in English, especially as the next message begins in the next verse again
with The Lord says. The decision to leave it out in the TEV restructuring
is perfectly correct so far as the meaning is concerned. On the other
hand, this mentioning of the source of the message both at the beginning
and the end is part of the power and rhythm of the passage in Hebrew.
Also, it is an important part of the way in which the book of Amos is
organized. It would not be too difficult to keep this second indicator
of the source in English if the whole passage is translated accordingly.
We already suggested, for example, that in English part (1) in verse 3
could be strengthened. Now part (6) can be tied in with it like this:

(1) "Here is what the Lord says:... (6) That is what the Lord says!" (1) "Here is the word of the Lord:... (6) That was the word of the Lord!" An example of such a restructuring of the TEV is to be found in Translating Amos, Section 5.3. In a prose translation these introductory and closing reminders of the source of the message should probably be set off in some way on separate lines or with special type. In some languages, of course, indicating the source of a message at the end is completely normal, if not required.

1:6-8

RSV	TEV
	Philistia
6 Thus says the LORD:	6 The LORD says, "The people of
"For three transgressions of	Gaza have sinned again and again,
Gaza,	and for this I will certainly
and for four, I will not	punish them. They carried off a
revoke the punishment,*b*	whole nation and sold them as
because they carried into	slaves to the people of Edom.
exile a whole people	7 So I will send fire upon the city
to deliver them up to Edom.	walls of Gaza and burn down its
7 So I will send a fire upon the	fortresses. 8 I will remove the
wall of Gaza,	rulers of the cities of Ashdod
and it shall devour her	and Ashkelon. I will punish the
strongholds.	city of Ekron, and all the Philis-
8 I will cut off the inhabitants	tines who are left will die."
from Ashdod,	
and him that holds the	
scepter from Ashkelon;	
I will turn my hand against	
Ekron;	
and the remnant of the	
Philistines shall perish,"	
says the Lord GOD.	

*b*Heb *cause it to return*

The same numbering for the different parts of the message will be used as were used in discussing the message to Syria. Except where the Hebrew is different, as much as possible the wording in translation should be the same also. However, the translator should not follow the earlier message mechanically but should think about how it sounds and how the whole passage fits together. It may be that the translation of the earlier message should be revised in keeping with things that are thought of in this one or later on.

1.6

(1-2) The Lord says...punish them. See verse 3. It may be useful to mark Gaza as a town: "the people of the town of Gaza."

(3) Because they carried into exile a whole people (Hebrew: because of their deporting an entire exile)/They carried off a whole nation. (Compare NEB: "because they deported a whole band of exiles.") Such an abstract wording as the Hebrew presents problems in many languages, and the group or groups which were carried off should often be expressed in translation.[16] It may not have been a whole nation which was carried off, however. It is better to speak of "whole groups" (NAB), or even of "whole villages." Thus the translation might be something like "because they captured/carried off (as captives) the population of whole villages."

To deliver them up to Edom/and sold them as slaves to the people of Edom. The attention is on the violence and the inhuman conduct to which the captives were submitted, and not on the commercial aspect of selling slaves. However, many languages require a specific translation, and a rendering such as sold sometimes cannot be avoided.

Them. To use some other translation than nation avoids another problem which the TEV has here. Sold them (plural) refers back to nation (singular).

(4) I will send fire upon the city walls of Gaza and burn down its fortresses. See verse 4.

(5) I will remove the rulers of the cities of Ashdod and Ashkelon. See verse 5. It should be shown that Ashdod and Ashkelon are cities. It should also be clear in context that they and Ekron along with Gaza are cities of the Philistines.

I will turn my hand against Ekron;/I will punish the city of Ekron. (See also Smith-Goodspeed, NAB, NEB). Hand here means "power."[17] If similar picture language can be used in the translation, it should be. If not, then some other kind of picture language expressing the idea of "power and punishment" should be used if possible. If no picture language is suitable, the translation will have to be direct as it is in the TEV. Compare Mft: "I strike my blows at Ekron." Ekron may also have to be qualified as the city of Ekron.

The remnant of the Philistines/all the Philistines who are left. The remnant of the Philistines does not mean those who have not been mentioned in the preceding verses, but those who might have escaped the punishment. The TEV restructuring is helpful.

(6) Says the Lord God. Unlike verse 5, the Hebrew text here has an additional word, God. However, whatever the reason for this difference,[18] the use of exactly the same form as in verse 5 is perfectly correct in the translation. (See also under 3.7)

1.9-10

RSV

9 Thus says the LORD:
  "For three transgressions of
    Tyre,
  and for four, I will not
    revoke the punishment;[b]
  because they delivered up a
    whole people to Edom,
  and did not remember the
    covenant of brother-
    hood.
10 So I will send a fire upon
    the wall of Tyre,
  and it shall devour her
    strongholds."

TEV

Tyre
  9 The LORD says, "The people of
Tyre have sinned again and again,
and for this I will certainly
punish them. They carried off a
whole nation into exile in the
land of Edom, and did not keep the
treaty of friendship they had made.
10 So I will send fire upon the
city walls of Tyre and burn down
its fortresses."

[b]Heb *cause it to return*

The message about Tyre differs slightly from the preceding ones about Syria and Philistia. Part (3), giving the specific illustrations of the people's crimes, starts in the same way as the others in Hebrew, but this time it is shorter and continues with a different grammatical construction. Parts (5) and (6) are completely missing.

1.9

(1-2) The Lord says...punish them. See verse 3. Tyre may be indicated as a "town."

(3) Because they delivered up a whole people to Edom (Hebrew: because of their handing over an entire exile to Edom)/They carried off a whole nation into exile in the land of Edom. The Hebrew uses the same words as in verse 6, so the translator should consult the discussion there. However, he should be careful of the meaning of this part of verse 9. The Hebrew involves two kernel sentences: (a) someone exiled/deported/took captive whole (groups of people); and (b) they (the people of Tyre/the rulers of Tyre) handed them over/sold them to Edom. The problems are in (a). (1) The nationality of the captives is not shown. Were they Israelites[19] or not?[20] Could they have been Phoenicians (people of the same country captured by their fellow people of Tyre)? (2) There is no historical evidence for any extensive slave raiding by the Phoenicians, but there is evidence for slave commerce. So perhaps the subject of (a) differs from that of (b). Maybe the slave raiders were Aramean. (3) The translation of the TEV is wrong as it implies capture by the Phoenicians and because it indicates that a whole people were carried off, which is not the meaning.[21]

Although a clear understanding of the first kernel is impossible, the best solution for translation would probably be something like: "because they delivered/sold whole groups of people (or: the population of whole villages) as captives/slaves to the people of Edom" (compare especially NAB).

And did not remember the covenant of brotherhood./and did not keep the treaty of friendship they had made. Although this is an independent sentence in both Hebrew and TEV, it is just another way of looking at the same events. This relationship should be made clear one way or another in the translation. NEB, for example, has done this by saying, "because, forgetting the ties of kinship, they delivered..." Another way might be by a word or a grammatical link between the two different sentences: "so (in so doing) they..."

Remember/keep. Keep is the right meaning of the Hebrew word in this context as it does not mean a mental process ("remember") but personal action.[22] Covenant of brotherhood, however, is more difficult, especially since this is the only place in the Old Testament where the expression occurs. Which covenant and between whom?[23] Most commentators think of the political treaty between King Hiram of Tyre and King Solomon (1 Kgs 5.12), and this understanding is translated in TEV the treaty of friendship they had made.[24] But the political treaty between Hiram and Solomon was more than 200 years before that, which makes this understanding rather doubtful.[25] Because of the uncertainties, a general translation such as "so they did not keep/honor the obligations brothers have toward each other" would be best. If something like this cannot be done, then the TEV solution should be followed.

(4) So I will send fire upon...fortresses. See verse 4.

RSV	TEV
	Edom

11 Thus says the LORD:
"For three transgressions
    of Edom,
and for four, I will not
    revoke the punishment,[b]
because he pursued his broth-
    er with the sword,
and cast off all pity,
and his anger tore perpetu-
    ally,
and he kept his wrath,[d]
    for ever.
12 So I will send a fire upon Teman,
    and it shall devour the
    strongholds of Bozrah."
	11 The LORD says, "The people
	of Edom have sinned again and again,
	and for this I will certainly punish
	them. They hunted down their broth-
	ers,[a] the Israelites, and showed
	them no mercy. Their anger had no
	limits, and they never let it die.
	12 So I will send fire upon the
	city of Teman and burn down the
	fortresses of Bozrah."

[a]THEIR BROTHERS: *The Israelites were descended from Jacob, who was the brother of Esau, the ancestor of the Edomites.*

[b]Heb *cause it to return*

[d]Gk Syr Vg: Heb *his wrath kept*

The message about Edom is almost the same as the preceding one about Tyre. The main difference is in part (3). After starting with the same grammatical construction in Hebrew, part (3) is developed a little differently. Parts (5) and (6) again are missing.

1.11

(1-2) The Lord says...punish them. See verse 3.

(3) Because he pursued his brother with the sword,/They hunted down their brothers, the Israelites. Hunted down may be a good solution for pursued...with the sword in other languages as well. Showing how the hunting was done may contribute to the emotional tone in some languages: "because, sword in hand, they hunted their kinsmen down" (NEB; compare Mft). If "hunting" vocabulary cannot be used for action toward people, the translation might be "they put their brothers to flight (or: they chased their brothers) by means of the sword."

For brothers the translator should use a very broad term including all fellow nationals or tribesmen. It may be necessary to state who their brothers are: the Israelites. The Edomites were descended from Esau, Jacob's brother (Gen 36.1-19).

And cast off all pity (Hebrew: destroyed his mercy),/and showed them no mercy. The Hebrew idiom cannot be translated directly into most languages. Sometimes a verb with a similar meaning can be used to create a similar picture: for example, "to stifle" in English (compare Smith-Goodspeed, Mft, NEB), "étouffer" in French, etc. But in a majority of languages even this would be impossible so a descriptive phrase has to be used as in TEV, or, even more directly: "and refused to be merciful." In this particular context the specific meaning of the Hebrew noun for mercy is "brotherly feelings," "brotherly love."[26] As many cultures have a specific term in this area, it may be possible to translate "they did not (want to) love them as brothers."

And his anger tore perpetually, and he kept his wrath for ever./ Their anger had no limits and they never let it die. The Hebrew text here is not clear, but may be understood as follows: "he (Edom) persisted in his anger and kept his wrath to the end" (NAB), or: "his anger persisted forever and his wrath to the end."[27] This is the basis for the TEV. In some translations the parallel information may be combined into one short sentence: "their anger never stopped/died down." TEV uses die for anger because it is clear and forceful in English. In each case the translator will have to look for an appropriate natural expression. Even a flat rendering such as: "they continued to be angry with them" may be necessary.[28]

1.12

(4) So I will send fire upon the city of Teman and burn down the fortresses of Bozrah. See verse 4.[29] TEV indicates that Teman is a city, but Teman and Bozrah could be taken as names of towns, regions, or both, so it is better not to be specific, if possible. As the fortresses of Bozrah are not included in Teman, and as there is a certain distance between the towns or regions, the translation should not say that the fire sent on Teman will burn up the fortresses of Bozrah, as RSV and other modern translations (except TEV) do.

1.13-15

RSV	TEV
	Ammon
13 Thus says the LORD:	13 The LORD says, "The people
"For three transgressions of	of Ammon have sinned again and
the Ammonites,	again, and for this I will certain-
and for four, I will not	ly punish them. In their wars for
revoke the punishment;*b*	more territory they even ripped
because they have ripped up	open pregnant women in Gilead.
women with child in	14 So I will send fire upon the
Gilead,	city walls of Rabbah and burn down
that they might enlarge	its fortresses. Then there will be
their border.	shouts on the day of battle, and
14 So I will kindle a fire in the	the fighting will rage like a storm.
wall of Rabbah,	15 Their king and his officers will
and it shall devour her	go into exile."
strongholds,	
with shouting in the day of	
battle,	
with a tempest in the day	
of the whirlwind;	
15 and their king shall go into	
exile,	
he and his princes together,"	
says the LORD.	

*b*Heb *cause it to return*

    All six parts are present in this message about Ammon as they were in the messages about Syria and Philistia.

1.13

    (1-2) <u>The Lord says...punish them</u>. See verse 3.
    (3) <u>Because they have ripped up[30] women with child in Gilead, that they might enlarge their border/In their wars for more territory they even ripped open pregnant women in Gilead</u>. The meaning is that when the Ammonites were fighting for more land they killed much of the population of Gilead and in so doing were especially cruel to pregnant women. Both events of "enlarging the territory" and committing atrocities happened at the same time, so the translator may have to say something like: "because, while extending their territory, they ripped open..." (compare NAB, Mft). <u>Pregnant women in Gilead</u> sometimes has to be translated as "pregnant women living in the land of Gilead."[31]

1.14

    (4) <u>So I will send fire...fortresses</u>. See verse 4. This time the Hebrew shows another slight variation: "I will set fire to" instead of

the usual "I will send fire on." This variation makes almost no change
in meaning, so the translator may use the phrase which he has used elsewhere if it seems best.[32]

 With shouting in the day of battle, with a tempest in the day of the
whirlwind;/Then there will be shouts on the day of battle, and the fighting will rage like a storm. In this case the battle of which the fire is
a part is mentioned. The Hebrew parallelism makes clear that "whirlwind"
is a picture of the heavy fighting. Since a translation such as tempest in
the day of the whirlwind makes little sense in most languages, the TEV
type solution is helpful. The translator should also make sure that the
relation between shouts and battle is clear. The shouts are part of the
noise of the confused fighting and the failing defenses.

1.15

 (5) And their king shall go into exile, he and his princes together/
Their king and his officers will go into exile. Their king is, of course,
the king of the Ammonites. Because this word is so far from the word to
which it refers, in some languages it would be better to state the relationship: "the king of (the people of) Ammon," or even "the king of
Rabbah."

 Officers translates a very general Hebrew term which includes court
officials, counsellors, military and other authorities. In many languages
a term such as "notables" or "big people" would be the right equivalent.

 Exile. See verse 6.[33]

 (6) Says the Lord. See verse 5.

2.1-3

RSV	TEV
	Moab

2 Thus says the LORD:
   "For three transgressions of
       Moab,
  and for four, I will not
       revoke the punishment;[e]
  because he burned to lime
      the bones of the king of Edom.
2 So I will send a fire upon Moab,
    and it shall devour the
       strongholds of Kerioth,
  and Moab shall die amid uproar,
    amid shouting and the sound
       of the trumpet;
3 I will cut off the ruler from
     its midst,
  and will slay all its princes
    with him,"
               says the LORD.
	2 The LORD says, "The people of
	Moab have sinned again and again,
	and for this I will certainly
	punish them. They dishonored the
	bones of the king of Edom by burn-
	ing them to ashes. 2 I will send
	fire upon the land of Moab and burn
	down the fortresses of Kerioth. The
	people of Moab will die in the
	noise of battle while soldiers are
	shouting and trumpets are sounding.
	3 I will kill the ruler of Moab
	and all the leaders of the land."

[e]Heb *cause it to return*

All six of the characteristic parts of this series are present in
this message about Moab. A sample restructuring of this passage is given
in Translating Amos, Section 5.2.

2.1

(1-2) The Lord says...punish them. See 1.3.

(3) Because he burned to lime the bones of the king of Edom./They
dishonored the bones of the king of Edom by burning them to ashes. The
historical situation that underlines this accusation is not known to us.
However, the act did not take place immediately after the death of the
unknown king, but some time later, along with the opening of his tomb.
So the particular crime is not in the act of burning, but in the opening
up of the tomb and taking out the bones. Such an act was felt to be a
serious offense, and not only by the ancient Semites![34]

The bones were burned so completely that their ashes became as fine
and as white as lime. This is how the meaning can be most easily expressed in many languages.[35] It is probable, however, that the Hebrew
also refers to an additional crime: that the Moabites used the ashes of
the king of Edom as one of the materials for plastering their houses. In
one ancient translation this possibility has been expressed directly:
"and plastered them in the lime on its house."[36] This understanding has
also been kept in the footnote of the NEB. So the restructuring suggested
in Translating Amos, Section 5, can also serve as a model for languages
where it would be convenient and effective: "burning his bones to make
lime."

2.2

(4) I will send fire...fortresses of Kerioth. See 1.10,14. In one
ancient translation Kerioth was not taken as a proper name but as meaning "towns"[37] (compare NEB: "fire that shall consume the palaces in their
towns"). There is historical evidence for the existence of a town Kerioth,[38] however, and it would be better to translate as such: "the fortresses of the town of Kerioth."

And Moab shall die amid uproar, amid shouting and the sound of the
trumpet/The people of Moab will die in the noise of battle while soldiers
are shouting and trumpets are sounding. The TEV has made much of the meaning clear. Moab has been translated as The people of Moab. Uproar is in
fact the noise of battle. The shouting involves people, so soldiers are
shouting. The sound of the trumpet is translated trumpets are sounding.
In some languages someone will have to do the blowing so "soldiers are
shouting and blowing trumpets." All three events happen at the same time,
and TEV expresses this relationship with while. The meaning of the shouting and trumpet blowing should not be misleading. As would be true in
many cultures, the shouting probably had a magical function and was intended to chase evil spirits.[39]

2.3

(5) I will cut off the ruler (Hebrew: judge) from its midst, and I
will slay all its princes (Hebrew: leaders) with him/I will kill the

ruler of Moab and all the leaders of the land. The TEV, with its prose
restructuring, has combined I will cut off and I will slay, which will
need to be done in many other languages as well. In most translations,
also, the word "judge" should not be translated literally, since in most
cultures the work of judging and of ruling is quite different. Ruler is
the meaning here.[40] Where no general term like ruler is possible, some
other more specific term may have to be used, but there is no clear indication as to the precise status of this ruler. From early times Moab had
been a monarchy (Num 23.7; Judges 3.12ff; 2 Kgs 3.4ff; Jer 27.3; Mesha
inscription 1.23), and the function of the ruler was certainly similar
to that of a king or chief (Mft: "monarch"; Smith-Goodspeed: "chieftain").

All the leaders of the land will, of course, sometimes be better
translated "all its leaders."

(6) Says the Lord. See 1.5.

2.4-5

RSV	TEV

RSV

4 Thus says the LORD:
     "For three transgressions of
          Judah,
        and for four, I will not
          revoke the punishment;[e]
     because they have rejected the
          law of the LORD,
        and have not kept his
          statutes,
     but their lies have led them
          astray,
        after which their fathers
          walked.
5 So I will send a fire upon
          Judah,
        and it shall devour the
          strongholds of Jerusalem."

TEV

Judah
     4 The LORD says, "The people of
Judah have sinned again and again,
and for this I will certainly punish them. They have despised my
teachings and have not kept my
commands. They have been led astray
by the same false gods that their
ancestors served. 5 So I will send
fire upon Judah and burn down the
fortresses of Jerusalem."

[e]Heb *cause it to return*

The message about Judah has the same parts as the messages about
Tyre (1.9-10) and Edom (1.11-12). It is particularly like that about Edom
in its grammatical construction in the third part. However, the same
structure expresses a message with very different content in some ways
from any of the preceding ones. Here there is no mention of crimes
against fellow men, only of crimes committed against God. This is particularly noticeable in the Hebrew because in verse 4 the Lord (who is
speaking) is referred to as the one being talked about.

2.4

(1-2) The Lord says...punish them. See 1.3.

(3) <u>Because they have rejected</u> (Hebrew: despised) <u>the law of the
Lord, and have not kept his statutes</u>/They have despised my teachings and
have not kept my commands. In most languages the translation of <u>the law of
the Lord...his...</u> has to be translated <u>my...my...</u>, since this is a section
in which the Lord is speaking. However, in Hebrew this stylistic irregularity has a purpose, and this purpose is lost when the irregularity is
smoothed out in translation. So, if it is at all possible to include the
word Lord so as to keep the Hebrew emphasis, this should be done: "because they despised the law of me, the Lord" or "because they despised
my teaching--the Lord's teaching!--and have not kept my commandments."

<u>They have despised my teachings</u> could be translated "they have re-
jected my teachings." But if at all possible, it is better to use an expression which keeps some of the meaning of "contempt" (NAB and NEB use
"spurned," which is good where it is not too high a level of language).

<u>Teachings</u> and <u>commands</u>. The Hebrew terms are difficult to translate.
In this particular context, the first Hebrew term means the whole of
God's will, and the second indicates specific rules.[41] No such distinction can be made in many languages. If a distinction exists, it is often
that between a "law" in some traditional and definite form, and a specific order given by some authority. There may also be a distinction between
unwritten customary law and specific orders.[42]

In cases like that, the local terms for traditional law, customary
law, etc., should be used as equivalents of <u>teachings</u>; a word for the
regulations of officials should be used as an equivalent for <u>commands</u>.
In cases where only one term can be used in the receptor language, the
sentence can be restructured: "because they have rejected my law." This
is not undertranslation since the two expressions are parallel in the
Hebrew text and there is a high degree of overlapping between their meanings.

<u>But their lies have led them astray, after which their fathers
walked.</u>/They have been led astray by the same false gods that their
ancestors served. Some modern English translations (RSV, Smith-Goodspeed,
NAB) translate <u>lies</u> literally, but this does not show the full meaning
of the Hebrew. The Hebrew word for <u>lies</u> is here a reference to <u>false gods</u>
or "idols," which are considered to be producers, and probably also products, of lies.[43] This reference has been made clear in some recent translations (Mft, NEB, TEV), and such a translation is to be preferred.
Whether it will be possible or necessary to qualify the "gods" as <u>false</u>
will depend upon the word which has been selected in the translation to
render <u>gods</u>. In some languages a diminutive plural "small gods" has been
used with the implication of "useless," "worthless," and such a translation may be sufficient.

"Walked after" is a picture for <u>served</u>. In some languages the kind
of grammatical construction will have to be changed: "the (false) gods
which their ancestors served have led them astray (or: have made them do
wrong)."

2.5

(4) <u>So I will send fire upon Judah and burn down the fortresses of
Jerusalem.</u>" See 1.4.

2.6-16

Five of the usual parts are present in this message to Israel (part
[4]--the standard punishment of war and fire--is missing), but three of
the five parts are different from the earlier messages in many ways. Only
part (1), the statement of the source of the message, and part (2), the
general reason for God's decision to punish the people, are the same in
wording as the earlier messages.

The fact that this message fits in with the series of messages where
the statements have been so much alike and yet that it is so different
in its content, emphasizes the significance of the differences. The challenge to a skillful translator is to make the reader sense that significance in his own language, in spite of the difficulties.

Section heading. See 1.3--3.2.

2.6a

RSV	TEV
	God's Judgment on Israel
6 Thus says the LORD:	6 The LORD says, "The people
"For three transgressions of	of Israel have sinned again and
Israel,	again, and for this I will certain-
and for four, I will not	ly punish them.
revoke the punishment;*e*	

*e*Heb *cause it to return*

(1-2) The Lord says...punish them. See 1.3. Since the message is
addressed to Israel, and is not simply about Israel (as the previous
messages were about the other peoples), the use of the people of Israel
and them may cause misunderstanding in some languages. It may sometimes
be necessary to translate so that God speaks directly here: "You people
of Israel...I will punish you." To do so brings up to verse 6 the change
which the Hebrew makes in verse 10.

However, if some way can be found to continue the style of the previous messages, as though God were still talking about someone else, and
then switch dramatically to the more direct form later, as the Hebrew
does, this may be very effective in many languages. TEV makes the switch
in verse 9, one verse before the Hebrew. In some languages it might be
best to bring it up even into the second part of verse 6. This would
strongly emphasize that although the message begins the same way as the
earlier ones, the implications for the hearers are not the same at all.

Wherever the change is made, special attention should be given to
the way in which it is made, with special emphasis in its wording. For
example: "you, my people, sell honest men into slavery..." or "and you,
the people of Israel, have sinned again and again."

2.6b-12

RSV	TEV

because they sell the righteous for silver,
 and the needy for a pair
 of shoes--
7 they that trample the head of
 the poor into the dust
 of the earth,
 and turn aside the way of
 the afflicted;
 a man and his father go in to
 the same maiden,
 so that my holy name is
 profaned;
8 they lay themselves down beside every altar
 upon garments taken in
 pledge;
 and in the house of their
 God they drink
 the wine of those who have
 been fined.
9 "Yet I destroyed the Amorite
 before them,
 whose height was like the
 height of the cedars,
 and who was as strong as
 the oaks;
 I destroyed his fruit above,
 and his roots beneath.
10 Also I brought you up out of
 the land of Egypt,
 and led you forty years in
 the wilderness,
 to possess the land of the
 Amorite.
11 And I raised up some of your
 sons for prophets,
 and some of your young men
 for Nazirites.
 Is it not indeed so, O people of Israel?"
 says the LORD.
12 "But you made the Nazirites
 drink wine,
 and commanded the prophets,
 saying, 'You shall not
 prophesy.'

They sell into slavery honest
men who cannot pay their debts,
poor men who cannot repay even the
price of a pair of sandals. 7 They
trample[b] down the weak and helpless
and push the poor out of the way.
A man and his father have intercourse with the same slave girl,
and so profane my holy name. 8 At
every place of worship men sleep
on clothing that they have taken
from the poor as security for debts.
In the temple of their God they
drink wine which they have taken
from those who owe them money.
 9 "And yet, my people, it was
for your sake that I totally destroyed the Amorites, men who were
as tall as cedar trees and as
strong as oaks. 10 I brought you
out of Egypt, led you through the
desert for forty years, and gave
you the land of the Amorites to be
your own. 11 I chose some of your
sons to be prophets and some of
your young men to be Nazirites.[c]
Isn't this true, people of Israel?
I, the LORD, have spoken. 12 But
you made the Nazirites drink wine,
and ordered the prophets not to
speak my message.

[b]trample; *Hebrew unclear.*

[c]NAZIRITES: *Israelites who showed
their devotion to God by taking
vows not to drink wine or beer or
cut their hair or touch corpses
(see Nu 6.1-8).*

[46]

(3) The third part of the message to Israel, containing the specific illustrations of Israel's crimes, starts with the familiar because they, with the crimes introduced in the usual way in the Hebrew grammar (2.6b), but there the similarity ends. Interwoven are social crimes and the fact that these are also crimes against God. The way in which these are organized may be seen in the Appendix, Section 3.1.

That the crimes against people are also crimes against God must be clear in the translation.

2.6b

Because they sell the righteous for silver, and the needy for a pair of shoes (Hebrew: sandals)--/They sell into slavery honest men who cannot pay their debts, poor men who cannot repay even the price of a pair of sandals. The Hebrew does not say who (in Israel) did the selling, which causes difficulty for translating into many languages. How this is decided depends on how the rest of the passage is understood. Did the same people sell the righteous as sold the needy, or did judges sell the righteous (by taking bribes) and creditors sell the "needy" into slavery to recover their debts?[44]

It does not seem likely that different people are doing the selling in the two cases, or even that one general group such as the corrupt upper classes are here divided into judges and creditors. It certainly is also unlikely that the same verb to sell should have been used once as picture language (for bribery) and once with its regular meaning. So there are two possible solutions: the ones who did the selling are either judges or creditors in both cases.

The easiest way of understanding the passage seems to be with the meaning of creditors. With it goes natural use of sell in both cases. Furthermore, the same people carry on into verse 7, and the rich can be understood as acting in both verses. Finally, it is not necessary to take righteous in a legal sense (compare Mft: "honest folk").[45]

In Hebrew the emphasis is first on the righteous, and then on a pair of sandals. So the point is first that for rich creditors money has more value than the personal qualifications of people, and second that even people who need help are victims for insignificant reasons. Translations of this passage should express a lot more of these meanings than they normally do. To sell has to be qualified as "to sell into slavery" or "to sell as slaves," and the meaning of "for money" and "for a pair of sandals" has to be stated clearly. TEV has done many of these things well, but who cannot repay even the price of a pair of sandals does not completely show that selling into slavery is the result of not repaying. Another way might be "because they can't pay back the small sum they owe for a pair of sandals."[46]

A pair of sandals[47] will have to be translated as "two sandals for two feet," or some other idiomatic way, in some languages.

2.7

They that trample the head of the poor into the dust of the earth/ They trample down the weak and helpless. The Hebrew for the word translated trample here is not clear. In some translations it has been taken

to mean (1) "long for," in which case the Hebrew would be "they long for
the dust of the earth on the head of the poor." This is the way the older
English translations have it: "that pant after the dust of the earth on
the head of the poor" King James Version (KJV). Such a translation of the
Hebrew has been understood in different ways: (a) as a picture of extreme
greed: the rich landowners even long to own the small quantity of earth
people throw on their heads as a sign of mourning;[48] (b) as a picture of
the way poor people are pushed down: the rich are only satisfied when
they see the poor in a miserable condition;[49] (c) as "they long for land
at the expense of the poor."[50]

In other translations the problem word has been understood as (2)
"crush," trample (upon) down, in which case the Hebrew text--after some
slight changes--could be translated literally as in the RSV, as well as
in most modern commentaries and English translations. The shortened form
in the TEV They trample down covers all the meaning of the Hebrew sentence as understood in the second interpretation. Leaving out the head...
into the dust of the earth reduces the picture language but does not
change the meaning. Mft, on the other hand, uses a comparison to keep the
picture: "they trample down the poor like dust."[51]

With our present knowledge, we cannot be sure which of these interpretations is best,[52] but (1a), (1b), and (2) may be followed equally
well in translation.

If interpretation (1a) is used, reason for the behavior may have to
be stated in many translations; for example, "they (the rich landowners)
even long to own the earth which poor people throw on their heads as a
sign of mourning."

Interpretation (1b) is less difficult for translation. Such a statement as "they like to see poor people mourning" or "they like to see
poor people throwing earth on their heads as a sign of mourning" can
easily be made.

If interpretation (2) is followed, TEV can usually be taken as a
model. Of course, the expression used to translate trample down must
imply oppression and not only physical "walking on." In some languages
the expression will be something like: "they rob the poor."

The poor...afflicted/the weak and helpless...poor. TEV has apparently
changed the order of these two terms. In the Hebrew it is the poor which
goes with trample, and "weak/oppressed/humble" which goes with push...out
of the way. In doing this, of course, the TEV has not changed the meaning
of the passage, since the expressions are parallel and are picture language for the same kind of action toward poor people who are not able to
defend themselves.

Turn aside the way of.../push...out of the way can be interpreted in
two different ways: (a) as a general statement like in TEV, and (b) as a
more specific act such as "they pervert the way (or: cause judgment) of
the weak." The more specific interpretation is made stronger by the
parallel expression in 5.12.[53] Here again it is difficult to decide, but
as the specific case is included in the general, it is perhaps preferable
to follow (a). In that case, if an expression like push...out of the way
is not natural and there is no similar use of picture language, the translation will have to say something like "they worry/trouble miserable
people" (compare Mft: "and humble souls they harry").

If interpretation (b) is preferred, some restructuring will be necessary, such as "they keep the miserable from getting justice."

A man and his father go in to the same maiden,/A man and his father have intercourse with the same slave girl. The men involved are a man and his father, which should not be translated as "father and son" (NEB) because the Hebrew implies "not only the son, but even the father."

The Hebrew go in to includes the meaning of sexual intercourse.[54] However, the attention seems to be less on the intercourse than on the way the woman is abused. The general theme is still that of mistreating the lower classes: "not only the son, but even the father, goes after the servant girl." In different languages, of course, the polite ways of expressing the sexual behavior will vary.

Slave girl is the right translation, rather than "prostitute" (NAB, JB note, Smith-Goodspeed). If temple prostitution was emphasized, we would expect to find verse 7b after verse 8.[55] Also, nowhere in the Old Testament does the word for "girl" mean "prostitute,"[56] nor anything equivalent in ancient translations.[57]

So that my holy name is profaned;/and so profane my holy name. This is the result of the treatment of the servant girl, expressed through a Hebrew particle translated and so.[58] Profane can often be translated by a word equivalent to English "defile." In languages in which it is hard to find an acceptable equivalent for holy, the translator can simply say "profane/defile/dishonor my name." Since the name stands for God himself, the translation can say something like "profane/defile/dishonor me."

2.8

They lay themselves down beside every altar upon garments taken in pledge;[59]/At every place of worship men sleep on clothing that they have taken from the poor as security for debts. In many languages beside every altar should be translated something like At every place of worship or "at all the places where they worship God." The sentence, however, raises several questions which are left unanswered: (a) why is the clothing at the place of worship? and (b) why do people lie down at the altars, and why on this clothing?[60] The translator cannot answer these questions, but he should word the translation in such a way that the reader sees all that is pictured as a misuse of the place of worship as well as a mistreatment of the poor, whose clothing (taken in pledge during the day) was to be returned at nighttime (Exo 22.26; Deut 24.12ff). For example, "even in their places of worship they lie down on clothing unlawfully kept from the poor as security for debts."

The Hebrew word for clothing should be taken here as a general word which includes every kind of garment. TEV has translated taken in pledge clearly and in less technical language as have taken...security for debts. In many cases a less technical term such as "guarantee" will have to be used in the receptor language, even if technical terms are available. Many societies do have a well-developed vocabulary for different kinds of pledges, but they may have meanings which are so tied in with the receptor culture that they cannot suitably reflect the Biblical situation.

In the house of their God/In the temple of their God. This may also mean "the house of their gods" (See NEB margin, Smith-Goodspeed). If God is used, house can be translated temple, although in many languages, of course, "house of God" will be standard terminology for temple. It should be clear that in this context it is the house of the God who is speaking, and in many languages the translation would better be "my house" or "my temple." Such a translation also helps in verse 9.

The temple of their God is, of course, fully equivalent with every place of worship, and the whole verse can sometimes be tied together by stating this setting only once, if that is better. However, in Hebrew the repetition of profane my holy name, at every place of worship and in the temple of their God emphasizes that this is not only injustice to man but also unfaithfulness to God.

They drink the wine of those who have been fined/they drink wine which they have taken from those who owe them money. TEV is based on the parallel in verse 8a, and such an interpretation is possible.[61] It is more probable, however, that the fines are those paid to the (temple) community, and this money was used for drunken parties in the sacred places instead of for those who received damage! It is quite possible that the fines were paid in wine rather than money.[62] This is the standard interpretation of the commentaries and the modern English translations. In translation this meaning might be expressed as "they drink the wine they got from people they have fined" Translators' Old Testament (TT).

In this context wine is a rather general word for any strong, intoxicating drink, and it is not necessary to use a borrowed word to make this drink more specific. The translator can use the local word for "palm wine," "rice wine," "millet beer," etc.[63]

2.9-12

At this point in the listing of the sins of the people of Israel, God reminds them of his special relationship to them and of his care for them in the past. This comes to a climax in verse 11:
   "Israel, you know that is true, don't you?
   It's the Lord who is reminding you!"
In translations where God has been speaking disrespectfully of the sinning nations (see under 1.3 [2]), it may be good for that style to change here and for this passage to Israel to be in a warmer style, more sorrowful than angry.

But this passage is difficult and needs special care by the translator (see the English restructuring in Translating Amos, Section 2.3); it is a very important passage in Amos' total message. One difficulty lies in the way it is organized in Hebrew (see Appendix, Section 3.1). It seems out of place in the list of Israel's sins, and part of it seems backwards as we read it in most translations. Salvation from Egypt (verse 10) actually came before the opening up of the land of Canaan (verse 9). Such backwards order is not possible in some languages, or it may be awkward and have to be changed (compare Mft). Even in languages where going back to a previous event is perfectly natural and makes a good translation, the two events should be carefully related. RSV and NEB, for example, do not do so, and leave the second mention of the Amorites in verse 10 as a weak repetition. TEV, in the way it constructs the sentences, more skillfully relates the events of Egypt and the desert as background to the events connected with the Amorites; the final mention of the Amorites is a stronger ending, better tied with verse 9. Many languages have words or expressions to relate things which are out of order in this way. Verse 9 describes what God has done to the Amorites on behalf of Israel, verse 10 what God has done to Israel itself. So in some languages the change can be underlined through the use of an emphatic pronoun: "And you, my people, I brought you..."

A second major problem for some languages is the one already mentioned under 2.6a; in verse 10 in Hebrew God now speaks directly to the people of Israel. See the earlier discussion.

A third problem is that the I which comes near the beginning of verse 9 is emphatic in Hebrew. It helps to indicate the sharp contrast between the people, who have been unfaithful, and God's faithfulness. Languages differ in how they express such emphasis and contrast. Some do it with special pronouns, some with changes in order, some with special expressions or additional words. In English, for example: "it was I" (NEB, NAB), "I, myself," or "I was the one."

Verse 10 also has an emphatic I, but at least partly with a different purpose. It is to make clear that verse 10 does not follow verse 9 in time, as discussed earlier. However, even though an emphatic wording may not be needed for that reason in the language of the translation (because the change in time is handled in some other way), still the contrast present in verse 9 is also present here, and for many languages the emphasis will need to be preserved (see NEB). A great deal will depend on how the two verses are tied together.

In many languages, also, long quotations are confusing, and the speaker has to be mentioned periodically. Where that is true, the beginning of verse 9 is likely to be such a place: "and the Lord continues to say," "and the Lord also says."

2.9

Before them,/for your sake. In contrast to what has been done in most modern translations, the Hebrew should be understood as showing the reason for God's action (like the TEV), not the place (like the RSV)(compare Hos 10.15; Gen 6.13; Deut 28.20).

Destroyed. In translation the term must be one which can be used for people. This destruction is that of war: death, loss of home and possessions, exile.

Amorite/Amorites lived in Canaan at the time when the people of Israel conquered it. Where it is helpful, the translation may say "your/their enemies, the Amorites."

Whose height was like the height of the cedars, and who was as strong as the oaks/men who were as tall as cedar trees and as strong as oaks. Such full comparisons are usually not hard to translate except for the terms cedar trees[64] and oaks.[65]

In either case, where the specific kind of Biblical tree is not known, the best solution is probably to take a general word for "tree" (provided it includes the possibility of tall trees and strong trees), and to build the comparison around it. Something like "as tall as the tallest trees, and strong as the greatest trees" might do. Or the two comparisons can be combined: "as tall, as strong as the greatest tree."

A second possible solution would be to borrow the words cedar and oak and write them according to the sound patterns of the language of

the translation: "tall as the tree called cedar," etc. Still a third
possibility is to take local trees which are tall and strong. Such a solution would not be as good if this were a particular tree of historical
importance, but as a basis for comparison like this, it is a possibility.
Still another possibility is to say something like "strong as big trees
like the mahogany tree." Or yet again, some of the information could be
put in a footnote so that the kind of tree could be better understood
without including inaccurate information in the text.

I destroyed his fruit above, and his roots beneath. This picture is
not kept in the TEV but included in the earlier use of totally destroyed
because this was a standard Canaanite and Hebrew idiom,[66] and the meaning
of the expression as a whole should be translated and not the meanings of
the individual words.[67] If the Hebrew idiom can be replaced by an equivalent idiom in your language, it should be done. In English we could say:
"I destroyed them root and branch" (Robinson, TT); in German: "ich rotte
sie mit Stumpf und Stiel aus," etc. If it is not possible to find an
equivalent idiom, the meaning of the total expression should be translated in a general way, as TEV has done.

2.10

I brought you up out of the land of Egypt/I brought you out of Egypt.
The word brought, which involves motion, will certainly require an indicator of direction in many languages (see discussion in Translating Amos,
Section 3). Hebrew has up out. In order to determine what would be most
appropriate in the language of the translation, the translator will need
to think about the relationship of Egypt to Israel. In some cases it may
also be useful to qualify Egypt as "land" or "country."

And led you forty years in the wilderness,/led you through the desert
for forty years. "Did you go" is translated led, but the Hebrew in this
particular context has two parts to its meaning: "guidance" and "care."[68]
In some languages the second meaning can be made clearer by using a verb
equivalent to English "accompany."

The Hebrew word translated by desert does not indicate a sandy desert
but rough uninhabited land with patches of grass which would provide a
certain amount of pasture for animals. "Uninhabited" is the most important
part of the meaning, and lack of vegetation is secondary. Most languages
have specific words for an uninhabited area such as "grasslands," "rocky
region," "place where no house is," etc.[69]

To possess the land of the Amorite./and gave you the land of the
Amorites. This sentence can be translated "that you might seize/have the
land of the Amorites" (see Smith-Goodspeed). On the other hand, this
event takes place under the leadership of the Lord, as stated in verse 9.
God is doing the action so the sentence can be translated as in TEV.

2.11

And I raised up some of your sons for prophets, and some of your
young men for Nazirites/I chose some of your sons to be prophets and
some of your young men to be Nazirites. The Hebrew verb has the meaning of
"constitute," "appoint,"[70] so it is possible to translate: "I appointed
some of your sons to be prophets, and some of your young men to be

Nazirites" (TT). On the other hand, the Hebrew "appoint" includes both "call"[71] and "choose." Thus, a rendering "I called..." or I chose is equally possible.

Prophets is usually difficult to translate. The Old Testament word for "prophet" should not be different in the translation from that used in the New Testament, but if the New Testament word is not satisfactory it should be changed so that both Testaments use a satisfactory word. It is useful to work out together words for a whole group of related and distinct terms such as prophet, seer, apostle, disciple, etc., or to revise words already in use.

Normally there are three different possibilities for the translation of prophet: (1) an expression for foretelling the future; (2) an expression which describes the prophet as a revealer of God's will and word; and (3) a loan word borrowed from Greek or some language in the area of the translation. This last solution (borrowing) should not be used unless the word is already known in the language, and with the correct meaning. The meaning which the term is likely to get in the process of borrowing is not likely to be the Biblical meaning.

The first solution (foretelling the future) is easy to follow, as all cultures have terms equivalent to "soothsayer," "fortune teller," etc. However, while not denying that the Hebrew term includes foretelling the future, the more important part is its meaning of the revelation of God's word;[72] and the term for "soothsayer" would doubtless convey meanings that have nothing to do with the Biblical message.

The second solution (descriptive phrase for revealing God's will and word) is therefore usually the best: "who speaks the things of God," "interpreter for God," "God's sent-word person," etc. The problem with descriptive phrases is keeping them concise as well as accurate. This is especially necessary with such words as prophet which occur so frequently in the Bible.[73] (See also the restructuring in Translating Amos, Section 2.3.)

Occasionally there may be a fourth alternative for prophet. Some traditional societies have a type of wise person who is quite distinct from the fortune teller. Through word revelation and without use of magic ritual he reveals hidden connections between things that happen and their causes. If the various meanings associated with the term for such a person are all right, the term can be used for prophet.

Nazirites should not normally be translated, but should be spelled according to the sound system of the language. Even if some descriptive expression is used, it will not convey the very particular meaning of the term. In either case, additional qualifications such as "were people (men) called Nazirites" will be necessary. An explanation will often be needed in a footnote or in the glossary. For example: "The Nazirite was someone set apart for the service of God. He was not allowed to cut his hair or to drink wine. He had to take several vows which are described in the law of the Nazirite: Num 6.1-21." (Compare the TEV note).

Is it not indeed so, O people (Hebrew: sons) of Israel?" says (Hebrew: message of) the Lord./Isn't this true, people of Israel? I, the Lord, have spoken. The climactic, emphatic quality of these reminders that God is talking to his people has already been discussed (2.9-12), as has the fact that they interrupt the flow of discussion of the Nazirites and prophets.[74]

The translator should try to make this climax strong, but he may
have to change its location in order to do it. The climactic position
may be after verse 12. The language which he uses in the translation
should also be forceful.

Some languages will not allow questions which do not have answers
such as Isn't this true, people of Israel? Or in some languages such
questions may be weak. In that case, a strong positive exclamation may
have to be used, such as "You Israelites will not deny that!" (TT) or a
statement followed by a question: "You know that is true, don't you,
people of Israel"?

"Message of the Lord" has been translated as an independent sentence
in TEV: I, the Lord, have spoken. In many languages such a translation
may sound awkward, especially if this line is not placed after verse 12.
It may look as though the Lord, having indicated that he has spoken,
continues to speak in an apparently unfinished discourse! If the question
is to be maintained, it may be easier to translate: "Isn't this true,
people of Israel? I, the Lord, ask you." (compare Mft). Other possibilities: "It's your Lord speaking," "I am your Lord, reminding you that
this is true." The two sentences can be combined: "You know that what I
am saying is true, don't you, people of Israel"?

2.12

In languages where long quotations are confusing or where the mention
of the Lord speaking in verse 11 will sound like the end of a quotation,
the speaker can be introduced here again: "And the Lord continues to say."

But you made the Nazirites drink wine may simply mean "but you made
the Nazirites break their vow."75

Wine, see verse 8.

And commanded the prophets, saying, "You shall not prophesy."/and
ordered the prophets not to speak my message. For some languages it will
be perfectly natural to have the direct words quoted as in Hebrew (see
RSV), even though this quotation is inside another quotation. In other
languages the direct quotation should be avoided, as it has been in the
TEV. Compare: "and forbade the prophets to prophesy" (TT). Prophesy can
best be rendered as speak my message or "speak my things," or, indirectly, "speak the things of God."

2.13-16

RSV	TEV
13 "Behold, I will press you down in your place, as a cart full of sheaves presses down. 14 Flight shall perish from the swift, and the strong shall not retain his strength, nor shall the mighty save his life;	13 And now I will crush you to the ground, and you will groan like a cart loaded with grain. 14 Not even fast runners will escape; strong men will lose their strength, and soldiers will not be able to save their own lives. 15 Bowmen will not stand their ground, fast runners will not get away, and men on horses will not escape with

15 he who handles the bow
        shall not stand,
    and he who is swift of
        foot shall not save
        himself,
    nor shall he who rides the
        horse save his life;
16 and he who is stout of heart
        among the mighty
    shall flee away naked
        in that day,"
                    says the LORD.

their lives. 16 On that day even
the bravest soldiers will drop
their weapons and run." The LORD
has spoken.

(5) This is the part of the message to Israel which gives the particular punishment the nation will receive. This part is again considerably longer here than in the messages to the other nations, and is different in content. Instead of promises of destruction for people and leaders, the punishment at first seems weak and mild: loss of strength, loss of ability to fight, inability to hold up a heavy load. However, the implication in context is very powerful. Israel's strength came from its relationship to God. Now that Israel has broken that relationship, its strength will be gone.[76] (See Appendix, Section 3.1).

2.13

"Behold/And now. In Hebrew this is an expression which calls attention to something and often begins a strong final or climactic statement. Behold, of course, is not modern English, while and now is too weak, particularly with no paragraph break in the TEV. A paragraph break and "so then" might be better in English here. The equivalent in many languages is more like the literal Hebrew.

I will press you down (Hebrew: meaning of word uncertain) in your place as a cart full of sheaves presses down./I will crush you to the ground, and you will groan like a cart loaded with grain. The key word in this verse is not clear in Hebrew. Discounting suggestions to change the text, six different meanings have been proposed:[77]

(1) I will crush you (press you down) (RSV, TEV, NAB).[78]

(2) I will make it groan under you (so with slight variants Smith-Goodspeed, TT [alternative reading]; compare NEB).[79]

(3) I will split (the earth) under you.[80]

(4) I will bring you to a halt (TT).[81]

(5) I will make it shake (Zürcher Bibel [Zür]).[82]

(6) I make your steps collapse (Mft).[83]

Until more convincing evidence turns up it is not possible to say that any one of these is absolutely correct. Nevertheless, a choice has to be made, and it seems wise to choose one of the first three translations.[84] All three carry the thought of a catastrophe, and this is exactly what one expects to find on the basis of the punishment we expect here. Also, a cart loaded with grain indicates "harvest," which is often a Hebrew picture of God's judgment.

The balanced organization of the Hebrew lines probably gives more weight to meaning (2), since this part of the balanced system has to do with Israel's weakness without God (Appendix). If this meaning is followed, some kind of clear statement will be needed such as "(when I punish you) you will groan (with weakness) as a cart overloaded with grain groans." In some languages, of course, the same word cannot be used for the pain of something alive and the sound of a cart, which may weaken the picture somewhat: "...you will groan...as a cart...squeaks/creaks."

The word for cart should stand for any type of vehicle without motor and capable of carrying grain. It is often easier to say that the cart is loaded/overloaded with grain than to say that it is full of sheaves.

In Hebrew the focus is on the weight.[85] Every language has its own ways of indicating that the cart is "overloaded." It is not enough, however, to translate simply "a full load" (NEB), omitting the grain which represents harvest and judgment.

If translation (1) is chosen, the first part of TEV can be followed: I will crush you to the ground "the way a cart full of grain is loaded down (or: is overloaded)."

TEV, however, combines translations (1) and (2), using (1) for the first part and (2) for the second part of the verse, which is rather doubtful.

Translation (3) is a difficult picture to translate: "I will split the earth under you as a cart loaded with grain splits the earth," as it is not clear what meaning this picture would have in the context.

2.14

Flight (Hebrew: a refuge) shall perish from the swift/Not even fast runners will escape. In many languages some form of restructuring will be necessary, such as "swift runners will find no refuge" (TT), or Not even fast runners will escape, "he who is quick will not escape," etc. There has been a slight shift in the language from earlier verses. God is now talking about, not directly to, people once more, so far as the grammar is concerned: "the swift," not "you who are swift" (see discussion under 2.6a). In English there is no problem, as these various people are examples of the you in verse 13. However, in some languages it would be better to translate "you fast runners" or "your fast runners" or "the fast runners among you." This continues through verse 16.

The strong shall not retain (Hebrew: unfold) his strength/strong men will lose their strength. Another possibility for the Hebrew: "his strength will not strengthen the strong." In some languages one may have to say something like: "strong (or mighty) people will not be able to use their strength" or "the strong will become weak."

Nor shall the mighty save his life/and soldiers will not be able to save their own lives. Another possibility: "and the warriors will not be able to save (or: protect) themselves."

2.15

He who handles the bow shall not stand/Bowmen will not stand their ground. TEV uses an English idiom "to stand one's ground" meaning "to maintain one's position in battle." This is exactly the meaning of the Hebrew verb. However, idioms can rarely be translated literally, so usually a translator will have to describe the action: "the men who shoot the bow in battle will be forced to retreat," or "the bowmen will not wait," meaning that they will not even be able to take time to aim, or "they will not stand firm" (see Smith-Goodspeed, TT).

Not all languages have a specific word for Bowmen. Often a descriptive phrase has to be used as in Hebrew "he who handles the bow." The translator may have to say, for example, "he who holds the bow in his hand" or "he who fights with a bow." If the bow is not known, the translator may have to use a more generic term for weapon.

He who is swift of foot shall not save himself,/not even fast runners will escape. Many languages have expressions similar to swift of foot, such as "men who have strong legs," etc.

Nor shall he who rides the horse save his life/men on horses will not escape with their lives. It will be necessary in many cases to use a descriptive phrase for men on horses, especially when horses are not used in the local culture. Normally they will at least be known, and there will be some term for them. Using horses in battle may be less widely known than horses themselves. In such cases the use of the horses may have to be clear: "men who ride horses as they fight their enemies."

2.16

In that day,"/On that day. TEV changes the order from the end of verse 16 to the beginning. It should be located where it is natural. However, this is not a way of expressing the simple idea that the events took place on the same day. That day in Amos (see also 8.3,9,13; compare: the day 3.14; the evil day 6.3) is The Day of the Lord (5.18,20) and always has a sound of danger and judgment, except in 9.11-15 where it is just the opposite.[86] Translation should show that this is a special day, and if possible the connection between these different references to the Day of the Lord should not be hidden by the wording. A way of translating this expression meaningfully might be "the day/time when the Lord/I will act/judge/punish."

He who is stout of heart among the mighty (Hebrew: and the strong with regard to his heart[87] among the warriors)/even the bravest soldiers. The part of the body used to indicate strength and courage will differ from language to language.

Even rightly marks the climax reached at the end of the section. Other languages may have other ways of doing this.

Flee away naked/drop their weapons and run." Even though a literal translation flee naked is possible (Smith-Goodspeed, NAB, Mft: "shall strip"), it is better to take the expression in the sense of "leaving behind one's weapons":[88] "will flee without his weapons" (TT) or "shall be stripped of his arms" (NEB) or even as "he shall fling away his weapons" (Robinson).

(6) Says the Lord/The Lord has spoken. The final part giving the source of the message, is slightly different from earlier messages (1.5, 1.8, etc.) in the Hebrew. It is more emphatic and closes not only this message but all eight messages of this section of Amos. In the translation it is good to have a slightly different, slightly more emphatic expression than was used earlier. If, for example, "that is what the Lord says" was used before, then "this is the message from the Lord himself" might be good here. NEB has "It is the word of the Lord" in earlier verses and "This

is the very word of the Lord" here. TEV, which did not repeat this part each time in the earlier occurrences, now has The Lord has spoken here.

3.1-2

	RSV	TEV

<table>
<tr><td>

3 Hear this word that the LORD has spoken against you, O people of Israel, against the whole family which I brought up out of the land of Egypt:
2 "You only have I known
    of all the families of
      the earth;
  therefore I will punish you
    for all your iniquities.

</td><td>

3 People of Israel, listen to this message which the LORD has spoken about you, the whole nation that he brought out of Egypt: 2 "Of all the nations on earth, you are the only one I have known and cared for. That is what makes your sins so terrible, and that is why I must punish you for them."

</td></tr>
</table>

The theme of this passage goes with that which immediately precedes more than with that which immediately follows, so we have included it with the messages about Israel and the nations in this Handbook.[89] The section which follows (3.3-8) is a clearly independent section with its questions and its emphasis on the role of the prophet rather than on Israel, and with its talking about the Lord (as in 2.9-16) rather than the Lord talking. The tone of 3.1-2 continues more sorrowful than angry, and the translation should carry this feeling. It makes more clear the point developed in 2.6-16 that Israel's punishment results especially from the breaking of the special relationship to God. The expression Hear this word, furthermore, and other similar ones begin the conclusion of various sections of Amos (see Appendix, Section 1.21), and the structure of the section ties closely with what goes before (see Appendix, Section 3.2).

In spite of the fact that this passage ties more closely with what precedes than what follows, none of the existing translations, except possibly for TEV, seem to group it that way. The TEV could be taken more than one way. Because there is no section heading in the TEV, 3.1-2 could be considered as the final paragraph of a larger section, 1.3--3.2, or as the final paragraph of a smaller section, 2.6--3.2.

Actually, 3.1-2 summarizes almost the total content of Amos' prophecy, so that it could have found a legitimate place elsewhere in the book, even at the beginning of the book as its general theme. In the general organization of the book, Amos 3.1-2 may well be a transition from the section on Israel among the nations to a continuing message to Israel in particular. It does end the particular attention to the theme of Israel's sins and punishment, which is picked up again in 8.4-14.

Section heading. For translations which are not trying to show the structure of the book through the use of section headings, a separate section heading may be used for 3.1-2, if this seems helpful in the translation (compare JB). A suitable title for 3.1-2 would be "God Punishes His Own People," emphasizing the connection with what goes before.

In those translations where the headings do show the structure, something like "Basis for Israel's Guilt" or "Why God Punished His Own People" might be helpful in showing the relationship.

Hear this word that the Lord has spoken against you, O people of
Israel, against the whole family which I brought up out of the land of
Egypt:/People of Israel, listen to this message which the Lord has spoken
about you, the whole nation that he brought out of Egypt. Because of the
important relationship between this passage and the previous one (see
3.1-2), it would be helpful in many languages to show the relationship
with a word like "so."

The Hebrew gives translators a problem because it changes from Amos
speaking to God speaking right within the same sentence. Such a rapid
change happens often in prophetic writings, and the reason may be that
the prophet identifies himself completely with the message of the Lord.

However, this kind of change is often awkward and grammatically
unacceptable in other languages. There are three ways of dealing with it
in translation: (a) the Lord may speak from the beginning: "I, the Lord";
(b) the Lord may begin to speak in the second half of the verse, as in
Hebrew, with a change to indicate whose family is being talked about: "I
led your whole family out of Egypt"; (c) the Lord does not begin to speak
until the next verse so that Amos continues speaking throughout verse 1:
the whole nation that he brought out of Egypt. (c) is the best solution.
It is a simple matter of a change of pronoun and gives little problem.[90]

People of Israel. TEV moves this to the first of the sentence. In
each translation it should be given a natural position in keeping with
language usage.

Message which the Lord has spoken. To "speak" a message is not fully
natural in English, and other wordings may be better in other languages
as well: "Listen to this message from the Lord about you, people of
Israel!", "Listen to what the Lord has to say about you."

Brought out. One way in which the sorrowful tone of this passage can
be strengthened in some languages is through the use of a word which is
warmer than brought out in English: "rescued" or "led out" or some other
term that implies personal involvement.

Whole family/whole nation. Whole nation or "whole race" (Mft) or
"all the people" is the meaning of the Hebrew.

If the solution to the problem of verse 1 is to have the Lord begin
speaking at verse 2, then an expression like "The Lord says" or "He says"
may be needed here to introduce verse 2. It must be clear also that the
following words are spoken now, not during the time when the people were
being brought out of Egypt.

You only/"Of all the nations on earth, you...only. The TEV is a correct translation of the Hebrew here. The meaning is not "more than" the
other nations.[91]

Have I known/I have known and cared for. The Hebrew word for "known"
has several important parts to its meaning, including personal knowledge,
intimate knowledge, care, and choice. In this particular context the
meaning of intimate knowledge and care should be translated. I have known
and cared for, "cared for" (NEB, Mft), "I have known intimately" (TT).
The Hebrew, furthermore, has considerable overlapping with another Hebrew

word for "choose," "elect,"[92] so that it may very well be translated "I have chosen." In fact, this may be the best translation in many languages, as very often a verb to "choose" implies personal intimate knowledge and care. The way in which this is expressed should contribute to the tone of sorrow: "the only ones I have really known and cared for," "the only ones I have ever really chosen and cared for as my own."

This knowledge and care of the Lord does not refer only to the past,[93] but also to his revelation which continues in the present: "I have always cared for," "I am continually caring." In some languages the continuation could be expressed through two different tenses: "I have cared and care for."

Therefore/That is why. The meaning is that God punishes because he knows and cares for. Because the Lord knows the people of Israel intimately and cares for them, the people in its turn should know the Lord intimately and want to do his will. Because of his special care, their sins are more terrible.

Iniquities/sins. The Hebrew word is different from the one used in chapters 1 and 2. There the emphasis was on the evil nature of man, whereas here (and only here in Amos) the emphasis is on the damage caused by doing wrong or the guilt of the person who causes damage through doing wrong.[94] "Guilty behavior" or "doing wrong" would be good translations, although it may be difficult to make this kind of difference in many languages.

3.3--4.3 THE PROPHET'S ROLE AND COMMISSION

This major division has two independent parts with very little connection except that they both have to do with prophets (3.3-8: the prophet's role, and 3.9--4.3: the prophet's commission to proclaim and testify). They are also balanced later in Amos by a section on the prophet's
experiences in 7.1--8.3, including Amos' role and commission as a prophet (see Appendix, Figures 3,5). 3.3-8 and 3.9--4.3 each has its own
structure and should be translated without trying to tie the two
closely together.

Section heading. For translations where the structure of the book
of Amos is being shown in the section headings, a major heading will be
needed here, together with sub-headings for the two smaller parts (see
Translating Amos, Section 2.4). "The Prophet's Role and Commission" is
hard to translate into many languages. It may be possible, however, to
say something like "What God Wants the Prophet to Do" or "The Work of
the Man Who Speaks for God." Whatever is chosen should fit with the
headings of the two parts which make up this larger section. Possibilities for each of these will be discussed later.

3.3-8

RSV	TEV
	THE PROPHET'S TASK
3 "Do two walk together,	3 Do two men start traveling to-
unless they have made an	gether without arranging to meet?
appointment?	4 Does a lion roar in the forest
4 Does a lion roar in the forest,	unless he has found a victim?
when he has no prey?	Does a young lion growl in his
Does a young lion cry out from	den unless he has caught something?
his den,	5 Does a bird get caught in a
if he has taken nothing?	trap if the trap has not been
5 Does a bird fall in a snare	baited?
on the earth,	Does a trap spring unless some-
when there is no trap for it?	thing sets it off?
Does a snare spring up from	6 Does the war trumpet sound in
the ground,	a city without making the people
when it has taken nothing?	afraid?
6 Is a trumpet blown in a city,	Does disaster strike a city
and the people are not	unless the LORD sends it?
afraid?	7 The Sovereign LORD never does
Does evil befall a city,	anything without revealing his plan
unless the LORD has done it?	to his servants, the prophets.
7 Surely the Lord GOD does	8 When a lion roars, who can
nothing,	keep from being afraid?
without revealing his secret	When the Sovereign LORD speaks,
to his servants the prophets.	who can keep from proclaiming his
8 The lion has roared;	message?
who will not fear?	
The Lord GOD has spoken;	
who can but prophesy?"	

[61]

The unity of 3.3-8 has been seriously questioned by many scholars.[1]
At first it seems like a series of only partly related questions, some
of which repeat each other and some of which do not seem to fit together.
Verse 7 is not even a question.[2] However, there are strong relationships
that give unity to 3.3-8 in spite of the difficulties. We have tried to
show some of the basis for unity in the Appendix, Section 3.3.

The overall meaning of the passage is that disaster shows God's
judgment, and prophecy is God's warning to people. The emphasis is on
what the Lord uses the prophet for: to show God's plan (verse 7). This
meaning is expressed in a way difficult to translate. It is shown by a
combination of picture language and questions without answers. So far as
the pictures are concerned, the translator has to make sure that they are
clear and that they carry over the proper meaning in his language. This
will be discussed at various points in the following treatment.

So far as the questions are concerned, they can be a difficult
problem in many languages because they really have the meaning of statements. In contrast with other Semitic languages, such as Arabic, such
questions without answers are not very frequent in Hebrew.[3] Where they
occur, the emotional reaction of the hearers and readers is stimulated.[4]
Besides, in this passage the chain of such questions building up to a
climax also gives more force to the message than would a single statement.

In some languages the answers to the questions must be stated.[5] The
translator will have to answer "No" to the first seven questions, and
"Nobody" to the last two. If there is a problem of the answers becoming
monotonous, perhaps some of the questions can be grouped to avoid repeating an answer too much. Care should be taken, furthermore, that the wording of the answer is in keeping with the emotional force of the question:
Does a lion roar...? "Of course it doesn't!" Does a young lion growl...?
"Never!"

In other languages it will not be possible to use questions in this
way at all, even with answers. In those cases the meaning of the questions
may be expressed in negative statements: "Two men do not start traveling
together without arranging to meet," etc. A still better way, if it makes
for good style in the language of the translation is to add the question
at the end of a statement: "Two men do not start traveling together without arranging to meet, do they?" In some cases, again, this will have to
be followed by an answer.

Whatever a translator does, he must make sure that the translation
is forceful and lively, with strong impact on his readers. If at all
possible, this section should be written in poetry, since the meter and
the rich pictures of the Hebrew are clear indication of its poetic
character. However, a prose text with a strong impact is better than
poetry without such force. In some languages the form of a proverb may
be appropriate.

For some languages another important difficulty with this passage
is that in many of the pictures the cause or condition of what happens
is expressed after the result or consequence. This is true except in
3.6a and 3.8. For example: Does a bird get caught in a trap (consequence)
if the trap has not been baited? (condition). However, in actual life the
conditions or causes actually take place before the consequences, and in
some languages backwards order is awkward or misleading, if it can be

understood at all. In such cases various kinds of restructuring will be
required: "If someone does not bait a trap, a bird will not get caught
in it. Isn't that right?" "The hunter does not bait the trap; does the
bird get caught?" "Before a trap has been baited, does a bird get caught?"

Whether or not the order is a problem, as just described, each language will have its own ways of showing the relationship between condition and consequence: "if...not," "unless," etc. However, the change between the two orders is important in Hebrew for helping to emphasize the
climax of a series (see discussion under 3.6a and 3.8). If all the questions are translated in the same order of condition and consequence,
some other way of showing that climax will be necessary.

Section heading. The section heading here should be based on the
theme of the conclusion (verse 8) and not on the themes of the earlier
verses. "The Role of the Prophet," "What the Prophet Does," "The Prophet
Announces God's Message," The Prophet's Task are possibilities.

3.3

"Do two walk together, unless they have made an appointment?/ Do
two men start traveling together without arranging to meet? In many languages the speaker will have to be indicated: "Amos said again," "Another
time, Amos said...," etc.

Made an appointment/arranging to meet translates a Hebrew word which
has two parts to its meaning: (a) "to arrange" and (b) "to meet." Existing translations differ mainly as to the meaning they use.[6] RSV and TEV
make both parts of the meaning clear. This seems to be the best solution.
If only one meaning is translated,[7] it should be "meet" and not "arrange,"
in spite of all the English translations, since the emphasis is upon the
meeting and not upon the arranging. Note that the TEV can be understood
in more than one way. The correct way is that the men arranged to meet
before they started traveling together, not that they arranged to meet
(again) after they started traveling together.

3.4

Does a lion roar in the forest, when he has no prey? Does a young
lion cry out from his den, if he has taken nothing?/ Does a lion roar
in the forest unless he has found a victim? Does a young lion growl in
his den unless he has caught something? These two pictures are not
exactly the same. The lion's roar in the first picture is the ferocious
roar with which the lion attacks an animal he is going to kill and eat.
When someone hears this roar, he knows that the lion has found his victim.
In the second picture, however, it is the lion's contented growl when
he has dragged his food to his den.

Translation problems are mainly in vocabulary. In Hebrew there are
two distinct nouns for a lion and a young lion, the first one a general
term, the second more specific. The young lion is not a cub or whelp (for
which there is also a specific term in Hebrew); he is old enough to go
hunting. Many languages, like English, will not have a range of specific
terms for lions, so the translator will have to use some word like 'young'
if he wants to bring out the distinction. However, in Hebrew the age of
the lion is not important. There is no reason against translating a lion

twice, if that sounds better. This is exactly what has been done in TT, which adds a footnote: "Hebrew has two different words for a full-grown lion here. The second indicates one which is younger than the first." Such a note, however, is not necessary. In some cases, translating as lion twice will sound better because the two questions will be more balanced, or, if young lion has an adjective, then the other term should have an adjective, too, like: "old lion," or "mature lion."

Finally, if the language has no word for lion, a more general term for "wild beast" can be used. It would be possible to add some comparative description such as "wild beast like a leopard," but such a description may be disturbing rather than helpful, especially if the translation is in poetic form.

The Hebrew word translated by forest is a rather general term covering such specific terms as "scrub," "bush," "thicket," and "forest." In this context "scrub" is meant. If the receptor language has no specific word for this type of vegetation, a more general equivalent of "savannah" can be used.

The Hebrew term translated as den is a general term for "dwelling place," used here for the place where a wild beast lives. The lion's den is a hollow in the ground, hidden behind shrubs.[8] Again, if the language lacks a specific term the translator may use a more general word for dwelling place, as in Hebrew.

3.5

Does a bird fall in a snare on the earth, when there is no trap for it? Does a snare spring up from the ground when it has taken nothing?/ Does a bird get caught in a trap if the trap has not been baited? Does a trap spring unless something sets it off? The snare/trap probably consisted of two rectangular frames flat on the ground and covered with a net. When the bird touched some sort of mechanism, the frames snapped together, holding the bird in the net which was folded around it.[9] A complication which can be seen in some English translations is that possibly the word for trap came into the Hebrew by a copying mistake. The ancient Greek translation does not have any such word.[10] We do not give this information to suggest that the translator not translate the Hebrew as it now is (with trap), but to show where some other translations come from.

Trap/baited. There are four different ways of understanding this word:

(a) "Bait," "lure."[11] Most English translations take this meaning. For example, in addition to TEV: "Is a bird brought to earth by a snare when there is no lure for it?" (NAB); "Does a bird swoop to a trap on the ground if there is no bait in it?" (TT); "Does a bird drop into the trap unless the trap is baited?" (Mft).

(b) The trigger, or mechanism which releases the trap:[12] "Does a bird fall into a trap on the ground if the striker is not set for it?" (NEB).

(c) A boomerang or throwing stick.[13] If this is the meaning, then the additional word for trap is impossible, as discussed above: "Does a bird fall on the ground unless a thrown stick has hit it?" (Zür).

(d) A "snare."[14] "Does a bird fall to the ground when there is no snare for it?" (Smith-Goodspeed).

Although it is recommended that the translator choose (a) or (b) as the meaning of the present Hebrew text, it is impossible to say that one of these meanings is correct and the others not. Translators may even be happy with the range of choice, because each culture will have its own ways of catching birds, and one Hebrew meaning may be easier to translate than another. Even then, some degree of cultural translation may be necessary. If, for example, in a certain culture only bird lime is used, with termites in it as bait, it may be necessary to say something like: "Does a bird swoop to the bird lime unless there are termites in it?" Note that in such a translation local specific items are used for trap and bait. Or if the culture is unacquainted with the type of trap intended in the Hebrew, but knows of other types of snare: "Does a snare move if nothing has fallen in it?" Here a general word "to move" is used for the specific spring up. In such cases, the parallel between "falling down" and "springing up" is lost. But it may be impossible to avoid that.

The consequence-condition relationship may have to be brought out more clearly in some languages than in Hebrew. So in TEV the result of the falling is the consequence: Does a trap spring... and the condition has been indicated by unless: unless something sets it off.

3.6

Is a trumpet blown in a city, and the people are not afraid? Does evil befall a city unless the Lord has done it?/Does the war trumpet sound in a city without making the people afraid? Does disaster strike a city unless the Lord sends it? In spite of the similarities between these two questions,[15] there is a very important division in the text between them (Appendix, Section 3.3). The first question ends a series about the relation of natural creatures to each other (man to man, animals to animals, men to animals). The second starts a series about the relation of God to man.[16]

The first question, furthermore, ends the series which states the general premise (that nothing happens without a reason), whereas the second begins the specific premise (that disaster comes from the Lord). The order of the parts of the first question is different from the rest of the first series, as well as from the second question. That is, it has a condition-consequence order, whereas the second one uses the earlier sequence of consequence-condition. This change, along with a new question word in Hebrew, helps to emphasize that the first question in verse 6 is the climax of the first series.

If a similar change would produce the same results in the translation, the change in Hebrew order of condition-consequence should be followed. But if such a change would result in awkward or inconvenient style, or if all of the questions have been translated with condition-consequence because that is more natural in the language, the climactic emphasis should be shown in some other way. For example, if the questions are being answered in the translation, the answer here could be more emphatic: "Most certainly not!" If statements are being used instead of questions, there are other possibilities: "How well you know that people in the city are afraid when the war trumpet sounds!"

3.6

Otherwise, there are not many translation problems in this verse. It is not enough to translate as in the RSV: Is a trumpet blown in a city (see also NAB, Smith-Goodspeed). The Hebrew word here means war trumpet, and without that the reason for the fear and the condition-consequence relation is lost. Some cultural adaptation may be necessary since different instruments such as bells or drums are the warnings for war in other places. It is not music which is intended. Sometimes a more general statement can be made to avoid the cultural difficulties. TT is good in this respect: "If the alarm is sounded in a city." However, not all languages have such a possibility, and in any case the picture in the question must be a strong and lively one.

Trumpet. See 2.2.

3.7

Surely the Lord God does nothing, without revealing his secret to his servants the prophets./The Sovereign Lord never does anything without revealing his plan to his servants, the prophets. As has already been shown, verse 7 is a secondary element in which the relationship between the second question of verse 6 (unless the Lord sends it) and verse 8 (who can keep from proclaiming his message) has been made clear. The way in which this verse connects or links should be clear in the translation. That is the intention of "No more does" (JB); "For" (NEB). Other possibilities in English would include "Neither does," "No, nor does."

Lord God (Hebrew: my master, Yahweh)/Sovereign Lord. In many languages it makes no sense to combine words for Lord and God. The phrase "my master, Yahweh" makes sense in Hebrew because "Yahweh" is the personal name for God. But in translating this into most languages the meaning would come out something like "my master, the Lord," which simply says much the same thing twice and is not really different from Lord except perhaps for being a bit more emphatic. To translate as "Lord" alone is certainly correct, and often the best solution. In some languages the Hebrew name of "Yahweh" is used in combinations like this (spelled, of course, in a way that is natural for the language of the translation). This gives a translation along the lines of "my Lord, Yahweh" or "Yahweh, who is my Lord."

The Hebrew vocabulary of this sentence is rather theological and technical. Although it will be good to maintain this kind and level of language in translations where it is appropriate to the reader, sometimes such a statement as revealing his plan is impossible. In many languages "without telling his servants the prophets" (Mft) would be better.

Prophets. See 2.11.

Servants in connection with prophets is a standard Old Testament combination which occurs frequently in other prophetic and historical writings. Just as the king has high-ranking officers in his service, so does the Lord: his officers are his prophets.[17] In this context it is the status of the prophet, not the act of serving, that is being emphasized. Where languages have distinctive terms for servant according to what they do or their social position[18] it may be easy to select an appropriate equivalent term. In other languages it is necessary to translate as "ones-who-work-for-him," "helpers," etc.

[66]

3.8

The lion has roared; who will not fear? The Lord God has spoken; who can but prophesy?/When a lion roars, who can keep from being afraid? When the Sovereign Lord speaks, who can keep from proclaiming his message? This is the conclusion to the series of questions and the order changes to condition-consequence as in the first question of verse 6. Again, the change helps to create a sense of climax.[19] On ways of translating so that there will be a sense of climax in the translation, see the discussion of verse 6a.

The lion of verse 4 comes back in the first half of verse 8, but the theme is different. Instead of an animal-animal relationship, the picture now is of an "animal" (a picture of the Lord)-man relationship (a relationship lacking until now). It prepares the reader for the final question. It is true, of course, that the lion is not identical with the Lord. So the first question should be translated keeping in mind the discussion of lion and roars in the commentary on 1.2. On the other hand, the fact that when a lion roars and when the Sovereign Lord speaks are parallel, and the fact that within the book of Amos lion and roar are pictures for the Lord and his speaking, make for strong unity between the two parts of the verse.[20]

Prophesy/proclaiming his message (see 2.12). For languages which require an indication of the speaker at the end of a major quotation, this may be one place for an expression such as "That is what Amos said," "said Amos," "He finished saying," etc.

3.9-4.3

This section is considered a unit, even though there are different messages within it. Various things tie it together:

(1) The theme of doom through the section.

(2) The sequence of warnings concerning Samaria (3.12), Bethel (3.14), and Samaria again (4.1). In fact, the section is introduced by a command that the rulers of Egypt and Ashdod be called to witness Samaria's sin (verse 9). Samaria (political center) and Bethel (religious center) are representative of Israel as a whole. The emphasis is not on two different places but on representatives of the same larger place.[21]

(3) There are two commissions in the passage: Announce to those who live in...Egypt and Ashdod (3.9), and Listen, now, and warn the descendants of Jacob (3.13).

(4) There is some similarity in the organization of the two halves of this section:

3.9-10 Proclaim...	3.13 Hear, and testify...
...says the Lord...	...says the Lord God, the God of Hosts
3.11 Thus says the Lord God Theme: punishment by destruction	3.14-15 Theme: punishment by destruction says the Lord

[67]

3.12 Thus says the Lord	4.1-3
Theme: destruction of Samaria's people	Theme: destruction of Samaria's women
Picture: ...two legs...	Picture: ...cows of Bashan... says the Lord

Although the limits of the section are rather clear, it is more difficult to define paragraph boundaries within it. It would be possible to have six short paragraphs, as shown just above, or a pattern of four paragraphs combining the two commissions with what follows: 3.9-11,12,13-15; 4.1-3.

Section heading. One possibility for a section heading is the theme of doom or disaster, as in Smith-Goodspeed and TEV. However, Doom of Samaria has a kind of grammatical construction which is not natural to all languages. It may be preferable to translate doom by a verb and show who is doing it: "The Lord Pronounces Sentence Against Samaria" or "The Lord Condemns Samaria to Destruction." In some translations it may be good to qualify Samaria as a "town." Because Samaria and Bethel stand for the country "Israel" the latter may be used instead of Samaria.

Another possibility is to emphasize the call or commission which begins each of the halves of this section: "God's Call to Witness" or "God Tells the Prophets What to Do."

3.9-11

RSV

TEV

THE DOOM OF SAMARIA

9 Proclaim to the strongholds
  in Assyria,*f*
  and to the strongholds in
   the land of Egypt,
  and say, "Assemble yourselves
   upon the mountains of
   Samaria,
  and see the great tumults
   within her,
  and the oppressions in
   her midst."
10 "They do not know how to do
  right," says the LORD,
 "those who store up violence
  and robbery in their
  strongholds."
11 Therefore thus says the Lord
  GOD:
 "An adversary shall surround
  the land,
 and bring down your defenses
  from you,
 and your strongholds shall
  be plundered."

9 Announce to those who live in
the palaces of Egypt and Ashdod:
"Gather together in the hills
around Samaria and see the great
disorder and the crimes being
committed there."
10 The LORD says, "These people
fill their mansions with things
taken by crime and violence. They
don't even know how to be honest.
11 And so an enemy will surround
their land, destroy their defenses,
and plunder their mansions."

f Gk: Heb *Ashdod*

[68]

Who is speaking? If we take verse 9 alone, it sounds like Amos is
speaking--but to whom? The listeners might be imaginary messengers
(compare Isa 40.1) or even the leaders of Samaria who are called by Amos
to send messengers to Ashdod and Egypt.

In those languages where the primary message of this passage will
be clear without precisely indicating who is speaking and to whom, there
should be no attempt to add the information. However, many translators
cannot avoid making a decision. In that case, it should either be "Amos
said to the leaders of Samaria: 'Send messengers to those who live in
the palaces of Ashdod and Egypt and announce to them'" or "God said to
the prophet:..."

The Hebrew picture is that the announcement will sound out over the
palaces, or that the messengers will cry out standing on the flat roofs
of the palaces. However, it is clear that the inhabitants themselves are
being called, so TEV translates correctly: Announce to those who live in
the palaces. These observers from the foreign nations will be independent
witnesses of the guilt of Samaria.

In some languages a word like announce or "tell" or proclaim cannot
be followed by a quotation. In such cases the literal Hebrew may be followed: "and say to them," or the quotation may be made indirect: "announce
to...that they should gather together..."

Older English versions such as RSV, Smith-Goodspeed and Mft have
"Assyria" instead of Ashdod. Ashdod should be followed since this is the
Hebrew (NAB, NEB, TT, TEV).[22] It may be necessary to say "the town of
Ashdod" and in some instances even "the land of Egypt," as in Hebrew.

Upon the mountains of Samaria/in the hills around Samaria. Mountains
of Samaria probably refers to the mountains around Samaria. Samaria itself was located on a hill approximately 460 meters high, and on the
east side of the town some of the mountains reached 500-700 meters. The
distance between these mountains and Samaria was about four kilometers,
too far to see what really happened in town. However, the picture is not
to be taken literally, but as a poetic one. The noun in Hebrew, in spite
of its plural form, may have a singular meaning,[23] and saying "Gather
together on the mountain of Samaria" could mean the same as "Gather together in the town of Samaria."

On the other hand, vividness and interest is lost if such direct
translation is necessary. The picture may well be one of spectators on
the mountainside as though in a stadium watching the action below. If it
is possible to maintain that kind of picture and not distort the meaning,
it would be good to do so. In fact, the picture might possibly be
strengthened in some translations: "Gather on the mountains around Samaria
and watch how the people terrify each other..."

Tumults/disorder (see also NAB, TT, Mft) is a translation of a Hebrew
word in the plural, which makes the meaning stronger.[24] The opposite of
this term in Hebrew would be the well-known word shalom meaning "peace"
and "order." On the other hand, because of the violence in this context
the Hebrew word here can be translated by "terror."[25] In any case, some
restructuring may be necessary such as "see how they terrify each other."

The oppression in her midst/the crimes being committed there. The
RSV is the usual translation, but the Hebrew word can also mean "oppressed

people." In translation it may be necessary to say "how people are oppressed" or "how one oppresses the other." It is also possible to take the Hebrew word as "acts of violence," which is the basis of TEV: the crimes being committed there.

3.10

"They do not know how to do right," says the Lord, "those who store up violence and robbery in their strongholds."/The Lord says, "These people fill their mansions with things taken by crime and violence. They don't even know how to be honest. The tone of this verse and the next is scornful and disrespectful.

TEV has done some major restructuring. The Lord says has been put at the beginning, and the order of the two halves of the verse has been changed to give the example of what people do (stealing and violence) before the general statement that They don't even know how to be honest. The whole picture is made clearer: not violence and robbery are stored up, but the result of robbery and violence: things taken by crime and violence. The emphasis of the Hebrew on the word know is brought out: they don't even know.

To what extent such restructuring will help in another translation depends entirely upon the language. Is the evidence or example better first, or the conclusion based on that evidence? The use of violence and robbery for the goods gained by violence and robbery has a strong effect in Hebrew. It intensifies the accusation. However, in many languages store up violence and robbery makes no sense, or is even ungrammatical. Some of the strength of the accusation can sometimes be expressed through changes in order: crime and violence or "robbery and murder." The colorless word things could be translated with a word for "loot" or some such expression for things gained through violent action.

3.11

Therefore thus says the Lord God:. This new mention of the speaker helps in Hebrew because there is a change from talking about the people of Israel (verse 10) to talking to them (verse 11). Such a change, common in Hebrew, is frequently confusing and awkward in other languages. The TEV has therefore restructured verse 11 so as to have the Lord still talking about the people of Israel, and so the speaker does not need to be mentioned again.

"An adversary shall surround the land,/And so an enemy will surround their land. This is the best way of understanding the Hebrew, although there are problems.[26]

And bring down your defenses (Hebrew: strength) from you/destroy their defenses. One possible translation is: "and strip you of your strength" (NAB), or if the translation has God speaking about the people of Israel: "and strip them of their strength" or "make them weak." On the other hand, the Hebrew word for "strength" may mean "fortifications," "defenses." So TEV has destroy their defenses. Since many languages do not have a general word for defenses or for certain types of fortifications, the nearest equivalent expression may be "destroy the places where they hide/protect themselves."

RSV	TEV

RSV

12 Thus says the LORD: "As the shepherd rescues from the mouth of the lion two legs, or a piece of an ear, so shall the people of Israel who dwell in Samaria be rescued, with the corner of a couch and part*g* of a bed."

*g*The meaning of the Hebrew word is uncertain

TEV

12 The LORD says, "As a shepherd recovers only two legs or an ear of a sheep that a lion has eaten, so only a few will survive of Samaria's people, who now recline on luxurious couches.*d*

*d*luxurious couches; *Hebrew unclear.*

As was pointed out earlier, verse 12 forms a separate paragraph since it is a new saying and has no clear connection with the preceding paragraph or the following paragraph.[27] The tone of the passage is that of someone who is saying the opposite of what he actually means (irony). The translator should try very hard to convey this tone. It is as though Amos was answering people who said that God would rescue his people. Amos' meaning here is that of course God will "rescue" them, just like a shepherd "rescues" the remains of a sheep when a lion has finished with it!

As TEV and RSV footnotes show, the Hebrew of the last part of verse 12 is not clear. In order to show why different translations are different, we first give two other translations of the verse. The KJV is quite literal; the NEB reflects the meaning in the context, and this is what is recommended for the translator to follow:

KJV

As the shepherd taketh out of the mouth of the lion two legs, or a piece of an ear; so shall the children of Israel be taken out that dwell in Samaria in the corner of a bed, and in Damascus in a couch.

NEB

As a shepherd rescues out of the jaws of a lion two shin bones or the tip of an ear, so shall the Israelites who live in Samaria be rescued like a corner of a couch or a chip from the leg of a bed.

The problem of grammar: how does the last part ("in the corner of a bed...a couch" [KJV]) relate to the rest?[28] Some translators relate it to "dwell in Samaria": "the Israelites...who loll on corners of diwans within Samaria, on silken cushions of a couch" (Mft); "the Israelites who sit in Samaria on beautiful beds and luxurious couches" (TT; see also BJ).

A better solution is to make "in the corner of a bed...a couch" relate to "taken out" or "rescued" because of the parallel with the first part of the verse:[29]

First part: "rescued...two shin bones or the tip of an ear"
Second part: "rescued...corner of a couch or chip from...a bed" (NEB). Most modern English translations have taken this solution to the grammatical problem: so shall the people of Israel who dwell in Samaria be rescued,

with the corner of a couch and part of a bed. (RSV); "so will the Israelites be rescued, who dwell in Samaria, along with the corner of a couch,
and the leg of a bed" (Smith-Goodspeed[30]); "So the Israelites who dwell
in Samaria shall escape with the corner of a couch or a piece of a cot"
(NAB).

The problem of comparison: what is compared with what? In the RSV,
NAB, and Smith-Goodspeed mentioned above, the comparison is between the
shepherd who can only save a useless pair of bones or a piece of an ear
of a devoured sheep and the Israelites who can save for themselves no
more than a few worthless pieces of furniture.[31] In the case of other
translations, however, the comparison is between the insignificant part
of the animal that is rescued and the small part of Israel that will be
saved: "only a very few will be rescued" (TT) and only a few will
survive.[32]

But all these translations may miss the point since the emphasis in
the picture itself is not on "saving" Israel or "being saved." When an
animal was killed by wild beasts it was the duty of the shepherd to bring
some remains of the animal to the owner to show him how it had been killed.
If the shepherd was unable to do that, he had to pay the owner for the
animal.[33] So the remains of the animal are nothing but pitiful evidence
of its destruction. "Rescue" or "save," therefore, is the opposite of what
it really means.[34] The picture is that all that will be left of the
Israelites in Samaria are just enough pieces of broken belongings to give
pitiful evidence of their complete destruction.

The problem of vocabulary: what does "in Damascus" (KJV) have to do
with it? This probably results from a mistake in writing the Hebrew
vowels (written much later than the consonants). Without the vowels, the
consonants can be understood as two Hebrew words meaning "piece of a
leg."[35]

So, taking the best solution to each of the three problems, this is
how the Hebrew can be understood: "So shall the Israelites who dwell in
Samaria be 'rescued'--in the form of a corner of a couch, and of a piece
of a leg of a bed!" That is the basis of the NEB quoted above, and will
be used as the basis for the discussion of translation problems below.

In many languages, however, an equivalent verb for "to save" or "to
rescue" cannot be used, for the simple reason that the use of such a word
will not be understood to mean the opposite of what it does mean, as would
be necessary here. In some cases an equivalent of "to save" can be written
between inverted commas (quotation marks), but this will only help experi-
enced readers. People who hear the Scripture read will not see the punc-
tuation. Sometimes a different verb may help, one which translates another
part of the meaning of the Hebrew word. For example, "Just as a shepherd
snatches from the lion's mouth two legs or a piece of an ear; even so
shall the sons of Israel who dwell in Samaria be snatched out: nothing
more than a piece of a couch and a part from a bed's leg."[36]

The reader can perhaps be helped to understand that the prophet is
speaking in an opposite way from what he says by making a contrast between "rescue" and "snatch out": "Just like a shepherd snatches nothing
more than two legs or a piece of an ear from the lion's mouth, the people
of Israel who live in Samaria will also be rescued--nothing but a piece
of a couch, and part of the leg of a bed." Or: "A shepherd brings back
only two legs of a sheep, or only its ear after a lion has finished eat-

ing it. That is how the people of Israel will be saved (or: someone will save the people of Israel) also; there will be nothing more left than a piece of a couch, and part of the leg of a bed."

Different languages require different parts of the picture to be made clear. Sometimes the translator has to say "two legs or a piece of an ear of a sheep" or "of his sheep" (NAB), or, since the particular kind of animal is not the important point, simply "of an animal." The one doing the snatching may have to be expressed: "someone will snatch out the Israelites..." Also, the word mouth really stands for something that happens, and so it may be better to say that a lion has eaten.

Shepherd. See 1.2.

Two legs. The Hebrew word has the meaning of "shank-bones" (Smith-Goodspeed) or "shin bones" (NEB) in some contexts, but there seems to be no reason to be so specific here. A general translation of two legs or "two bones" is enough.

The Assyrian bed was richly carved,[37] and perhaps the beds of the Israelites in Samaria were much the same. It is not completely clear what is meant by "corner or side of a couch." This may be the head or the foot of the bed. The details are not important for the picture. Some languages do have specific words for the part of the bed which supports the head as well as for the leg. If not, the information can be made more general and also shorter; for example, "as pieces of a bed/sleeping-platform."[38]

3.13-15

RSV	TEV
13 "Hear, and testify against the house of Jacob," says the Lord GOD, the God of hosts, 14 "that on the day I punish Israel for his trans- gressions, I will punish the altars of Bethel, and the horns of the altar shall be cut off and fall to the ground. 15 I will smite the winter house with the summer house; and the houses of ivory shall perish, and the great houses[h] shall come to an end," says the LORD.	13 Listen now, and warn the descendants of Jacob," says the Sovereign LORD Almighty. 14 "On the day when I punish the people of Israel for their sins, I will de- stroy the altars of Bethel. The cor- ners of every altar will be broken off and will fall to the ground. 15 I will destroy winter houses and summer houses. The houses decorated with ivory will fall in ruins; every large house will be destroyed."

[h]Or many houses

Verse 3.13 begins the second part of this section (see under 3.9--4.3). Notice that the TEV ties verse 13 with verse 12 by including it in

the same paragraph and in the same message (see also NEB). However, on
the basis of the parallels which we have already pointed out between the
two halves of this section, it certainly seems better to understand verse
13 as beginning a new part of this section.

The passage begins with another commission, followed in verses 14
and 15 with the theme of punishment, this time by the destruction of
buildings. The Lord is the speaker, but the people to whom he is speaking
are not named. It is clear that they will be witnesses of the punishment
and that they are called upon to listen to the announcement of this punishment. It is possible that the witnesses of the punishment are the same
people as the witnesses of the guilt in verse 9.

3.13

Testify against/warn. The Hebrew, because of its particular construction here, means warn, not "testify against."

The house of Jacob/the descendants of Jacob. House or "family" in
Hebrew often represents the nation.[39] Though house of Jacob is equivalent
to "Israelites," the name of Jacob should be kept in the translation. He
may have been mentioned here because of the sanctuary of Bethel (verse 14)
which he established, and he is associated with God's choosing the Israelites. However, as a translation, "the family of Jacob" (NEB) may be
misleading. The descendants of Jacob (so also TT) is better.[40]

The Lord God, the God of hosts/the Sovereign Lord Almighty. For the
translation of Lord God, see 3.7.

God of hosts is the standard translation of almost all modern English
versions. However, what hosts means is far from clear. Some think of the
armies of Israel which the Lord leads, others of heavenly armies, including the angels and the stars. Because of this uncertainty, the kind of
army cannot be made clear in translation. However, to translate simply
"armies" is certainly misleading.[41] But whatever the meaning of the expression may be, there always seems to be an element of "power" in it,
and so the best solution is to translate this meaning: "the powerful God,"
Lord Almighty.[42]

3.14

That on the day I punish/On the day when I punish. This is not a
simple time reference, and should not be translated merely as "when I
punish" (see 2.16).

Punish/punish and destroy are translations of the same Hebrew word
(see 3.2). The difference in English translation is necessary because you
cannot "punish" altars in English (RSV, Mft; compare Smith-Goodspeed).
The same is true in many other languages. The only solution is to use an
equivalent of such a verb as destroy because the immediate context makes
clear that utter destruction is meant.

Altars may be hard to translate where no parallels to the "altar" of
the Bible exist. Some possible translations include: "the thing on which
(sacred) offerings are placed" or "places of sacrifice."

Bethel should be called a "town" ("the town of Bethel") so that it
will not sound like the name of a God in this context.[43]

[74]

Horns of the altar/the corners of every altar. These were horn-like
projections at the corners of the altar. Although most English translations use the traditional expression horns of the altar, it makes little
sense in modern English and will be completely impossible in most languages. It would be possible to translate "the projections in the form
of horns on the corners of the place of sacrifice (or: of the thing on
which offerings are placed)," but there is no need for something so long
and involved; the emphasis is not on the shape. For this reason TEV translates the corners of every altar, which makes clear the location instead
of the shape. This will be a good solution in many languages. However,
much will depend on the word which is used for "altar." The reader may
need a picture to help him in cases where there is nothing in his own
background which makes it possible for him to visualize the altar.

The importance of this act of destroying the "altar-horns" is that
they represented a place of safety. The Hebrew means that even this way
of escape will be destroyed. Such background information should be provided, and this can best be done in a footnote: "According to such Bible
passages as 1 Kgs 1.50 and 2.28, a fugitive secured himself from arrest
or violence by catching hold of altar-horns (the corners of the altar)."
It may also be possible to translate: "Every hiding place will be destroyed."

In many languages, God, who does the cutting down, will have to be
mentioned: "I will cut off the corners of the altar and they will fall
to the ground" or "I will destroy every hiding place."

3.15

Most scholars understand winter houses and summer houses to mean
that rich people had separate homes in different climates.[44] In many
areas of the world winter houses and summer houses will make little sense.
"House for the rainy season" and "house for the dry season" will not help,
either, if such things do not exist. Sometimes the best equivalent is
"town houses" and "country (village) houses" or "village houses" and
"field houses." The emphasis, of course, is not on the kind of house but
on the widespread destruction. Where no suitable distinction can be made,
translate simply "I will destroy their big houses and their little houses"
or "their brick houses and their thatch houses."

Houses of ivory/houses decorated with ivory. Houses of ivory does
not mean "houses built with ivory." In Hebrew ivory is "(elephants')
teeth," and such an expression will be the usual one in many languages.

And the great houses shall come to an end/every large house will be
destroyed. The meaning of "many houses will be destroyed" (see Smith-
Goodspeed, Mft, NAB; marginal reading RSV) is also possible in Hebrew.
"Large houses" would be adding some information, whereas "many houses"
would summarize what was said before. The translation "many houses"[45] is
better because it underlines the thoroughness of the destruction which is
a main theme of this paragraph.[46]

Shall come to an end/will be destroyed. Other possibilities: "be
demolished" (NEB), "be no more" (NAB). God is the one doing the action:
"I will destroy."

Says the Lord has been omitted in TEV since the speaker has already
been identified in the beginning of the paragraph (verse 13). (See 1.5.)

In many languages an equivalent of the Hebrew will be necessary or helpful, especially because it is Amos, and not God, who continues speaking
in the next paragraph.

However, in Amos this phrase coming at the end of messages does more
than indicate the speaker. It indicates the end of a message and the
authority of that message (see 1.5,8,15; 2.3,16). Some translations emphasize this purpose by a statement such as "This is the very word of the
Lord" (NEB), "It is the Lord who is speaking" (compare JB).

4.1-3

RSV	TEV
4 "Hear this word, you cows of Bashan, who are in the mountain of Samaria, who oppress the poor, who crush the needy, who say to their husbands, 'Bring, that we may drink!' 2 The Lord GOD has sworn by his holiness that, behold, the days are coming upon you, when they shall take you away with hooks, even the last of you with fishhooks. 3 And you shall go out through the breaches, every one straight before her; and you shall be cast forth into Harmon," says the LORD.	4 Listen to this, you women of Samaria, who grow fat like the well-fed cows of Bashan, who mis-treat the weak, oppress the poor, and demand that your husbands keep you supplied with liquor! 2 As the Sovereign LORD is holy, he has promised, "The days will come when they will drag you away with hooks; every one of you will be like a fish on a hook. 3 You will be dragged to the nearest break in the wall and thrown out."*e*

*eHebrew has an additional word,
the meaning of which is unclear.*

This final paragraph of this section is spoken by Amos.[47] Because
of the change of speaker or because of the new message some languages
will need to show who is speaking: "Amos said" or "Amos continued, saying:"

In this message Amos quotes two other speakers: the women in verse 1
and the Lord in verses 2 and 3. This creates problems for translation
into some languages (especially when it is necessary to show Amos as the
speaker at the beginning). Every language has its own ways of expressing
quotations inside quotations, even if that way is never to do it! There
will normally have to be shifts in pronouns to take care of it.

Amos is speaking to a certain class of women in Samaria. In verse 1
they are shown in their characteristic guilty behavior, mistreating the
poor, and in verses 2 and 3 they themselves are being destroyed.

This time the announcement of punishment is not introduced simply by naming God as the source of the message, but by an oath which stresses the fact that God's judgment cannot be changed.

4.1

"Hear this word, you cows of Bashan, who are in the mountain of Samaria,/Listen to this, you women of Samaria, who grow fat like the well-fed cows of Bashan. The most important translation problem is how to handle the picture and comparison cows of Bashan. There is no doubt about the persons to whom the cows are being compared. They are the women of the leading class of the capital.[48] In the translation this must be made clear by saying something like you women of Samaria. If the receptor language has a specific word for women who belong to the upper classes of society (like the British English "lady"), the use of such a special term may be good. However, it may also be unnecessary since the social position of these women is clearly shown in the passage.

The basis of the comparison is not so clear. Nowhere else in the Old Testament are women called cows; perhaps the expression belonged to the stock-breeder's way of talking. Bashan was very fertile country east of the river Jordan stretching from the river Yarmuk in the south up to Hermon in the north (see map). It was, among other things, famous for its excellent cows.

With this little knowledge, there seem to be several possibilities to provide the basis for the comparison: "nobility,"[49] "excessive demand" (since it is said that the cows of Bashan required much attention from their herdsmen),[50] but most likely "plumpness"[51] or "fatness" (as the cattle of Bashan had been characterized as "fattened cattle" in Ezek 39.18).[52] There is at least some overlapping between the last two possibilities.

It is, of course, impossible to translate the picture and comparison literally in languages in which human beings are never compared to animals, or in which cows are completely unknown, or where they are never thought of as fat or well cared for. The TEV who grow fat like the well-fed cows of Bashan will be a good solution in many cases. If the language has no specific word for "cows," a more general term for "cattle" or "domestic animals" or "animals fit to be eaten"[53] can be used.

Unfortunately, we cannot be sure what the emotional force of the Hebrew picture was. It sounds scornful in English, but in some other modern languages it would be a compliment, since fatness is a sign of beauty. It is even possible that Amos used a compliment in order to catch the attention of the women before expressing God's judgment. On the other hand, lack of knowledge makes it impossible to be sure just how faithful any translation is to the original emotional force.

Weak and poor. See 2.6 and 2.7.

Who say to their husbands (Hebrew: lords), "Bring, that we may drink!"/and demand that your husbands keep you supplied with liquor! Whether the women should be quoted directly (as in Hebrew, RSV) or not (as in TEV) will depend on the requirements of the language. In either case there may be adaptations needed in the pronouns[54] (see also Mft, NEB, NAB, TT).

Say to/demand. "Saying" in Hebrew means an order here, and so some languages may want to translate it as such.

Husbands. Hebrew "lords" clearly refers to husbands (RSV, Mft, TT, TEV), but uses a rare word[55] which brings out that these husbands who obeyed the women's commands were supposed to be "masters" but really acted like servants!

Of course, "your lords" (NEB, NAB) makes little sense or even gives the wrong meaning in modern English. However, in many languages there are different words for husband, one of which may indicate a "master" relationship. So a term like "master of the compound" may be currently used. If there is one, such a term should be used in translation here.

Bring is addressed to one person in Hebrew, as each woman addresses her own husband. In other languages it will be necessary for the command to be addressed to several people because there is more than one husband. In that case the pronoun will probably have to be changed: "bring (plural) us wine to drink"[56] or "bring us wine that we may drink." The "us" should not include the husbands if the language has that distinction in pronouns.

That we may drink/keep you supplied with liquor. If what was drunk should be stated, use "wine" if possible (so Mft, TT). If there is no term for wine, then a general term for "fermented fruit juice" or even a cultural equivalent can be used in this context.

4.2

The Lord God has sworn by his holiness/As the Sovereign Lord is holy, he has promised. Nowhere else in the book of Amos does the Lord God swear by his holiness and only one other time in the whole of the Old Testament (Psa 89.35). In 6.8 the Lord God swears by "his life" or by himself, and the meaning is much the same. In this context the moral part of holiness seems emphasized, and that is why TEV translates As the Sovereign Lord is holy, he has promised.

Another possibility is that this oath and the one in 6.8 can be translated in the same way: "The Lord God has sworn by his life/himself," especially if this is a kind of oath in the receptor language. Where no word for "swearing" exists or where it has to be avoided, one can say "declared" or, better, promised to make clear that this particular declaration refers to the future.

Holy belongs to the specialized vocabulary of theology and presents a problem for the translator. It is usually not satisfactory to use a word for "clean," since this normally means "free from dirt." In many cases, a word for "right" or "righteous" is the nearest possible equivalent. Many times the clearest translation of holy emphasizes the Biblical fact that holiness comes from relationship to God;[57] Holy Spirit is often translated as "God's Spirit," etc. This leads to a translation such as "As surely as he is God, the Lord God swears" (compare Mft); "With his authority as God, the Lord God swears."

The following words are the Lord's, as quoted by Amos, and some of the same problems as those of the women speaking in verse 1 will have to be solved. TEV translates the words as spoken directly by God, but it could have translated just as well in an indirect way: "...he has promised that the day will come..." (see RSV, NEB). The question of how to translate this quotation must be considered along with the question of says the Lord at the end of verse 3.

That, behold, the days are coming upon you,/"The days will come. The Hebrew for that, behold gives emphasis to what follows.[58] In English this could be expressed by such a word as "surely": "The days will surely come." One should simply make sure that the translation is emphatic.

The days will come may not be translated literally in all languages. A way should be found to indicate an indefinite future period: "There will be a time," "One of these days," "Not very long from now," etc. One should try to avoid too indefinite an expression like "some time." In making any necessary adaptation, however, see 2.16, and it is important to keep in mind the day of the Lord (5.18,20) and in/on that day (8.3,9, 13; 9.11) which occur later in this book and in other books of the Old Testament. If it is possible to translate "the days will come" in such a way that it will help the reader to see a connection with those phrases, this should certainly be done.

When they shall take you away with hooks, even the last of you with fishhooks,/they will drag you away with hooks; every one of you will be like a fish on a hook. They does not refer to the husbands, as it would appear in TEV and RSV! The meaning is general: "men" (NEB), "people," "someone," or "you will be dragged away" (see JB, Mft).

The picture now changes. This time the women of Samaria are compared to fish caught and taken away. The women will be taken away into exile with force and cruelty.[59]

Hooks, fishhooks/hooks, hook. These are two different words in Hebrew and we cannot be sure exactly what they mean. For the first word such different meanings as hooks,[60] shields,[61] and snares[62] have been proposed. And for the second word such different meanings as fishhooks[63] and fish baskets.[64] However, because of the comparison to fish, meanings not having to do with fishing do not need to be considered. The two words may have meant much the same thing. Much the same action may have been spoken of twice: Take you away with hooks, even the last of you with fishhooks is not saying two different things but putting a different emphasis on the same point.

Because we do not know the precise meaning of the terms, it is better to choose a general one which covers different types of fishing tools and which can be used in both parts of the comparison. Of course, if the language only has a few specific words, one of these will have to be taken. Where people do not know about fish or fishing it may sometimes be possible to use a short descriptive phrase such as "things which live in the water." However, this will draw people's attention away from the real comparison, even if the "capture" is made clear: "everyone of you will be like creatures that lived in the water and which have been seized with a hook" is not likely to picture the deportation of people.

But even if the two terms were fairly distinct, the differences between them are not what is being emphasized. The essential point is that nobody will escape deportation. It may be better to change the picture to one that is known: "drag you away with a ring in your nose," "drag you away in a chicken coop," "drag you away with a rope around your neck," etc. TEV makes the comparison clearer with the use of like: everyone of you will be like a fish on a hook. Each language has its ways of making comparisons.

And you shall go out through the breaches,[65] every one straight before her/you will be dragged to the nearest break in the wall. As the
women do not go of their own free will, most translations should show
that the action was done to them:[66] you will be dragged to or "they
(people, the enemy) will take you through." The breaches are "broken down
places" in the (city) wall (compare Mft, NAB, NEB, TT). On wall, in countries where town walls are unknown, see 1.5.

Everyone straight before her implies that there are so many breaks
in the wall that almost every woman is near one. So they can leave the
city "by the most direct way" (NAB) without having to pass by the city
gates. Since the Hebrew shows the direction of the movement, a translation such as "you will each be taken straight out through the breaks in
the wall" or "each one...through a break" may be the best solution. The
nearest break in the wall may also be a good solution in some languages.

And you shall be cast forth into Harmon,"/and thrown out."[67] If
those who were doing the action were shown in the earlier part of the
sentence this should, of course, be continued: "(they) will throw you
out."

TEV states in a footnote that the Hebrew adds a word whose meaning
is not clear. There are three different ways of handling this:

(1) Omit the particular word and give a footnote like the TEV. Only
this one word should be left out. It is certainly not right to leave out
the whole of verse 3 as sometimes has been done (Zür).

(2) Write the Hebrew word in the letters of the receptor language
because it is most probably the name for some place we do not know about.
Although the practice of doing this is very old[68] we are not sure just
what Hebrew spelling should be followed; Harmon and "Haharmon" are both
possible. Also, we do not know whether "country," "region," "mountain,"
or "town," etc., can be used in the translation to make the name more
meaningful.

(3) Use the best suggestion available for a slight change in the
Hebrew,[69] which is to understand this word to be the name of the well-
known mountain "Hermon." It is very similar to the present Hebrew spelling and is the mountain of Bashan, so this message would begin and end
with a reference to the same territory. Hermon would not be the place of
exile. It is "into the direction of." However, Hermon is on the road to
Assyria and in 5.27 there is another example of such a vague geographical
direction: "beyond Damascus." Many scholars think this change is correct,[70]
and it has been followed in several translations (Mft: "chased to Mount
Hermon"; BJ: "et vous serez repoussées vers l'Hermon"; Dhorme and
others).[71] If the translator wants to follow this third possibility, he
may qualify "Hermon" as a "hill" or "mountain."

Says the Lord. See 3.15.

This is one section, as can be seen in the overall pattern of the book of Amos (Appendix, Figures 3,5), but it is made up of three loosely-connected messages (verses 4-5, 6-11, 12). The third message (verse 12) is an emphatic conclusion to 6-11, or even to 4-11. It also helps to prepare for the hymn in verse 13 because verse 13 describes the power of God.

Because verse 12 is a separate message it can be given a separate paragraph (BJ). Or, because it is an emphatic conclusion it can be in the same paragraph as the end of the second message (TEV). It will depend a lot on the way the poetry of Amos is handled in the translation.[1]

Section heading. Because of the weak connections between them, some translators use separate section headings for the different messages,[2] but when this is done the overall pattern gets lost. So it is much better to use one title for the total section, verses 4-13, as has been done in TEV. A title such as "Israel Fails to Learn" or "Israel Does Not Learn God's Lessons" covers the different themes of the different parts (the continuation of the failure, the failure itself, and its consequences).

4.4-5

RSV | TEV

ISRAEL'S FAILURE TO LEARN

4 "Come to Bethel, and transgress;
        to Gilgal, and multiply
            transgression;
    bring your sacrifices every
            morning,
        your tithes every three days;
5 offer a sacrifice of thanks-
            giving of that which is
            leavened,
        and proclaim freewill
            offerings,
            publish them;
        for so you love to do, O
            people of Israel!"
                says the Lord GOD.

4 The Sovereign LORD says,
"People of Israel, go to the holy place in Bethel and sin, if you must! Go to Gilgal and sin with all your might! Go ahead and bring animals to be sacrificed morning after morning, and bring your tithes every third day. 5 Go on and offer your bread in thanksgiving to God, and brag about the extra offerings you bring! This is the kind of thing you love to do.

In Hebrew the message is very carefully organized with meter[3] and is worded so that the Jewish hearers will be reminded of the law (for example, Lev 7.22-25); there are commands to the people and then a sentence beginning with "for." But Amos is using this type of religious expression with very different purpose.[4] His tone is very sarcastic. Amos is speaking scornfully of the way the people misuse their religion and their worship, and make it a part of their sin. It starts as though it were a call to worship in the holy places of Israel, but quickly the call to worship turns to a shocking accusation.

The sarcastic tone of this passage may be harder to translate than

are the details. The reader must realize that Amos is saying that the
people sin when they worship, and that the sacrifices they perform in
worship (or the motives with which they sacrifice) are their sins. In
some languages the call or command to worship may be translated as an
accusation, which is the real meaning:

> You people of Israel, you love to come to worship God in Bethel,
> and when you do, you sin! You love to go on to worship at Gilgal,
> and there you multiply your sins! You sin when you bring your
> animals... You sin when you bring your tithes... You sin when you
> offer bread to thank God. And then you even love to brag about
> the little extra offerings you bring! That's what you are like,
> people of Israel! (In this example, "love to" was translated
> throughout the passage rather than only at the end.)

Says the Lord God/The Sovereign Lord says. The Hebrew does not show
who the speaker is until the end of verse 5, where it has says the Lord
God, an expression which shows again the source and authority of Amos'
message. In English it certainly helps to have the speaker mentioned at
the beginning (TEV), and this will be true in many other languages. In
some languages it will be necessary to show also that Amos is really the
one speaking for God at this point: "Amos said again:..." In that case it
might be best to end verse 5 with something like "That is the message
from the Lord," or "I have spoken the words of the Lord."

O people of Israel!"/"People of Israel. Again, the Hebrew does not
say to whom the message is spoken until the end (see RSV). But for English, and for many other languages, translating the expression at the
beginning helps to make the passage clearer and is more natural, at
least in a simple style of language.

4.4

"Come/Go. The choice of go or come depends upon the system of showing directions in a language. As we said in Translating Amos, Section 3,
Bethel itself is the viewpoint place of the book of Amos. In some languages where this makes a difference, it may be best to translate "come to
Bethel" and "go to Gilgal."

To Bethel.../Gilgal,/the holy place in Bethel...Gilgal. Hebrew has
only Bethel and Gilgal, but these towns are named because important places
of worship were there, and this worship in these holy places is being emphasized in the passage. Other languages will usually need to follow TEV
and make this meaning clear for Bethel, and probably for Gilgal as well.
Another possibility for holy place would be "God's place" or "the place
where people worship God" or "God's house." The holy place was at a small
distance from the town of Bethel on the east side, and Gilgal was approximately 30 kilometers southeast of Bethel in the Jordan Valley.[5]

Transgress/sin translates a Hebrew verb which is used only here in
the book of Amos. (On the noun, see 1.3.) "Rebellion" is an important
part of the meaning in this context. The NEB has translated with such an
emphasis: "Come to Bethel--and rebel! Come to Gilgal--and rebel the more!"
A translator who follows this example will usually have to make clear
against whom the rebellion is taking place: "rebel against me." However,
in some situations a translation of "rebel" would be misleading because
of political situations which make it sound good instead of bad. "Disobey"

might be another possibility: "(You) come to my house at Bethel--and disobey me! (You) go (and) worship me at Gilgal--and disobey me all the more!"

If you must. By the use of these words TEV is trying to make it clear that God is not really commanding the people to sin, but the English expression may not help very much and probably cannot be translated. The suggestion under 4.4-5 is probably more helpful.

Multiply/with all your might! The Hebrew indicates some increase in frequency of time or quality. Some languages have grammatical ways of showing such meaning. In other cases it will be necessary to express the meaning in a word or phrase: "sin the more" (NAB), "commit still more sins" (TT), "pile sin on sin" (Mft), sin with all your might, etc.

Every morning...every three days;/morning after morning...every third day (see also Smith-Goodspeed, NAB, TT). This way of understanding the Hebrew sees it as an extreme exaggeration,[6] because the custom was to bring a sacrifice once a year, and the tithe payment every third year. The majority of scholars,[7] however, understand the Hebrew to mean that people brought their sacrifice on the morning of the day after their arrival and their tithe payments on the following day, the third one (counted from the day of arrival) or two days after arrival. "Bring your sacrifices for the morning, your tithes within three days" (NEB, Traduction Oecuménique de la Bible [TOB]).

Some languages may have specific words for "tomorrow" or even "early tomorrow morning" and for "the day after tomorrow," and these can sometimes be used. However, such expressions might make the translation sound like Amos is speaking to the people at the entrance of the holy place the moment of their arrival (for which there is no evidence); if so, it would be better to look for another expression. Other languages may simply count the days, but they may differ as to the point from which they start counting. So "third day" may have to be translated "second day."

Bring your sacrifices/Go ahead and bring animals to be sacrificed. The Hebrew means the sacrifice of animals, which TEV makes clear. If one must indicate who does the sacrificing, then: "Bring your animals for the priest to sacrifice."[8] Where there are no special words for sacrifice one may have to say "bring animals to be killed."[9] It may or may not be necessary to show that this is a gift for God according to whether the setting of the holy place and worship does or does not make this clear.[10]

Go ahead and is simply an English way of expressing the urging which God is pretending to do.

Your tithes/bring your tithes. In all modern English translations the technical term "tithes" has been used, since the word has become part of English religious vocabulary. Even where this is the case, however, it may be helpful to give a more detailed explanation of the term in the glossary, basing the explanation on TEV. Where Islamic influence is strong, translators in local languages have sometimes used an Arabic loan word (zakat), although zakat is a social tax for the benefit of the poor and not necessarily ten percent. In Israel the poor were helped by the tithes (Deut 14.28 and following, and Deut 26.12-15), but these were mainly for the benefit of the priests.[11] However, there are important historical and local differences in the practice of the payment of these "taxes" which make them roughly equivalent. Elsewhere a descriptive phrase will have to be used, such as "bring/pay/offer a tenth of what you have earned" or "a tenth of your crops."

[83]

4.5

Offer a sacrifice of thanksgiving of that which is leavened (Hebrew: Burn[12]/make go up in smoke[13] what is leavened[14] as a thank offering)/ offer your bread in thanksgiving to God. To burn something does not usually mean a sacrifice or an offering in other languages. Neither is burning the main point here, so in translation a more general term such as offer, "bring," or "give" is usually better. Leavened here stands for bread, of which it is one characteristic. There is no emphasis on the leavening, which should not be used in translation if bread is used instead. Where languages have no specific word for bread or use a loan word for a western kind of bread, a general word for "food" should be used (compare NAB: "leavened food").

The "thank offering" is a sacrifice that is offered in thankfulness for one reason or another. Possible translation: "bring your food as a gift to express your thankfulness (or: to thank God)."

Freewill offerings/extra offerings. These are like the "thank offering"[15] in that they are not required but are given when the worshiper wants to give them. Possible translations: "voluntary offerings" (Smith-Goodspeed), "spontaneous offerings," "offerings/gifts brought out of your own free will," or extra offerings.

And proclaim...publish/brag about. As is clear from This is the kind of thing you love to do, the emphasis is on the "worshiper's" attempt to impress other people rather than to obey God. This meaning must be made clear in translation. In some languages it will be very natural to do so by putting two verbs together as in Hebrew: "announce, boast about your extra offerings."

4.6-11

This message has five paragraphs (verse 6, verses 7-8, verse 9, verse 10, and verse 11). Each paragraph begins with a description of a particular kind of punishment which the Lord has used[16] in the past and ends with "yet you did not come back to me, says the Lord."

Each paragraph makes the same point. In each one the Lord says that he purposely punished people in a particular way to make them realize his power and to make them come back to him. But they refused to return to him, and this is their real guilt. This meaning must be clear in the translation, so the part which repeats at the end of each paragraph can be translated (at least the first time): "but that did not make you come back to me." After that, it could be translated Still you did not come back to me, unless it is important to keep the repetition the same in each paragraph for the emotional effect.[17]

Each paragraph describes a different punishment: famine, drought, damage to crops, death (from plague and battle) and destruction. The passage is very much like Lev 26, Deut 28, and (in the mention of the particular theme of return) 1 Kgs 8.31-53.[18] Some of these punishments are closely connected with each other, like the first two, since drought is often the reason for famine. For that reason TEV combines the first two subsections in one paragraph.

But regardless of how this passage is organized in the translation, the effect of the repetition of the yet you did not return to me is to give a feeling of disappointment and sorrow which contrasts strongly with the sarcasm of the previous message. It is very important that this emotion be felt in the translation.

There is little regular meter and rhythm in these messages, and only rarely is there strict parallelism. Poetry and prose alternate, and prose becomes predominant towards the end.[19] There is therefore no particular reason for translating this passage as poetry, but that decision should be based as much on the language of the translation as on the Hebrew.

As elsewhere in Amos, the repetition of says the Lord after each paragraph is awkward for many languages, although it works well in others. TEV has left out all of the repetitions except the last one (verse 11), and it is perfectly clear that the Lord continues speaking from verse 5. However, TEV might be stronger by including "says the Lord" at the end of verse 6, and making the beginning of verse 7 a new paragraph. This would emphasize the similarity of the different messages and round off the group of messages by having "says the Lord" both at the beginning and the end. In some cases "the Lord says" should go at the very beginning: "The Lord Eternal declares" (Mft). In some languages, of course, Amos' speaking will have to be indicated also; for example: "Amos spoke again (or continued with) these messages:"

4.6

RSV	TEV

6 "I gave you cleanness of teeth
    in all your cities,
    and lack of bread in all
    your places,
yet you did not return to me,"
    says the LORD.
	6 "I was the one who brought
	famine to all your cities, yet
	you did not come back to me.

The Hebrew begins with a word which gives a connection with the preceding section. The connection itself is roughly as follows (the parts in [ ] are a summary, not a translation):

verses 4-5 [You love to sin even when you are "worshiping" me.]
the connection: a Hebrew conjunction meaning "and even though"
verses 6-11 [I have repeatedly tried to make you repent by the punishments I sent you; you refused.]

In many translations no connection is expressed directly in words (see RSV, Mft, NEB, TEV) because 4-5 and 6-11 were separate messages, not connected when they were originally spoken. However, the place itself of the two messages one after the other in the present text suggests a connection to the reader now. The original separation is no longer true. If the use of connecting words is either necessary or preferable in any language, such a connection should be made. In languages where no connection has to be made in words, it is possible (but probably less helpful) not to express the connection.[20]

"I/"I was the one who. (Compare NEB: "It was I who.") The Hebrew puts particular emphasis on the I by using a separate pronoun as well as including it in the verb. To express such an emphasis, many languages have emphatic pronouns or other systems which can be used, in some cases very much like the Hebrew.

Gave you cleanness of teeth/brought famine. The unusual Hebrew expression cleanness of teeth is a picture[21] or idiom for famine. Though the expression occurs only here, its meaning is certain because of lack of bread which follows in the next line. A literal translation (like RSV, Smith-Goodspeed) does not make sense, however, and a translation based on a literal understanding of the expression, such as can be found in NAB ("though I have made your teeth clean of food") and NEB ("kept teeth idle"), is misleading.[22] If the language happens to have ways of expressing famine as a picture in a simple way, the translator should use it so that the impact of the original picture does not get completely lost in translation; for example: "I made your ribs protrude and your bellies swell." However, this will often not be possible, so usually the meaning famine has to be translated directly. Some languages have no noun for famine, so the translation should be something like "I made (caused) that you had nothing to eat."[23]

And lack of bread in all your places,/so that you had no food. This repeats the same point about famine in another way, and in some translations the two pictures should be combined or partly combined, as they have been in TEV.

On the other hand, it is possible that in all your places is deliberately more general than all your cities, in order to emphasize the wide area of the famine: "not only in the towns, but also in the country" (so Mft: "your towns," "over all the land"). So the passage could be condensed in another way (especially in languages which have no noun for famine) by saying, for example, "I made (caused) that you had nothing to eat either in your towns or in the country" or "I made (caused) that you had nothing to eat wherever you lived." In languages which make a difference between a recent past and a remote past, the remote (if it is not a mythical or legendary remote past) should be used.

For another way of expressing yet you did not come back to me as "but that did not make you come back to me," see 4.6-11. The Hebrew uses a rather strong word meaning that the movement completely reaches its mark: "all the way back..." Some languages have grammatical ways to express that particular emphasis. In languages which relate directions to a viewpoint place (Bethel, from which Amos is speaking) rather than a viewpoint person (God, who is speaking), the translation may be "go back to me" or "return, go to me."

4.7-8

RSV	TEV
7 "And I also withheld the rain from you when there were yet three months to the harvest; I would send rain upon one city, and send no rain upon another city;	7 I kept it from raining when your crops needed it most. I sent rain on one city, but not on another. Rain fell on one field,

one field would be rained
    upon,
  and the field on which it
    did not rain withered;
8 so two or three cities wandered
    to one city
  to drink water, and were not
    satisfied;
yet you did not return to me,"
          says the LORD.

but another field dried up. 8 Weak
with thirst, the people of several
cities went to a city where they
hoped to find water, but there was
not enough to drink. Still you did
not come back to me.

In the second paragraph the picture is one of drought. As was pointed out in 4.6-11, verses 6 and 7-8 could be combined in one paragraph
since the lack of rain (verse 7) causes the thirst (verse 8) and the
famine (verse 6). From that point of view verse 6 is a general or topical
statement for which verses 7-8 give detail and explanation about the cause
of the famine. To bring about this relationship of the cause to the effect
more clearly, in some languages a translator may prefer to change the
order by putting verse 6 after verses 7-8.[24]

4.7

I also withheld the rain from you/I kept it from raining. God's control over the weather is expressed differently in different languages.
One may have to say "I caused (made/gave) that it did not rain" or "I did
not allow rain to fall (arrive)." The same type of problem comes later in
the verse, where it can be translated "I would cause the rain to fall on
one city, but would not allow it to fall on another city."
When there were yet three months to the harvest;/when your crops
needed it most. This means that the "latter rain" of the spring (March-
April), which is so necessary for the grain harvest three months later
(May-June), did not fall.[25] However, the timing is related to the climate
in the Middle East and will not necessarily be understood in other areas.
For that reason TEV qualifies the information by saying when your crops
needed it most. In such a translation something about the Middle Eastern
culture is left out, but it could easily be included as well: "three
months before the harvest, when your crops needed it most."
There may be no specific word for harvest in a language, but it can
be described as "the time when grain was cut."[26]

4.8

So two or three cities wandered to one city to drink water, and were
not satisfied;/Weak with thirst, the people of several cities went to a
city where they hoped to find water, but there was not enough to drink.
Two or three cities means the people of several cities, and in languages
where cities cannot stand for people or be described as doing things like
people, it will be necessary to translate as in TEV (compare also NEB and
TT).
The Hebrew word for wander or went indicates also a state of exhaus-
tion for which "staggered" might be an English equivalent. However, apart
from the difficulty of finding a close, natural equivalent, the translator

may need to make the reason for the wandering (thirst) clear in the translation and say something like weak with thirst, they went...where they hoped to find. In some languages the natural expression for this state will be "sick of thirst" or "thirsty nearly dead."

One city/a city. Another town than their own.

On the expressions repeated in each of these paragraphs (yet you did not return to me, says the Lord), see 4.6-11.

4.9

RSV	TEV
9 "I smote you with blight and mildew; I laid waste[i] your gardens and your vineyards; your fig trees and your olive trees the locust devoured; yet you did not return to me," says the LORD.	9 "I sent a scorching wind to dry up your crops. The locusts ate up all your gardens and vineyards, your fig trees and olive trees. Still you did not come back to me.

[i]Cn: Heb *the multitude of*

"I smote you with blight and mildew;/"I sent a scorching wind to dry up your crops. Blight and mildew (even if they are known) give the impression that some sort of diseases are intended, and smote you seems to refer to human diseases.[27]

But in fact in this picture people are only indirectly the victims, and the diseases are diseases of the crops: "I caused blight and mildew to destroy your crops." In some languages it may be possible to have such technical terms like blight and mildew in the translation and to give an explanation in a glossary. However, in most cases there will be no such terms, or they will be known only by crop specialists. The blight was caused by the hot desert wind. The cause of the mildew is not as certain, but there is a strong possibility that it was caused by worms.[28] This makes it possible to translate: "I sent a hot wind and worms to destroy your crops." TEV has only a scorching wind (compare also TT: "a burning wind" and NAB: "searing wind").

I laid waste your gardens and your vineyards;/all your gardens and vineyards. The majority of scholars change[29] the Hebrew slightly to something which means "I dried up" or I have laid waste (see Smith-Goodspeed, Mft, NEB, TT).[30] With this change the text to be translated is: "I have dried up your gardens and vineyards."

In some languages vineyards can be translated by such expressions as "field/garden with vines," "grape garden," "place-for-grapes," "wine garden," etc. In other places a word for vineyards may have to be introduced as a loan word from the dominant language in the area. Elsewhere it may be necessary to use a cultural equivalent such as "field/garden of palmwine-trees," in which case the expression should correspond if at all possible with the word for "wine" used in 2.12 (see the commentary there).

Sometimes the closest equivalent will simply be general terms such as "gardens and plantations" or "fields and gardens" or "vegetable gardens and fruit gardens." Sometimes both expressions will have to be contained in one word "gardens."

Likewise, fig trees and olive trees may be unknown, and it is often necessary to borrow the meaningless names for these trees from the dominant language in the area. An explanatory word such as "tree" should be included as well. Some languages may have a general term for all kinds of cultivated fruit trees, though no specific name for olive trees and fig trees, in which case such a term can be used: "the locusts ate up your fruit trees." Sometimes a kind of wild fig tree or olive tree is known, but since they are never cultivated, the words for this kind of tree cannot be used.

Where locusts are unknown, one can use an explanatory word such as "insects called locusts" or simply a general term "a kind of insect."

For the repeated parts of this paragraph, see 4.6-11.

4.10

<table>
<tr><td align="center">RSV</td><td align="center">TEV</td></tr>
<tr>
<td>10 "I sent among you a pestilence after the manner of Egypt;
I slew your young men with the sword;
I carried away your horses;^j
and I made the stench of your camp go up into your nostrils;
yet you did not return to me,"
says the LORD.</td>
<td>10 "I sent a plague on you like the one I sent on Egypt. I killed your young men in battle and took your horses away. I filled your nostrils with the stink of dead bodies in your camps. Still you did not come back to me.</td>
</tr>
</table>

*j*Heb *with the captivity of your horses*

This paragraph is about two disasters which are closely connected with each other: disease and war.[31] Perhaps the structure of this paragraph is parallel to that of 3.6-8 where famine was mentioned first, though it was clearly the result of the drought talked about afterwards. In the same way disease can be seen as the result of war, more particularly as caused by the rotting bodies at the battlefield camps.

As was the case in the first paragraph(s), the relationship will need to be expressed by a different order of the sentences in some languages. For example, the first sentence could be put after the picture of decaying bodies in camp, with something to show the connection. However, for some languages the rather unconnected series of pictures may help to give the feeling of the chaos of war and a people taken by a widespread disease.

"I sent among you a pestilence after the manner of Egypt;/"I sent a plague on you like the one I sent on Egypt. After the manner of Egypt may be understood in two different ways: (1) "an Egyptian plague" (so

Mft, TT) in the sense that Egypt had an unhealthy climate with infectious illnesses; or more probably (2) one of the ten plagues of Egypt (compare Exo 9.3-9,15). There is no advantage in this case to translating in so general a way that more than one meaning is possible. It is better simply to use the best knowledge we have. This gives a translation such as <u>I sent a plague on you like the one I sent on Egypt</u>.

<u>Plague</u> refers to the bubonic plague, a severe disease spread from rats to people by fleas. If the language has a word for such a violent form of illness, it should be used. Sometimes the plague itself is known but may be referred to by some indirect or euphemistic term which can be used in translation. If, on the other hand, there is no specific word for the plague, a more general term such as "epidemic" can be used.

<u>I slew your young men with the sword; I carried away</u> (Hebrew: with the captivity of) <u>your horses;/I killed your young men</u> in battle, and <u>took your horses away</u>. <u>Sword</u> represents <u>battle</u>, and such a picture may be quite clear in some languages. In others it should be changed to a more direct <u>I killed your young men in battle</u>, or, more exactly, "I made (caused/gave) your young men (to) die in battle."

The reference to the horses can be understood in two ways: either the horses were captured and killed (so Smith-Goodspeed: "I slew your young men with the sword, together with your captured horses," and basically Mft, NEB, TT), or they are only captured (so RSV, NAB, TEV). The latter seems much more probable because horses were rare and very expensive! So a translation might be "I gave your horses as booty (to your enemies)" or "I let your horses be captured" (compare NAB).

If there is a specific word for "war-horses" in the language, it should be used.[32]

<u>I made the stench of your camp go up</u> (namely[33]) <u>into your nostrils;</u> /<u>I filled your nostrils with the stink</u> of dead bodies in your camps. This sentence can be restructured according to the needs of the receptor language as in the TEV, or as "I made (caused/did) you smell the bad odor of the dead bodies/corpses in your camps."[34]

For the repeated parts of this paragraph, see 4.6-11.

4.11

RSV	TEV
11 "I overthrew some of you, as when God overthrew Sodom and Gomorrah, and you were as a brand plucked out of the burning; yet you did not return to me," says the LORD.	11 "I destroyed some of you as I destroyed Sodom and Gomorrah. Those of you who survived were like a burning stick saved from a fire. Still you did not come back to me," says the LORD.

"<u>I overthrew some of you</u>, /"<u>I destroyed some of you</u>. Another way of understanding the Hebrew meaning is "I brought destruction amongst you" (NEB), but that can hardly be translated without restructuring as something like <u>I destroyed some of you</u>. The way the destruction took place is not stated, and although many commentators think of an earthquake[35] it is better not to try to include that in the translation like Mft did: "I sent you a shattering earthquake."

As when God overthrew Sodom and Gomorrah,/as I destroyed Sodom and Gomorrah. God refers to himself as God here rather than "I," which happens frequently in the Hebrew, especially since God overthrew Sodom and Gomorrah is doubtless a fixed phrase. In cases like this, God should be translated as "I" (TEV and TT) to avoid misunderstanding. One may want to show that Sodom and Gomorrah are "cities."

And you were as a brand plucked out of the burning;/Those of you who survived were like a burning stick saved from a fire. Almost the same expression occurs in Zech 3.2, which shows that this was a proverbial saying for a person saved from great danger. This saying became proverbial in English, also, which influenced the RSV and Smith-Goodspeed translations. However, this expression is no longer common in modern English and does not exist in other languages. The TEV translation makes the meaning clear and can be followed in most languages. Other possibilities include: "Those of you who were not destroyed (or: whom I did not destroy) barely escaped (or: were almost destroyed also) like when someone saves a stick from the fire, even after it has already begun to burn."

On the other hand, a language may have a different proverbial expression which means the same thing, and the translator can use that to give a picture with some of the emotion of the original picture.

If a translation such as I destroyed some of you is used in the first part of the paragraph, the contrast between those destroyed and those saved may be brought out by saying something like "But/on the other hand you were..."

For the repeated part, see the preceding paragraphs.

4.12

	RSV	TEV

12 "Therefore thus I will do to you, O Israel; because I will do this to you, prepare to meet your God, O Israel!"

12 "So then, people of Israel, I am going to punish you. And because I am going to do this, get ready to face my judgment!"

Thus I will do to you,/I am going to punish you. This is a transitional verse and for the way to relate it to the other passages and paragraphs, see 4.4-13.

The verse is rather difficult because we cannot be sure what this (or thus) refers to. All commentators agree that this cannot refer directly back to one of the punishments in the preceding paragraphs since all these things took place before. They also agree that this does not seem to refer to future events described in the beginning of the next chapter because these form a different section of the book, and verses 12-13 are the end of a section. Some scholars think that this problem came about through changes which were made by early scribes.[36] A more natural explanation is that this refers to some threatening gesture or to something the first hearers could see on the spot and which did not need any explanation to those who could see it.[37]

All this may help to understand the text, but it will certainly not help the translation as we do not know what the gesture was, anyhow. So the translation may have to be vague and unsatisfactory. Nevertheless, if it is impossible for the receptor language to refer to the punishment as this, the translator will have to say something like "I am going to punish you severely." Such a rendering would be based on purely translational considerations.

TEV has tried to solve the problem by translating first I am going to punish you, and then this in the next sentence refers back to the punishment. However, this restructuring causes unnecessary and awkward repetition. It might be better to say: "So then, people of Israel, I am going to punish you. Get ready to face..."

Prepare to meet your God/get ready to face my judgment! The meeting with God refers to judgment and punishment, so has to be qualified in translation: "face your God" (TT) or face my judgment. In some languages it will be good to say something like "prepare yourself to meet God, who will judge you." Your God is a fixed saying, like God destroyed Sodom and Gomorrah in 4.11. It can be translated in various ways: my judgment; "me, your God"; "me, your God, who will judge you"; "me, as I judge you."

This is the end of the Lord's speaking until 5.3. If the receptor language indicates such an ending, see the discussion at 1.2.

4.13 THE POWER OF GOD TO CREATE

This is a very brief section balancing 1.2 (see Appendix, Section 1.1).

Section heading. No heading may be needed if there is no attempt in the translation to show the structure of Amos. If there is a heading, it should contrast with that of 1.2: "God Is Able to Create," "God Is the One Who Creates/Makes All Things."

4.13

RSV	TEV
13 For lo, he who forms the mountains, and creates the wind, and declares to man what is his thought; who makes the morning darkness, and treads on the heights of the earth— the LORD, the God of hosts, is his name!	13 God is the one who made the mountains and created the winds. He makes his thoughts known to man; he changes day into night. He walks on the heights of the earth. This is his name: the LORD God Almighty!

This verse describes the character and power of the God who brings judgment. It is in the poetry of a hymn (like 1.2) which recognizes God's power and praises him at the same time.[1]

Whatever style was used in 1.2 should be used here also. The sample text in English meter given in Translating Amos, Section 5.1, shows how Hebrew meter[2] can be restructured to the poetry of other languages without loss of meaning.

Like 1.2 this verse has Amos speaking directly, not quoting the Lord. It may be necessary to show this at the beginning or the end of the verse, or both, if that is best in the receptor language.

Lo. The Hebrew is the same as behold in 2.13. Here it helps to indicate that the passage is a climactic statement near the end of Part 1 of Amos (Appendix, Figure 5), but in addition carries some meaning of wonder and awe. TEV does not have any transition, and it is difficult to find a suitable transitional phrase in English. ("What do you know!" carries the meaning but is too colloquial.) A restructuring of the passage could move the idea of wonder to near the end: "Yes, that very one is the Lord, the mighty God!" "For" (JB) is probably a little weak. A possibility in modern English might be "Yes..." The translator in another language may be able to find some suitable transitional expression.

Forms/made. Made and created[3] have practically the same meaning in Hebrew. One is related to the picture of the potter who "forms" the clay, which is why most English translations use "form." In many languages a general word like "to make" will have to be used, perhaps even twice.

Creates the wind/created the winds. The Hebrew word translated by wind can also be translated by "spirit." It is very likely that both meanings[4] are present in the poem because the meaning "wind" connects this sentence with the one before it about the creation of natural things like mountains, and the meaning "spirit" or "spirit of man" connects it with the following sentence He makes his thoughts known to man. Normally, this double meaning is lost in translation.[5] All English translations have wind. However, it may be possible or even necessary to keep the double meaning of the Hebrew word by a double translation: "God is the one who made mountains and winds. He created the spirit of human beings and makes his thoughts known to them." Whether or not it is best to give a double translation depends upon the way the translation is restructured.

Declares to man what is his thought;/He makes his thoughts known to man. Grammatically the his in Hebrew can be understood to refer to God or to man, and this ambiguity will be carried over into other languages, unless something is done to make the meaning clear. Unlike the case of "wind-spirit," two meanings are not intended here, and a decision about which meaning to use has to be made. Although some commentators think that his refers to man,[6] it is more probable that it refers to God in view of the vocabulary used.[7] Mft, for example, capitalizes "His": "and reveals His inner mind to man."

Who makes the morning darkness/he changes day into night. Hebrew manuscripts do not all agree here. Most are like the RSV, but a few are slightly different and can be translated as "who makes dawn and darkness" (Smith-Goodspeed [S-G], Mft, NAB). It is hard to say which manuscript should be translated. The parallel in 5.8 (probably originally part of the same hymn) makes "who makes the morning darkness" more probable. So also TT "who changes the dawn to dusk"; NEB "who darkens the dawn with thick clouds"; TEV he changes day into night.[8]

And (who) treads (marches/strides) on (over) the heights of the earth/He walks on the heights of the earth. This is a picture of the rule of God over the earth. He is shown to be Lord by his moving over its highest places. If such an understanding can be obtained by keeping the picture, it would be best to do so, especially when translating as poetry. On the other hand, if the Hebrew picture does not give a correct understanding in a receptor language, something like "he rules over all the earth" is a possibility.

The Lord, the God of Hosts/the Lord God Almighty. See 3.13.

The Lord...is his name/This is his name. This expression presents a general problem for all translators (see Translators Handbook on Ruth, 1.6). Here Amos is not telling the people what God's name is. Rather, he is saying something like "It is the Lord himself who does this!" The creative action of verse 13 reveals the character of the God who rescued the people from Egypt and established a special relationship with them.

There is an additional problem in the fact that the Lord is not a name but a title. So consequently, in English and many other languages "His name is the Lord" is a peculiar expression. A translation such as that suggested above may solve the problem. Combined with the God of Hosts the translation could be "It is the (al)mighty Lord himself who does this" or "Our powerful Lord is the one who does all this." A similar expression ("Yahweh [is] his name") occurs in 5.8.

5.1-3 CONCLUSION: LAMENT FOR ISRAEL

This brief message forms the conclusion to Part 1 of Amos, as de-
cribed in the Appendix, Section 1.1. At the same time it balances the
introductory message of Part 3.

Section heading. The section heading may be worded so as to show
something of the balance with verses 16-17. One possibility here would be
"The Prophet Sings a Funeral Song," with "Israel Sings Funeral Songs" in
5.16-17, or "Amos Cries for the Dead" as against "Israel Cries for the
Dead." If there is a special word in the language for the mourning which
accompanies death or a funeral, it might be suitable: "Mourning for the
Dead" (both places) or "Amos Mourns" and "Israel Mourns."

5.1-3

RSV	TEV
	A CALL TO REPENTANCE
5 Hear this word which I take up over you in lamentation, O house of Israel:	5 Listen, people of Israel, to this funeral song which I sing over you:
2 "Fallen, no more to rise, is the virgin Israel; forsaken on her land, with none to raise her up."	2 Virgin Israel has fallen, Never to rise again! She lies abandoned on the ground, And no one helps her up.
3 For thus says the Lord GOD: "The city that went forth a thousand shall have a hundred left, and that which went forth a hundred shall have ten left to the house of Israel."	3 The Sovereign LORD says, "A city in Israel sends out a thousand soldiers, but only a hundred return; another city sends out a hundred, but only ten come back."

The unity of this section is not very clear. Verses 1 and 2 belong
together as introduction to a funeral song followed by the funeral song
itself, but in verse 3 the speaker changes from Amos to the Lord and the
subject changes from Israel to a city.[1] TEV has translated verse 3 as
completely separate, although the three verses form a unit of some sort.
The meter of the funeral song continues in part of verse 3, where the
theme of dying is also made more clear. It is typical for the prophet to
show the authority of his announcement of judgment by quoting the Lord.
What happens to a city may simply be an illustration of what happens to
the nation as a whole. So verse 3 may be taken as the reason for the
funeral song. The structure of verses 1-3 is well balanced (see Appendix,
Section 3.4), and the theme of verses 1-3 balances that of verses 16-17
in the larger organization of the book (Appendix, Figures 3, 5).

This is a passage which some translators may want to translate in a
balanced way (as suggested in Translating Amos, Section 2.2), if that is
effective in the receptor language.

[95]

5.1

Hear this word which I take up over you in lamentation, O house of
Israel:/Listen, people of Israel, to this funeral song which I sing over
you:
Hear this word/Listen. As in other places in Amos, this expression
begins a concluding section (Appendix, Section 1.21). In this case it
would be well to indicate that fact with the use of a word like "so."
House of Israel shows to whom the message is being spoken, and in
many languages it is natural to put such an expression at the beginning,
or at least near the beginning, of the sentence, like TEV. In addition,
a picture such as house of Israel will often be clear only in a translation such as people of Israel.
Since the Lord starts to speak in verse 3, Amos is the speaker of
verses 1 and 2. In some languages this should be shown by translating
"which I, Amos, sing over you" or by introducing the whole sentence with
"Amos said": or "Amos continued, saying," or "Amos spoke again."
The translation may also need to show that the funeral song is Amos'
message by saying, for example, "this, my funeral song."[2]
The funeral song or "mourning song" was the chief funeral ceremony
in Israel. It was a poem of grief on the death of a kinsman, friend or
leader. In Amos this kind of song for an individual is changed into one
for the people of Israel as a whole, so it becomes a political mourning
song. The "dead" over whom Amos sings his song are the living people to
whom Amos is speaking. In this way they listen to the announcement of
their own death.[3]
Funeral customs differ, and the idea of a "song" in connection with
a funeral is entirely strange in some cultures. It may even be contra-
dictory because songs are associated with joy or work or play, but not
with death. In such cases the translation should have something like
"Listen to what I say in mourning over your death." There may be some
kind of specific term which would be usable. If there are poems or
speeches recited or composed rather than sung, adaptation should be made
along that line.

5.2

If verse 1 speaks of a funeral song, verse 2 should sound like one.
That is, it should have the style of a funeral song in the language of
the translation.[4] If song is not used in verse 1, then whatever is indicated there should be true of the style in verse 2, whether poem, statement, etc.
If verse 2 is to be a funeral song or poetry of any kind in translation, the translator will have to use imagination and creativity in restructuring into the patterns of the language, and still translate faith-
fully (see Translating Amos, Section 5).
Fallen, no more to rise, is the virgin Israel;/Israel has fallen,
never to rise again. This statement presents several translation problems.
In many languages it is not possible to talk about a nation as though it
were a person.[5] Normally, in such cases, the translator tries to show the
basis of the comparison.[6] For example, one possibility is "The nation of

Israel is like a young woman: in spite of her youth she has fallen and will not get up again." But in this case there is no agreement about what the basis of comparison really is, as can be seen from the different commentaries.

In some languages the best solution is not to translate the picture at all and to say something like "the nation/people of Israel has/have fallen." Such a translation loses something, but the loss may be more in feeling than in ideas.

Fallen. The Hebrew picture is one of violent death. It was commonly used in funeral songs with the meaning of "fallen by the sword" (compare 2 Sam 1.19,25,27; Lam 2.21; Jer 9.22). This meaning often has to be made clear in translation, or people will think that the fall is due to an accident. One way is to show what causes the fall: "killed by the sword, Israel has fallen." Another is to use a different verb, such as "struck down" instead of "fallen."

The Hebrew verb is in the perfect, indicating a past completed action. This means that what will happen to the hearers in the future is presented as an already accomplished fact and the effect on Amos' hearers was something like someone reading in the newspaper that he is dead.[7] In translation one may have to use future tenses to emphasize the absolute certainty that the message will come true.

Forsaken on her land, with none to raise her up."/She lies abandoned on the ground, And no one helps her up. The meaning is "she lies abandoned on her own soil," and it would be better to say "on her own soil" (or "in their own country," if "the people of Israel" is used earlier), since this makes clear the invasion of the country by foreign armies.

5.3

For thus says the Lord God: "The city that went forth a thousand shall have a hundred left, and that which went forth a hundred shall have ten left to the house of Israel."/The Sovereign Lord says, "A city in Israel sends out a thousand soldiers, but only a hundred return; another city sends out a hundred, but only ten come back." The place of to the house of Israel at the end of the verse is a problem in the Hebrew. The meaning does not fit where it is, although it balances O house of Israel in 5.1 (see Appendix, Figure 14). TT has moved it: "For this is what the Lord God has said to the nation of Israel," which makes it like verse 4.[8]

Such an understanding of the Hebrew is not necessarily any help in translation, however. It may simply be repetitious to say: "For this is what the Lord says to the nation of Israel." The people to whom the message is spoken in verse 3 are the same as those in the preceding verses, so in many languages they do not need to be stated again. This is why TEV translates: The Sovereign Lord says (compare Mft).

Lord God/Sovereign Lord. See 3.7.

Unlike TEV, it may be advisable to indicate the connection between this verse and the preceding one by stating clearly that verse 3 gives the basis for verse 2. In English this can be expressed by such a particle as for [NAB, S-G, Mft], or the connection can even be made stronger by something like "It's just as the Lord says." Other languages have their own ways of making this relationship clear.

The message itself certainly needs some restructuring in many languages. The quotation of the Lord will sometimes be a problem, tied as it is to Amos' own words in verse 2. One possibility is to say "For the Lord Eternal has declared that..." (Mft).

The typical Hebrew expression <u>the city that went forth a thousand</u> (or as a thousand, with a thousand)[9] can seldom be translated literally. <u>The city</u> may need to be translated as <u>A city in Israel</u> or "her city," if the picture of verse 2 is kept. That <u>went out</u> refers to battle may be made clear by speaking of <u>soldiers</u> or by "to go out to battle" (TT) or "marched out to war" (NEB).[10]

A city cannot do something like "sending" or "going forth" in all languages, so in TT: "A thousand men will go out to battle from a town, but a hundred will survive, a hundred men will go out to battle from a (another[11]) town, but ten will survive."

Some languages may have technical terms like "battalion," "company" and "platoon" which would clearly indicate that they are the military forces of a town.[12] However, technical terms should be broadly used and ones that do not fit the Hebrew setting should be avoided. The important thing is how many men were killed. The forces were cut to a tenth of their original strength.

5.4-15 POSSIBILITY OF SALVATION: ISRAEL'S PERIL

This passage, which forms Part 2 of Amos (see Appendix, Section 1.1), at first seems to have very little organization. Different subjects follow each other and sometimes there is little connection between them, or things that do seem to go together are separated with something else between. But there is an organization to this section just the same, and here the passages are so short that it is relatively easy to make it possible for the reader to see what it is. Some of the structure can here be shown by translation, paragraphing, and in other ways than by headings alone (see Translating Amos, Section 2).

Section heading. For those translations which have headings for each of the three major parts of Amos (Translating Amos, Section 2.4), it may be possible to choose something like "Israel Is in Great Danger, But She May Seek God" or "Israel Can Be Saved from Great Danger." In that case there should also be headings for the individual smaller sections, as discussed below.

In translations where the structure of the book is not shown in the headings, a general heading here such as one of those above, or simply "Brief Messages to Israel" or Call to Repentance can be used, and there may not need to be any headings for the smaller sections.

5.4-6

RSV	TEV
4 For thus says the LORD to the house of Israel: "Seek me and live; 5 but do not seek Bethel, and do not enter into Gilgal or cross over to Beersheba; for Gilgal shall surely go into exile, and Bethel shall come to nought." 6 Seek the LORD and live, lest he break out like fire in the house of Joseph, and it devour, with none to quench it for Bethel,	4 The LORD says to the people of Israel, "Come to me, and you will live. 5 Do not go to Beersheba to worship. Do not try to find me at Bethel--Bethel will come to nothing. Do not go to Gilgal--her people are doomed to exile." 6 Go to the LORD, and you will live. If you do not go, he will sweep down like fire on the people of Israel. The fire will burn up the people of Bethel, and no one will be able to put it out.

It is clear that 5.4-6 forms a unit.[1] This can be seen in the way it is organized (Appendix, Section 3.5) and by the fact that it is balanced with a similar pattern in seek good and not evil (5.14-15). There is a problem, though, with where this section ends. Both RSV and TEV consider it to end with verse 7 on the basis that the warning in verse 6 continues in the following verse. However, on the basis of the overall structure of the book (Appendix, Figures 3, 5), verse 7 seems to be a separate, very short section (see below). It may be, however, that in translation it would be better to combine it with verse 6, especially if the translator is not making any attempt to show the balanced organization of the book. There are also problems in verse 6. The familiar confusion between the Lord speaking and the prophet speaking takes place again, and the style and grammar also change.

The challenge in translating this section is to carry over to the modern reader some of the meaning and emotional force of the passage, which is full of picture language related to Israel's history of relationship to God, made more complicated by poetic language and organization. All this will be explained as each verse is taken up below.

One possible restructuring for English was given in Translating Amos, Section 2.2. This restructuring kept an organization similar to that of the Hebrew for verses 4-6, laying out the lines on the page to help the reader see that organization. However, there the wording of the TEV was used as much as possible.

Here follow two further restructurings which go beyond TEV in showing some of the implicit meanings in the text as we will discuss them below. By making these explicit it is possible to emphasize the relationship between the ideas in the balanced pattern of the Hebrew passage. The first follows the Hebrew order of patterning, while the second does not.

Neither of these restructurings is English poetry, but they are both patterned prose which tries to bring out something of the original patterning, even if only weakly. They may give some idea of how to proceed in another language and provide a model in addition to RSV and TEV.

(5.4-6)

The Lord says to the people of Israel:
"Come back and be my people again, so you can live!
    Don't stay in 'God's House'a to pray any more;
    Don't gather at Gilgal;
    Don't hunt for your help way off in Beersheba;
    No, Gilgal will be your gate into exile,
    And 'God's House' will be haunted!
Come back to follow your Lord, so you can live!"
    "And if not," said Amos,
"God's fire will sweep down
    on you people in Israel,
    burning the ones
    who live in 'God's House'--
A fire you cannot put out."

aHebrew: Bethel, which means "God's House."

*   *   *   *   *

The Lord says to the people of Israel:
"Come back and be my people again, so you can live!
    Don't stay in 'God's House'a to pray any more--
      it's going to be haunted!

Don't gather at Gilgal;
    it's going to be your gate into exile!
Don't hunt for your help way off in Beersheba--
    No, just
Come back to follow your Lord so you can live!"
    "And if not," said Amos,
"God's fire will sweep down on you people of Israel,
    a fire you cannot put out;
burning the people who live in 'God's House.'"

[a]Hebrew: <u>Bethel</u>, which means "God's House."

<u>Section heading</u>. If the various sections within 5.4-15 are given headings to show their organization, then this part could be entitled something like "God Warns Israel to Come to Him" or "Come to God so that You May Live." The parallel heading in 5.14-15 could be "God Warns Israel to Do Good" or "Do Good so that You May Live."

<u>5.4</u>

<u>For thus says the Lord/The Lord says</u>. The opening word in Hebrew introduces a separate saying and does not show a relationship with the preceding paragraph. In contrast with older translations which had "for" (RSV, S-G), it seems better in many languages not to translate this word at all. Note some of the translations in addition to TEV: "These are the words of the Lord to the people of Israel" (NEB) and "This is what the Lord has said to the nation of Israel" (TT); (compare also Mft: "Here is the Eternal's message for the house of Israel"). On the structural importance of this phrase, see Appendix, Section 1.3.

<u>The house of Israel/the people of Israel</u>. See 5.1.

"<u>Seek me and live/"Come to me, and you will live</u>. Often a verb "to seek" implies a search for something or someone lost or inaccessible, which is, of course, not the case here. The best translation in some languages is <u>come to me</u> (so also TT) or, more clearly, "come (back) to worship me" or "come to me for help," "come to me for advice" (compare NEB: "resort to me").[2] "Turn back" is a possibility in some languages.

Of these, "come/turn (back) to worship me" may be the easiest to fit into the context because of the contrast with places of worship in Bethel, Gilgal, and Beersheba. However, a term for "worship" is not enough if it simply means a ritual. Some possibilities: "come and let me be your Lord" or "come back to being my people."

The Hebrew has two commands, of which "seek" is the condition and "live" the consequence:[3] <u>Come to me, and you will live</u> or "Come and let me be your Lord. Then you will live," or even "If you come to me for help, you will live" or "Come back to be my people, so you can live." <u>You will live</u> may have to be expressed as "you will remain alive," "you will survive (my judgment)," or in some languages it may be better to translate "so you may not die." In translating this sentence it is important to keep in mind the parallel sentence in verse 6.

5.5

This verse is a real challenge to the translator because it should not only be clear but should also deal effectively with the balance of ideas (see 5.4-6). For an example of how the balance can be unnecessarily destroyed, see NEB.

On the other hand, if this kind of organization would have the effect of weakening the force of the message in a language, the translation must be restructured. TEV does this by putting the middle part about Beersheba first, since this is the only part which does not have a matching part. Then the two parts about Bethel are combined, and the ones about Gilgal are combined. This may be a very useful way to translate in other languages (see the second restructuring in 5.4-6, and Translating Amos, Section 2.2).

However, the order in which these different parts are translated may differ from language to language, and in some cases the ways of showing directions which are characteristic of the language may influence the order. Bethel is the viewpoint place of the book (see Translating Amos, Section 3), and Gilgal is 30 kilometers southwest of Bethel in the Jordan Valley. Beersheba, on the other hand, is in the extreme south of the neighboring territory of Judah (see the map). So the normal ways of showing such relationships in some languages may favor the order Bethel--Gilgal--Beersheba, or the reverse.

It is not only the balanced arrangement of the Hebrew which strengthened the message for the original hearer and reader, but also the play upon words and the repetition of sounds in Gilgal shall surely go into exile. Even those who do not know Hebrew can see the repetition if the Hebrew sounds are written out as follows: haggilgāl gāloh yigleh. The sequence gl is repeated four times, and each word begins or ends with h.

It is very hard, if not impossible, to translate with equivalent sound combinations in other languages. The effect is usually silly rather than forceful. So Mft: "for Gilgal shall have a galling exile." The best example can perhaps be found in Wellhausen's German translation: "Gilgal wird zum Galgen gehn" ("Gilgal will go to the gallows").[4] If the translator can find a dynamic pun in his language, it may be very helpful, but the pun should not be an artificial one, because an artificial pun is worse than no pun at all. What makes the play on words even more difficult is that the Hebrew reminds the people of Israel of things the modern reader may not know. Gilgal was the place where the land was symbolically given to Israel (Josh 4.20 and following) and now becomes the place where the land is to be lost. It may be very difficult to make this important part of the meaning clear without a footnote. Also, in many languages it is impossible to say for Gilgal shall surely go into exile, since a place cannot go into exile. One often has to say: "the people of Gilgal" (TT) or her people.[5] One could identify Gilgal: "where you first entered this land" and balance "gate into exile" against "entered."

Bethel shall come to nought."/Bethel will come to nothing. Here the impact comes from the fact that Bethel means "the house of God" in Hebrew, and it will come to nothing. In many languages will come to nothing has to be translated something like "be annihilated" or "be destroyed," unless, again, the translator is able to create an effective contrast in his language. A good example of such a contrast is again Wellhausen's translation: "Bethel wird des Teufels werden" ("Bethel will become the devil's," or perhaps better, "Bethel will go to the devil"). Another translation which can perhaps be used as a cultural model is "Bethel becomes a house of ogres,"[6] drawing on the idea that ogres and demons dwell in the ruins of destroyed cities. But none of these will really work unless the reader knows that Bethel means "house of God" or such information is supplied in the translation. It could be possible, for instance, to translate: "the house of God (the place called 'house of God') will become a place where bad spirits live," or "haunted."

In translation, the different verbs for "going" should be chosen in relation to Bethel as the viewpoint place and the directional system of the receptor language. It may not be enough to say Do not go to Beersheba to worship. It is true that go is not particularly emphasized here, but the precise meaning is "to cross the border (to go to)," and such precise geographical information may have to be clear. Also, instead of saying Do not try to find me at Bethel, one may have to say something like "do not go/come for help to Bethel" (TT), "do not go/come to pray at Bethel." In some cases such information as "the sanctuary (holy place) of Beersheba," etc., may have to be stated.

5.6

Seek the Lord and live/Go to the Lord, and you will live. Here again there is a change from the Lord speaking to the prophet speaking. If the translator is not trying to translate so that the balanced organization of 4b-6a will be clear in translation, the change of speaker will present little problem. However, if one is trying to get an effect like the Hebrew balance in translation, the change can be difficult. One way, if necessary, is to move the beginning of Amos' own words to verse 6b, and have the Lord continue to speak here.

Lest/If you do not go. It is much better to start with a new sentence here. The relations between the two sentences should, however, be clearly stated. The following judgment depends on the way in which people will act; for instance, If you do not go... or simply "if not..."

Lest he break out like fire in the house of Joseph, and it devour, with none to quench it for Bethel/If you do not, he will sweep down like fire on the people of Israel. The fire will burn up the people of Bethel, and no one will be able to put it out. The Hebrew sentence structure is not very clear, as can be seen from the RSV.[7] However, an analysis into the kernel sentences and a restructuring of these sentences to an acceptable level[8] in the language will certainly give a translation not very different from that of TEV. Instead of saying he will sweep down, the translator may have to say "he will come like a great fire burning."

House of Joseph/the people of Israel.[9] In TEV the tribes of Ephraim and Manasseh have been replaced by the whole group to which house of Joseph refers.

5.7

RSV	TEV
7 O you who turn justice to wormwood, and cast down righteousness to the earth!	7 You are doomed, you that twist justice and cheat people out of their rights!

This verse is often considered to be a continuation of verse 6, as has been pointed out in 5.4-6. However, it balances another warning in 5.10-13 (Appendix, Figures 3, 5); some scholars, not having seen the balance, have been troubled by the fact that the two warnings are separated by a hymn to the power of God (5.8-9). They have therefore moved verse 7 to come before verse 10, as in NAB, NEB, Mft, TT. It is possible, of course, that such a move may be necessary in order to translate in some languages, but that is a question of translation, not of the Hebrew organization.

Section heading. In spite of the fact that this section is so short, a heading here helps to show the balance in those translations where this is done: "Warning to Sinners" or "Amos Warns Those Who Are Unjust" are possibilities.

O you/You are doomed. The meaning of the Hebrew seems to be that of an exclamation, like "Woe to those who" (NAB).[10] Though such an expression sounds old-fashioned in English (and so has been avoided in TEV), it would be perfectly natural in many languages.

Who turn justice to wormwood/that twist justice. Wormwood[11] is a plant which may grow to the size of a bush, and the juice of its leaves has a bitter taste.[12] So "bitter" is the basis for the comparison: "you have changed justice into a very bitter herb" or "you who make justice a bitter thing" (Mft), "you who turn justice to gall" (S-G). In many languages the comparison cannot be made at all; some possibilities: you that twist justice or "you that distort what is right."

And cast down righteousness to the earth/and cheat people out of their rights. The Hebrew words for "justice" and righteousness are very similar in meaning, and commentaries usually try hard to define a difference, but in most cases it would not be possible to make a distinction in other languages. Sometimes the translator can use terms with the same general meaning, such as "you that treat as evil what is good, and despise what is right." Other times the only solution is to combine the two expressions: "you that distort what is right and trample on it with your feet." Though TEV translation is possible for English, it can hardly be used as a translational model because of the English idiom it uses.

5.8-9

RSV	TEV
8 He who made the Pleiades and Orion, and turns deep darkness into the morning,	8 The LORD made the stars, the Pleiades and Orion. He turns darkness into daylight

and darkens the day into
  night,
who calls for the waters of
  the sea,
and pours them out upon
  the surface of the earth,
the LORD is his name,
9 who makes destruction flash
  forth against the strong,
so that destruction comes
  upon the fortress.

and day into night.
He calls for the waters of the
  sea
and pours them out on the
  earth.
His name is the LORD.
9 He brings destruction on the
  mighty and their
  strongholds.

This is another section of hymn like 1.2 and 4.13. In translation, the style should be like them also. The basic problem in this passage is the relationship between verse 8 and verse 9. His name is the Lord. He brings destruction on the mighty and their strongholds seems to have no connection with what has gone before.[13] This is caused by two different problems. For one thing, The Lord is his name is included between the two parts of the hymn when it would seem to make more sense at the end (like 4.13). The reason for its coming where it does, however, is that it is the turning point of the balanced organization of the whole book of Amos, and by having it inside the hymn the first part of the hymn (creation) balances the second part (destruction).

The second problem is that even leaving the question of The Lord is his name aside, some people find it difficult to see how the message of verse 9 relates to verse 8. However, read as poetic pictures there is a relation. Everything up to The Lord is his name is a series of pictures of the power of the Lord who made the universe and keeps it working in its regular way, with its regular changes.[14] Verse 9 is a picture of the power of the Lord to punish and destroy. But more than that, who calls for the waters of the sea, and pours them out upon the surface of the earth is not only a picture of God's working in his regular way through rain but is also a picture of a flood, which suggests destruction and makes a link between the creative power of God (verse 8) and the destructive power of God (verse 9).

Section heading. Translations which show the structure of Amos in their headings should have a heading here and should try to include some of the wording of the headings of both 1.2 and 4.13-14: "God Can Create and Destroy," "It is God Who Creates the World and Punishes People."

He who made the Pleiades and Orion/The Lord made the stars, the Pleiades and Orion. If a language does not have names for the Pleiades and Orion, they will have to be described as stars or "constellations."[15] Another possibility is "the stars of springtime and autumn," or "stars of autumn and springtime," which is the Hebrew order since the setting of the Pleiades introduces the winter and Orion is associated with the summer.[16] The theme of change makes it probable that a change of season is implied. However, such a translation will not work where languages have no equivalent for "autumn" and "spring."

And turns deep darkness into the morning, and darkens the day into night,/He turns darkness into daylight, and day into night. See 4.13.

Who calls for the waters of the sea, and pours them out upon the surface of the earth,/He calls for the waters of the sea and pours them out on the earth. In many languages it is not possible to call the sea. The translator might say something like "He draws/gathers/sends for the waters of the sea" (see TT) or "He takes the water from the sea and pours it out over the earth."

The Lord is his name/His name is the Lord. For the significance of this expression, see 4.13. The problem here is where to put it for the modern reader so that the translation will make its importance clear without being confusing. One possibility is to put it at the end of verse 9. However, if that is done, it should be made prominent through the wording: "The Lord is the one who does it!" or "It is the Lord himself who does this!" A second possibility is to put it at the beginning of verse 8. TT does this, but does not make it prominent enough: "It is the Lord who made..."[17] "The Lord!" could be put both at the beginning and at the end as an exclamation. This keeps a balanced organization, but in a different way from the Hebrew, and makes the expression prominent in the passage.

Who makes destruction flash forth against the strong, so that destruction comes upon the fortress./He brings destruction on the mighty and their strongholds.[18] In simple language a restructured translation may run as follows: "He strikes down the strong (people) and destroys their forts." The picture is a punishment by destruction, as in so much of Amos. The translator can use picture language that comes from lightning or flood if it is suitable.

On fortress, see the discussion of another Hebrew word with similar meaning in 1.4.

5.10-13

RSV	TEV
10 They hate him who reproves in the gate, and they abhor him who speaks the truth. 11 Therefore because you trample upon the poor and take from him exactions of wheat, you have built houses of hewn stone, but you shall not dwell in them; you have planted pleasant vineyards, but you shall not drink their wine. 12 For I know how many are your transgressions, and how great are your sins--	10 You people hate anyone who challenges injustice and speaks the whole truth in court. 11 You have oppressed the poor and robbed them of their grain. And so you will not live in the fine stone houses you build or drink wine from the beautiful vineyards you plant. 12 I know how terrible your sins are and how many crimes you have

you who afflict the righteous,
who take a bribe,
and turn aside the needy
in the gate.
13 Therefore he who is prudent
will keep silent in such
a time;
for it is an evil time.

committed. You persecute good men,
take bribes, and prevent the poor
from getting justice in the courts.
13 And so, keeping quiet in such
evil times is the smart thing to
do!

This paragraph has a complicated organization in Hebrew[19] (see Appendix, Section 3.6) which makes translation difficult. But the same organization helps to see the relationship between the parts.[20] Verses 11-12 are a warning to those people who hate in verse 10. Because of their crimes they will not be able to benefit from their wealth and luxury; instead, God is going to destroy them. Then verse 13 is a warning to those people in verse 10 who are hated. Because the times are so bad, it would be safer for them if they did not challenge injustice or speak the whole truth in court (verse 10).

It is possible to make the relationships between the parts of this organization much clearer in English and many other languages by the use of paragraphing and connecting words (Translating Amos, Section 2.3), together with some change in order. Here is one example of what might be done:

10You people hate anyone who challenges injustice and speaks the whole truth in court.

11-12--I know how terrible your sins are, and how many crimes you have committed. You persecute good people. You oppress the poor and rob them of their grain. By taking bribes you prevent them from getting justice in the courts. These are some of the reasons why you will not live in the fine stone houses you build, or drink wine from the beautiful vineyards you plant.--

13Yes, the smart thing for the truthful witness to do is to keep quiet in such evil times as these.

Section heading. If a heading is used to show the balance with 5.7, the wording should be similar: "Warning to Sinners and Righteous" or "Amos Warns Wise People and Unjust People."

5.10

They hate him who reproves in the gate, and they abhor him who speaks the truth./You people hate anyone who challenges injustice and speaks the whole truth in court. In this verse the Hebrew speaks about the ones who are doing the hating (see RSV), but in the next verse changes and speaks directly to them. The Hebrew continues speaking directly to them until verse 13 (which balances verse 10); in verse 13 it speaks about people once more, but they are different people.

TEV simplifies the passage by speaking to the people right from the beginning. This makes the passage much easier and avoids the problem that in some languages the use of they could mean nothing else than the strong who were destroyed in verse 9. Such a translation would certainly be wrong.

The setting of verse 10 is gate, which means the large space inside the city gate where court cases were judged.[21] Since the place itself is not being emphasized in this context, court makes a better translation in English. Court should be translated in such a way that it indicates local judgment, not the judgment of a far-off national government. In some languages this will be "palaver house" or "village council" or "meeting of the elders," etc.

The Hebrew has two words, to hate and to abhor, and the translator may want to look for two equivalent verbs if that would be best for the style of the translation. On the other hand, the words mean the same thing except for emotional differences between them,[22] and may be combined into one word, as in TEV.

It is hard to know who is being hated and abhorred in this verse.[23] Probably they are people with the qualities translated in the TEV: anyone who challenges injustice and speaks the whole truth in court. In translating like this, however, in some languages it will be necessary to show whose injustice is intended: "he who shows (reproves) your injustice" (compare Mft: "who exposes you") or "anyone who shows how unjust/unfair you are."

It is not fully clear whether the person who challenges injustice is the same as the one who speaks the whole truth. More likely they are different (judges who speak out against injustice, and witnesses who refuse to lie), but sometimes it will be easier to translate with only one kind of hated person: "he who shows your injustice in speaking the (whole) truth."

5.11

Because the balanced organization of the Hebrew is complicated, TEV has restructured it some. In TEV, verse 11a is a separate sentence stating the wrong behavior. Then the results of such behavior (And so) are given. Since the result is you will not live in..., that has been emphasized rather than you will build houses.[24] The point is that the people to whom Amos is speaking will not enjoy the fruits of their luxury because destruction is coming.

In some languages such a restructuring may not be helpful. After verse 11a the order of the Hebrew is the order of the events as they take place, and the relationship between the events can be expressed grammatically: "...building houses...you will not live in them, planting vineyards... you shall not drink their wine," or "although you build houses...you will not live in them; although you plant vineyards, you will not drink wine made from their grapes."

Therefore because you trample upon the poor/You have oppressed the poor. The meaning[25] is expressed in a picture in Hebrew, more directly in TEV. The translator may want to find picture language which will carry the meaning.

And take from him exactions of wheat,/robbed them of their grain. The idea of forcing people is well expressed by the verb rob, but other languages will use different constructions such as "you have taken with force their grain for nothing."

You have built houses of hewn stone/fine stone houses you build. There are still places where houses of hewn stone are a sign of great luxury. Where this is not so, the luxurious character of the houses will have to be shown in a different way, as in TEV for example. In some languages there are different words for ordinary houses and great luxurious homes like "mansions." The use of a term for such a luxurious home may carry the meaning of luxury where the fact of stone does not.

For wine and vineyards, see 4.9.

5.12

For I know how many are your transgressions, and how great are your sins/I know how terrible your sins are and how many crimes you have committed. Many languages make no difference between sins and crimes. One possibility: "I know how bad your crimes/sins are and how often you do them."

You who afflict the righteous,/you persecute good men. On righteous, see 2.6b. This is an accusation of being harsh and unfair to the ordinary, powerless person, who has done nothing wrong.

Who takes a bribe/take bribes. Every language has its ways of expressing the idea of a bribe: "take money under the table," "expect presents," etc.

Turn aside the needy in the gate/keep the poor from getting justice in the courts. TEV is a correct, meaningful translation of the Hebrew.[26] In some languages, however, this injustice to the poor is expressed in a way very similar to that of the Hebrew; for example: "you overthrow the poor in the palaver house."

5.13

Therefore he who is prudent will keep silent in such a time; for it is an evil time/And so, keeping quiet in such evil times is the smart thing to do. This verse has presented numerous problems of interpretation.[27] It does not fit into the context very clearly unless the reader sees it as balancing verse 10 (see 5.10-13). With the organization of verses 10-13 in mind, the prudent of verse 13 are those who reprove and speak the truth in verse 10. They are hated for what they say (verse 10), so they would be wise to keep quiet. Notice, however, that the people referred to here are not the people who are the center of attention in verses 10-12 but the ones whom they hate in verse 10. The attention of the passage has shifted. The connection could be made clearer by a translation such as "but those that you hate would be wise to keep silent (not to speak out) in such evil times."

5.14-15

RSV	TEV

14 Seek good, and not evil,
    that you may live;
  and so the LORD, the God of
    hosts, will be with you,
    as you have said.
15 Hate evil, and love good,
    and establish justice in
    the gate;
	14 Make it your aim to do what is right, not what is evil, so that you may live. Then the LORD God Almighty really will be with you, as you claim he is. 15 Hate what is evil, love what is right, and see that justice prevails in the courts. Perhaps the LORD will be

it may be that the LORD, the
    God of hosts,
will be gracious to the
    remnant of Joseph.
	merciful to the people of this
	nation who are still left alive.

These verses not only balance verses 4-6 with their similar theme, but they also have a similar organization in Hebrew (see Appendix, Section 3.5). They have sometimes been considered an interpretation of verses 4-6.[28] However, this passage is not as difficult to translate as verses 4-6 because the first half is not tied to the second half in the same complicated way, and there are not so many allusions to things which the modern reader may not know.

In Translating Amos, Section 2.2, a restructuring was given for this passage, to try to highlight the balanced structure. There the wording of TEV was used as closely as possible, but here is a further restructuring which uses some of the pointers made in the discussion of the text below:

(5.14-15)

Come back to doing right instead of evil--
    So you can live!
    And the mighty Lord
    Will really live with you
    As you say he does.
Hate evil, love what is right--
    See that justice is done in the courts!
    Perhaps the mighty Lord
    Will really be merciful
    To those who are left of his people, Israel.

<u>Section heading</u>. See 5.4-6.

5.14

<u>Seek good, and not evil, that you may live/Make it your aim to do what is right, not what is evil, so that you may live</u>. On seek, see 5.4. The meaning of the Hebrew in this context is "to be concerned about," "to devote oneself to":[29] "be concerned about what is good," "devote yourself to what is good," "strive after what is good," <u>Make it your aim to do what is right</u>, etc. To keep the balance of wording with 4-6, a possible translation is "come back (or: turn back) to doing right instead of evil."

<u>And not evil/not what is evil</u>. In some languages the verb may have to be repeated or another word with similar meaning used: "strive after what is good instead of pursuing what is evil." In some languages the negative should be first: "don't do evil things but work for what is right."

<u>That you may live/so that you may live</u>. See 5.4.

<u>The Lord, the God of hosts/the Lord God Almighty</u>. See 3.13.

<u>Will be with you/really will be with you</u>. Some languages say "stay" or "live with you." Others may use such expressions as "be/stay where you live," "be/stay alongside you," etc. The important thing is that the

picture express the meaning of God's power and help. In many languages
the Lord...will be with you does this, but in other cases one may have
to translate more directly: "will help you."

As you have said/as you claim he is. A fuller statement of the meaning would be "just like you regularly/habitually say that he is with you
(or helping you)." How much of this will need to be expressed directly
depends on the grammar of the receptor language.

5.15

Hate evil, and love good, and establish justice in the gate/Hate
what is evil, love what is right, and see that justice prevails in the
courts. Establish ("set up") justice is the exact opposite of cast down
righteousness in verse 7. Many languages do not use such a word as "to
set up" or establish for justice, and TEV translates directly as see that
justice prevails in the courts (compare NAB: "and let justice prevail at
the gate"). One possibility is to say something like "do what is right in
your palaver house (or: in the decisions of the elders)."

Will be gracious/will be merciful. For this context, the word chosen
in translation should indicate kindness or mercy toward someone who
deserves severe punishment.

To the remnant of Joseph/the people of this nation who are still left
alive. For Joseph, meaning "the (people) of Israel," see 5.6. In a message addressed to Israelites it may be better in many languages to continue speaking directly to them: (the people of) this nation (or: "your
nation"). However, some translators may prefer a translation which keeps
the term Joseph (if it is clear), because it balances verse 6: "what is
left of the descendants of Joseph" (so TT: "those of Joseph's descendants
who survive"). For the meaning and translation of remnant, see also 1.8.

This section begins the third major part of Amos (Appendix, Figure 5). For the organization of the section itself, see Appendix, Section 3.4. This would be a good passage to translate with a balanced pattern in those languages where such a structure would be effective (see Translating Amos, Section 2.2).

Section heading. For translations where the structure of Amos is shown in the section headings (Translating Amos, Section 2.4), two headings will be needed here, one for the major part (5.16--9.15) and the other for this small section (5.16-17). The heading for the major part should relate to that of 1.1--5.3: "Israel's Punishment; The Prophet's Involvement" or "God Will Punish Israel; The Prophet Is God's Messenger." For possible headings to 5.16-17, see 5.1-3.

5.16-17

RSV	TEV

16 Therefore thus says the LORD,
    the God of hosts,
    the Lord:
"In all the squares there shall
    be wailing;
    and in all the streets they
      shall say, 'Alas! alas!'
They shall call the farmers to
    mourning
    and to wailing those who are
      skilled in lamentation,
17 and in all vineyards there
      shall be wailing,
    for I will pass through
    the midst of you,"
        says the LORD.
	16 And so the Sovereign LORD Almighty says, "There will be wailing and cries of sorrow in the city streets. Even farmers will be called to mourn the dead along with those who are paid to mourn. 17 There will be wailing in all the vineyards. All this will take place because I am coming to punish you." The LORD has spoken.

5.16

Therefore/And so. The reason for the mourning is the death (verse 3) which results from God's punishment (verse 6b), and the reason for the punishment is Israel's sin, as mentioned in almost every passage of Amos. But all this is based on the fact that the Lord who has had a special relationship to Israel (2.6--3.2; The Lord is his name, 5.8) can change that relationship just as he changes the seasons (5.8), and his protection can change to his destruction (5.9). Thus, And so does not refer back to the preceding verse, as readers in many languages would expect. On the other hand, it is impossible to translate clearly all the connections we have just pointed out. For many languages the translation can be something like "because of your sins" or "because you have disobeyed me" or "because of all this."

The Lord, the God of hosts/the Sovereign Lord Almighty. See 3.13.

"In all the squares there shall be wailing; and in all the streets they shall say, 'Alas! alas! (Hebrew: Ho! ho!)'/"There will be wailing and cries of sorrow in the city streets. TEV has combined the two parallel sentences into one, and this may have to be done in some other prose translations. But whether translated as prose or poetry, in many languages it will be better to keep the cry of the mourners and use a natural equivalent in the receptor language for the "Ho! ho!" of the Hebrew. All this may result in such a translation as "People will mourn in all the public squares and streets of the town, saying..."

In this passage the Lord is still talking to the people of Israel (see the end of verse 17), but he is talking to the ones who will be dead, and not to the mourners. In some languages it may be clearer to translate: "There will be wailing and cries of sorrow for you..." or "People will mourn for you in all the public places..."

They shall call the farmers to mourning and to wailing those who are skilled in lamentation,[1]/Even farmers will be called to mourn the dead along with those who are paid to mourn. Farmers probably were simple farm workers or landless serfs.[2] The poor people who have suffered the injustices of which Amos speaks are called in to bury their oppressors! If possible, the translation should use an expression for such a lower working class or "country people." If the translation must have a descriptive phrase, such as "those who till the soil" (and this does not imply class distinctions), something like "the poor, who till the soil" may suffice.

Many societies have people (those who are skilled in lamentation whose work it is to mourn at funerals. They may be referred to by some sort of descriptive phrase like "those who sing the funeral songs." In order to bring out the professional character of this group, TEV translates those who are paid to mourn. It might be better to translate as "those whose work is to mourn," etc., because we know little about the payment, and it is certainly not being emphasized. Mentioning the payment raises false questions about whether the farm workers were paid for mourning or not. The point seems to be that so many people are dying that there are not enough experts to perform the funerals, and the oppressed people have to be called in to wail for their dead oppressors. Some translations may not only have to state that certain people are called, but also that they actually come to mourn; for example, "People will call the poor who till the soil, and they will come/go to mourn for you; people will call those who sing the funeral songs, and they will come/go to sing when you are dead."

5.17

And in all vineyards there shall be wailing/There will be wailing in all the vineyards. "People will be wailing in all the vineyards"(see verse 16).[3] In many societies, even if the vineyards are known, the idea of wailing in such places is culturally very strange.[4] There should, perhaps, be some form of explanatory note saying that vineyards were normally places of laughing and fun, especially when grapes were harvested; wailing in the vineyards thus creates a very effective contrast for the original hearers. One possible translation might be "people will be wailing instead of laughing/playing in all the vineyards."

For I will pass through the midst of you"/All this will take place because I am coming to punish you." All this will take place makes clear that the conclusion refers to the whole paragraph and not only to the last sentence. Pass through means punishment here. Some translations could keep the poetic picture by saying something like the TT: "because I shall pass through your country to punish you." Otherwise, because I am coming to punish you is possible. In some languages the translation will be more natural with "when" instead of because.

This is one section, as can be seen in the overall pattern of the Book of Amos (Appendix, Figures 3, 5). It is made up of two shorter sections (5.18-27 and 6.1-14) with some parallels of wording. The tone of the whole section is one of warning and doom, set in part by the repeated expressions woe to (5.18; 6.4) and I hate, I despise...I take no delight (5.21) and I abhor...and hate (6.8). The alternative to what the Lord hates is justice and righteousness (5.24; 6.12).

Section heading. Because the section starts here and not at 6.1, it would be better not to follow the TEV section headings. The theme which runs through the section is that Israel's confidence, its expectation of safety, is based on the wrong things: the day of the Lord, religious festivals, prosperity, national power, etc. "Israel's False Sense of Security" may be difficult to translate in some languages. Other possibilities are "Israel Trusts the Wrong Things," "Israel Trusts (or: Has Confidence) Falsely."

If section 5.18-6.14 is too long and needs to be given two section headings or subheadings, then the one for 5.18-27 could be "Israel Has Confidence in False Religion" or "Israel's Religion Is Not True." If these would be too difficult, another possibility is "Nobody Can Escape from the Lord."

5.18-20

RSV	TEV

18 Woe to you who desire the day
         of the LORD!
     Why would you have the day
         of the LORD?
   It is darkness, and not light;
19   as if a man fled from a
         lion,
     and a bear met him;
   or went into the house and
         leaned with his hand
         against the wall,
     and a serpent bit him.
20 Is not the day of the LORD
         darkness, and not light,
     and gloom with no bright-
         ness in it?

18 How terrible it will be for you who long for the day of the LORD! What good will that day do you? For you it will be a day of darkness and not of light. 19 It will be like a man who runs from a lion and meets a bear! Or like a man who comes home and puts his hand on the wall--only to be bitten by a snake! 20 The day of the LORD will bring darkness and not light; it will be a day of gloom, without any brightness.

This is the first paragraph in a subsection which continues to verse 27. There is no strong connection with what goes before. The passage is still about death, but here death is the result of false hope in the day of the Lord.

The paragraph opens with a general announcement of disaster to come (verse 18a). Then comes a question which implies that hope is false (verse 18b). The paragraph ends with a similar question (verse 20) and

between the two is a short illustration of an unlucky man who escapes
from two dangerous animals, only to be killed by a snake bite in his
own home, where he thought he was safe (verse 19).

5.18

Woe to you who desire (Hebrew: long for) the day of the Lord/How
terrible it will be for you who long for the day of the Lord. Some translations should indicate the speaker of this new section: "Another time
Amos said...," etc. Many languages have an equivalent to woe (see 5.7).
In other languages (like English, where such an equivalent is not natural)
the meaning of the Hebrew has to be expressed in another way: How terrible
it will be for you, "Fools who..." (NEB), "The Lord will punish you
terribly, you people who are longing for the time of his judgment" or
"...who eagerly hope that the day of the Lord will come soon."
The day of the Lord.[1] See 2.16.
Why would you have the day of the Lord?/What good will that day do
you? The Hebrew question asks what advantage the day of the Lord will
bring,[2] as in TEV. Another possible translation is "What will the day of
the Lord (or: the time when the Lord acts/judges/punishes) mean to you?"
(NEB, and with minor variants also NAB, S-G, and TT). Of course, in some
languages a day cannot do or mean something to somebody, so a possible
translation is "What do you expect to happen on the day of the Lord?" If
someone cannot answer his own question, the translation may have to be
"That day certainly will not do you much good!" or "It will be a day of
disaster rather than good."
It is darkness, and not light/For you it will be a day of darkness
and not of light. This is the answer to the question. If darkness and
light are not natural pictures of disaster and good in the language of
the translation, care will be needed here and in verse 20. A translation
like this might be possible: "How terrible it will be for you who long
for the day/time when the Lord will judge Israel. What good will that
day/time do you? (or: That day/time will certainly not do you much good!)
When the Lord judges you it will bring/cause disaster rather than good
like a storm brings/causes darkness rather than light" or "Instead of
blessing you the Lord will judge you; he will bring/cause disaster..."
If necessary, of course, the picture can be omitted entirely, and only
its meaning translated.

5.19

As if a man fled from a lion, and a bear met him; or went into the
house and leaned with his hand against the wall, and a serpent bit him/
It will be like a man who runs from a lion and meets a bear! Or like a
man who comes home and puts his hand on the wall--only to be bitten by a
snake. In many languages it is necessary to state exactly what is being
compared. For some scholars the comparison is between the day of the Lord
and the unlucky man. That is what TEV does: It will be like a man...;
another possibility: "For you it will be like when a man..." However,
the comparison might also be between the hearers and the unlucky man. "You
will be like a man..." (TT).
But what seems to show the meaning of the Hebrew syntax best is that

the as relates to the question in verse 20 in the following way: "Just as a man (has these experiences), will not the day of the Lord also bring darkness and not light?" In that case it also illustrates the meaning of darkness and light in verse 18.

The translator will have to make a decision on the basis of the possibilities in the receptor language and the level of translation which he intends. For the third solution he may need to indicate the comparison in verse 20, and start verse 19 simply with "A man..." or he may be able to tie the comparison directly to the end of verse 18: "like when a man..." In many languages the only solution may be a comparison in which men are compared with men: "In that day you will be like a man..."

A more important question is whether the verse makes two separate comparisons or only one in which the disasters happened one after the other. All modern English translations, except Mft, have two comparisons, in spite of the fact that the overwhelming majority of scholars[3] are in favor of only one comparison.[4] So it is Mft's translation which should be used as a model: "a man runs from a lion, and a bear springs at him; he hides indoors and, resting his hand on the wall, a serpent bites him." It may be helpful to use an expression like "Then" between the two parts.

Lion. See 3.4. The Syrian bear may have been fiercer and more savage than the lion. In areas in which the bear is unknown the translator may use the name of another dangerous animal or simply state that "another wild/dangerous animal meets him" or "he meets another wild animal."

In many languages it may be necessary to say why the man puts his hand on the wall. This is no doubt because he is exhausted (something which is not clear if there are two separate comparisons) and because he feels secure at home. "Leans on the wall to rest" is a possible translation.

The Hebrew word for snake is rather general and does not name any of the twenty kinds of poisonous snakes in Palestine. However, death is implied, and the translator should select a poisonous snake in the receptor language, if a more general term would not show this.

5.20

Is not the day of the Lord darkness, and not light, and gloom with no brightness in it/The day of the Lord will bring darkness and not light; it will be a day of gloom, without any brightness. The Hebrew either asks one double question or else asks a single question and answers it. Most translations and commentaries take the first way, as in the RSV.[5] The other possibility is: "Is not the day of the Lord darkness and not light? Yes, it is gloom without any brightness."[6] The meaning is the same in either case, and the answer to the question is "yes" in either case.

Where questions of this kind do not exist or are not clear or appropriate, there are three different ways to translate: (a) the whole verse can be translated as a statement as in TEV and in NEB; (b) the first part can be translated as a question and the second as the answer to that question; (c) the whole verse can be translated as a question, and an answer such as "Yes, it will be like that" can be added. Questions like this really have the meaning of forceful statements in Hebrew, not of questions (see 3.3-8). The choice should be based on the style of the receptor language and the impact on the readers. In many languages a future tense should be used.

On translating the picture of darkness and light, see 5.18. It may not be possible to say that the day/time (when the Lord will judge) will bring darkness, since a day cannot do something in many languages: "The day/time...will be dark." Gloom, without any brightness can sometimes be translated more easily as "black without any ray of light in it."

It may be helpful to bring out the connection with the previous verse by making a comparison here: "That is how it really will be on the day when the Lord will judge Israel. It will be dark, not light..." Or, if the basis of the comparison is not clear: "On the day when the Lord judges Israel you will not have the good you expect. It will be dark..."

Since the next subsection has the Lord speaking, some translations will need to show that Amos' own words end here: "he said," "Amos finished speaking," etc.

5.21-24

RSV	TEV
21 "I hate, I despise your feasts, and I take no delight in your solemn assemblies. 22 Even though you offer me your burnt offerings and cereal offerings, I will not accept them, and the peace offerings of your fatted beasts I will not look upon. 23 Take away from me the noise of your songs; to the melody of your harps I will not listen. 24 But let justice roll down like waters, and righteousness like an everflowing stream.	21 The LORD says, "I hate your religious festivals; I cannot stand them! 22 When you bring me burnt offerings and grain offerings, I will not accept them; I will not accept the animals you have fattened to bring me as offerings. 23 Stop your noisy songs; I do not want to listen to your harps. 24 Instead, let justice flow like a stream, and righteousness like a river that never goes dry.

This subsection ties in with the previous one, not only on the basis of the overall patterning shown in the Appendix, Figures 3, 5, but also in similar ideas: the religion the people practice is not what God wants (5.21-24), just as the day of the Lord which they expect is not what they will get (5.18-20).[7]

In this paragraph the Lord first rejects Israelite worship again, as he did in 4.4-5. This is stated in general terms (verse 21) and then in specific ones (verse 22). These statements are followed by the Lord urging people to stop doing specific things typical of their worship (verse 23), and then to start behaving in a way that reflects God's will, expressed in general terms (verse 24).

I hate, I despise your feasts, and I take no delight in (Hebrew: I
cannot smell) your solemn assemblies (Hebrew: your assemblies)/The Lord
says, "I hate your religious festivals; I cannot stand them. Although the
Hebrew does not say so directly, the Lord is now speaking and this must
be expressed in translation in many languages, especially since Amos is
the speaker in the preceding section (verses 18-20).

In Hebrew, when there is a sequence of two verbs (I hate, I despise)
without a word relating them, only one event is meant,[8] so TEV uses only
one verb I hate, and this will be necessary in many other languages. But
the Hebrew repetition is very forceful and produces an emphasis which is
important to the whole section. If repetition is not sufficient the translation should have a strong word for hate or should qualify the verb in
some way.

Hate. There may be a problem in choosing the right word. In verse 10
the same verb was used of hating a person, which is no problem. But here
it is not a person who is being hated, and in many languages it is not
possible to use the same word. The translation should be something which
means dislike of what people do. There may even be a lively expression
like "feel the shudder of repugnance (which runs down one's spine) at
something disgusting."[9] Or, to use an English idiom which may not be
translatable either: "Your feasts make me sick!"

Originally, "smell" was used literally when it was said that the Lord
smelled sacrifices (with pleasure) (Gen 8.21; Lev 26.31; 1 Sam 26.19).
Here it is clearly used as a picture. If the translator cannot keep the
picture with the same meaning or replace it by a similar one, he will have
to say something like I cannot stand, "I cannot bear/tolerate."

Feasts and assemblies. The two words mean about the same thing here.
TEV therefore uses only one term, religious festivals. It is necessary to
say religious in cultures where there is a distinction between those
feasts which are religious and those which are not. In other cultures
feasts are normally religious and there is no need to add the information,
especially since the context shows that these feasts are of a religious
character.

The translator should choose strong terms or restructure the sentence
so that it is as forceful as possible. Repetition or use of synonyms often
leads to forcefulness in modern languages, as it does in Hebrew. One
possibility in English (not TEV style) would be "I loathe your religious
festivals, and your pious meetings make me sick!"

5.22

Even though you offer me your burnt offerings and cereal offerings,
I will not accept them, and the peace offerings of your fatted beasts I
will not look upon/When you bring me burnt offerings and grain offerings,
I will not accept them: I will not accept the animals you have fattened
to bring me as offerings.[10] The three specific Hebrew words for offerings
used here are not often directly translatable, because not all peoples
offer such sacrificial gifts. For many parts of the Old Testament the
translator has to develop new terms. In this context, however, it may be
better not to make a distinction in the first part of the verse: "When

you bring me (any kind of/different kinds of) offerings I will not
accept them." If it is necessary to make up new terms for these offerings,
the translator should do this in a way that is natural for the receptor
language but should avoid long descriptive and interpretative phrases.[11]
Burnt offerings were sacrifices in which the whole animal was burned up
completely on the altar, being "sent up" to God in smoke. Cereal offer-
ings/grain offerings were presentations of grain, offered to God as from
an inferior to a superior. Sometimes it is possible to translate with
such concise expressions as "thing-sacrifice to burn (or: by burning)"
and "thing to give." In other languages it is not possible to speak of
"offerings" but only of "gifts," and so the translation should be something like "burnt gift," "food gift," etc.

It is not certain what specific kind of offering is meant by the
third Hebrew term as can be seen from the different translations which
have been used: "Peace offerings" (RSV, NAB), "thank-offerings" (S-G),
"shared-offerings" (NEB, TT). There is a possibility that it was the
offering for the end of the feast.[12] The fat of the animal was burnt
on the altar and offered to the Lord; the rest of the animal was eaten
by the people. The important part is certainly the fat offered and not
the meal.[13] TEV gives a meaningful restructuring the animals you have
fattened to bring me as offerings; this can serve as a model. I will not
accept is literally in Hebrew I will not look upon, "I will not notice."
Such verbs are used to mean rejection in many languages.

5.23

The grammatical form of the imperative (take away) in this sentence
is singular. However, the command should be understood as addressed to
all and should be translated in most languages as spoken to many people.

Take away from me the noise of your songs/Stop your noisy songs. It
must be clear in the translation that the singing is a part of the religious worship, part of the festival. The context may be enough to make
this clear, but if not, some possibilities are "Stop the noisy songs of
your worship" or "Stop trying to worship me with noisy singing." English
has other ways of expressing the meaning of this command: "Away with your
noisy songs!" (NAB), "No more of your hymns for me!" (Mft), "Spare me the
sound of your songs" (NEB). In some other languages it would be better to
translate instead "Go away with the noise of your songs," "Stop singing
your noisy songs," "Stop bothering me with the noisy singing which you
use to worship me." In some languages the expression may be close to the
Hebrew: "the noise you make by singing (or: when you sing)."

To the melody of your harps (Hebrew: lutes) I will not listen./I do
not want to listen to your harps. Melody of or "music of" is not expressed
in TEV (compare Mft) because it is understood in English. In many languages one may have to speak of the "voice" or "sound" or "cry" or "noise"
of musical instruments. In some languages will is expressed in the present:
"I do not listen to." After the nose (verse 21b) and the eyes (verse 22b)
now the ears are closed.

The musical instrument mentioned here was probably what could be
called a "lyre" or "lute" in English. It was a stringed instrument with
different numbers of strings (up to ten) and with a sounding box at the
top.[14] Some degree of cultural adaptation must be made in translation,

since cultures differ among each other in the shape, the number of strings, and the function of their instruments. One will have to select an equivalent instrument in the receptor language.

5.24

But let justice roll down like waters, and righteousness like an everflowing stream/Instead, let justice flow like a stream, and righteousness like a river that never goes dry. This verse contrasts with the preceding one, expressed in some English translations by words like Instead, But or "No" (Mft). In many languages one should use an equivalent word to express the contrast.

Justice and righteousness. See 5.7. As everywhere else in Amos, human justice and righteousness are intended.[15]

Powerful as the verse is in Hebrew and English, it may be very difficult to get an equivalent translation in many languages. There may be no direct equivalent of let... or "may..." and it may be impossible to compare justice and righteousness to a stream. Some possibilities are "You must always be just and do right" or "It is good that justice be like..."

The everflowing[16] stream contrasts with one that becomes dry during the dry season, so TEV reads a river that never goes dry. This makes the meaning of the comparison clear and would be helpful in many geographic areas where there may even be different words for seasonal and non-seasonal streams, as well as in areas in which a stream is always "everflowing." It expresses the permanent character of righteousness in a more powerful way.

One possible way of translating this verse might be "Instead/but/on the other hand, never stop treating the poor people justly, like a great river never stops flowing; always do what is right, as surely as water always flows downward."

5.25-27

RSV	TEV
25 "Did you bring to me sacrifices and offerings the forty years in the wilderness, O house of Israel? 26 You shall take up Sakkuth your king, and Kaiwan your star-god, your images,[k] which you made for yourselves; 27 therefore I will take you into exile beyond Damascus," says the LORD, whose name is the God of hosts.	25 "People of Israel, I did not demand sacrifices and offerings during those forty years that I led you through the desert. 26 But now, because you have worshiped images of Sakkuth, your king god, and of Kaiwan, your star god, you will have to carry those images 27 when I take you into exile in a land beyond Damascus," says the LORD, whose name is Almighty God.

[k]Heb *your images, your star-god*

In Hebrew the relationship of verse 26 to its immediate context is not at all clear. Everything depends on the interpretation given to the verb with which verse 26 begins.

(a) Some scholars consider it to be past and parallel to the verb in verse 25. In that case verse 26 simply continues the question of verse 25: "Did you then (that is, at that time) carry the images of your deities?" implying "as you do now."

(b) Others also take it to be past, but as a contrast with and answer to verse 25: "No! But you have carried..." This interpretation is found in at least one of the ancient versions[17] and in some modern translations (S-G, Dhorme), but it has rightly been abandoned by more recent research.[18]

(c) A third group understands it as future, parallel with the opening verb of verse 27, with verse 27 continuing the statement of verse 26. (27) "I will take you into exile...(26) and you will carry with you..."

So there is a difficult choice between interpretations (a) and (c). Scholars are more divided on this than are the existing modern translations, which generally follow interpretation (c).[19] If only the linguistic arguments are considered (not historical and theological ones), interpretation (a) is better.[20] In that interpretation the subject and time of the verb are the same in 25 and 26, and all the things being talked about in the two verses are in the same area of meaning. Also interpretation (c) conflicts with the overall discourse structure of Amos, in which action by the Lord is always mentioned before the consequences which it has for the people.

To follow interpretation (a), the translator will either have to translate verses 25-26 as one continuous question or statement, or as two separate ones. It is usually better to make it two, or the sentence would become too long and too involved. (On translating such questions as these, which are not really questions but have the meaning of emphatic statements, see 3.3-8.) Here the answer to the questions is "No." Depending on the usage in the receptor language, the translator can either retain the questions and give the negative answer to them (once after verse 26, or twice after verse 25 and verse 26) or he can make two negative statements. Examples of these alternative solutions would be:

1. "...did you have to bring me...? Certainly not! Did you carry...? No! But now you do, and that is why..."

2. "During those forty years that I led you through the desert I did not demand that you bring me sacrifices and offerings. Neither did you then worship the images of your... But now you do, and I am going to take you into exile..."

On the other hand, to follow interpretation (c), the translator can treat verse 25 as a single question or statement, and connect 26 with 27, as in TEV.

Almost the whole of this paragraph is quoted in Acts 7.42-43. There are significant differences in text and interpretation, so the translator should pay special attention to the helps available for this situation.[21]

This is the longest section of Amos so far treated as prose in RSV (but not so treated by all translators--see NEB, Mft, NAB). If the translation makes a distinction between prose and poetry, the translator should remember the issues discussed in Translating Amos, Section 5, and decide what would be the best way to handle this particular passage.

5.25

The major problems in translating this verse were discussed in
5.25-27.
O house of Israel?/"People of Israel. See 5.1.
"Did you bring to me/I did not demand. This is a reference to an
ideal time in the desert when Israel showed its relationship to the Lord
by faithfulness to him, not by forms of worship like offerings and sacrifices. RSV could sound like a condemnation of Israel for not bringing
sacrifices and offerings, which is clearly not what is meant. TEV improves
this by making clear that the Lord did not demand sacrifices and offerings, but this changes the point slightly, because the emphasis in Hebrew
is not on what the Lord demanded but on Israel's action. Perhaps a translation like "you did not have to show your faithfulness to me by sacrifices and offerings during those forty years..." could be used.
The forty years in the wilderness/those forty years that I led you
through the desert. TEV has made the time and place relationships clear,
and other translations should probably do the same. See 2.10.
Sacrifices and offerings. This Hebrew word for sacrifice was not
included in verse 22. Offerings refer to offerings of plants and grains
and sacrifices to animal offerings in general. Together they cover the
whole range of what was offered. However, where a language does not have
a number of different words for different kinds of offerings, the translator may have to use the same kind of concise expression that was suggested for verse 22, and in some languages he will need to use one word
or expression to cover both Hebrew words here.

5.26

You shall take up (Hebrew: did you take up [?]) Sakkuth your king,
and Kaiwan your star-god, your images (Hebrew: your images, the star of
your god), which you made for yourselves/But now, because you have wor-
shiped images of Sakkuth, your king god, and of Kaiwan, your star god,
you will have to carry those images. Considerable restructuring of this
verse will be necessary in any translation.[22] For the relationships of
this verse with the immediate context and for other major problems in the
translation, especially when this verse is connected with the preceding
one, see 5.25-27. When this verse is taken together with the following
one, TEV can be used as a model.[23]
God will have to be rendered as "idol." In this context the gods
must be portable. Most languages do not make a distinction between images
and gods.[24] In addition, in many cases it is extremely difficult to express such a notion as king god or star god. One possible translation:
"your idols, which you call Sakkuth and Kaiwan."
Take up/carry. Some languages have at least twenty different terms
depending on the method of carrying: in the hand, on the shoulders, on
the head, with the help of something, alone or sharing the load, etc.
They may even have different vocabulary for carrying sacred items.[25] In
this case the Hebrew word probably implies that the idol was on the end
of some kind of upright support.[26]

[123]

5.27

If one follows interpretation (c), verse 27 can be related to verse 26 in the way it has been done by TEV. If interpretation (a) is followed, verse 27 will have to start with a new sentence, introduced with something like "So," "Therefore," or "That is why," which is in fact the meaning of the first part of the Hebrew word.

I will take you into exile. See 1.6. In many cases one will have to translate as "I will make you slaves" or "I will make you captives."

Beyond Damascus/in a land beyond Damascus. The Hebrew means "in a land which is farther than the town of Damascus." The actual distance is not important in the meaning, and it is not clear how far the people were to be taken beyond Damascus. Even if this is a reference to Assyria, such information should not be stated in the translation, since the author intends it to be vague.

Says the Lord, whose name is the God of hosts/says the Lord, whose name is Almighty God. See 3.13; 4.13. This can often be better translated as an independent sentence (compare NEB): "It is the Lord God, whom people call the powerful chief, who says this."

6.1-14

This chapter can be considered the second subsection about Israel's false sense of security. This time the security is not in false religion, but in human power and prosperity, and in the cities and buildings which result from them. This subsection, furthermore, has three smaller subsections which parallel those of 5.18-27 in the use of such expressions as How terrible (6.1-7), I hate (6.8-11), and People of Israel (6.12-14). The three subsections each end with the announcement of a specific punishment. (There are other such announcements within some of them.)

There are paragraph divisions within these subsections, as will be seen below. The paragraph divisions suggested here are sometimes different from those in TEV and more like what is found in most recent commentaries and in some modern translations (compare NEB and BJ).

Section heading. If a separate section heading or subheading is used for 5.18-27, another will be needed here. It would be good, in that case, to have a heading here which would be somewhat parallel to the one used there. Some possibilities are: "Israel Has Confidence in False Power" or "Israel's Power Will Not Last" or "The Lord Will Destroy the People of Israel."

6.1-7

RSV	TEV
	THE DESTRUCTION OF ISRAEL
6 "Woe to those who are at ease in Zion, and to those who feel secure on the mountain of	6 How terrible it will be for you that have such an easy life in Zion and for you that feel safe in

Samaria,
the notable men of the first of
the nations,
to whom the house of Israel
come!
2 Pass over to Calneh, and see;
and thence go to Hamath the
great;
then go down to Gath of the
Philistines.
Are they better than these
kingdoms:
Or is their territory greater
than your territory?
3 O you who put far away the evil
day,
and bring near the seat of
violence?
4 Woe to those who lie upon beds
of ivory,
and stretch themselves upon
their couches,
and eat lambs from the flock,
and calves from the midst
of the stall;
5 who sing idle songs to the
sound of the harp,
and like David invent for
themselves instruments
of music;
6 who drink wine in bowls,
and anoint themselves with
the finest oils,
but are not grieved over the
ruin of Joseph!
7 Therefore they shall now be the
first of those to go
into exile,
and the revelry of those who
stretch themselves shall
pass away."

Samaria--you great men of this
great nation Israel, you to whom
the people go for help! 2 Go and
look at the city of Calneh. Then
go on to the great city of Hamath
and on down to the Philistine city
of Gath. Were they any better than
the kingdoms of Judah and Israel?
Was their territory larger than
yours? 3 You refuse to admit that
a day of disaster is coming, but
what you do only brings that day
closer. 4 How terrible it will be
for you that stretch out on your
luxurious couches, feasting on veal
and lamb! 5 You like to compose
songs, as David did, and play them
on harps. 6 You drink wine by the
bowlful and use the finest perfumes,
but you do not mourn over the ruin
of Israel. 7 So you will be the
first to go into exile. Your feasts
and banquets will come to an end.

The translator should probably divide this subsection into more than one paragraph, depending on how he translates it. The passage seems to be organized as follows:

6.1 Woe to those who feel secure in their political position.
6.2 Quoted example of their sense of security.
6.3 [Woe to] you [who] would avoid thinking about destruction to come.
6.4-6 Example of lack of concern.
6.7 The punishment (what the "woe" is for).

The major paragraph break would seem, therefore, to be at verse 3. The *Woe to* or *How terrible* in verse 1 carries over also to verse 3, and although it is not repeated there in Hebrew, translators should usually repeat it there, and sometimes in other places as well. (RSV and TEV repeat it at 6.4, instead.) The emphasis in verses 1-2 is on prosperity and political power, whereas that in verses 3-6 is on a fuller picture of a life of luxury.

Furthermore, there are some problems in knowing just who is speaking in every case in this subsection. No doubt Amos is speaking in verses 1 and 3-6, for the pronouncement of woe is always the word of the prophet. In languages where a clear identification of the speaker is important, the translator should introduce verse 1 with something like "Amos said" or "Amos also said," especially since the Lord was the last mentioned speaker.

Verse 2, however, is probably a quotation which Amos is putting in the mouth of the wealthy and powerful Israelite leaders (see 6.2). In that case, verse 2 should also be a separate paragraph, beginning "You say..." or "You like to say..."

On the other hand, it is not so easy to identify the speaker of verse 7. Normally, the punishment is stated by the Lord, and this is made clear in the text.[27] In some languages it will be important to show that the Lord is now speaking by making a new paragraph and beginning it with something like "Therefore the Lord says:..." In fact, the expression says the Lord, the God of hosts from verse 8 could be used, as it is not needed there (see 6.8).

Amos is probably speaking directly to the people of the ruling class. This is clear from the use of you in verse 3. Otherwise the Hebrew uses those and they. TEV and NEB have translated the whole passage with you, and most translators should do the same. If for some reason the use of "those" or "they" is better in a receptor language, then verse 3 should probably be translated with "Those who" as well, to keep the manner of speaking the same throughout.

Except for verses 2 and 7, this subsection is an accusation. First of all, it speaks of the proud self-confidence of the ruling class (verses 1-3), including a possible quotation (verse 2) which makes the description stronger by dramatizing the attitude of the people. Then, in verses 4-6a, there is a change to the luxurious life of those leading classes, ending with the lack of concern of the leaders (verse 6b). Finally, the announcement of the punishment (verse 7) is connected with the preceding accusations in the usual way with an introductory Therefore or So. Certain key words which were used earlier in the unit are used again: first (verse 1) and stretch themselves (verse 4), so that verse 7 picks up the two topics of verses 1-6 to end the unit.

6.1

"Woe to/How terrible. See 5.7 and 5.18. In many languages it would be better to translate this verse with more than one sentence. Woe to may then have to be repeated in the beginning of the second sentence: "woe to you great men..."

The mention of Zion creates certain problems of interpretation which are dealt with at length in the commentaries (see also 1.2). However, these questions have nothing to do with translation.[28]

On the mountain of Samaria/in Samaria. See 4.1. The particular geographical position of Samaria is not important here, so a translation like in Samaria or "in the town of Samaria" is all right.

At ease...feel secure/have such an easy life...feel safe. The same two Hebrew expressions occur as a pair in Isa 32.9-18 also. Their meanings overlap to a great extent and can be translated as "at ease/careless" and "secure/untroubled." Possible translations are "to live in peace" and "to rest quietly." "Peace" in this context means "peace of mind" and many languages may have expressions like "to sit down in one's heart," "to have a song in the body," "to be cool," "to have a stomach which is smoothed," etc.[29]

The notable (Hebrew: distinguished, prominent) men of the first of the nations/great men of this great nation Israel. First does not mean first in time, as has been wrongly suggested in some English translations (Mft: "leaders of this most ancient race"; NAB: "Leaders of a nation favored from the first"). In most languages the translator can restructure much as in TEV.

To whom the house of Israel come (Hebrew: and they come to them the house of Israel)/you to whom the people go for help. The Hebrew raises questions which are difficult to answer. Who comes to whom and why? Is house of Israel coming? Is it an explanation of "them," or is Amos speaking to the house of Israel? Does "them" refer back to the leaders or to the nations? Why do they--whoever they are--come? For help, for judgment, to honor?[30] Traditionally, the text has been understood to mean that the people of Israel come to their leaders for help (so S-G, NEB: "resort"; NAB: "have recourse"; TEV: go for help). The translation should therefore follow the solution of the TEV. However, for "go" or "come" the translator should use what is natural for the language. The Hebrew verb can be understood to mean "come again and again" and some languages should perhaps express this idea of repetition: "keep going/coming," "come/go again and again."

6.2

Pass over to Calneh, and see; and thence go to Hamath the great; then go down to Gath of the Philistines. Are they better than these kingdoms? Or is their territory greater than your territory,/Go and look at the city of Calneh. Then go on to the great city of Hamath and on down to the Philistine city of Gath. Were they any better than the kingdoms of Judah and Israel? Was their territory larger than yours? Two main interpretations have been given for this verse: (1) That these are Amos' own words addressed to the leaders of Israel, as a warning to remember nations which were greater than theirs and yet had met their doom. This is probably not the correct meaning.[31] (2) It is a quotation put by Amos in the mouths of the rulers to show their unlimited boasting. The leaders tell the people to compare how well off Israel is in comparison with other nations. The translator will have to make a choice between these meanings. In many languages he cannot simply reproduce the questions and so maintain a vague meaning. In fact, he often has to provide definite answers to the questions or express the meaning in statements.

TEV is not a good model to follow here.[32] The best solution is to make a statement like: "You say to your people: go and look at the city of Calneh; then go on to the great city of Hamath, and on down to the

Philistine city of Gath. See how none of these countries is as strong
and as large as the kingdoms of Judah and Israel!" Or, "You say: let our
people go...and see how..."

It will be necessary to pay special attention to the choice between
"come" and "go," particularly in languages with a highly developed directional system (see Translating Amos, Section 3). Hamath was a city-state
in upper Syria on the Orontes River. Unfortunately, the city of Calneh
has not yet been found. All we know is that it was north of Hamath.33
With Bethel as the viewpoint place of the book of Amos, the movement is
first to the north (Calneh), from there to the south (Hamath), then
further to the south and even slightly to the southwest, since Gath is
located southwest of Bethel.

The usual translation better may be misleading, because the Hebrew
word does not have a moral meaning here. Something like "prosperous" or
"strong" (TT) is more suitable.

6.3

O you who put far away the evil day,/You refuse to admit that a day
of disaster is coming. As mentioned in 6.1-7, the equivalent of woe to
should be included here again (6.1) and as often as necessary through
verse 6.

According to some, the Hebrew implies the use of magic acts and
spells,34 but the evidence is not strong enough to make this a basis for
translation. More likely this is a picture of refusing to think about
such a day, as in TEV (and TT: "you refuse to think of the day when
disaster will come"). In some languages, of course, the Hebrew picture
is understood with the correct meaning, and one can translate "you chase
far away the day of disaster" or "you chase the day of disaster, it has
gone far" without necessarily having to express such information as "from
your mind." However, even then one may need to indicate that this is only
wishful thinking by some such translation as "you think you have chased
the day of disaster, that it has gone far, but..."

And bring near the seat of violence/but what you do only brings that
day closer. The Hebrew word for seat is difficult to understand and many
changes of text have been proposed. None of them is supported by any of
the ancient translations, however. The only useful solution is to take
seat in the sense of "throne" and to understand "throne" as meaning
"reign"35 or "rule." So NAB: "yet you hasten the reign of violence" and
TT: "you are bringing nearer the time when violent men will reign." This
reign of violence is brought nearer through the actions of the leaders
and that fact may have to be stated (compare TEV). In many languages it
is impossible to speak of a "reign of violence" and/or you cannot "bring
near" such a reign. One possibility: "but you yourselves, by the way you
act, will cause violent people to come (and destroy you)."36

6.4

"Woe to.../How terrible... See 6.1-7.

Lie...stretch themselves...eat/stretch out...feasting. The leaders
are lying down while they are eating. The custom in Israel had always
been to sit on rugs or seats to eat. The practice of reclining for meals,

which is mentioned here for the first time, was no doubt foreign. The translation should not sound as though the eating precedes the lying on beds, like a nap. On the other hand, the idea of lying down to eat may shock the reader of the translation and lead to misunderstanding. It may be helpful therefore to make a short cultural note something like this: "The custom of lying down on couches when eating is mentioned here for the first time. At the time of the New Testament, it had become a more general custom. See, for example, Matt 9.10 and 26.7."

Stretch themselves/stretch out. This refers to the way in which people lie down. They "sprawl" (so Mft, NEB, TT).[37] A descriptive phrase such as "you lay down your bodies as lazy people" is possible. Sometimes the use of idioms for "lazy people," like "people with dead hands," may help to make the translation as colorful as the Hebrew.

Beds of ivory/luxurious couches. The meaning is "beds decorated with ivory" (TT) or "beds inlaid with ivory" (NEB).[38] (See 3.12, 15). Here the important point, of course, is the expensiveness and luxury of these beds, not the particular kind of decoration. Where that would not be clear, beds of ivory should be translated as "luxurious beds" or "expensive beds."

The Hebrew uses two different words with similar meaning for beds and most English translations use different words like "beds" and "couches." The translator may have to combine them into one, as in the TEV couches, or use the same word twice. If the same word is used twice, some quality of the bed can be added the second time, to make it seem less repetitive, something like "soft beds," perhaps.

Lambs from the flock, and calves from the midst of the stall (Hebrew: place where they are tied up)/feasting on veal and lamb. The meaning is that of "choice lamb" and "fat calves." (Veal means the meat of a calf.) TEV prefers to show the kind of eating (feasting) and does not express the idea of the quality of the food. NEB does both: "feasting on lambs from the flock and fatted calves," which includes more information than may be necessary. In most languages it is better to use an ordinary verb "to eat" and to bring out the special quality of the meat. If different words for "eat" are used according to who is eating, the choice should reflect the fact that the prominent people of the country are described here.[39]

6.5

Who sing idle songs to the sound (Hebrew: upon the mouth of) of the harp (or: lute), and like David invent for themselves instruments of music;/You like to compose songs, as David did, and play them on harps. Translations of this verse differ very much because the Hebrew is not clear. It is easier if we start with the second part of this sentence: like David invent for themselves instruments of music. Many translations (RSV, NEB, TT, Dhorme, BJ) translate this literally, but not many commentators think that is the right meaning[40] because it makes no sense either within this paragraph or in the wider historical context of the Old Testament.

For that reason, the great majority of scholars have proposed very minor changes of the Hebrew.[41] Not all scholars would propose exactly the same change, but all give a common understanding of the text, as in S-G:

"and compose songs for themselves like David," Mft: "composing airs like David himself" and TEV: You like to compose songs, as David did. This meaning should be translated in spite of the minor changes in the Hebrew that are involved.

In the first part of the Hebrew verse, only the meaning "to the sound of (upon the mouth of) the lute" is sure. The precise meaning of the Hebrew verb (which is found only here in the Old Testament) is not clear.[42] No definite solution can be offered here, but all the various meanings proposed for the word involve the meaning of "to sing" or "to play," and it seems safe to use one of these, as in TEV: and play them on harps.

TEV has changed the order of the two halves of the verse since composing songs normally precedes their singing or playing. This change would be helpful in many languages.

Invent/compose. Some languages have no special term for composing music. In some situations the nearest idea is "improvising"; or it may be necessary to translate "you like to sing new songs, which nobody sang before, and play them on harps."

Harps. See 5.23.

Who drink wine in bowls (Hebrew: Who drink from wine bowls),/You drink wine by the bowlful. The English translations express the fact that it was wine which was drunk and most other translations should do the same.[43] It is the quantity which is important here, as translated by TEV (see also NEB).[44]

Bowls. Some kind of cultural adaptation may be necessary, of course. In some cultures, for example, it is possible to use a word for a particular kind of large calabash, or a general word for calabash which qualified as "big" and "filled."

Wine. See 2.12.

And anoint themselves with the finest oils/and use the finest perfumes. Where local custom includes rubbing oil on the body, and where the purpose of doing so is much the same, the Hebrew should be followed literally, as in the RSV. In many societies this is part of the preparations for a festival, as it was in Hebrew culture, and it will be understood in the same way as a sign of gladness. In Hebrew culture anointing was given up in case of mourning, and this is important for understanding what follows. Where anointing the body is not known or has a different meaning, the cultural adaptation used in TEV may be followed.

But are not grieved (Hebrew: do not become ill) over the ruin of Joseph/but you do not mourn over the ruin of Israel. NAB kept the Hebrew picture in its translation ("yet they are not made ill by the collapse of Joseph") and in some other languages this might work well: "but the ruin of Joseph does not make you ill." In other cases, the picture should not be kept, and one should use a verb like "to worry," "to be grieved," mourn, etc., or an idiom from the receptor language. The ruin of Joseph should usually be translated as "the ruin of Joseph's descendants" (TT) or "the ruin of the house/clan/line of Joseph" or as the ruin of Israel (see 5.6 and 5.15).

In either case, the ruin is a future event, and the translation should not sound like it has already taken place: "because Israel is doomed," "because Israel will be destroyed."

6.7

    Therefore they shall now be the first (Hebrew: at the head) of those to go into exile/So you will be the first to go into exile. In many languages the Hebrew picture would be good: "you will be at the head/front of those who are taken away as captives."

    Exile. See 1.15.

    Therefore...now/So. The Hebrew word normally translated "now" does not seem to refer to time here.[45] The meaning is that of so.

    First. This word is similar to the Hebrew word as in verse 1: first of the nations. Now they have become "first of the exiles." If there is any way of preserving this parallel in the translation without awkwardness or lack of clarity, it would be important to do so. However, since the meaning is different in the two cases (great in verse 1, and "at the head of the line" here), it will often not be possible.

    The revelry of those who stretch themselves shall pass away."/Your feasts and banquets will come to an end. The Hebrew word translated by RSV (and also by NEB) as revelry is not completely clear.[46] In view of the immediate context and the reference to verse 4, stretch themselves, it seems best to understand it as feast: "and the feasting of those who sprawl at ease will be ended" (TT).

    Stretch themselves. The Hebrew word here is the same as the one used in verse 4 and is repeated so that the topic of verses 1-3 (first) and the topic of verses 4-6a are mentioned again here at the conclusion of this subsection. Unlike the case of first, however, the meaning of stretch themselves is the same in both cases, and so it can be translated here exactly the same way as in verse 4. However, there may be no expression of "sprawl" which is suitable for either passages, except for such long, cumbersome expressions as "to lay down your bodies as lazy people on beds." Although English can use one single verb, the widely differing English translations show that even there translators felt a need to handle the Hebrew word differently in the two cases. So TEV uses banquets referring to the whole of the event in which the "sprawling idlers" take part. Such restructurings, however, are often not very helpful for translators in other languages, since such words as feasts and banquets frequently have no literal equivalents elsewhere. In some cases it may be best to say: "your joy, (the joy of) you who live such a good life, will end,"[47] "your fun will be finished!"

6.8-11

    This section is parallel to 5.21-24 in its use of the expression I hate (verse 8). It continues the general theme of 5.18-6.14 that Israel's sense of security is false by saying that there is no security in the basic human institutions of city, home, and family. These are taken up in distinct paragraphs: mansions and city (verse 8), house (verses 9-10), houses (verse 11).

RSV	TEV
8 The Lord GOD has sworn by himself (says the LORD, the God of hosts): "I abhor the pride of Jacob, and hate his strongholds; and I will deliver up the city and all that is in it."	8 The Sovereign LORD Almighty has given this solemn warning: "I hate the pride of the people of Israel; I despise their luxurious mansions. I will give their capital city and everything in it to the enemy."

This short paragraph is about the destruction of the city. First there is an oath, which shows the Lord to be the speaker, followed by a message from the Lord. The first part of the message shows God's attitude toward Israel's guilt; the latter part promises the punishment.

In Hebrew the oath is followed with a second introductory sentence: says the Lord, the God of hosts, repeating what is already in the previous sentence, which is why it has been put between parentheses in RSV and TT. Translationally, it seems better either not to translate this sentence at all or to combine the extra information God of hosts with the preceding oath (as in TEV). See 3.13. It would be better yet to put this sentence at the end of verse 7 as in S-G and Mft (see 6.1-14).

6.8

The Lord God has sworn by himself (Hebrew: his life)/The Sovereign Lord Almighty has given this solemn warning. See 3.7; 4.2.[48] In some cases there is no need to make a distinction between promise (4.2) and warning as the TEV has done. In other languages, however, "promise" is always for good and "warning" is for evil, so that the distinction should be made.

"I abhor...hate/"I hate. See 5.21.

The pride of Jacob/The pride of the people of Israel. See 3.13, where it is suggested the translator keep the name of Jacob. The reasons given for that passage do not apply here, and it may be clearer to translate people of Israel. Pride of Jacob may have been a proverbial expression for the first readers, but it is practically meaningless for the average reader today.

Strongholds/luxurious mansions. These were symbols of Israel's pride. Other translations which have been used include "palaces" and even "buildings with several stories."[49] Where languages do not have close equivalents, see 1.4.

And I will deliver up the city and all that is in it/I will give their capital city and everything in it to the enemy. City can only refer to Samaria, and TEV is correct in translating their capital city. In many languages the translator will have to state to what or to whom the city has been abandoned. The same Hebrew word was used in 1.6 with the specific meaning of "to give completely into the power of the enemy," and this meaning is used here also in TT and TEV.[50] In many cases it would be best to say "their enemies."[51]

RSV	TEV
9 And if ten men remain in one house, they shall die. 10 And when a man's kinsman, he who burns him,^{l} shall take him up to bring the bones out of the house, and shall say to him who is in the innermost parts of the house, "Is there still any one with you?" he shall say, "No"; and he shall say, "Hush! We must not mention the name of the LORD." 11 For behold, the LORD commands, 　　and the great house shall be 　　　　smitten into fragments, 　　and the little house into 　　　　bits.	9 If there are ten men left in a family, they will die. 10 The dead man's relative, who was also in charge of the funeral, will take the body out of the house. The relative will call to whomever is still left in the house, "Is anyone else there with you?" The person will answer, "No!" Then the relative will say, "Be quiet! We must be careful not even to mention the LORD'S name."^{f} 11 When the LORD gives the command, houses large and small will be smashed to pieces.

^{l}Or who makes a burning for him

^{f}Verse 10 in Hebrew is unclear.

This unit deals with one theme, the end of the house, the home, and, by implication, the family. None of these provides security. The passage consists of several paragraphs based on changes in speakers in the conversation. So far as meaning is concerned, the connection with 6.8 is rather close, for after the destruction of the city with its dwelling places, its mansions, the destruction of houses forms a rather natural sequence. In other ways, however, 6.8 and 6.9-11 are very different. Verses 9-10 are written in prose and not in verse. They consist of a piece of a story, including a brief, dramatic conversation. Then in verse 11 the poetry begins again, with a general statement of the Lord's punishment through destruction.

Unlike the paragraph division in TEV and RSV, but like NEB, verse 11 should be included in this unit, but as a separate paragraph. In this section (6.1-14) each of the subsections (verses 1-7,8-11,12-14) ends with the announcement of punishment. The only difference in verse 11 is that the punishment is not expressed directly by the Lord. Besides, verse 11 refers again to house as in verse 9.

It is not fully clear who is speaking at various points in this unit.[52] It seems slightly more probable that the prophet (not the Lord) is speaking throughout the passage, and in some languages verse 9 should begin with something like "Amos said" or "Amos said again." It is still more difficult to know who is speaking to whom in the brief conversation. That will be discussed under verse 10.

RSV translates verses 9-10 as prose. See the comments on 5.25-27.

And if ten men remain in one house, they shall die/If there are ten men left in a family, they will die. There is no necessity to understand men in the sense of "male" and to wonder (as some commentators do) why there were so many males in the house. "People" is often more natural.

It is possible that the ten people were members of one family, but

[133]

the Hebrew word house should not be taken to mean family here. The use of the Hebrew word for in and the repeated use of the word for house, clearly meaning "building" in verse 10, indicate that "house" is best, as in all other English translations.[53]

It is possible to understand the reason for the ten people remaining in the house as their being left alive from some earlier, unstated disaster and looking for security by hiding in a house. But the security is false (in keeping with the theme of 5.18--6.14), and they die there. In some languages this should be made clear: "If ten men try to keep safe by staying/hiding together in a house they will die just the same (or: nevertheless die)."

The translator who consults S-G may be puzzled by the translation "and they die, one being left over." This comes from one of the ancient translations[54] and should not be followed.

6.10

This verse is not at all clear. None of the very different English translations can definitely be considered the right one.

One of the major problems is that we do not know who the story is about or who the people are that speak to each other in it.[55]

And when a man's kinsman, he who burns him (Hebrew: and will take him his uncle and he who burns him), shall take.../The dead man's relative, who was also in charge of the funeral, will take... In most English translations the uncle does the taking, and "his" refers to one of the dead people. In that case the general statement of verse 9 is being developed with an example. In spite of the problems, this is the best solution.

However, two uncertainties remain. Does "his uncle and he who burns him" refer to the same person or to two different people, and does the Hebrew grammatical construction, which occurs only here, really mean "he who burns him?"

If "uncle" and "he who burns him" are different people, then the conversation can be between them, as one of them searches inside the house. If not, the relative must speak to a survivor.[56] The only English translation which has the uncle and "embalmer" as two different people (NEB), has them both speak to a survivor. It is impossible to know from the Hebrew which interpretation is correct. However, the translator must make a decision, perhaps on the basis of the dominant translation in the area.

As to the meaning of "he who burns him," the Hebrew has been taken to mean several sometimes-unrelated things: (a) corpse-burner (RSV); (b) the one who burns spices in honor of the dead (alternative reading of RSV: "who makes a burning for him"); S-G: "who is to burn a sacrifice for him"; and, more generally expressed, who was also in charge of the funeral, "who performs his funeral rites" (TT);[57] (c) embalmer (NEB);[58] (d) relative in general, or specifically the mother's brother along with the father's brother, who is mentioned first.[59]

Of these, meaning (c) seems unlikely. In spite of the English translations, (b) is also improbable, since the custom of burning spices in honor of the dead was probably used only for royal people. Each of the remaining meanings, "corpse-burner" and "relative," is supported by one

of the ancient translations.[60] Here again, it is impossible to tell which
of the two meanings to choose. Against the meaning "corpse-burner" is the
fact that cremation was never an accepted funeral practice among the Israelites, except in the case of an epidemic. It would have to be assumed
that at a time of plague corpses could be burned because of the unusual
disaster.

Meaning (a), "he who burns him," combined with the preceding "uncle,"
can be translated: "When a dead man's uncle comes to take out the body
and burn it..." This "uncle" is the "father's brother." In societies
where only the mother's brother has any role in funeral ceremonies, a
short cultural note will be necessary.

If meaning (a) is accepted, but "he who burns him" is combined with
a second person, the translation may be something like "When a dead man's
uncle comes to take out the body together with him who will burn it..."

For meaning (d) the translation would be something like "When the
uncle and another member of the family of a dead man come to take out the
body..." or "When a dead man's relative comes to take out the body..."

And shall say to him who is in the innermost parts of the house/The
relative will call to whomever is still left in the house. The conversation should be translated according to the decisions made about who is
involved. The person speaking may be outside at the door or just inside
the house. The person who answers is inside the house, and if he is taken
to be a survivor, it may be that he is hiding there.

"Is there still anyone with you?" he shall say, "No"; and he shall
say, "Hush! We must not mention the name of the Lord"/"Is anyone else
there with you?" The person will answer, "No!" Then the relative will say,
"Be quiet! We must be careful not even to mention the Lord's name." For
some translations, like NEB, NAB, S-G and Dhorme, the conversation ends
with Hush (spoken by the uncle and not by a survivor, as in NEB), and
then the prophet adds a kind of commentary: "For the name of the Lord must
not be mentioned." In other translations, such as RSV, TT, TEV, JB, the
last sentence is still spoken by the relative. Whichever interpretation
is followed, the translation should be clear, not just from the use of
quotation marks (which cannot be heard when the passage is read aloud).
When the last sentence is taken as part of the conversation, the statement is as true for the speaker as it is for the person spoken to.
Therefore RSV and TEV use we. If the receptor language makes such a distinction, the word for we should, of course, be the one which includes
the person spoken to.

Why the relative says what he does is also not very clear, but he
seems to be afraid that the person hiding there may for some reason
carelessly use the Lord's name and so call the Lord's attention to them
and bring destruction upon them: "We must be careful not to call the
Lord's attention to us by mentioning his name."

6.11

For behold. See 2.13; 4.13. Again TEV does not make any connection,
and does not show that this is the climactic statement in 6.8-11. A
good translation in English would be "So it is that..."

The Lord commands, and the great house shall be smitten into fragments, and the little house into bits./When the Lord gives the command,

houses large and small will be smashed to pieces. It is possible to interpret this verse in more than one way. The verb in the first sentence could
be taken to mean "the Lord is the one who commands!" and then the Lord
could be taken as the one doing the shattering. More likely, however, he
commands someone to do the shattering.[61] In the light of the message of
the whole book and of this particular section (see verse 14), the one
commanded is probably an enemy nation or enemy army.[62]

It may be advisable to say this clearly in translation. However,
since we do not know the specific cause of the destruction, it would be
best to avoid stating who is doing the shattering.[63] The translation can
be as in RSV and TEV, or something like "the great house will fall into
ruins, and the small house will break."

Some of the repetition of ideas has been combined in TEV and expressed
only once: houses large and small will be smashed to pieces. This is a
good example for languages in which parallelism is unnatural or leads to
bad style. But in many languages it would be better style not to combine
these.

The Hebrew words for fragments and bits are parallel in their vowel
sounds, as can be seen from the following transcription: resisim and
beqi^c im. This contributes to the poetic effect, and should be kept in
mind when translating as poetry.[64]

6.12-14

RSV	TEV

12 Do horses run upon rocks?
    Does one plow the sea with
        oxen?[m]
  But you have turned justice
      into poison
    and the fruit of righteous-
      ness into wormwood--
13 you who rejoice in Lo-debar,[n]
    who say, "Have we not by
      our own strength
      taken Karnaim[o] for our-
      selves?"
14 "For behold, I will raise up
      against you a nation,
   O house of Israel," says
      the LORD, the God of
      hosts;
  "and they shall oppress you
      from the entrance of
      Hamath
    to the Brook of the Arabah."
	12 Do horses gallop on rocks?
	Do men plow the sea with oxen? Yet
	you have turned justice into poison,
	and right into wrong.
	   13 You brag about capturing the
	town of Lodebar.[g] You boast, "We
	were strong enough to take
	Karnaim."[h]
	   14 The LORD God Almighty himself
	says, "People of Israel, I am going
	to send a foreign army to occupy
	your country. It will oppress you
	from Hamath Pass in the north to
	the Brook of the Arabah in the
	south."
	
	[g]LODEBAR: *This name sounds like the
	  Hebrew for "nothing."*
	
	[h]KARNAIM: *The name of this small
	  town means "horns," a symbol of
	  strength.*

[m]MT *does one plow with oxen?*
[n]Or *a thing of nought*
[o]Or *horns*

This final subsection consists of two rather distinct units, verse 12 (one paragraph) and verses 13-14 (different paragraphs for different speakers). One reason for combining them into a unit is the fact that chapter six parallels 5.18-27 in various ways, as discussed under 5.18-6.14. It is also possible to see some connection in meaning between them: impossible things like horses running on cliffs and oxen plowing the sea don't happen, do they? But you make the impossible happen: you make right come out wrong! (verse 12). Also you are so powerful you conquered Karnaim, and it's impossible for you to be defeated, isn't it? (verse 13). Well, Almighty God makes the impossible happen, too. A foreign army will occupy your whole country. (See also Appendix, Section 3.7, where the verses fit together neatly into a pattern.)

However, it is also possible that there is not enough evidence to make this kind of connection between verse 12 and what follows. Some may prefer to keep it as a separate unit, with a separate topic about the end of the normal order of things in the world.[65]

6.12

Amos continues as the speaker here. The verse is composed of two questions to which the answer is "no" (verse 12a) and two statements (verse 12b). The first part of the verse asks if the impossible could happen, the latter part says that the impossible is happening, that the leaders of Israel are doing it, and that this is a terrible evil. The effect is very powerful. One should look for a good way of creating the same effect in the receptor language even if questions cannot be used in this way. Keep in mind the discussion on 3.3-8.

Do horses run upon rocks?/Do horses gallop on rocks? The answer to the first question is "Of course not." Horses do not run on cliffs or rocks because of their hoofs. The word used for rocks should not mean small stones, but great boulders or expanses of rock. Besides, in those days horses were used only for pulling war chariots in the lowlands. One may have to translate "Horses cannot run on rocks/cliffs, can they?" or "Horses cannot run on rocks/cliffs."

Horses. See 2.15.

Does one plow the sea with oxen/Do men plow the sea with oxen. The Hebrew is "does one[66] plow with oxen?" but that does not fit, because the answer to that would be "Of course one does!" Most scholars and nearly all translators solve the problem by dividing the consonants of the last Hebrew word in such a way that they mean "with oxen the sea."[67] If oxen are unknown, or plowing with oxen is unknown, the translator may have to use the name of another, somewhat related animal or even an entirely different animal, but one which can be used for plowing, or he may say simply "Do you plow the sea?" In other cases, he may be obliged to use a borrowed word, showing that it is the name of an animal, and then explain something about the animal in a footnote, such as: "An ox is an animal about (so many times) the size of (another animal of the receptor culture). It is taken care of by men and is used to pull heavy loads and plows."

Where animals are not used for agricultural work and plows are unknown, a possible translation would be: "People do not make a garden in the sea/water/river (do they?)" or "Animals do not work for men in the sea." A short explanation of Hebrew farming custom may then be put in a footnote if necessary.

But you have turned justice into poison/Yet you have turned justice
into poison. See the similar statement in 5.7. However, there justice was
turned to wormwood and here wormwood comes at the end of the next statement. Here it is not fully clear from the Hebrew just what justice is
turned into. The Hebrew word occurs elsewhere as the name of a plant
which people thought was, and may have been, poisonous.[68] It is also used
with the meaning "snake poison."[69] Poison, therefore, is the meaning which
should be translated.

And the fruit of righteousness into wormwood/and right into wrong.
Wormwood. See 5.7. A parallel solution may be found here. There is a
slight difference, however, since in 6.12 there are two pictures, fruit
and wormwood: "Righteousness, which is like a pleasant tasting fruit, is
changed into bitter wormwood." It may sometimes be possible to give a
rather literal translation of the Hebrew in which a particular bitter
plant known to the readers is used for wormwood. However, in that case the
meaning of the picture must still be clear. In other cases it will be necessary to translate the meaning directly. TEV understands fruit as a metaphor for "result" and translates and right into wrong.

6.13-14

Whether or not there is a direct connection between 6.12 and 6.13-14,
this is a unit in itself (see 6.12-14). It is about the end of the victori-
ous army, the most powerful basis for a false sense of security. Like 6.1-7
and 6.8-10 it also deals with the end of the pride and self-confidence of
the people. It is this pride (verse 13) which goes before the fall (verse
14).

Amos continues to speak here and he mentions the self-congratulation
of the people, their complete confidence in their military power, as an
accusation against them. He quotes their boasting just as he did before
(see 6.2), and for the same reason. This quotation is a question also, but
this time the answer is "Yes," and it can be translated as a strong positive statement. The accusation is followed by the usual announcement of a
concrete punishment with the Lord speaking. The people to whom Amos and
then the Lord speak are still the ruling classes.

6.13

You who rejoice in Lo-debar/You brag about capturing the town of
Lodebar. The Hebrew word for rejoice certainly implies "rejoicing arro-
gantly" here. Depending on what particular meaning one wishes to stress,
such different translations as "exult," "be/are jubilant" (TT,NEB), "are
so proud" (Mft), and brag are possible in English. Many languages have
particular idioms to express such feelings, such as "your heart is sweet."

The reason for joy is to be found later in the verse and should be
made clear as capturing the town of Lodebar; a possible translation might
be "you are proud because you have captured the town of Lodebar."

Lodebar was a town on the left bank of the Jordan River, south of the
Sea of Galilee and north-northeast of Bethel, the viewpoint place of the
book (see Translating Amos, Section 3). It should be clear that Lodebar is
a town.

Who say, "Have we not by our own strength taken Karnaim for our-selves?"/You boast, "We were strong enough to take Karnaim." In Hebrew the first person plural suffixes make the sentence sound very boastful. This could be captured in English by translating something like, "We captured Karnaim; we were strong enough to do it ourselves." By our own strength can often be emphasized: "It is by our own strength..." The use of boast also helps in English, and one may have something equivalent.

Karnaim is the name of a town. It was situated northeast of Lodebar, approximately halfway between Damascus and Amman. In TEV Karnaim is not called a "town" because it seemed unnecessary after speaking of the town of Lodebar. But in many languages one will have to say "the town of Karnaim."

S-G and NEB have very different translations here. NEB, for example, has "you who are jubilant over a nothing and boast, 'Have we not won power by our own strength?'" Such a translation is possible, because the Hebrew name Lodebar sounds like the Hebrew word for "nothing," and the name Karnaim is the same as the word for "horns," a picture of "power." Many ancient translations also take this interpretation.[70] However, it is not recommended. The context makes concrete military victories likely, and there is probably a word play. So it is better to keep the proper names in the translation and give two short footnotes like those in TEV.

6.14

"For behold. See 6.11. Here, however, it is important to translate in such a way that the contrast between the boasting false security of 6.13 and the reality of punishment in 6.14 is clear. In English the use of "But" or "In the same way" to begin the verse would be helpful, and the same thing may be best in the language of the translation.

I will raise up against you a nation, O house of Israel," says the Lord, the God of hosts/The Lord God Almighty himself says, "People of Israel, I am going to send a foreign army to occupy your country. The RSV follows the Hebrew closely, except that in Hebrew a nation comes after God of hosts. The position of says the Lord, the God of hosts seems very strange in Hebrew[71] until it is seen as the center of a balanced parallel (Appendix, Section 3.7) as with so many other things which seem out of order in Amos. However, in translation it should be put in wherever is best in the language of the translation; in many cases this would be at the beginning, like the TEV. Then O house of Israel/People of Israel would come in whatever is the natural position within the saying itself.

I will raise up against you a nation/I am going to send a foreign army to occupy your country. Against you implies an attack and this must often be made clear: "I will cause a nation to attack you." Nation can frequently be translated by "tribe," the more so as war is often a tribal affair. On the other hand, nation certainly is a picture in which the whole (people) stands for a part (soldiers). So a translation as army is good also.

"And they shall oppress you from...to.../It will oppress you from... to... This part of the verse, which describes the results of the attack and the loss of security, can best be translated as an independent sentence. There may be difficulty finding an expression for oppress: "That nation/tribe/army will dominate you (or: occupy your country) from... to..." The idea of "oppression" must of course be one of the main meanings of whatever expression is used.

The entrance of Hamath to the Brook of the Arabah/from Hamath Pass in the north to the Brook of the Arabah in the south. The geographic names present some problems as can be seen from the different translations in English.[72] The place or area of Hamath is probably to be found somewhere between Lebanon and the Antilebanon (see Translating Amos, Section 3). The brook of the Arabah cannot be identified with certainty, but it is probably in the area of the Dead Sea. Anyway, the two expressions taken together represent the northern and southern limits of the kingdom. In translation, it is very useful at least to help the reader by saying something like in the north and in the south. Also, the unknown "brook of the Arabah" could be replaced by a widely known "Dead Sea," or a footnote could help the reader with any necessary geographic information.

7.1-9 THE PROPHET'S EXPERIENCES

This section tells of some experiences which Amos had in seeing three
visions which were messages from God. The section therefore consists of
three stories, including brief conversations in each one. It is balanced
by another section (8.1-3), which tells of a fourth such vision (Appendix,
Figures 3, 5).

The four stories about visions are all told in a similar way: each
begins with almost exactly the same words (Thus the Lord God showed me).
Then it describes what Amos saw in the vision (in all cases introduced by
behold). Each closes with a conversation between Amos and the Lord.
However, the four stories can be divided into two pairs. In the first
pair (7.1-3 and 4-6) Amos sees something happen which represents the destruction of Israel; he immediately prays that the Lord will not destroy
the people. The Lord then changes his mind and agrees not to destroy them.
The conversations of this first pair are almost the same in their wording.

In each of the stories of the second pair (7.7-9 and 8.1-3) Amos sees
an object. The meaning of the object is not immediately clear and the Lord
starts the conversation in both cases with the question What do you see?
After Amos describes briefly what he sees, the Lord interprets the meaning of the object (with similar wording in the two cases), using the object as a basis for a picture or a play on words to announce the destruction of Israel. The conclusion of the second pair of visions is exactly
the opposite from the conclusion of the first pair of visions; God does
not change his mind. He will carry out the punishment. The way in which he
states that the punishment must happen (I will not change my mind again)
shows that the conclusions here are related to those of the first pair,
which in turn makes the unity of this group of stories stronger.

With the exception of 7.9 and 8.3, which have other differences (see
below), these stories are not written in verse but in prose. There is no
grammatical parallelism (the most distinguishing feature of Hebrew poetry)
within each story, although, as we have just pointed out, there is parallelism between the stories. It is hard also to find any metrical form. On
the other hand, the prose style of the Hebrew is concise and effective.

In translation, these stories should be strong and dignified prose,
with real emotional impact. The four visions should be translated together, so that the parallels between them are handled in a stylistically
effective way. The translation should not be mechanically parallel but
should gain the same effect in its language which the Hebrew parallels
give in Hebrew.

Section heading. In translations which try to show the structure of
Amos by the use of headings, one is needed here for 7.1-9 (See Translating Amos, Section 2.4). Some possible such headings would be "The
Prophet's Experiences," "What the Prophet Sees," or "God's Message Comes
to the Prophet." It could also be useful to have a subheading for each
story. In cases where the structure is not being shown in the headings,
a heading for each vision would be enough.

7.1-3

	RSV		TEV

A VISION OF LOCUSTS

RSV

7 Thus the Lord GOD showed me: behold, he was forming locusts in the beginning of the shooting up of the latter growth; and lo, it was the latter growth after the king's mowings. 2 When they had finished eating the grass of the land, I said,
"O Lord GOD, forgive, I beseech thee!
How can Jacob stand?
He is so small!"
3 The LORD repented concerning this;
"It shall not be," said the LORD.

TEV

7 I had a vision from the Sovereign LORD. In it I saw him create a swarm of locusts just after the king's share of the hay had been cut and the grass was starting to grow again. 2 In my vision I saw the locusts eat up every green thing in the land, and then I said, "Sovereign LORD, forgive your people! How can they survive? They are so small and weak!"
3 The LORD changed his mind and said, "What you saw will not take place."

Section heading. It may be diffult in some languages to make a suitable heading for this story without employing a long sentence. This would be true in translating A Vision of Locusts (TEV, NAB) into many languages. One way of handling the headings for the individual visions might be to number them. In that case the heading here could be something like "First Vision: The Locusts" or "What Amos Saw the First Time." The choice for a heading here should be influenced by what parallel headings can be found for the other three visions. For example, if the expression for plumb line (7.7-9) is long and awkward so that it cannot be used as a heading where it occurs, then a heading with locust should not be used here.

7.1

Thus the Lord God showed me/I had a vision from the Sovereign Lord. Amos is speaking again; that fact will have to be made clear in some languages. This is also the beginning of a very short story, and in many languages it should start like a story starts: "One time," "One day," "It happened," etc. The Hebrew has Thus in a prominent position at the beginning of the story. The translation should have a similar effect: "Here is what the Lord God showed me," "This is what..." or "Listen to what..." Sometimes it is necessary to be a little more specific and say: "showed me in a vision."

Behold...and lo. The usage here is slightly different from 2.13, 4.13, and 6.14 because here the expression does not show a concluding, climactic statement, but points to something unusual, something worth seeing. One way of translating this effect in English would be to say "what was he doing but (creating...)" or "he was actually creating..." The translation will be stronger if it has an equivalent effect. Some languages have ways of doing this in the grammar itself.

He (Hebrew: someone) was forming (Hebrew: a swarm of) locusts in the beginning of the shooting up of the latter growth; and lo, it was the latter growth after the king's mowings/In it I saw him create a swarm of locusts just after the king's share of the hay had been cut and the grass was starting to grow again. A comparison of RSV and TEV will show that in the Hebrew structure (RSV) two events (forming and shooting up) happen at the same time, and that additional information is given afterwards to show when this took place. TEV restructures this same information in a very different way. In many languages something which is more like the Hebrew sentence structure may be the more dramatic, effective style.

The person who is doing the forming is not named in Hebrew, because the things formed are being emphasized instead. It is clear, however, that the Lord himself is doing it, and this information must often be stated in a translation. This can be done without a wrong emphasis by saying something like I saw him create a swarm of locusts.[1]

Locusts/a swarm of locusts. The TEV seems to be the correct translation of the single Hebrew word (see all recent English translations).[2] Because this took place in the spring it is possible that these were locusts at the stage before they changed into adult form. They seem to eat more then than at any other time. There are many different Hebrew words for locust, but it is hard to know what their different meanings were.

As far as translation is concerned, see 4.9. In some cases it will be necessary to use the same word as was used there even though the Hebrew term is different. To add something like a swarm of may be helpful.

Latter growth/starting to grow again. The meaning is not certain. It may have meant the crops which came as the result of the rains late in the spring (Mft: "spring-crops...royal crop"; TT: "main crop...first crop"; NEB "late corn...early crop") or it may have been what grows after making hay[3] (S-G: "aftermath...mowings"; grass...hay).

King's mowings/the king's share of the hay. Unfortunately such a custom is not mentioned anywhere else in the Old Testament. However it has generally been understood to mean that the king had the first grass of spring cut for his horses.[4] In a later period the Roman rulers of Syria claimed such a right during the months of March-April,[5] and even in modern times the Turkish government required the same from the peasants.[6]

In many languages the translation must say what was mowed, which means choosing between "grain" and "grass." Although the evidence for "grass" seems to be slightly greater, "grain" is still possible.

Here is a possible restructuring of the whole thing: "(I saw him create a swarm of locusts) just after the grass/grain had been cut (or: the farmers had cut the grass/grain) for the king. It was at the very moment when the new young grass started to grow again."

7.2

When they had finished eating the grass of the land/In my vision I saw the locusts eat up every green thing in the land. The Hebrew sentence is not complete, something like "And it would have happened that, if they had eaten up everything green in the land..." This could be restructured as "What would have happened, had they eaten up everything green in the land!"[7] However, the great majority of scholars believed the spelling of the Hebrew should be changed to something which would mean "While they were eating...I said" (NAB) or "When they were on the point of eating...

I said."[8] Many languages express such events which take place at the same
time by something like "The locusts were on the point of eating everything
green in the land, I said..."

The grass/every green thing. The Hebrew word means not only grass, but
all green plants. It may be necessary to choose a particular kind of plant
like "grass" if the language does not have such a general term for vegetation (so also S-G and NAB).

I said/and then I said. In what follows Amos is asking God to spare
Israel from the fate which he sees in the picture of the locusts eating
everything green. In some languages I said may not be strong enough: "I
begged (the Lord)," "I pleaded," etc., using a word for speaking to someone on behalf of someone else.

The emotional tone of what Amos says is very important in translation
here. Amos' tender concern should be felt in the translation, in contrast
to his anger and scorn in Chapter 6. Also, in some languages people speak
differently when talking to God or a king and when talking with other
people. Amos' words must sound suitable (Translating Amos, Section 4).

O Lord God, forgive/Sovereign Lord, forgive your people. In many languages to use a word like "forgive" means that it is necessary to state
who is to be forgiven, as in TEV. What the translator does will depend,
of course, on the way he translates this meaning. In some languages there
are descriptive phrases such as "to think about (something) no longer."
Others use pictures like "to wash away" or "to turn one's back on sins,"
"to make the heart soft," "to heal the neck." In some cases there are such
cultural equivalents as "spit is returned to the ground (for someone) (by
God)."[9]

How can Jacob stand[10]/How can they survive. As elsewhere Jacob stands
for "Israel" (see 3.13; 6.8). If something like your people was supplied
in the preceding sentence, a pronoun as in TEV may be enough; otherwise
something like "descendants of Jacob," "(people of) Israel," etc. Stand
can best be translated as survive (so also TT).

He is so small/They are so small and weak. Another good English word
would be "helpless" (TT).

7.3

The Lord repented concerning this/The Lord changed his mind. A transitional word or expression may be needed to show the relationship of this
sentence to what went before, according to the language: "then," "so," or
"because of what Amos said."

Here, as so often in the Old Testament, God is spoken of as though he
were a human being. Such expressions often give trouble to translators.
The major meaning here is "change of mind," with additional meanings of
personal involvement, emotional awareness, and sensitivity to others. When
the Lord is doing it there does not seem to be any meaning of regret or
sorrow.[11] In most languages there is no serious trouble translating changed
his mind, using such idiomatic expressions as "turning backwards in his
thoughts," etc.

It shall not be/and said, "What you saw will not take place." The
tense here will have to fit what is used in 7.2 and what would be natural
in this context in the language. Another possibility in English would be
"No, it's not going to happen."

7.4-6

RSV	TEV

A VISION OF FIRE

4 Thus the Lord GOD showed me:
behold, the Lord GOD was calling
for a judgment by fire, and it devoured the great deep and was eating up the land. 5 Then I said,
  "O Lord GOD, cease, I beseech
      thee!
    How can Jacob stand?
    He is so small!"
6 The LORD repented concerning
     this;
    "This also shall not be,"
     said the Lord GOD.

4 I had another vision from the
Sovereign LORD. In it I saw him
preparing to punish his people with
fire. The fire burned up the great
ocean under the earth and started
to burn up the land. 5 Then I said,
"Stop, Lord GOD! How can your people survive? They are so small and
weak!"
    6 The LORD changed his mind
again and said, "This will not take
place either."

For the basic pattern of this story about a vision see 7.1-8.3. As
much as possible it should be translated in the same way as the previous
story, but the translator should be sure both are natural and effective in
the receptor language.

Section heading. Whatever is done here should be parallel to 7.1-3.
If the visions are numbered as suggested there, the subtitle here could be
"Second Vision: The Fire," or "What Amos Saw the Second Time."

7.4

Thus the Lord God showed me: behold/I had another vision from the
Sovereign Lord. See 7.1. It may be necessary to show the change of speaker, as the Lord spoke last. Since this is a second vision, it will often
be better to say "showed me again in a vision," another vision, etc.

Behold. See 7.1.

The Lord God was calling for a judgment by fire (Hebrew: He was calling to punish by fire, the Lord God, or: He was calling the fire to punish, the Lord God),/In it I saw him preparing to punish his people with
fire. The Hebrew grammar presents problems,[12] but the meaning is shown
well in TEV, except that especially in light of 1.4 and other such passages in Amos, the reader may not realize that in this context fire is a
picture of the heat of the sun in the summer. The translation can be something like "The Lord God showed me how he caused the burning heat of the
sun to punish his people."

And it devoured the great deep/The fire burned up the great ocean
under the earth. This refers to the great ocean which people of the ancient
East believed lies under the earth as the source of springs and rivers.
The usual translations such as "great deep" (RSV, Mft, S-G) or "great
abyss" (NAB, NEB) are not very meaningful to modern readers. "The great
ocean" (TT) is misleading since the expression will be understood in its
modern geographic sense. So a descriptive phrase like the great ocean
under the earth is often the best solution. Many languages have to use a
phrase for ocean like "vast extension of water." It may be helpful to
give readers a cultural note such as was included in an early edition of

TEV Amos: "The ancient Hebrews believed that under the earth there was a great body of water which sometimes broke through the earth's surface." In addition, references can be given to Gen 7.11; 49.25; Psa 36.6; Isa 51.10. In some languages neither burned up the great ocean nor devoured the great deep will make any sense. The translation may have to say "dried up."

And was eating up the land./and started to burn up the land. This is in fact the cultivated land (S-G: "plow-land"; Mft: "the tilled land"); many languages will have a specific term for it. If burn up the land or eating up the land is an impossible picture even in a vision like this, other possibilities may be "made the farmlands very dry" or "made the farmlands like dust."

7.5

Then I said, "O Lord God, cease, I beseech thee! How can Jacob stand? He is so small!"/Then I said, "Stop, Lord God! How can your people survive? They are so small and weak!" What Amos said is exactly the same as verse 2b except for cease here instead of forgive (verse 2). The Hebrew means "Don't do it" or Stop (so also TT). In many languages it will be necessary to say "stop the heat" or "stop doing this," etc.

7.6

The Lord repented concerning this: "This also shall not be," said the Lord God/The Lord changed his mind again and said, "This will not take place either. See verse 3. In Hebrew the two verses are the same except for the addition of this also.

7.7-9

RSV	TEV

TEV

A VISION OF A PLUMB LINE

7 He showed me: behold, the Lord was standing beside a wall built with a plumb line, with a plumb line in his hand. 8 And the LORD said to me, "Amos, what do you see?" And I said, "A plumb line." Then the Lord said,
"Behold, I am setting a plumb
line in the midst of my
people Israel;
I will never again pass
by them;
9 the high places of Isaac shall
be made desolate,
and the sanctuaries of Israel
shall be laid waste,
and I will rise against the
house of Jeroboam with
the sword."

7 I had another vision from the LORD. In it I saw him standing beside a wall that had been built with the use of a plumb line, and there was a plumb line in his hand. 8 He asked me, "Amos, what do you see?"

"A plumb line," I answered.

Then he said, "I am using it to show that my people are like a wall that is out of line. I will not change my mind again about punishing them. 9 The places where Isaac's descendants worship will be destroyed. The holy places of Israel will be left in ruins. I will bring the dynasty of King Jeroboam to an end."

Here begins the second kind of story about Amos' visions; this section and the parallel one in 8.1-3 consist of two units. Verses 7-8 are in prose in Hebrew, with verse 9 in poetry.[13] In fact, in some ways verse 9 belongs both with this section and the one which follows. It is related to verse 8 by the overall discourse structure (Appendix, Figure 5), by continuing the Lord speaking, and by telling what the punishment of verse 8 will be. On the other hand, it introduces the story of verses 10-17, mentioning themes which are taken up again there: Isaac in verse 16b; the sanctuary in verse 13b and Jeroboam in verse 11a.

In translation it might be useful to show that the conversation ends with verse 8 and that verse 9 has a transitional character by not making it one continuous saying by the Lord as in TEV. Translating verses 7-8 as prose and verse 9 as poetry would not be enough. The best way would seem to be to print verse 9 as a separate paragraph, introduced by something like "The Lord (also) said," or begin verse 9, "I will destroy the places ..."

Section heading. It may be difficult to find a suitable subtitle because the thing which Amos saw in this vision, the plumb line, is unknown in many areas (see below). Some possibilities are "Third Vision: A Plumb Line," "Third Vision: A Cord to Measure the Straightness of the Wall," or "What Amos Saw the Third Time."

7.7

He showed me: behold, the Lord was standing/I had another vision from the Lord. In it I saw him standing. On the change of speaker and the fact that this is another vision, see 7.4. Here the Hebrew text is shorter than the other visions.[14] Like in the other visions, the Lord is the one who showed Amos, and translations have to say so in most languages (so rightly Mft, NAB, TEV). This will probably mean changing to a pronoun in what follows: I saw him standing;[15] "The Lord Eternal showed me this, showed me himself standing..." (Mft); "Then the Lord God showed me this: he was standing..." (NAB).

Behold. See 7.1.

Beside a wall built with a plumb line (Hebrew: a wall of a plumb line), with a plumb line in his hand./beside a wall that had been built with the use of a plumb line, and there was a plumb line in his hand. The Lord is seen as standing on or by a wall which in Hebrew is called "a wall of a plumb line" (if plumb line is itself correct--see below). RSV and TEV as well as TT all try to make sense out of this by saying something like a wall...built with the use of a plumb line. On the other hand it may be better to follow most modern English translations (S-G, Mft, NAB, NEB) as well as many commentators[16] who have something like "standing by a wall with a plumb line in his hand." They consider "of a plumb line" to be the result of a copying mistake.

Plumb line. The translation is not fully certain[17] but no other suggestion is as good.[18] A plumb line is a cord with a lead weight used by builders to be sure that walls are straight up and down. In many cultures the only similar tool is the water-level, and such Pidgin English words as "wataplan" have often become part of the vocabulary. This measures the horizontal rather than the vertical, but might serve the purpose for the picture in this vision. A better solution would sometimes be to use a

short descriptive phrase. In addition, some kind of illustration to show
the shape and use of the tool might be helpful.

A possible way of translating into some languages would be "The Lord
caused me to see again in a vision. I saw him on the top of a wall
stretching out the cord to see whether the wall was straight."

7.8

And the Lord said to me,/He asked me. Since said introduces a question here, in many languages it would be more natural to use a word for
ask.

"Amos, what do you see?" And I said, "A plumb line." Then the Lord
said, "Behold, I am setting a plumb line in the midst of my people Israel;/"Amos, what do you see?" "A plumb line," I answered. Then he said, "I
am using it to show that my people are like a wall that is out of line.
One translation problem here is that my people Israel is compared with a
wall[19] but this is not stated directly.[20] It has been partially expressed
in such translations as Mft: "With a plumb line I test my people" and TT:
"I am holding a plumb line against my people Israel," but the comparison
must be made fully clear in many languages, as in TEV: I am using it to
show that my people are like a wall that is out of line. The final restructuring in any language will differ in detail. One possibility would
be something like "This cord is to show that my people Israel is not
straight like a straight wall."[21]

Another problem is that to be crooked in a physical sense may not
give a picture of sin or injustice. A good translation might be something
like "When you stretch this cord beside a wall you can see clearly that
the wall is not straight. I have seen the sin of my people Israel just as
clearly."

I will never again pass by them;/I will not change my mind again
about punishing them. The meaning of the Hebrew is "I will forgive them no
longer" (NAB), "I will never pardon them again" (TT). I will not change my
mind again about punishing them expresses the relationship between this
conclusion and that of the preceding stories (see 7.1-8.3). A possible
translation: "I will never change my mind again but will surely punish
them." Sometimes it is necessary to make the relationship clear between
the first and last part of what the Lord says: "Because this is so (or
"because they are not straight yet" or "because of their sins"), I will
no longer forgive them."

"Forgive." See 7.2.
Behold. See 7.1.

7.9

For the special character of this verse and its poetic structure, see
7.7-9.

The high places of Isaac/The places where Isaac's descendants worship. High places refers to places of worship which are located on hills.
Originally the high place was simply a burial mound with worship related
to dead people, but later this developed into a fertility cult.[22] The
Israelites took over the custom of worshiping at the high places from
the Canaanites with the difference that they did not worship Baal but
the Lord.[23]

Isaac stands for the people of the northern kingdom of Israel, and there will be misunderstanding if it is not translated as Isaac's descendants.

High places of Isaac means the places where Isaac's descendants worship and this will have to be spelled out in most languages. It may also be necessary to say whom they are worshiping: "me" (that is, God).

Worship. There are often good equivalents, such as "to cut one's personality down before," "to rub (earth) on one's body" (an expression of homage and a recognition of kingship), etc.[24]

Shall be made desolate,/will be destroyed. Many translations will have to say something like "Someone (or: people/the enemy) will destroy the places where the descendants of Isaac worship me/(their) God." It is not the location on the hills which is important here, so TEV may be right in not mentioning high places. Another possibility, however, is "the places on the top of the hills where Isaac's descendants worship."

And the sanctuaries of Israel shall be laid waste,/The holy places of Israel will be left in ruins. These are the more important state places of worship in the northern kingdom. Sanctuaries of Israel means "the sanctuaries in Israel." (Note the difference from high places of Isaac just above.)

Holy. This is difficult to translate, as was pointed out in 4.2. Sometimes a short descriptive phrase like "houses of God" or "houses where people worship God" can be used. In other cases there may be cultural equivalents like "festival longhouse (of God)," etc.[25]

And I will rise against the house of Jeroboam with the sword."/I will bring the dynasty of King Jeroboam to an end." Rise against may often be translated "attack" or "defeat" (see 6.14).

With the sword. See 1.11.

It would be helpful to many readers to show that Jeroboam was a king.

This story, which breaks into the sequence of stories about visions,
is different in several ways. (On the way in which it fits in the structure of Amos, see Appendix, Section 1.1.) It is not about a vision, and
Amos is not telling about his own experience; someone else (most probably
a pupil of the prophet) is telling about an encounter between Amos and a
certain priest named Amaziah. There is important information about Amos
himself here (verses 14-15), but that is not the point in the story. In
fact, it is Amaziah, not Amos, who is more important. Amos' experience
with Amaziah shows the opposition of the religious leaders to the word
of the Lord and gives Amos another chance to speak the word of the Lord,
this time directly to a religious leader (verse 17). Amos tells him of
punishment to come to him and his family,[1] just as the stories about the
visions end with the promise of punishment to the nation in general.

The story has three scenes (10-11, 12-13, and 14-17), which should be
handled by the translator as three paragraphs, with an additional paragraph containing the word of the Lord (16-17) in the third scene. In the
first two scenes Amaziah is prominent, but in the last one he is in the
background.

The first two short scenes introduce and prepare the third one. In
the first one the priest makes a report to the king warning that Amos is
dangerous. In the second, the priest tries to get Amos to go away. Amos
replies to both of these in the third scene. He makes a statement about
himself and why he is prophesying (verses 14-15). This shows that Amaziah's
attack is not really against Amos but against the Lord who sent Amos. Without mentioning the king, the problem of authority raised by Amaziah in the
earlier scenes has been solved. The Lord, a higher authority, is acting.
So then Amos speaks the word of the Lord to Amaziah (16-17), using what
Amaziah has just said (verse 13) to show his guilt. Then comes the annouce-
ment of punishment (verse 17) spoken by the Lord.

Section heading. If there is no attempt to show the structure of Amos
in the section headings, then something like "Amos Disputes/Answers
Amaziah" or "The Palaver between Amaziah and Amos" would be enough. However, in translations where the structure of the book is being shown in
the headings, it would be better to have a heading which is the same, or
similar to, that of 3.3--4.3.

7.10-11

RSV	TEV
	AMOS AND AMAZIAH
10 Then Amaziah the priest of Bethel sent to Jeroboam king of Israel, saying, "Amos has con-spired against you in the midst of the house of Israel; the land is not able to bear all his words. 11 For thus Amos has said, 'Jeroboam shall die by	10 Amaziah, the priest of Bethel, then sent a report to King Jeroboam of Israel: "Amos is plotting against you among the people. His speeches will destroy the country. 11 This is what he says: 'Jeroboam will die in

<table>
<tr><td>the sword,
and Israel must go into
   exile
away from his land.'"</td><td>battle, and the people of Israel
will be taken away from their land
into exile.'"</td></tr>
</table>

The priest of Bethel. On the question of the need for a title for
Amaziah and the kind of language he should use, see Translating Amos,
Section 4, and the discussion under Amos in 1.1. Amaziah was not the only
priest at the place of worship in Bethel. A translation of "chief priest"
would be better to indicate the real position Amaziah held.[2] In many languages, of course, the problem is to find any good equivalent for priest.
Sometimes there is a cultural term, but too many unwanted meanings may be
related to it. In certain cultures specific terms for priests exist, especially in relation to their sacrificial work, such as "knife men." Such
a functional expression may be more acceptable, but such a term is rather
limited because the function of Hebrew priests is not restricted to the
offering of sacrifices. But there may be no other choice than something
limited like "one who presents sacrifices," "one who takes the name of
the sacrifice," "one who speaks to God," "spokesman of the people before
God," etc. Sometimes borrowed terms can be employed, like the Arabic malim,
where it is widely known, but generally this cannot be recommended.

Amaziah may have to be introduced here with some expression like
"There was a priest, Amaziah, who was the chief priest in the temple at
Bethel" or "Have Amaziah..."

Sent to Jeroboam king of Israel, saying,/sent a report to King
Jeroboam of Israel. Something has to be sent, and what is sent often has
to be made clear in translation. So, for example, "sent word" (Mft, NAB),
sent a report, "reported" (NEB). In other languages, a translation something like "he caused (someone) to tell" might be used.

"Amos has conspired against you in the midst of the house of Israel;
/"Amos is plotting against you among the people. The language should be
appropriate for a high priest to write to a king.

Many languages do not have specific verbs for plotting or "conspiring."
However, this human activity is common everywhere, and there is some way
to talk about it. One possibility is a short descriptive phrase like "to
prepare bad things against someone." The accusation is that Amos was plotting within the territory of the king ("right here in the kingdom of
Israel"), not that he was plotting with the people against the king.

The land is not able to bear all his words./His speeches will destroy
the country. The land stands for "the people of the land," so a good
translation might be "The people cannot resist his many words." However,
in many languages it is necessary to say what will happen because they
cannot resist: "The people cannot resist his many words which will destroy
the country." Amaziah is speaking his own thoughts rather than those of
the people.

7.11

For thus Amos has said, 'Jeroboam shall die by the sword,/This is
what he says: 'Jeroboam will die in battle. In this verse Amaziah supports
his report to Jeroboam by quoting what Amos has said. A quotation inside a
quotation is sometimes difficult. See 1.2 and 4.1. To eliminate the inside

quotation it is possible to translate something like "Amos is saying that your majesty/you will..."

By the sword/in battle. See 4.10.

And Israel must go into exile away from his land.'"/and the people of Israel will be taken away from their land into exile.'" On exile, see 5.5,27; 6.7. An alternative rendering would be: "Enemies will force/ cause the people of Israel to leave their country and to become captives far away."

7.12-13

RSV	TEV
12 And Amaziah said to Amos, "O seer, go, flee away to the land of Judah, and eat bread there, and prophesy there; 13 but never again prophesy at Bethel, for it is the king's sanctuary, and it is a temple of the kingdom."	12 Amaziah then said to Amos, "That's enough, prophet! Go on back to Judah and do your preaching there. Let *them* pay you for it. 13 Don't prophesy here at Bethel any more. This is the king's place of worship, the national temple."

This is the second scene discussed under 7.10-17. It should be a new paragraph. We are not told what the relation of this scene is to the previous one. The translation, however, will depend on how that relationship is pictured. Is Amaziah doing what the king ordered in his reply? This is not very likely, since Amaziah's report had to be sent by messenger to Samaria, which would mean a delay of several days. Amaziah seems to have acted on his own account, and seems to have tried to get Amos to leave the kingdom before the king could act.

The translator should be careful not to see more in this than the Hebrew text allows. Notice the RSV: O seer, go, flee away to the land of Judah, and eat bread there, and prophesy there. In Hebrew the tone is neutral, without indicators of emotion.

Many English translations, on the contrary, make Amaziah sound angry or scolding: "Off with you, visionary" (NAB); "You dreamer! Be off to Judah and earn your living there; play the prophet there" (Mft); "Be off, you seer! Off with you to Judah!" (NEB); That's enough, prophet! It is doubtful that such translations are equivalent. The Hebrew word for seer did not have a derogatory tone, and such people were not looked down on in Hebrew culture.[3] Also, the Hebrew eat bread for "earn a living" is not derogatory. On the contrary, the grammatical form in combination with the Hebrew verb for "to flee away"[4] shows some kindheartedness in Amaziah's words.

So the translation should not use strong and negative language. It could be something like "Leave from here, you who see visions, save yourself in the country of Judah; speak there the message of God; they will give you your bread/food and you will eat it."

There is also a possibility that Amaziah is using the fact of his report to Jeroboam as a lever to get Amos to leave. Whether Jeroboam reacts or not, if Amaziah gets Amos out, he accomplishes his purpose: "Why don't you escape to Judah while there is time? You can always prophesy

there and make your living. But don't you dare stay around here and
prophesy at Bethel any more! This is the national temple, the place
where the king worships."

And Amaziah said to Amos,/Amaziah then said to Amos. In some cases
the style used by Amaziah in speaking to Amos will have to be different
from that used with the king in the previous scene. How he speaks to Amos
will depend on the decision concerning his motives, as discussed just
above.

Seer,/prophet! These two words overlap in meaning so that prophet
can be justified in English. For the translation of prophet and prophesy,
see 2.11, 12.

Go, flee away to the land of Judah,/Go on back to Judah. Many languages use more than one verb in a row, as the Hebrew does, but not necessarily in the same order.

And eat bread there,/Let them pay you for it. Prophetic work included the right to be supported by the community. TEV changes the order to
show the relation between the activities. Other translations should probably do the same. On the other hand, although Let them pay you for it may
be a necessary translation for money economies, in many cultures and eat
bread there, "and let them feed you" or "get your rice from them" would
be better.

TEV prints them in special type to emphasize it so that the sentence
will not be understood wrongly as "Let them pay you for it" (the most
normal reading in English). Such a device is not recommended in a common-
language translation. The same effect could have been made by a different
wording: "You can get your pay from them," "Let the people there pay you."

And prophesy there;/and do your preaching there. See 2.11,12. There
does not seem to be any need to use preaching here, as TEV has done, although the meanings overlap.

7.13

But never again prophesy at Bethel,/Don't prophesy here at Bethel
any more. See verse 12. It is the place Bethel which is important here,
not the prophetic activity as such. The translation should have the same
effect, as does TEV here at Bethel.

For it is the king's sanctuary, and it is a temple (Hebrew: house)
of the kingdom."/This is the king's place of worship, the national temple." The king's sanctuary is the place where the king himself worships,
as in TEV: This is the king's place of worship. Some scholars think
"house of the kingdom" refers to a royal residence, and translate "royal
palace" (S-G, NEB). However, there is no evidence that Bethel was one of
Jeroboam's residences. Therefore "house" is more generally understood as
temple. This can then be translated "royal temple" (NAB, TT) or national
temple (so also Mft). In many languages it will simply come out as "temple of the king." One of the equivalents proposed in verse 9 can be used
to translate temple.

The king's sanctuary and a temple of the kingdom therefore do not
mean exactly the same thing, but they refer to the same place, as is
clear in TEV. Some translations may have to say something like "the national temple where the king worships (God)" or "the place where the king

worships (God), that is, the national temple." If the best way of translating national temple or temple of the kingdom is "the king's temple,"
as discussed above, the translator may not be able to make the distinction and it would all come out as "the place where the king worships
(God)."

7.14-15

RSV	TEV
14 Then Amos answered Amaziah, "I am no prophet, nor a prophet's son;p but I am a herdsman, and a dresser of sycamore trees, 15 and the LORD took me from following the flock, and the LORD said to me, 'Go, prophesy to my people Israel.'	14 Amos answered, "I am not the kind of prophet who prophesies for pay. I am a herdsman, and I take care of fig trees. 15 But the LORD took me from my work as a shepherd and ordered me to go and prophesy to his people Israel.

pOr *one of the sons of the prophets*

Amos begins his reply by telling why he is prophesying. He is speaking to the high priest, and if the language requires a special style for
that, it should be used here.

Amos answered Amaziah, "I am no prophet, nor a prophet's son (or:
one of the sons of the prophet);/Amos answered, "I am not the kind of
prophet who prophesies for pay. Scholars disagree on the translation of
this verse. In recent English translations some have Amos speaking in the
present tense (RSV, S-G, Mft, TEV) and others in the past tense (NAB).[5]
The problem is that the Hebrew wording has no verbs, so that in English
translation either a present or a past of the verb "to be" has to be
supplied.

If the present tense is chosen, Amos is saying that he is not a
prophet and even the order of the Lord to prophesy (verse 15) does not
change this. In that case he is making a distinction between the office
of prophet and the act of prophesying. If the past tense is chosen, Amos
is saying that he was not a prophet, but became one when called by the
Lord.

Scholars are almost equally divided,[6] but it seems more satisfactory
to use a present tense, because it fits the grammar and context better.[7]

A prophet's son does not mean the physical son of the prophet, but a
member of a group of prophets (S-G; "member of a prophetic order"; Mft:
"member of any prophet's guild"). Amos is saying that he is not a professional prophet. Therefore in answer to verses 12-13, TEV has him say
I am not the kind of prophet who prophesies for pay. This restructuring
is helpful for languages where it might be possible to say, for example,
"I am not of those prophets who live from the fruit of the message of
God," etc.

But I am a herdsman,/I am a herdsman.[8] The translation should fit
with shepherd (see I.1). In many cases it will be necessary to use the
same term here. Many languages have such a word as "herd," and it may
be enough to say "I have herds" or "I take care of herds" or "I get my

bread/rice/food/pay from caring for herds (of sheep)," etc.

And a dresser of sycamore trees (or: figs),/and I take care of fig trees. "A dresser of sycamore-figs" (NEB) or "someone who raises (dresses) figs of sycamore trees." A general statement such as I take care of fig trees may be sufficient. In some languages it may be best to say simply "I have a field of fig trees,"9 especially if care for them would be understood.

The sycamore tree belongs to the same family as the mulberry and fig trees. It was a broad heavy tree 7.50 to 15 meters high, growing especially in the plains of Palestine. Its fruit looks like figs, but the taste is unpleasant.10

Fig trees. See 4.9.

7.15

And the Lord took me from following the flock, and the Lord said to me, 'Go, prophesy to my people Israel.'/But the Lord took me from my work as a shepherd and ordered me to go and prophesy to his people Israel. These sentences contrast with the preceding ones and should usually be introduced by a word like English but. In Hebrew the Lord is repeated twice here in contrast with the I in verse 14. This emphasizes the authority on which Amos acts and should come out clearly in translation. In TEV this contrast would be strengthened by repeating the Lord: "I am not the kind of prophet...I am a herdsman, and I take care of fig trees. But the Lord took me...and the Lord ordered me..."

In some societies where keeping animals is common, there might be a similar idiom to from following the flock.

Whether or not Amos should quote the Lord directly depends on the language (see 1.2; 4.1; 7.11). One possibility here is "the Lord sent me to tell his message to his people Israel."

7.16-17

RSV	TEV
16 "Now therefore hear the word of the LORD. You say, 'Do not prophesy against Israel, and do not preach against the house of Isaac.' 17 Therefore thus says the LORD: 'Your wife shall be a harlot in the city, and your sons and your daughters shall fall by the sword, and your land shall be	16 So now listen to what the LORD says. You tell me to stop prophesying, to stop raving against the people of Israel. 17 And so, Amaziah, the LORD says to you, 'Your wife will become a prostitute in the city, and your children will be killed in war. Your land will be

[155]

parceled out by line;	divided up and given to others,
you yourself shall die in an	and you yourself will die in a
unclean land,	heathen country. And the people
and Israel shall surely go	of Israel will certainly be taken
into exile away from	away from their own land into
its land.'"	exile.'"

A new paragraph should begin here, introducing a new message from the Lord. In Hebrew it is in poetry. (See 7.10-17).

7.16

"Now therefore hear the word of the Lord. You say, 'Do not prophesy against Israel, and do not preach against the house of Isaac.'/So now listen to what the Lord says. You tell me to stop prophesying, to stop raving against the people of Israel. Again the translator will have to decide whether to have a quotation (like RSV) or indirect speech (like TEV).

Hear the word of the Lord./So now...Listen to what the Lord says. Expressions of this type are used in Amos at the beginning of a concluding section (Appendix, Section 1.21). The transition could be shown in many languages by a word like "so," as in TEV.

Israel and house of Isaac are the same, so TEV has simply the people of Israel. However, the translator may want to keep the reference to Isaac (see verse 9). This may partly depend on how the rest of the sentence is translated.

Prophesy...preach against (Hebrew: let drip)/prophesying...raving against. The meanings of these words are very similar in Hebrew. "Let drip" includes the meaning of "speaking with strong emotion." In this context "let drip" has no negative meanings and should not be translated like raving or "drivelling on" (NEB). "Speaking out" might be an acceptable equivalent in English. If there is no equivalent except something long and elaborate or with some kind of negative meaning, an emotionally neutral term like preach (RSV, NAB) or "speak"[11] would be better. The two expressions can be combined in some translations: "stop prophesying against the people..."

Against. Some possibilities for restructuring: "do not speak the bad message of God," "do not denounce the descendants of Isaac" (TT), "don't say bad things about the people of Israel."

7.17

Therefore/And so, Amaziah. The relationship between verses 16 and 17 must be clear, both in its change of speakers and in the fact that verse 17 results from what happens in verse 16. "For that reason, (the Lord says to you) Amaziah..." "because you say that, Amaziah."

Thus says the Lord:/the Lord says to you. See 1.3.

By the sword,/in war. See verse 11.

Your land shall be parceled out by line;/Your land will be divided up and given to others.

This means that Amaziah's private property becomes the property of the conquerors, who will divide it among the new families of immigrants.

[156]

The (measuring) line12 is not important to the meaning so that it does not need to be included if it is a problem. However, the information and given to others is important to the meaning, though it is not stated directly in Hebrew. To show who is doing the action, it is possible to use an impersonal subject "someone will divide..." or "the conquerors of the land will divide..."

An unclean land,/a heathen country. Neither of the two translations is very helpful for other languages. In most cases one should simply say: "a foreign country" (Mft).

And Israel shall surely go into exile away from its land.'"/And the people of Israel will certainly be taken away from their own land into exile.'" See verse 11b. For some languages this promise of punishment will be much clearer if the order of events in translation fits the order in which they will happen: "Your children will die in war, your country will be conquered, and your land will be divided up and given to those who conquer you; your wife will become a prostitute in the city, and you yourself will be taken away to die in a foreign land. Yes, the people of Israel will be taken away into exile."

RSV

8 Thus the Lord GOD showed me: behold, a basket of summer fruit.^{q}
2 And he said, "Amos, what do you
see?" And I said, "A basket of
summer fruit."^{q} Then the LORD said
to me,
   "The end^r has come upon my
      people Israel;
   I will never again pass by
      them.
3 The songs of the temple^s shall
      become wailings in that
      day,"
           says the Lord GOD;
"the dead bodies shall be many;
  in every place they shall be
    cast out in silence."^{t}

^{q}*qayits*

^{r}*qets*

^{s}Or *palace*

^{t}Or *be silent!*

TEV

A VISION OF A BASKET OF FRUIT

8 I had another vision from the
Sovereign LORD. In it I saw a basket of fruit. 2 The LORD asked,
"Amos, what do you see?"
   "A basket of fruit," I answered.
   The LORD said to me, "The end^i
has come for my people Israel. I
will not change my mind again about
punishing them. 3 On that day the
songs in the palace will become
cries of mourning. There will be
dead bodies everywhere. They will
be cast out in silence."^{j}

^{i}END: *The Hebrew words for "end"
and "fruit" sound alike.*

^{j}out in silence; *or* out. Silence!

This fourth story about a vision is organized in much the same way
as the third one (see 7.7-9). An important difference from the third
vision, however, is that here there is a pun, a play on words, because
of the similarity in Hebrew between summer fruit and end.[1]
    Like 7.7-9, this section consists of two units, with the vision it-
self (8.1-2) in prose, and an additional transitional statement (8.3) in
poetry. Verse 3 even starts off in much the same way as 7.9. The Lord is
speaking; the verse has the same function as 7.9, making the punishment
of verse 2 more specific, and introducing the section 8.4-14, where themes
of verse 3 occur again (for example, in verse 10). Whatever way the transitional character of 7.9 was handled earlier, the same should be done
here.[2]
    Section heading. For translations in which the structure of Amos is
not shown in the headings: "Fourth Vision: A Basket of Fruit" or "What
Amos Saw the Fourth Time." For translations in which the structure is
being shown, the heading should be like that of 7.1-9 to show the balance.

8.1

Thus the Lord God showed me: behold, a basket of summer fruit./I had
another vision from the Sovereign Lord. In it I saw a basket of fruit.
See 7.1; 7.4; 7.7. Even though the story of this vision is separated from
the others, the translation should follow the same pattern. However, because of the distance from the others something may be needed to tie them
together: "Here is what the Lord showed me in still another vision: it was
a basket of fruit."

Behold. See 7.1.

Basket. The Hebrew term[3] was no doubt a general one for receptacle.[4]
The translation should have a general word if possible, one which would
be appropriate for showing fruit for sale in the market place, carrying
it, or storing it. If no kind of basket is suitable, then any container
used for the purpose would be all right.

Fruit. The Hebrew word is the same as for "summer" and means here
"that which the summer produces." It is wrong to translate as summer fruit
(RSV, S-G, TT), since it suggests a contrast with some other seasonal
fruit. Some translations have "ripe fruit" (Mft, NAB; compare NEB: "ripe
summer fruit"), in order to make a pun in the English text of the next
verse. There would be no point in translating "ripe" in languages where
"the time is ripe" (verse 2) is not an idiom. Most languages have a general term for fruit. If not, a specific kind of fruit can be used in
translation. In Hebrew probably the fruit here is "figs."[5]

8.2

And he said,/The Lord asked. See 7.8. Here, in addition, it may be
better to translate he as the Lord and/or indicate that he spoke to "me,"
depending on what is best in the language.[6]

"Amos, what do you see?" And I said,/"Amos, what do you see?"...I
answered. Unless there is some reason in the language why it should not
be done, the wording here should be the same as in 7.8.

"A basket of summer fruit." Then the Lord said to me, "The end has
come upon my people Israel;/"A basket of fruit,"... The Lord said to me,
"The end has come for my people Israel. There is a pun between the Hebrew
words for summer fruit (qayits) and end (qets).[7] In order to make some
kind of pun in English, some translations have "ripe fruit" in verse 1,
and here they have "the time is ripe" (NAB, NEB) or "so is the doom ripe"
(Mft). However, puns are almost never translatable; only occasionally is
there a suitable equivalent, as with "ripe." To make up a pun which
sounds unnatural is no help. Usually it is better to translate the Hebrew
rather literally (the end has come) and add a short note that the Hebrew
words for "end" and "fruit" are similar, as is done in TEV. Of course,
the end has come should not be translated literally, but perhaps something
like "the time is finished," "this is the end" or "(my people Israel)
will not continue any longer," etc.

I will never again pass by them./I will not change my mind again
about punishing them. The wording is the same as in 7.8.

For the special character of this verse, see 8.1-3; 7.7-9.

On that day. For the special meaning of this expression, see 2.16. TEV has done some restructuring by putting the expression at the beginning, since it is the time setting of the whole verse (so also NEB, TT). This will also be the natural position in many other languages as well.

Says the Lord God has been omitted in TEV because there is no change of speaker. Other translations should not necessarily do this, but in some languages it may be better to put it at the end of the verse to show the end of the unit (so TT). If verse 3 is printed as a separate paragraph according to the suggestion in 7.7-9, "The Lord God says" may be used as an introductory sentence before the time setting.

The songs of the temple shall become wailings/the songs in the palace will become cries of mourning. This gives the traditional interpretation of the Hebrew (except for the palace), but it is probably not right. Because of the context the great majority of scholars change the Hebrew text slightly to "the singing women in the palace shall howl" (NEB, and the same interpretation in TT).[8] This is the interpretation which should be followed. A possible translation is "The women who were singing in the palace will wail instead."

"The dead bodies shall be many; in every place they shall be cast out in silence."/There will be dead bodies everywhere. They will be cast out in silence." This gives the reasons for the mourning. There are so many dead and not enough place to bury them. TEV has combined these two ideas into There will be dead bodies everywhere. NEB takes these to be the words which the women were wailing.

In silence. (Hebrew: Silence! or Hush!) Compare 6.10. But who is speaking? The Lord? The singing women (NEB)? Or a reader who expressed his feelings in a marginal note? It seems impossible to know. The best way to make some sense out of this might be to say "not a sound will be heard."

The punishment of Israel, which was always present among other themes
in all the major sections of Amos from 3.3 to 8.3, here emerges as the
major theme once more, balancing other sections (Appendix, Figures 3, 5).
In this section the first message (8.4-6) again mentions Israel's sins,
using some of the same pictures as in 2.6--3.2.

Then follows a paragraph consisting of 8.7-8, which introduces the
punishment subsection (8.7--9.4) of this large section. This is followed
by three paragraphs with pictures of punishment, beginning with on that
day (8.9-10), the days are coming (8.11-12), and in that day (8.13-14).
In the last two, the time of the Lord's judgment is shown as a time of
lack of the Lord's help.

Finally the punishment subsection ends with another vision of the
Lord announcing punishment (9.1-4).[1] It brings the section to a climax
with its pictures of the impossibility of escape.

Section heading. In some cases one section heading for 8.4--9.4 may
be enough. In other cases additional subheadings at various points may be
needed, as will be discussed below. The heading of the larger section
should relate to 1.3--3.2 or 5.18--6.14 as much as possible. For example,
"God Judges/Will Punish the People of Israel."

8.4-6

RSV	TEV
	ISRAEL'S DOOM
4 Hear this, you who trample upon the needy, and bring the poor of the land to an end,	4 Listen to this, you that trample on the needy and try to destroy the poor of the country. 5 You say to yourselves, "We can hardly wait for the holy days to be over so that we can sell our grain. When will the Sabbath end, so that we can start selling again? Then we can overcharge, use false measures, and fix the scales to cheat our customers. 6 We can sell worthless wheat at a high price. We'll find a poor man who can't pay his debts, not even the price of a pair of sandals, and we'll buy him as a slave."
5 saying, "When will the new moon be over, that we may sell grain? And the sabbath, that we may offer wheat for sale, that we may make the ephah small and the shekel great, and deal deceitfully with false balances,	
6 that we may buy the poor for silver and the needy for a pair of sandals, and sell the refuse of the wheat?"	

For another restructuring of this passage in English and some discussion of the reasons for it, see Translating Amos, Section 5.1. The

paragraph opens with Amos calling to his audience (verse 4). In some cases the translation may need to show this by "Amos said:" or "Then Amos said:", both because this begins a new major section and because the last speaker was the Lord.

Attention here is on the people to whom Amos is speaking, the wealthy merchants. He tells what they are like by what he says about them directly in speaking to them, and by quoting them to show their deeds and motives (verses 5-6).[2] The merchants live only for their commerce (verse 5a), which consists of fraud (verses 5b, 6a) and trade in human misery (verse 6b). The last theme takes up again the opening theme of "trampling on the needy" in verse 4.

Section heading. If a subheading is used here it could be "The Sins of the Rich People" or "The Rich People Sin."

8.4

Hear this,/Listen to this.[3] Compare 3.1; 4.1; 5.1. This wording begins a concluding section in Amos (Appendix, Section 1.21) and in many languages should have a word like "so."

You who trample upon the needy,/you that trample on the needy. See 2.7. It may be better to indicate who the you refers to by saying "you merchants."

And bring the poor of the land to an end,/and try to destroy the poor of the country. The destruction of the poor is the purpose of trampling on the needy, and this has to be made clear in the translation. Poor of the country may have to be rendered as "poor people in the country/nation" or simply as "poor people."

8.5-6

The quotation (see 8.4-6) starts with verse 5 and continues to the end of the paragraph.[4] In Hebrew it consists of two questions without answers, the second one rather long. The point of the questions is to show how the merchants want the time set aside for worshiping God to end quickly so they can get back to cheating people in business again. A great deal of restructuring is needed because the passage is otherwise too difficult in most languages. Shorter sentences can be used, and questions can be alternated with statements, as has been done in such translations as NAB and TEV. The restructuring in Translating Amos, Section 5.1, handles it as a series of accusations.

Another problem is that and sell the refuse of the wheat (6c) seems out of place. TEV and NEB put it at the beginning of verse 6. Another possibility is in verse 5, as will be discussed below.

8.5

Saying,/You say to yourselves. Although you say to yourselves (so also TT) may be a good solution in some languages, in others it is impossible to speak to oneself, and the translation may have to be "you think" or "you say." If only part of the quotation is translated as a question, care must be taken with such a specific verb as "to ask" (so NAB). On the other hand, if there is a word like "mutter" (Mft) or "say in secret," that would be good.

"When will...be over,/"We can hardly wait...to be over. The choice
between question or statement was discussed in 8.5-6. It depends on what
is effective in the language of the translation. The important thing is
for the reader to feel the impatience of the merchants without having to
depend on tone of voice, etc. It may be best to make this impatience
explicit in the translation: we can hardly wait, "you can't wait."

New moon/holy days. In many cultural situations it will be possible
to say new moon in the translation,although it may also be necessary to
show that it is a "feast": "the feast of the new moon." Even if a feast
of the new moon is not known, in some cases people will easily understand that certain activity was forbidden on such feast days, and they
will not need a general description such as holy days (not to be confused
in English with holidays!).

That we may sell grain? And the sabbath, that we may offer (Hebrew:
open) wheat for sale,/so that we can sell our grain. When will the Sabbath end, so that we can start selling again? The Hebrew picture is that
of opening the storehouse where the wheat is kept: "that we may open our
storehouses/shops to sell wheat" or simply "that we can start selling
wheat again." Generally, it is better to translate sabbath with "rest
day" or "day for resting," which has the advantage of making a meaningful
contrast in this particular passage.[5] In some languages there is difficulty with the similarity of this question to the question just above.
TEV has not mentioned "grain" or "wheat" the second time. Some translations may need to combine the two questions, or emphasize different
features of them. For example, "...to open our shops...to sell our wheat."

In some translations it would be best to move the end of verse 6
(and sell the refuse of the wheat) here for smoothness of the flow of
ideas (see 8.5-6).[6] What is done will depend on the way in which the first
half of verse 5 was translated. It may be possible to say, for example,
"that we may open our storehouses in order to sell the refuse of wheat
(or: worthless wheat)," "that we can start selling grain again, even the
refuse of wheat." However, this solution does not emphasize the picture
as much as the final balanced position in Hebrew emphasizes it, and some
stronger wording might be better, like TEV We can sell worthless wheat at
a high price or "You even take what you sweep from the floor of the wheat
bin and sell it to the hungry at a high price." Of course, if the end of
verse 6 is moved here, verses 5-6 should be numbered together.

That we may make the ephah small and the shekel great, and deal
deceitfully with false balances, (Hebrew: to twist the balances of false-
hood)/Then we can overcharge, use false measures, and fix the scales to
cheat our customers. The ephah was a measure of capacity.[7] It was changed
in one way or another so that the customer did not get all he should get.
In the time of Amos money was unknown. So the shekel, a weight of limestone (probably about 11 grams) was used to weigh bars, rings, etc. of
valuable metal which were used in commerce. When the weight of the shekel
was enlarged in one way or another, the price the customer had to pay was
too high.

The important part of the meaning is not in the particular measure
and weight, but in the examples of cheating. So there is no need to keep
the difficult terms ephah and shekel in the translation. Possibilities
include "measures" (compare Mft, TEV) and "weights" (Mft) or some cultural

equivalent for ephah (compare NEB: "giving short measure in the bushel"); the effect of the cheating with the shekel can be indicated: "too high a price." For example, "Then we make the measures (or cultural equivalent) small and the price of things big."

A third possibility of cheating customers was in using false balances. One of the scales was made heavier or the beam was twisted so that the balance became false: fix the scales to cheat or "cheat by tampering with the scales" (Mft), etc.

In a culture where standardized measures, weights, and balances are not known, or not all known, some of these pictures may have to be combined into general expressions of cheating, or there may be some equivalent idiom or picture in the language.

<u>8.6</u>

An alternative place for and sell the refuse of the wheat (end of the verse) is at the beginning of verse 6, as in TEV and NEB (see also 8.5-6; 8.5).

That we may buy the poor for silver and the needy for a pair of sandals,/We'll find a poor man who can't pay his debts, not even the price of a pair of sandals, and we'll buy him as a slave." This picture is very much like that of 2.6 except that here it speaks of buying rather than selling, and here it is the poor rather than the righteous who are being described. According to the explanations given in 2.6, the translation here might run something like 'We will buy poor people as slaves because they cannot pay their debts, even if the debt is so small as that of a pair of sandals."

<u>8.7-14</u>

Section heading. If subheadings are included in this section, one here could be "How the Lord Will Punish" or "Kinds of Punishment."

<u>8.7-8</u>

RSV	TEV

7 The LORD has sworn by the
        pride of Jacob:
"Surely I will never forget
        any of their deeds.
8 Shall not the land tremble on
        this account,
    and every one mourn who
        dwells in it,
    and all of it rise like
        the Nile,
        and be tossed about and
            sink again,
        like the Nile of Egypt?"
	7 The LORD, the God of Israel,
	has sworn, "I will never forget
	their evil deeds. 8 And so the
	earth will quake, and everyone in
	the land will be in distress. The
	whole country will be shaken; it
	will rise and fall like the Nile
	River.

This paragraph introduces the pictures of punishment, the result of the sins illustrated in the preceding paragraph. The punishment is first described in a general and negative way: the Lord will never forget the evil deeds mentioned in the preceding paragraph (verse 7). What this means in positive and specific terms is explained in verse 8 and in the following paragraphs.

8.7

The Lord has sworn by the pride of Jacob:/The Lord, the God of Israel, has sworn. Sworn here is in the sense of taking an oath, not the usual English meaning of "swear" (see 6.8). In almost all modern English translations the Hebrew is translated literally and without meaning, as in RSV. In most languages it makes no sense to swear by someone's pride, any more than it does in English.[8] It is even questionable whether that is what the Hebrew really means. In the Old Testament the Lord never swears by something or somebody else, but always by himself or by something which is identical with himself. If this rule is applied here, the Lord swears by himself as pride of Jacob.[9] From here it is only one step to the TEV The Lord, the God of Israel, has sworn.

However, the TEV translation is not really enough. Pride of Jacob was probably not a common title for the Lord, so the information in it is of some importance. The suggested translation would be something like "The Lord, of whom Israel is so proud (whom Israel honors/glorifies), has sworn/promised..."

In some languages a word meaning "say" or "promise" will be needed in addition to one meaning "take an oath," to show that what follows is the content of the oath.

"Surely I will never forget any of their deeds./"I will never forget their evil deeds. Evil may be unnecessary after 8.4-6, where Israel's crimes are described.

8.8

In Hebrew this verse consists of a question to which the answer should be "Yes."[10] In some cases the translation can make the first half of the verse a question and the second half a positive answer to the question, perhaps introduced by "Yes." However, in many languages questions like shall not the land tremble are unusual or extremely difficult and should often be translated as direct statements, as in TEV.

On this account (Hebrew: because of this),/And so. In Hebrew the connection between this verse and verse 7 is unusual and grammatically difficult.[11] In this context this can best be taken as referring to all of 8.4-7. It may be best to translate "because of their evil deeds," and so..., or "that is why...," etc.

Shall not the land tremble/the earth will quake. See 1.1. The Lord causes this to happen, and some languages should say "I will make the earth quake..."

And all of it rise like the Nile (Hebrew: the river),[12] and be tossed about and sink[13] again, like the Nile of Egypt (Hebrew: river of Egypt)?"/The whole country will be shaken; it will rise and fall like the Nile River. All of it refers back to land, and so, if a new sentence begins here, it may be necessary to say "All earth" (NEB) or The whole country. It may also be necessary to repeat: The whole country will be shaken, "The whole country will move," etc. "The river" and "the river of Egypt" both refer to the Nile, and should sometimes be combined: it will rise and fall like the Nile River, "rising and falling like the Nile River," etc. Be tossed about can be kept in the translation, as in most English translations, but it can also be left out (as in Mft), since it probably is an addition.[14] The idea is already included in rise and fall.

8.9-10

RSV	TEV
9 "And on that day," says the Lord GOD, "I will make the sun go down at noon, and darken the earth in broad daylight. 10 I will turn your feasts into mourning, and all your songs into lamentation; I will bring sackcloth upon all loins, and baldness on every head; I will make it like the mourning for an only son, and the end of it like a bitter day.	9 The time is coming when I will make the sun go down at noon and the earth grow dark in daytime. I, the Sovereign LORD, have spoken. 10 I will turn your festivals into funerals and change your glad songs into cries of grief. I will make you shave your heads and wear sackcloth, and you will be like parents mourning for their only son. That day will be bitter to the end.

Says the Lord God,/I, the Sovereign Lord, have spoken. RSV follows the Hebrew sentence order. TEV puts the phrase at the end of verse 9, where it does not fit, since TEV has no paragraph break before verse 9. This expression should have been put either at the beginning of verse 9 or at the end of verse 10. For many other languages the natural place for this phrase is either at the beginning of a new paragraph like (TT) or at the end of verse 10.

"And on that day,"/The time is coming. This is again a reference to the day of the Lord (see 2.16; 5.18). If possible, the translation should not be so general as in TEV. It would be better to use the same expression as in 8.3 (on that day) or something like "when the day of my judgment comes" or "on the day when I will punish the people," etc.

I will make the sun go down at noon. This is a reference to an eclipse of the sun.[15] It is likely to present translation problems only where the expression for noon is something like "sun overhead." In such a case one possibility would be "I will make the sun go down when it should be overhead," or "I will make the sun disappear in the middle of the day."

And darken the earth in broad daylight./and the earth grow dark in daytime. Another possibility: "darkness will come/happen during the day-time."

8.10

Verse 10 continues the list of punishments, but there is no other immediate connection with verse 9. Attention now is on the sorrow that will result from punishment, not on disruptions in nature. For many languages a connection like "also" or "not only that but" will be needed between the verses.

I will turn your feasts into mourning,/I will turn your festivals into funerals. Festivals into funerals makes a very effective contrast in English, but in many cultures funerals may be considered a kind of feast. Some possibilities: "while you are feasting joyfully, I will make you start mourning" or "I will make/cause you not to feast joyfully, but to mourn."

And all your songs into lamentation;/and change your glad songs into cries of grief. For many languages TEV is an excellent model. However, in languages where "songs" are only cheerful it may be better to contrast "songs" and "lamentations."

I will bring sackcloth upon all loins, and baldness on every head;/ I will make you shave your heads and wear sackcloth. Two particular mourning customs are mentioned: (1) to put on clothing of coarse hairy material, wrapped around the waist; (2) to shave the head, either completely or in part.[16] Baldness on every head will usually be understood wrongly as natural baldness. I will make you shave your heads is better. Make you or "cause you" is often necessary because the Lord is not actually doing the shaving. In the same way it is usually best to say I will make you...wear sackcloth.

Sackcloth often has to be translated with a phrase like "rough coarse cloth around your waist." However, even then the reader may not understand that the shaving and sackcloth are customs of mourning for the dead. So it may be necessary to add something like "to show that you are mourning."

It is sometimes possible to use equivalent mourning customs from the culture of the translator, especially if they are not very different from the Hebrew ones: for example, "I will put the cord of mourning around your neck," which would be immediately understood in certain cultures.[17] However, there are dangers as well as advantages in such a cultural translation. Particular aspects of the Hebrew culture are lost, and there may be undesirable meanings.

I will make it like the mourning for an only son,/and you will be like parents mourning for their only son. The Hebrew translated by it refers to the total event.[18] One possibility: "I will make you mourn like someone whose only son has died." TEV also gives a good model.

And the end of it like a bitter day./That day will be bitter to the end. Here again it refers to the total event. The meaning is "on that day (from verse 9)...the end of everything will be like a day of tragedy" (compare TT) or "on that day...everything will end in tragedy." A possible translation might be something like "everything which happens will end with great sorrow."

8.11-14

In this subsection the Lord punishes his people by not helping them (see 8.4-9.4). The first paragraph mentions the absence of spiritual help

[167]

(verses 11-12); the second the absence of physical help (verse 13).

The theme of thirst which links verses 11-12 and 13-14 together is to be taken in its literal sense in verse 13 and as a picture of spiritual lack in verse 11. Neither the literal nor the spiritual thirst will be satisfied (verse 13 and verse 12). The result is that people will collapse (verse 13) and will fall and not rise again (verse 14).

This whole desperate situation is caused by the Lord himself (verse 11), who continues to speak through this section. The mention of beautiful girls and young men in verse 13 is a picture of people in general, to emphasize the greatness of the disaster. Even those people with the greatest strength and health will collapse. It is not the people themselves who are emphasized, but their actions, experiences, and words.

8.11-12

RSV	TEV

11 "Behold, the days are coming,"
   says the Lord GOD,
  "when I will send a famine
   on the land;
  not a famine of bread, nor a
   thirst for water,
  but of hearing the words of
   the LORD.
12 They shall wander from sea to
   sea,
  and from north to east;
  they shall run to and fro, to
   seek the word of the
   LORD,
  but they shall not find it.
	11 "The time is coming when I will send famine on the land. People will be hungry, but not for bread; they will be thirsty, but not for water. They will hunger and thirst for a message from the LORD. I, the Sovereign LORD, have spoken. 12 People will wander from the Dead Sea to the Mediterranean and then on around from the north to the east. They will look everywhere for a message from the LORD, but they will not find it.

8.11

Says the Lord God,/I, the Sovereign Lord, have spoken. See 8.9-10. Here the indication of speaker covers the whole subsection, verses 11-14.

"Behold. See 2.13.

The days are coming,"/"The time is coming. See 8.3. Here the expression has days instead of day, but the meaning of "the time of God's judgment/punishment" is the same.

"When I will send a famine on the land.;/when I will send famine on the land. I will send always refers to the Lord causing a disaster.19 Often a word meaning "cause" can be used instead: "I will make/cause a famine" or "I will cause hunger to fall on/enter the land," etc.

On the land may have to be translated "in the country" or "among the people."

Not a famine of bread, nor a thirst for water,/People will be hungry, but not for bread; they will be thirsty, but not for water. It may not always be necessary to break up the Hebrew sentence into a number of shorter sentences as has been done in TEV. In some languages a sentence closer to RSV would be more effective. This would be especially true when

a word can be used which means both "hunger" and "need." If hunger for
food and thirst for water are not suitable metaphors for the lack of a
message from God, it may be necessary to strengthen the picture by using
a word for "lack" here and in the rest of the verse: "not a lack of bread
or water, but a lack of a message from me."

Bread. If "bread" is not the basic food, a general word meaning
"food" should be used or else the word for the most important food, like
"rice" or "yams."

But of hearing the words of the Lord./They will hunger and thirst for
a message from the Lord. Since the Lord is speaking, it may be best to
translate "my message" or "a message from me, the Lord."[20]

8.12

They shall wander from sea to sea, and from north to east;/People
will wander from the Dead Sea to the Mediterranean and then on around
from the north to the east. On wander, see 4.8. In Hebrew, they (also S-G,
NAB) does not refer back to anyone who has been mentioned before. Whether
they or "men" (NEB, Mft) or people (also TT) or some impersonal pronoun is
used will depend on the translation of verse 13.

From sea to sea is normally taken to mean "from the Mediterranean to
the Dead Sea." In terms of a viewpoint-place like Bethel (or even Tekoa)
this would be the same as saying "from west to south." The only directions
which remain are from north to east! It would also be possible to take
from sea to sea in the reverse sense: from the Dead Sea to the Mediterranean. The movement would then be seen as a circle of wandering: South
(Dead Sea)--West(Mediterranean)--North(Lebanon)--East(Bashan), as in TEV.

The translator will have to use the directional systems of his language, keeping the viewpoint-place of the book (Bethel) constantly in
mind. In some languages this may lead to such a translation as "from north
to south" and "from east to west" (NEB, but on the wrong grounds) or vice
versa, depending on what is normally used in the language in question.
Sometimes equivalents like "sunrise" and "sunset" can be used for "east"
and "west," but it is usually much harder to find terms for "north" and
"south." If such distinctions as "up-stream" and "down-stream" or "north
wind" and "south wind" are not made in the language, it may be possible
to say, for example, "from east to west and in all other directions" or,
if necessary, "people will wander through the whole country."[21] (See
Translating Amos, Section 3.)

They shall run to and fro has much the same meaning as the Hebrew
word translated wander. The single word wander covers them both nicely
in English.

To seek/They will look everywhere. In this context seek means search
for something which is lost, and many languages will have specific words
for this.

The word of the Lord,/a message from the Lord. See 8.11. It may not
make sense in some languages to seek or look...for a message, because
look implies the use of the eyes, and message implies the use of the ears.
Instead, "look for someone who will tell them my message" or "try to hear
my message" are possibilities.

But they shall not find it./but they will not find it. Depending on
the translation of other parts of the verse, it may be good to say some-

thing like "but they will not hear from me" or "they will not hear me speak."

RSV	TEV
13 "In that day the fair virgins and the young men shall faint for thirst. 14 Those who swear by Ashimah of Samaria, and say, 'As thy god lives, O Dan,' and, 'As the way of Beer-sheba lives,' they shall fall, and never rise again."	13 On that day even healthy young men and women will collapse from thirst. 14 Those who swear by the idols of Samaria, who say, 'By the god of Dan' or 'By the god of Beersheba'--those people will fall and not rise again."

8.13

"In that day/On that day. See 2.16;8.9.

The fair virgins and the young men/healthy young men and women. The reference is to the entire nation, as represented by its strongest members.[22] TEV brings this out by adding even and healthy.[23]

Shall faint for thirst./will collapse from thirst. Thirst in this case is not metaphorical, that is, a lack of any response from the Lord,[24] but literal, that is, lack of water. In some cases the translation should be "die from thirst." It may be good to strengthen the contrast between 8.11-12 and 8.13-14, so that thirst will not be understood as spiritual lack here. For example, the TEV would make the difference clearer if verse 13 was translated "Moreover, on that day even healthy young men and women will collapse from lack of water."

8.14

This verse tells more fully who the people are in verse 13 and gives more specific reasons for their punishment. They are people who swear by other gods, who are more important to them than the Lord. The prediction of punishment is repeated at the end of the verse. The translation can say something like "these people will fall and never be able to rise again, because they swear..." or "these are the people who swear...they will fall..."[25]

Those who swear by...and say,/Those who swear by...who say. See 8.7. (Here, of course, it is not the Lord who is swearing.) In the first line of the Hebrew verse the people swear by something (or someone); in the second line the same people are introduced as speakers whose oaths are quoted. It may not be possible to do this in some languages. It may be necessary to quote the oath in all three cases, or not quote it in all three cases. If swearing of this kind is not known, other possibilities are "rely on" or "seek help from" in this particular context.

The short Hebrew oath (literally: "may live..." or "as...lives") was

shortened from "As surely as (name of deity) lives, I will (will not)
do..." In many cultures similar oath-sentences are used, though rarely
with the same wording as in Hebrew. Shortened forms are less frequent, so
that by the god of... cannot very often be used as a model for other languages. The only solution may be to follow the construction of the first
line in the second: "who swear by the god of Dan or the god of Beersheba."
To swear by may be translated as "They swear using the name of" or "...
through the power of" or "They say, 'May the idols of Samaria help me'"
or "...'In the name of the idols of Samaria'" or whatever the form of an
oath is in the language of the translation.

In some languages the problem may be that "swearing by" is not an
expression of loyalty or trust, as it is here. The translation should then
be something like "those who follow/obey other gods, and therefore swear
..." or even "those who rely on the idol of Samaria, and say 'the God of
Dan lives...'"

Ashimah (Hebrew: the guilt) of Samaria,/the idols of Samaria. "The
guilt of Samaria" is not found in the more recent English translations.
Most of them interpret the Hebrew word for "guilt" as having slightly
different vowels and so obtain the proper name Ashimah (S-G, TT) or, more
clearly, "Ashimah, goddess of Samaria" (NEB). This goddess is known from
2 Kings 17.30, which tells of the different peoples whom the Assyrians
allowed to settle in Samaria after the Israelites were captured. The people from Hamath in Syria brought their own goddess Ashimah with them.

However, "the guilt of Samaria" should probably be interpreted as
a prophetic way of speaking about the sacred image of the bull in Bethel,
or even in Samaria itself (compare Hos.8.5-6): the image shows the guilt
of the people. Mft speaks of the "god at Bethel," but if the place reference is correct, it is better to speak of the idols of Samaria. Better
yet is NAB: "the shameful idol of Samaria."

Idols. See 5.26.

'As thy god lives, O Dan,'/'By the god of Dan.' If it is not possible to quote an appropriate oath, the translation will have to be
something like "swear, using the name of the god of Dan" or "they rely on
the god of Dan."

'As the way of Beer-sheba lives,'/'By the god of Beersheba.' As the
way of Beer-sheba lives makes little sense. Possibly the meaning is that
people swear by the pilgrimage route to Beersheba in the same way that
Arabs still swear by the pilgrimage route to Mecca.[26] This is the way in
which some of the ancient translations understood the Hebrew[27] and in
which it has been translated in NEB: "By the sacred way to Beersheba." If
people do swear by such things in the language of the translation, there
might be reason to follow this interpretation.

However, this interpretation is still unsatisfactory, since a reference to a god would seem to be needed in this context. For that reason a
slight change in the Hebrew consonants has often been suggested,[28] and the
resulting word has been interpreted in different ways.[29] Such suggestions
all refer to a god of Beersheba and are supported by one of the ancient
translations, which has "your god, O Beersheba."[30] So a translation "By the
god of Beersheba" or "those who swear by the name of the god of Beersheba"
is possible. This is a choice between what is improbable and what is
uncertain.

9.1-4

RSV	TEV

THE LORD'S JUDGMENTS

RSV

9 I saw the LORD standing beside[u]
    the altar, and he said:
"Smite the capitals until the
    thresholds shake,
    and shatter them on the
        heads of all the people;[v]
and what are left of them I
    will slay with the sword;
    not one of them shall flee
        away,
    not one of them shall escape.
2 "Though they dig into Sheol,
    from there shall my hand
        take them;
though they climb up to heaven,
    from there I will bring
        them down.
3 Though they hide themselves on
    the top of Carmel,
    from there I will search
        out and take them;
and though they hide from my
    sight at the bottom of
    the sea,
    there I will command the
    serpent, and it shall
    bite them.
4 And though they go into cap-
    tivity before their
    enemies,
    there I will command the
    sword, and it shall
    slay them;
and I will set my eyes upon
    them
    for evil and not for good."

TEV

9 I saw the Lord standing by the
altar. He gave the command: "Strike
the tops of the Temple columns so
hard that the foundation will shake.
Break them off and let them fall on
the heads of the people. I will kill
the rest of the people in war. No one
will get away; not one will escape.
2 Even if they dig their way down to
the world of the dead, I will catch
them. Even if they climb up to
heaven, I will bring them down. 3 If
they hide on the top of Mount Carmel,
I will search for them and catch
them. If they hide from me at the
bottom of the sea, I will command
the sea monster[k] to bite them. 4 If
they are taken away into captivity
by their enemies, I will order them
put to death. I am determined to
destroy them, not to help them."

[k]SEA MONSTER: *It was believed that
the sea was inhabited by a great
monster. This creature, like all
others, was regarded as under
God's control.*

[u]Or *upon*

[v]Heb *all of them*

    Section heading: If subheadings are being used in this section (see
8.4--9.4), there should be one here: "Nobody Can Escape When the Lord
Judges/Punishes."
    Here Amos tells of another vision (see 7.1-8.3), but this one is
very different, and so there is no need to try to make it parallel to
the earlier visions.[31] For the internal structure of this paragraph, see

Appendix, Section 3.8, which may be of help especially when translating
as poetry. Since this paragraph involves directions ("away," "up," "down"),
the translator should remember that the viewpoint place is on the earth,
beside the altar. Movements and directions are seen from there.

9.1

I saw the Lord standing beside the altar,/I saw the Lord standing by
the altar.
Altar. See 3.14. The actual position is either by the altar (also
NEB, TT), beside the altar (also NAB), or "upon the altar" (S-G). Most
probably the Hebrew means by or in front of the altar, and suggests at
the same time that the Lord was a very large figure. In a higher level of
English than TEV this could be translated "towering above the altar" or
"looming over the altar." If it is hard to combine location and height in
the translation without using a longer expression, it would be possible to
say that the Lord stood by or "in front of" the altar and not express the
other meaning.
The content of the vision may be enough to indicate that no ordinary
seeing is meant, but in some cases it is necessary to say "I saw the Lord
in a vision, and he stood..."[32]
And he said:/He gave the command. It is impossible to know to whom
the Lord is speaking.[33] TEV translates he gave the command, because commands follow, but in many languages it is necessary to say to whom a command is given. In some cases the reader may think that Amos is the one to
whom the Lord is speaking,[34] which is not likely.
Capitals refers to a round decoration at the tops of the pillars of
the temple. TEV avoids the technical term capitals (RSV, S-G, NEB) and
speaks of the tops of the...columns (compare also TT: "the top of the
pillars" and Mft). In addition TEV makes clear that these columns belong
to a temple, which may be wise in other translations also, especially in
cultures where altars are not normally found in places of worship.
Temple. See 7.9, 13.
Columns. Where buildings are supported by posts of some kind the
translator should say something like: "Strike the center post of the temple..." If buildings supported by columns or posts are not known, then it
may be necessary to say "Strike the roof beams" in order to be able to
continue with the rest of the saying below.
Until the thresholds shake,/so hard that the foundation will shake.
In Hebrew it is clear that something shakes under the blow, but translations usually differ considerably as to what is shaken: thresholds (RSV,
S-G), "lintels" (TT) or "doorjambs" (NAB), "ceiling"[35] (Mft) or "the whole
porch" (NEB) or foundation. The meaning is probably either the foundations
or the roof structure.[36] However, the picture is of the whole building
shaking from the roof to the foundation until it collapses. This is what
must be made clear, with the particular choice of wording depending on the
translation of what follows.
And shatter them on the heads of all the people (Hebrew: all of
them);/Break them off and let them fall on the heads of the people. The
Hebrew is not at all clear in its details,[37] but the overall picture of
the building falling on the people inside can be seen and should be made
clear in translation. In many cases it will be impossible to break some-

[173]

thing off on the head of somebody and TEV gives a good solution and let them fall on the heads of...(so also TT).

The people are those present in the temple, and it may be necessary to say "of all who are there" (TT) or even "of all the worshippers" (Mft).

And what are left of them I will slay with the sword;/I will kill the rest of the people in war. See 4.10.

Not one of them shall flee away, not one of them shall escape./No one will get away; not one will escape. The only possible problem here is the repetition. In some languages it may be better to say it only once, but there is strong emotional force in the repetition, and this force should be carried over in the translation.

9.2

"Though/Even if. The impossibility of escape is now shown in exaggerated pictures, which TEV introduces by even if. Other languages can make use of similar wording.

They dig into (Hebrew: break through to)/they dig their way down to. "Force" is one of the important parts of the meaning of the Hebrew: "even if they tried to enter into...with force."

Sheol,/the world of the dead. In the Old Testament Sheol is the common gathering place for all the dead. According to Israelite understanding, there is a relationship between "grave" and "sheol." Where there is a grave, there is sheol, and where there is sheol there is a grave. However, sheol is not the sum of all the graves. It is often considered as a dark world where the dead gather, deep down under the earth, far deeper than the grave.[38] To take over the Hebrew word is not very meaningful and should be avoided. Some possible translations in English are world of the dead, "Death-land" (Mft), "nether world" (NAB). Very often it is possible to make use of existing concepts and beliefs in the culture. However, frequently the "land of the dead" or some other local equivalent will not have some important parts of the meaning of Sheol and some kind of note may be necessary. For example, "The Israelites thought that the dead came together in a land under the ground."

From there shall my hand take them;/I will catch them. In some instances, it is possible to keep the picture my hand (which stands for the whole person) in the translation: "My hand will bring them up from there" or "I will catch them with my hand and bring them up from there." The Hebrew has two events, "catching" and "pulling out." Sometimes one of the events does not have to be stated directly because it is understood, but sometimes it is better to express both. In some languages it is important to express the upward direction, from below to the speaker above.

Though they climb up to heaven, from there I will bring them down./Even if they climb up to heaven, I will bring them down. Here the directions are reversed. One possible translation would be "I will make them descend to earth."

9.3

Though they hide themselves on the top of Carmel, from there I will search out and take them;/If they hide on the top of Mount Carmel, I will search for them and catch them. The top of Carmel was an ideal hiding

place because of thick forests and more than two thousand limestone caves.
Such information should, however, not be stated in the translation. The
important thing is the balance of up with down. Normally it is important
to indicate that Carmel is a "mountain" or "hill."

TEV stops using even after verse 2, but in some languages it may be
better to use an equivalent expression in verses 3 and 4 also, in order
to emphasize the impossibility of escape.

And though they hide from my sight (Hebrew: my eyes) at the bottom of
the sea,/If they hide from me at the bottom of the sea. "My eyes," of
course, is a picture of God searching, and when understood as such can be
kept in the translation (S-G; compare RSV, TT: my sight; NAB: "my gaze").
In other cases it may be more natural to say from me (so also Mft, NEB).
Sometimes it would be possible not to state directly what they are hiding
from because it is clear from the context.[39]

It is not always easy to translate at the bottom of the sea.[40] In
cultures where the sea is not known, it may be necessary to say "on the
earth, after having gone into the water" or "...under the deep water" or
"...deep in the water."

There I will command the serpent, and it shall bite them./I will command the sea monster to bite them. This is the only case in this paragraph
where the picture is of the Lord using something else to accomplish what
he wants to do. However, it is not fully clear what the meaning is. The
English translations indicate the range of possibilities: serpent (also
S-G, NAB), "Serpent" (with capital S: TT), "Dragon" (Mft), or sea monster.
Since poisonous sea-serpents did not live in the Mediterranean, most
scholars think that this is the sea monster, called Rahab (Isa 51.9;
Psa 89.10; Job 9.13; 26.12) and Leviathan (Isa 27.1; Psa 74.14). On the
other hand, except for Isa 27.1, these passages do not have the Hebrew
word nāḥāsh which is used here, whereas this word and the word for bite
are both used in Amos 5.19: bitten by a snake. The translator will have
to make his translation on the basis of what makes sense in his language.
If it is possible to speak of a sea monster, it may still be necessary to
add a cultural note such as is given in TEV: "It was believed that the
sea was inhabited by a great monster. This creature, like all others, was
regarded as under God's control." In some languages there may be some
fearful creature in the sea, and it may be possible to use that here.
Often, however, it is necessary to use the general term for "snake."

9.4

And though they go into captivity before their enemies,/If they are
taken away into captivity by their enemies. The idea is that even if enemies capture them and drive whole groups of them away like herds of cattle
to another country, under their protection and under the protection of the
god of that country, there will be no escape from the Lord. If there is a
specific term for herding or driving cattle or other animals, the translation might be "if they are driven into captivity (like cattle) by their
enemies" (compare TT) or "if their enemies drive them into captivity
(like cattle)." If there is no such word for herding animals, then a more
general word like "lead" or "take away" can be used.

There I will command the sword, and it shall slay them;/I will order
them to be put to death. It is clear that the sword is the means used to

kill the people, but it is not clear who will do the killing. Almost certainly it is not the enemies who captured the people. For English and many other languages the TEV translation is good: I will order them to be put to death; other possibilities: "I will order people to kill them with the sword" or perhaps "I will make/cause that they perish through the sword (or: through violence/war)."

And I will set my eyes upon them for evil and not for good."/I am determined to destroy them, not to help them." In Hebrew "to set the eye upon someone" normally means "to look after somebody" or "to take care of someone" so that for good is part of the normal meaning. Here the expression "set the eye upon" has just the opposite meaning. I will set my eyes indicates a determination of the Lord; good means "help" and evil means "destruction" in this particular context. It is very unlikely that a literal translation will make sense. It will be necessary to use some kind of equivalent picture or to remove the metaphor and translate the meaning directly as in TEV.

RSV	TEV
5 The Lord, GOD of hosts,	5 The Sovereign LORD Almighty
he who touches the earth	touches the earth,
and it melts,	and it quakes;
and all who dwell in	all who live there mourn.
it mourn,	The whole world rises and
and all of it rises like	falls like the Nile River.
the Nile,	6 The LORD builds his home in
and sinks again, like	the heavens,
the Nile of Egypt;	and over the earth he puts
6 who builds his upper chambers	the dome of the sky.
in the heavens,	He calls for the waters of
and founds his vault upon	the sea
the earth;	and pours them out on the
who calls for the waters of	earth.
the sea,	His name is the LORD!
and pours them out upon	
the surface of the	
earth--	
the LORD is his name.	

Verses 5-6 are the last of four pieces of a hymn[1] which are found at various places in Amos (1.2; 4.13; 5.8-9). This piece comes between two sections of the book where the Lord is speaking. But he is not speaking here, and the transition should be clear and natural in translation. In some languages it will be important to say "Amos said" or "Amos then said," etc.

This passage should be translated in the same style as the three earlier hymn passages. All of them should be read over together in translation to make sure that they fit together smoothly. The long Hebrew sentence in verses 5-6 will have to be broken into several shorter sentences.

Section heading. The translator should use a section heading here only if he is using one for the other pieces of the hymn as well. In that case the wording should be similar.

9.5

The Lord, God of hosts,/The Sovereign Lord Almighty. See 3.13.

He who touches the earth and it melts, and all who dwell in it mourn, /touches the earth, and it quakes; all who live there mourn. Various English translations say that the earth melts (also S-G, TT, NAB), but in many languages this is impossible even in poetry! Verse 5 describes the effects of an earthquake, and the Hebrew should be translated "tremble" (Mft) or quakes (compare also the more literary "heave" of the NEB).[2]

In the Hebrew God does only one thing: he touches the earth. This causes the earth to quake, and the earthquake causes deaths for which the inhabitants of the earth mourn.[3] In some cases it may be possible to say something like "when he touches the earth, it trembles so that people mourn for those who die."

And all of it rises like the Nile, and sinks again, like the Nile of Egypt;/The whole world rises and falls like the Nile River. See 8.8, where much the same wording is used.[4] The relationship between this Hebrew line and the preceding lines is not too clear, except for the balanced parallelism (Appendix, Section 3.9). If this is a picture of the earthquake, balancing it and separated from it by the effect on people, it may be necessary to change the order in translation, putting the mourning after the earth moving like the Nile.[5]

9.6

Who builds his upper chambers in the heavens,/The Lord builds his home in the heavens. In Hebrew it is not clear what the Lord is building.[6] Most scholars understand the meaning to be "room" or "rooms."[7] The poetic picture is that of building a home, and something equivalent would make a good translation in other languages.

And founds his vault upon the earth;/and over the earth he puts the dome of the sky. Practically everybody agrees that it is a vault (also S-G, Mft) or dome which is really meant here. TEV translates the meaning clearly. (Compare also TT: "and sets the sky as a dome over the earth.") This is a useful model for many languages. However, there may be problems in others. People may have a different picture of how the earth and sky go together, and in some languages there may be no word for dome. One possibility for translation is something like "He makes the sky cover the earth."

Who calls for/He calls for. The rest of verse 6 is the same as 5.8b and, if possible, should be translated in the same way. However, in 9.6 the meaning may be destruction and punishment rather than creation (Appendix, Section 3.9).

The Lord is his name./His name is the Lord! See 4.13.

9.7-15 EPILOGUE: PUNISHMENT AND RE-CREATION OF ISRAEL

This final section of Amos consists of two subsections.[1] 9.7-10 emphasizes once more, destruction as punishment, but has, right in the middle of it, the qualification that the destruction will not be complete (verse 8b). Then 9.11-15 picks up the hint of hope in verse 8b and expands it into a promise that Israel will be brought back to God's blessing, to power and prosperity (verses 11-15).

Section heading. It may be possible to say "Destruction but Restoration" or "Restoration after Destruction" in a natural and easy way in the language, this would be a good heading for the section, whether the structure is being shown by headings or not. In most cases, however, this would be too difficult and the translator will have to search for a short, easy alternative such as "God Will Restore After He Destroys" or "God Will Bless After He Punishes." If separate headings for 9.7-10 and 9.11-15 are to be used, the heading here could be something like "The Lord Will Even Destroy His Own People."

9.7-10

This subsection, which is part of the closing section of the book, has many links with 9.1-4, the closing section of the main part of the book. Some of the vocabulary of verses 1-4 is taken up again in verses 7-10: evil in verse 4 occurs again in verse 10; I will set my eyes upon them (verse 4) is similar to verse 8 (Behold, the eyes of the Lord God are upon...); I will command (verses 3 and 4) is taken up again in verse 9; there may also be a relationship between shake as related to parts of the temple (verse 1) and shake as related to a sieve in verse 9, in spite of the difference of the Hebrew words.[2]

The main point in this section is that Israel's special position as God's people will not save it from punishment. It is no different from other nations.

The subsection can be divided naturally into two paragraphs (verses 7-8 and 9-10), or into three (with verse 8c, But I will not destroy all the descendants of Jacob, as the second of the three paragraphs).

9.7-8

RSV	TEV
7 "Are you not like the Ethiopians to me, O people of Israel?" says the LORD. "Did I not bring up Israel from the land of Egypt, and the Philistines from Caphtor and the Syrians from Kir? 8 Behold, the eyes of the Lord GOD are	7 The LORD says, "People of Israel, I think as much of the people of Sudan as I do of you. I brought the Philistines from Crete and the Syrians from Kir, just as I brought you from Egypt. 8 I, the Sovereign LORD, am watching this

[179]

upon the sinful kingdom, and I will destroy it from the surface of the ground; except that I will not utterly destroy the house of Jacob," says the LORD.	sinful kingdom of Israel, and I will destroy it from the face of the earth. But I will not destroy all the descendants of Jacob.

9.7

Says the Lord./The Lord says. The Lord is speaking again after a section in which he has not been speaking. It may be useful to introduce the speaker immediately, as in TEV.

O people of Israel?"/"People of Israel. The position of this expression depends on what is natural in the receptor language.

"Are you not like the Ethiopians to me...Did I not bring up Israel from the land of Egypt, and the Philistines from Caphtor and the Syrians from Kir?/I think as much of the people of Sudan as I do of you. I brought the Philistines from Crete and the Syrians from Kir, just as I brought you from Egypt. The emotional force here is very strong. God is telling the people of Israel that they are not so special after all. He has done as much for other people as he has done for them. Israel is put on the same level as the most distant and despised people (the Ethiopians) and is grouped with its worst enemies (Philistines and Syrians). It is important to try to get this emotional force in the translation.

The Hebrew questions both require "Yes" as an answer. The meaning is given well in TEV. On translating such rhetorical questions, see 3.3. TEV has translated entirely as statements and changed the order to make the comparison easier. In some cases it would be good to use combinations like "I brought the Philistine people from Crete and the Syrians from Kir, didn't I?" or to translate the first question as a statement: "To me you Israelites are no better than the Ethiopians." Then the second question may be translated as a question (so TT). Another possibility is "Are you anything more to me than the Ethiopians, you Israelites? Certainly I brought Israel up from Egypt! and I also brought the Philistines from Crete and the Syrians from Kir!" The translator should select what gives the most forceful translation. Furthermore, this verse should be translated in such a way that the relationship between it and the following verse is clear (see below).

Did I not bring up Israel/I brought you. The Hebrew represents God as though he were speaking about the people rather than to them. See the discussion of this in 4.11,12.

Ethiopians/people of Sudan. NEB takes over the Hebrew word as "Cushites," but all other modern English translations (except TEV) and some ancient translations[3] use the more meaningful Ethiopians, which is approximately correct. Since the Nubian tribes of Northern Sudan are also included, it is possible (but not quite as correct) to translate people of Sudan.

Caphtor/Crete. Most translations use the Hebrew name, but the meaning is probably Crete[4] (see also Mft), and that is what the translator should use.

Syrians from Kir. See 1.5.

9.8

It may be necessary to make clear the relationship of this verse to
the previous one. Verse 7 says that Israel really does not have as special
a position as it thinks, and verse 8 goes on to show that God is not going
to keep back from punishing it. The false idea that the people have a
special relationship to God is not going to save them. To show how these
ideas fit together it would be possible to say in English: "You certainly
don't think I will save you any more than the Ethiopians, do you? No, I
brought the Philistines from Crete and the Syrians from Kir, just like I
brought you up out of Egypt! In fact, as your Lord, I am watching you; I
am going to destroy your sinful nation--I'm going to sweep it off the
ground."

Behold. See 2.13; 6.14.

The eyes of the Lord God are upon/I, the Sovereign Lord, am watching.
In many languages God cannot say eyes of the Lord God, referring to himself (see 4.11,12). He can speak of "my eyes"5 or "look, the eyes of me,
the Lord God, are fixed upon..." or I...am watching. The meaning is that
God is watching because he expects wrong to be done. He does not trust
Israel. In English this feeling could be conveyed by "I am keeping my eye
on you."

The sinful kingdom,/this sinful kingdom of Israel. It is not very
clear what exactly is meant by the sinful kingdom. It may be this sinful
kingdom of Israel, which seems likely in the context, or "every sinful
kingdom," which would include Israel. A possible translation would be
"your country (or you people in Israel), which does/do evil things" or
"your sinful nation."

And I will destroy it from the surface of the ground;/and I will destroy it from the face of the earth. Some English translations use idioms
like from the face of the earth and "wipe it off the face of the earth"
(NEB; see also JB). The meaning is complete destruction so that there is
no one left on earth. There may be a similar idiom in some languages, or
else the translation could be "I will destroy you and remove you from the
earth." This should be made very strong, even though the next line contra-
dicts it. That is part of the dramatic and emotional force here.

Except that I will not uttterly destroy the house of Jacob,"/But I ,'
will not destroy all the descendants of Jacob. In the middle of this subsection, in which the Lord says that he will punish his own people, the
Israelites, comes a dramatic qualification that not everyone will be des-
troyed.6 In one way it is like a parenthesis, but should not be placed in
parentheses because it is very prominent with its central position and
the way it contrasts with what comes before and after. One way of showing
this would be to make it a separate paragraph (Translating Amos, Section
2.3). In any case, the translator should be careful to show the connection with what goes before in the translation.

The house of Jacob,"/the descendants of Jacob. In this case there
does not seem to be any particular reason for translating Jacob rather
than "Israel." Readers should not be led to think that two different
groups of people are being discussed.7

Says the Lord. TEV has omitted this, no doubt because the Lord is speaking and continues to speak. However, it helps to emphasize the dramatic contrast here and should be kept, especially if this part of the verse is in a separate paragraph. It may be better as a separate sentence: "It is I, the Lord, who says so" or "It is I, the Lord, who promises this."

9.9-10

RSV	TEV
9 "For lo, I will command, and shake the house of Israel among all the nations as one shakes with a sieve, but no pebble shall fall upon the earth. 10 All the sinners of my people shall die by the sword, who say, 'Evil shall not overtake or meet us.'	9 "I will give the command and shake the people of Israel like grain in a sieve. I will shake them among the nations to remove all who are worthless. 10 The sinners among my people will be killed in war-- all those who say, 'God will not let any harm come near us.'"

Whether or not the translation has a separate paragraph for the last part of the previous verse, there should probably be one here. The Lord continues to show how his own people will be punished.

9.9

"For lo. The Hebrew word is the same as for behold (see 2.13).

I will command,/"I will give the command. On the need to say to whom the command was given, see 6.11. Here again it is probably the enemy: "I will command the enemy and have/make/let them shake the people..."

And shake the house of Israel...as one shakes (Hebrew: as is shaken) with a sieve, but no pebble shall fall upon the earth./and shake the people of Israel like grain in a sieve. I will shake them...to remove all who are worthless. In order to translate meaningfully, one must decide what the picture is and with what it is being compared. The Hebrew word for sieve probably refers to a coarse type of sieve in which stones are kept while the grain passes through.8 The same type of sieve was also used by bricklayers, who separated the larger stones from the fine sand which they used for mortar. The picture used here could therefore be based on either grain or sand.9 It does not really matter which picture the translator chooses, since the important point is that not one of the stones gets through the sieve. They will all be caught and then discarded.

God is commanding the enemy to treat Israel like this: none of the sinners among the people of Israel will escape punishment, just as no stone gets through the sieve. It may be possible to translate "I will shake/sift the people of Israel like someone shakes sand (or: grain) in a sieve, through which not a single stone falls to the ground. I will shake/sift them to remove the bad people from among them."

Among all the nations/among the nations. This phrase is difficult to make fit in a meaningful way. Probably the best solution is to translate

something like "...when/as they (will) live among (other) nations..."
This phrase could be related to "shake/sift" in either of the restructured sentences suggested above.

9.10

By the sword,/in war--. See 4.10.
Who say,/all those who say. Whether or not the first part of this
verse is combined with verse 9, the translator must be careful of the
relationship between it and what goes before. It continues the theme
begun in verse 7 that the Lord is not treating the people of Israel any
differently from the other nations in spite of the fact that they are
"my people."
It may be helpful to start a new sentence and translate something
like "You/These are the same sinners who say..."
'Evil shall not overtake or meet us (Hebrew: You will not let disaster come near us or overtake us)."/'God will not let any harm come
near us.'" If there is a problem with a quotation inside another quotation, the translation can easily say something like "that God will not let
any harm come near you."
RSV has changed the Hebrew here,[10] but in this case it would be better to follow such translations as NEB and TT ("You will not let any
harm overtake us or meet us"), except that it may be necessary to show who
the "you" refers to. The most likely reference is to God himself, which is
in keeping with the theme of 9.7-10, that Israel is wrong in thinking God
will spare it because the people are God's own people. TEV is a good model:
God will not let any harm come near us. The two verbs in Hebrew (overtake
and meet) represent two parts of the same event, and should be translated
according to what is natural and effective in the language.

9.11-15

There is a clear distinction between verses 11-12 and verses 13-15;
they are separate messages and they should be made separate paragraphs.[11]
They do, however, have one strong central theme, that after its destruction Israel will some day be restored. That restoration is described as
a political renewal in verses 11-12 and as a blessing of the land in
verses 13-15.
The Lord is the speaker throughout the section, but it is not clear
to whom he is speaking. In some languages it will be necessary to translate so that God is speaking directly to the people of Israel and address-
ing them as "you."
The contrast between this section and the previous one (except for
verse 8c) is very great, and the translation may need to show this by an
expression meaning "but" or "on the other hand."
Depending on the style being used for Amos, it may be good to follow
TEV in translating verses 11-12 as prose and verses 13-15 as poetry.
Verse 12 is prose in Hebrew; the rest is poetry.
Section heading. If the translation is using different headings for
9.7-10 and 9.11-15, the section heading here would be "The Future Restoration of Israel," "God Restores Israel," or "God Will Bring Back Israel."

9.11-12

RSV	TEV

RSV

11 "In that day I will raise up
      the booth of David that
         is fallen
   and repair its breaches,
      and raise up its ruins,
      and rebuild it as in the
         days of old;
12 that they may possess the
      remant of Edom
      and all the nations who
         are called by my name,"
      says the LORD who does this.

TEV

THE FUTURE RESTORATION OF ISRAEL
      11 The LORD says, "A day is
coming when I will restore the
kingdom of David, which is like a
house fallen into ruins. I will
repair its walls and restore it. I
will rebuild it and make it as it
was long ago. 12 And so the people
of Israel will conquer what is left
of the land of Edom and all the nations that were once mine," says
the LORD, who will cause this to
happen.

9.11

The Lord says. The Hebrew does not mention the speaker at the beginning of this passage but only in verse 12. However, since verse 11 starts
a new section and verse 10 closes by quoting other speakers, it may be
important to indicate the speaker here rather than waiting for the end of
verse 12.

"In that day/"A day is coming. See 2.16. Here the meaning of that day
changes from "the day when the Lord will punish" to "the day when the
Lord/I will bless."

I will raise up the booth (or: hut) of David that is fallen/when I
will restore the kingdom of David, which is like a house fallen into ruins.
"Hut," of course, is a picture to which the kingdom is probably being compared. The point of similarity is almost certainly fallen. David's kingdom is now destroyed, broken down, like an old broken down building.12
The Kingdom of David refers to the people of Israel at the highest point
of their political and military power.

In English it is more natural to translate "hut" as house: "I will
restore David's fallen house" (NEB). TEV has made the comparison clear
in every way, which is what most translations need to do.

Kingdom of David may be difficult to translate meaningfully without
destroying the emotive overtones in the Hebrew. It is, of course, possible
to translate in a non-poetic way like "I will cause (you) the people of
Israel to become great/powerful again like they/you were in the time of
their/your King David. Now they/you are like a house that is in ruins
(or: has been broken down/destroyed by war)." A more forceful translation
might be "The/your great nation/kingdom of which David was king is now
like a house in ruins, but I will build it/you up again."

And repair its breaches, and raise up its ruins, and rebuild it as
in the days of old;/I will repair its walls and restore it. I will rebuild it and make it as it was long ago. In many languages it would be
more natural to say that walls are repaired rather than "I will repair
the gaps in its walls" (TT). In others, however, it is normal to say
that "gaps" or "holes" are repaired and not the walls. This verse has a

number of overlapping pictures of repair and restoration (repair, restore, rebuild, make it as it was), some of which may have to be combined in translation.

9.12

That they may possess the remnant of Edom and all the nations/And so the people of Israel will conquer what is left of the land of Edom and all the nations. The result of restoring the kingdom is that Israel's military and political power will be extended once more over its original territory. The Hebrew makes this clause a continuation of the sentence in verse 11, but it is often better to start a new sentence with something like And so...

Who they refers to is not clear in Hebrew. They could be the kings descended from David, but it is probably better to interpret them as the Israelites in general: the people of Israel (compare Mft: "the people" and TT: "his people").

The remnant of Edom means what is left of the land of Edom or "Edom's remaining territory" (TT) or "Edom, down to the last fragment (or: little bit)."

All the nations probably goes with the remnant of, that is, "what is left of all the nations/countries."[13]

Who are called by my name (Hebrew: over whom my name is called),"/ that were once mine."[14] TEV has the correct meaning. (Compare NEB: "who were once named mine"). It is also possible to say "which once belonged to me." However, in translation this should not sound like the people of Israel will be conquering countries which once belonged to God, thus taking away from God what belonged to him. TEV unfortunately could give this impression. The meaning is that under King David these countries had once been conquered by Israel, and because the Israelites who ruled them were God's people, these countries also belonged to the Lord. A translation could run something like: "And so, the/you people of Israel will (be able to) conquer again what is left of the country of Edom and of all the other countries you once ruled for me."

Says the Lord who does this./says the Lord, who will cause this to happen. See 1.5. In this case the expression says the Lord should not be left out even if the speaker has been named at the beginning of verse 11. Says the Lord is strengthened by who does this, which contributes to the climax as the book nears the end. One way of capturing the effect in English would be to say "That is what the Lord says--and that is what he will do."

9.13-15

RSV	TEV

13 "Behold, the days are coming,"
        says the LORD,
    "when the plowman shall
        overtake the reaper
    and the treader of grapes
        him who sows the seed;
	13 "The days are coming," says
	        the LORD,
	    "when grain will grow faster
	        than it can be harvested,
	    and grapes will grow faster
	        than the wine can be made.

[185]

the mountains shall drip
    sweet wine,
  and all the hills shall
    flow with it.
14 I will restore the fortunes
    of my people Israel,
  and they shall rebuild the
    ruined cities and
    inhabit them;
they shall plant vineyards and
    drink their wine,
  and they shall make gardens
    and eat their fruit.
15 I will plant them upon their
    land,
  and they shall never again
    be plucked up
  out of the land which I
    have given them,"
      says the LORD your God.
	The mountains will drip with
	    sweet wine,
	  and the hills will flow
	    with it.
	14 I will bring my people back
	    to their land.
	They will rebuild their
	    ruined cities and
	    live there;
	they will plant vineyards
	    and drink the wine;
	they will plant gardens
	    and eat what they grow.
	15 I will plant my people on the
	    land I gave them,
	  and they will not be pulled
	    up again."
	The LORD your God has spoken.

This is a final piece of poetry in which economic prosperity is described as a part of the restored kingdom. If only some parts of Amos are being translated as poetry, this should probably be one of those parts (see Translating Amos, Section 5.2).

9.13

"Behold. See 2.13.
The days are coming,". See 9.11.
Says the Lord. In this section the expression indicating the speaker comes both at the beginning and at the end, as is often the case earlier in the book. See 1.3,5. In translation, says the Lord should be kept in both places if at all possible, but if it is left out it would be better to leave it out here (where there is no change of speaker) than at the end of the passage where it is also the end of the book (see below).
"When the plowman shall overtake the reaper and the treader of grapes him who sows the seed;/"when grain will grow faster than it can be harvested, and grapes will grow faster than the wine can be made. The picture here is of great fertility. The crops will grow so fast that the plowman is hardly finished breaking up the earth for sowing before the grain is already ripe for harvest.[15] This would be a picture of the speed of growth of the crops. On the other hand, the second part of the picture shows that the grapes will be so abundant that pressing them out to make wine will not be finished when sowing time arrives. This is not a picture of speed of growth but of the overwhelming quantity of crops. In many languages, these pictures are very difficult to translate as such because Hebrew farming is not the same as that in many other cultures. The use of long phrases for various farming words would be very disturbing, especially in translating as poetry.
From this point of view TEV is a very useful model, especially in its translation of the first picture: when grain will grow faster than

it can be harvested. On the other hand, it cannot be used in the translation of the second picture, since it is not the speed of growth, but the quantity of crops which is important. So in many cases, the following kind of translation will have to be made: "See, the time is coming when the fertility of the earth will make things ripe in the fields so fast that there will be no time between planting and harvest; fruit will be so abundant that no one can ever finish pressing it to make wine (or: people can never use/eat it all)."

TEV translators may have wanted to translate with a parallel thought. This is certainly legitimate, but in that case the translation should have been the other way around, making abundance the point of the first picture as well. The Hebrew can easily be understood that way: the harvest, normally ripe by April-May, is so abundant that the cutting of it is not finished until October when plowing begins.[16]

The mountains shall drip sweet wine, and all the hills shall flow with it. (Hebrew: shall melt)/The mountains will drip with sweet wine, and the hills will flow with it. The translator who consults different translations of this Hebrew picture may be rather puzzled. All agree that the mountains are connected with new or fresh wine, but whereas for some this is also true of the hills (RSV, NAB, TEV); for others the hills "wave with corn" (NEB) or "are aflow with milk" (Mft).

The problem is in the picture of the hills "melting." This is an exaggerated picture. The thought may be that the grapes will hang so heavily in the mountain vineyards that the slopes will seem to drip and flow with fresh wine. Or it may picture the juice overflowing the vats in which the wine is pressed, and flowing down the slopes of the hills so that they become soft with mud. In many languages, it will be extremely difficult to translate this picture. One solution for the first half is to say "the juice of grapes (or: ripe fruit) shall drip down the mountains where they are growing" (see NAB). Since the same meaning is in the second picture ("the hills shall melt" and certainly not "corn" or "milk"!), translations can add "and flow down the slopes," or the second part of the Hebrew picture can be left without stating it directly.

9.14

I will restore the fortunes of my people Israel,/I will bring my people back to their land. The Hebrew is not clear. Most scholars take it to mean something like "reverse the fortunes of,"[17] as in RSV (also S-G, NEB); or "I will bring about the restoration of my people Israel" (NAB, TT).[18] TEV translates the same meaning more directly: I will bring my people back to their land. Some translations may have to say "you" or "you, my people."

And they shall rebuild...and drink their wine,/They will rebuild ...and drink the wine. This is the reversal of the punishment predicted in 5.11. However, 9.14 has the addition and they shall make gardens and eat their fruit./they will plant gardens and eat what they grow.

9.15

    <u>I will plant them upon their land, and they shall never again be plucked up out of the land which I have given them,</u>"/<u>I will plant my people on the land I gave them, and they will not be pulled up again.</u>" Them does not refer back to the <u>fruit</u> or <u>gardens</u> of the preceding verse, but to <u>my people</u>, which may need to be translated as "you." The pictures of "planting" and "pulling up" people may be impossible in some languages. So the translator will have to try to replace the Hebrew picture by one which will mean "restore" or "establish." Some languages may have such lively idioms as "press your rear end on the ground." Or it may be best to translate the meaning directly: "I will let/cause you to own your own land again, the land which I gave you, and I will never again let you be taken away from it."

    <u>Says the Lord your God.</u>/<u>The Lord your God has spoken.</u> See 9.12. If a forceful translation for this expression has been used throughout the book (see the comment at 1.5), it can be used here to give a strong, ringing final note to the whole book. In some languages it will be necessary to add, "Amos said" or "Amos finished speaking."

APPENDIX

In earlier parts of this Handbook frequent reference has been made
to the way in which the book of Amos is organized. In certain instances
suggestions have been made about translations which are based partly on
an understanding of the organization. Since some of this structure has
not been noticed before and is not to be found in the standard commentaries on Amos, evidence is here given for the overall pattern of the
book and for details of those passages where the structure was part of
the reason for particular suggestions to the translator. In no case is
the present description in any way a complete discourse analysis. It
simply supports statements and suggestions in the rest of the Handbook.

1. The overall structures of Amos

The organization of the whole book was discussed in Translating
Amos, Section 2. It has a bearing on how some of the parts are understood and could be used as a basis for the wording of section headings
throughout the book.

1.1 Balanced groups of messages in Amos

First of all, Amos is made up of messages and groups of messages
which are balanced against each other in the first and last halves of
the book. Take, for example, Amos 5.1-17 as displayed in Figure 1.[1] The
first three verses (5.1-3) are about wailing, mourning, lamentation. And
so are the last two verses (5.16-17). These are placed opposite each
other in Figure 1 and are labeled F and F' respectively. Correspondingly,
G and G' have a great deal in common.

Skipping H/H' for the moment, I and I' are two parts of a piece of
hymn about God's power, broken by J: the Lord is his name. I' is about
the Lord's power to destroy (and in the context of Amos, that means
punish). I is about his power to create.[2]

The similarity between H and H' is not as great as that between
the members of the other pairs. There is a great difference in length,
and not all of H' corresponds in meaning to H. However, verses 11 and
12 are a warning to sinners, and verse 13 is perhaps a warning to the
righteous who reprove the sinners in verse 10 (more on that in Appendix
Section 3.6). Verse 7 is often interpreted as a warning (see discussion
of Amos 5.7). Thus there is the possibility of some common meaning,
which is reinforced by the position of these messages in relation to
the others of Figure 1.

F <u>5</u> Hear this word which I take ▼
up over you in lamentation, O
house of Israel:
2 "Fallen, no more to rise,
   is the virgin Israel;
forsaken on her land
   with none to raise
   her up."
3 For thus says the Lord GOD;
"The city that went forth
   a thousand
shall have a hundred
   left,
and that which went forth
   a hundred
shall have ten left
to the house of Israel."

G 4 For thus says the LORD to
   the house of Israel:
"Seek me and live;
5   but do not seek Bethel,
and do not enter into Gilgal
   or cross over to
   Beer-sheba;
for Gilgal shall surely go
   into exile,
and Bethel shall come
   to nought."

6 Seek the LORD and live,
   lest he break out
   like fire in the
   house of Joseph,
   and it devour, with
   none to quench it
   for Bethel,

16 Therefore thus says the LORD, F'
   the God of hosts, the
   Lord:
"In all the squares there
   shall be wailing;
and in all the streets
   they shall say,
   'Alas! alas!'
They shall call the farmers
   to mourning
and to wailing those who
   are skilled in
   lamentation,
17 and in all vineyards there
   shall be wailing,
for I will pass through
   the midst of you,"
       says the LORD.

                          G'

14 Seek good, and not evil,
   that you may live;
and so the LORD, the God
   of hosts,
   will be with you,
   as you have said.
15 Hate evil, and love good,
   and establish justice in
   the gate;
it may be that the LORD, the
   God of hosts,
   will be gracious to the
   remnant of Joseph.

H

7 0 you who turn justice to
    wormwood,
  and cast down right-
    eousness to the
    earth!

| 10 They hate him who reproves   H'
    in the gate,
  and they abhor him who
    speaks the truth.
11 Therefore because you trample
    upon the poor
  and take from him exactions
    of wheat,
you have built houses of hewn
    stone,
  but you shall not dwell in
    them;
you have planted pleasant
    vineyards,
  but you shall not drink
    their wine.
12 For I know how many are your
    transgressions,
  and how great are your sins--
you who afflict the righteous,
    who take a bribe,
  and turn aside the needy
    in the gate.
13 Therefore he who is prudent
    will keep silent in
    such a time;
  for it is an evil time.

I 8 He who made the Pleiades
    and Orion,
  and turns deep darkness
    into the morning,
  and darkens the day
    into night,
who calls for the waters
    of the sea,
  and pours them out
    upon the surface
    of the earth,

I'

9 who makes destruction flash
    forth against the strong,
  so that destruction comes
    upon the fortress.

J the LORD is his name,

Figure 1

[191]

The balance in Amos 5.1-17 can be displayed in another way, as in Figure 2. This time there are headings instead of the text of the RSV. These headings have been chosen to show the major similarity of content between the passages which balance each other. They have been arranged to make the balance immediately visible, F with F', etc. This kind of pattern is a very common arrangement for biblical texts, long and short.[3] It is often called chiasmus (or chiasm) or inverted parallelism. We will speak of it as patterned recursion (or balanced recursion) in inverted order.

F Lament for Israel	5.1-3
G Seek God and live (i.e. avoid destruction)	5.4-6
H Warning to sinners	5.7
I The power of God to create	5.8a
J The Lord is his name	b
I' The power of God to punish	5.9
H' Warning to sinners and righteous	5.10-13
G' Seek good and live (i.e. obtain mercy)	5.14-15
F' Lament for Israel	5.16-17

Figure 2

Figure 3 goes on to show that Amos 5.1-17 is only the peak of a much larger structure of patterned recursions. However, the balanced sections in A-E and E'-A' are longer sections than those in F-J and J'-F', and the similarity of recursion is usually not as close as it is in F/F' or G/G', sometimes it is more like the weaker H/H'. Furthermore, the piece of hymn immediately preceding F (4.13) is not matched by anything

A Prologue: the prophet	1.1-2a
B The power of God to punish [hymn]	1.2b
C Israel's special guilt among the nations	1.3--3.2
D The prophet's role and commission	3.3--4.3
E Israel doesn't learn God's lessons	4.4-12
(B¹ The power of God to create [hymn])	4.13
F Lament for Israel	5.1-3
G Seek God and avoid destruction	5.4-6
H Warning to Sinners	5.7
₿¹ I The power of God to create [hymn]	5.8
J THE LORD IS HIS NAME	
₿' I' The power of God to punish [hymn]	5.9
H' Warning to sinners and righteous	5.10-13
G' Seek good and obtain mercy	5.14-15
F' Lament for Israel	5.16-17
E' Israel relies on false security	5.18--6.14
D' The prophet's experiences	7.1--8.3
C' The punishment of Israel	8.4--9.4
B'/B¹ The power of God to punish and create [hymn]	9.5-6
A' Epilogue: punishment and re-creation	9.7-15

Figure 3

right after F', which is why it is in parentheses in Figure 3. Also, I/I' match B/B' as well as each other. And there are other difficulties in this structure. It does not all fit neatly, and some people may not find it convincing. We therefore take up these problems to see where they lead.

1.2 Some problems

1.21 The position of 3.1-2

In Figure 3, 3.1-2 is included in C because it is still about Israel's special guilt and punishment (see also the evidence in the Appendix, Section 3.2); but for that matter the whole book is about Israel's punishment, highlighted in different ways. Some English translations make this passage the beginning of the next section (see discussion of Amos 3.1-2). They do so because it begins with Hear this word, which they consider to be an expression which begins a section, and it was even used for chapter division.[4] On the other hand, it is important to notice just when the occurrences of this expression actually do come in Amos in relation to Figure 3.

3.1 Hear this word. The case under consideration. We suggest that it begins the last segment of C (Figure 3).

4.1 Hear this word. Begins the last segment of D.

5.1 Hear this word. Begins F. We will come back to this in Appendix Section 1.22.

7.16 Hear the word of the Lord. Begins the last segment of the Amaziah episode in D'.

8.4 Hear this. Begins C', the last major section of oracles in the body of the book (leaving off prologue and epilogue).

The evidence therefore indicates the possibility that this particular expression is used at the beginning of a concluding section on some level or other (reserving judgment for the moment on 5.1, which does not quite fit).

1.22 The presence of 4.13; 5.1-3 as a concluding unit

The second problem with Figure 3 is that 4.13 does not balance anything in the second half of the book of Amos. We look for a piece of hymn at 5.17 or 18, but it is not there. On the other hand, 4.13 does balance 1.2, with the contrast of create against punish (destroy), a contrast picked up in I and I' (5.8-9) and then combined in B'/B¹ (9.5-6). Obviously these pieces of hymn are structurally very important, punctuating the beginning and the end of the body of this structure and framing the peak of it, except for 4.13, which seems out of place.

Of course, it frequently happens that in otherwise very nearly balanced recursion there are elements which do not fit. However, we saw in the previous section that section F (5.1-3) began with Hear this word, in spite of the fact that there is no indication in Figure 3 that it is a closing section like the others which begin with this expression. But if we did consider that it is a closing section of some unit, then 4.13 would also fit into a balanced structure, as in Figure 4.

[193]

```
A    a  Prologue: the prophet                          1.1-2a
B      b  The power of God to punish [hymn]            1.2b
C        c  Israel's special guilt among the nations  1.3--3.2
D          d  The prophet's role and commission       3.3--4.3
E        c'  Israel doesn't learn God's lessons        4.4-12
       b'  The power of God to create [hymn]           4.13
F    a'  Conclusion: lament for Israel                 5.1-3
```

Figure 4

That would mean that each of the sections A-F (Figure 3) has a place in an overall balanced recursion pattern for the whole book, but that 4.13 does not. At the same time, each of the sections A-F plus 4.13 also has a place in a smaller balanced recursion pattern a-a' (Figure 4).

1.3 Three balanced parts in Amos

As Figure 5 shows, the presence of the closing element in 5.1-3 and the balanced structure from 1.1--5.3 suggest that we consider this to be the first part of the whole book (Figure 5). If we do so, we notice that it is followed by a second part, with the same number of items in it (7) and a balanced structure which can be seen as running in reverse order to the first part. The second part, however, coincides completely with the larger structure of the book (Figure 3) rather than having an additional set of structural relationships. The third part is also shown as having a balanced structure.

We have already seen how the expression Hear this word, or variations on it, helps to relate some of the sections in Amos. Many of the sections also begin with Thus says the Lord (God). There are two longer forms of this expression, however, and these come exactly at the beginning of the second and third parts: For thus says the Lord to the House of Israel (5.4, at the beginning of the second part) and Therefore thus says the Lord, the God of Hosts, the Lord (5.16, at the beginning of the third part).5

More important, when we take a close look at the third part, it also has a balanced structure. D' of Figure 3 breaks into three sections in Figure 5. In the third part, the final section of hymn (9.5-6) also does not balance with anything, so that it has a place in the balanced structure of the whole book but not of the part, similar to the way in which the hymn in 4.13 has a place in the balance of the part but not of the whole book. All this is shown by the difference between the capital letters and the small letters in Figure 5.

Further evidence in support of both Figure 3 and Figure 5 is to be found indirectly in the more detailed analyses of individual sections which follow. However, in these we present only part of the evidence, only what is needed to support suggestions made in the Handbook.

[Part I	Israel's guilt; the prophet's responsibility]		1.1--5.3
A	a Prologue: the prophet		1.1-2a
B	b The power of God to punish [hymn]		1.2b
C	c Israel's special guilt among the nations		1.3--3.2
D	d The prophet's role and commission		3.3--4.2
E	c Israel doesn't learn God's lessons		4.4-12
-	b The power of God to create [hymn]		4.13
F	a^1 Lament for Israel (conclusion)		5.1-3

[Part II	Possibility of salvation; Israel's peril]	5.4-15
G	d^1 Seek God and avoid destruction	5.4-6
H	c^1 Warning to sinners	5.7
I	b The power of God to create [hymn]	5.8
J	e THE LORD IS HIS NAME	
I'	b The power of God to punish [hymn]	5.9
H'	c^1 Warning to sinners and righteous	5.10-13
G'	d^1 Seek good and obtain mercy	5.14-15

[Part I'	Israel's guilt and punishment; the prophet's involvement]	5.16--9.15
F'	a^1 Lament for Israel (introduction)	5.16-17
E'	c Israel relies on false security	5.18--6.14
	⎡ f The prophet's experiences: visions	7.1-9
D'	d The prophet's role and commission	7.10-17
	⎣ f The prophet's experiences: vision	8.1-3
C'	c^2 The punishment of Israel	8.4--9.4
B'/B^1'	(b the power of God to punish and create [hymn])	9.5-6
A'	a Epilogue: punishment and re-creation	9.7-15

Figure 5. a, a^1 = opening/closing section; b = hymn to the power of God; c, c^1, c^2 = Israel's guilt and punishment; d = the prophet's role and commission; d' = the prophet's positive message; f = the prophet's vision experiences.

2. Summary of the approach

Before going on to study the structure of individual passages, the translator will need to understand the principles behind the analyses and the ways in which the structures are shown on paper. Figure 6 illustrates some of this.

First of all, in Figure 6 the translation is a literal translation of the Hebrew. Hyphens between words indicate that in Hebrew this is all one word. () indicates that a word with grammatical use has not been translated. The reference (chapter and verse) is at the right, with 5a, 5b, etc., as convenient ways of referring to the "spans" into which the text has been divided.

The way in which the text has been organized on the page is called an "exploded text," and its purpose is to make certain relationships within the text clear. The letters of the alphabet at the left also help

[195]

to show these relationships, that is, the resemblance between spans a/a',
b/b', etc.

This resemblance which we find between spans is due to the fact that
there are "recursion ties" between them, and that the recursion is
"patterned." "Ties" are individual instances of "recursion," or repetition, on any level. In the cases of Figures 3 and 5 they were usually
major themes. In Figure 6 they are specific words and meanings, like
"seek," "live," "Bethel," etc.

In Figure 6 some of the recursion ties are "patterned" and others
are not. "Seek" in verses 4, 5a, and 6 provides a tie between each pair
of these lines, but it is only the one between verses 4 and 6 which fits
into a pattern. What creates the pattern in Figure 6 is the fact that
the text can be divided up into spans which show regularity in the way
the ties are arranged. In the case of Figures 3 and 5 the spans are
usually messages or groups of messages. The spans of Figure 6 are short
groups of words, but the principle is the same.

The patterned ties of Figure 6 can be isolated and presented as in
Figure 7. The words which have been left out of Figure 7 do not enter
into the forming of this pattern, although they do enter into other
structures of the text, ones not being noted here, like grammatical structures and logical ones.

```
a  Seek-me and-live;                                        5.4
   b  and-not seek Bethel,                                  5a
      c  and-Gilgal not shall-you-enter                     b
         d  and-Beersheba not shall-you-go-over-to          c
      c' for Gilgal () shall-surely-go-into-exile           d
   b'  and-Bethel shall-be for-nothing.                     e
a'  Seek () the-Lord and-live6                              6
```

Figure 6


```
a  Seek-me and-live                                         5.4
   b  and-      Bethel                                       5a
      c  Gilgal      (verb of motion)                        b
         d  (place name)      (verb of motion)               c
      c' Gilgal      (verb of motion)                        d
   b'  and-Bethel                                            e
a' Seek the-Lord and-live                                   6
```

Figure 7

But there is more patterned recursion in this text than Figure 7
shows. Some of it can be seen in Figure 8, which has an exploded text
with shorter spans. To the left of the text there is also a "graph"
consisting of "tie lines" and "span brackets" organized to show other
structural relationships than those explicit in the exploded text. The
tie lines are those in column 1. The span brackets are in column 2. The
span brackets enclose the same spans as those of Figure 7, and the tie

[196]

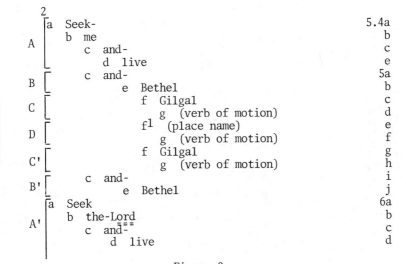

Figure 8

lines show the recursion ties of Figure 7. But in the exploded text of Figure 8 abcd/abcd is clearly a patterned set of recursions, a regular distribution of ties. So are ce/ce and fg/f¹g/fg. These patterns have the same order of ties in both occurrences, while the order in Figure 7 is inverted in the second half. It is possible to see the patterns of Figure 8 in Figure 7, and the pattern of Figure 7 in Figure 8, but each display is based on a different length of span and makes it easier to see one or the other of the patterns which exist there together. Whether this passage is displayed as in Figure 7 or as in Figure 8 depends on which level of structure is more important to show, but both are equally true of the text.

Some of the information in Figure 8 (and more) can, of course, be incorporated in Figure 6 by the use of span brackets. This is done in Figure 9. This makes explicit that there is a span, consisting of the shorter spans cdc', in which there is a recursion of verbs of motion. There is a larger span, surrounding and including the span with the verbs of motion, which contains recursions of place names. The span with recursions of place names breaks down into two spans, one of which is a Warning and the other a Threat. Surrounding these are spans consisting of Injunction (I) and Promise (P). These may be further abstracted as a sequence of spans with the pattern ABA, in which A = positive injunction, and B = negative injunction or pronouncement.

In Figures 5, 7 and 9, the symbol ' was used to distinguish one member of a recursion pair from another. This is convenient when the pattern is a simple one like these, but in Figure 8 it would be difficult to distinguish the four cases of c in this way, or the three cases of f or g. The symbol ', therefore, is usually not used in displays. In any case, its use is optional. The information about recursion is contained in the use of the letter of the alphabet or the end points in a tie line of a graph.

[197]

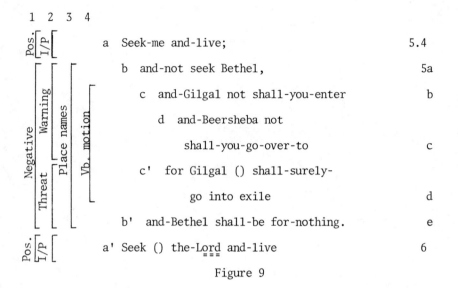

Figure 9

In Figure 8 a superscript number was used: f[1]. This does have signif-icance. The letter indicates that there is a recursion of something (in this case "proper name"). The superscript indicates that there is some structurally significant difference to this recursion (in this case the fact that it is not Gilgal).

Sometimes there is a pattern created by the structure where there is no semantic recursion. This is illustrated in Figure 10. In this case b = punishment and c = sinner who is to be punished. b[+] indicates a con-tinuation of a previous b (in this case 1.5f) rather than a recursion in a strict sense. This modification of the usual recursion pattern occurs from time to time. On the level of the exploded text at the right there

```
x              b   And-I-will-break                    1.5a
                   c   the-bar-of-Damascus,             b
               b   and-cut-off                          c
                   c   the-ruler from-Biqat-aven,       d
                   c   and-the-holder-of the-scepter
                           from-Beth-eden;              e
               b   so-they-will-go-exiled,              f
                   c   [will] the-people-of Syria,      g
y             b⁺  to-Kir,                               h
```

Figure 10

is no problem. However, as the pattern of tie lines in the graph makes clear, and as in so many other cases in Amos, there is a higher level recursion pattern as well. The end points of most of the tie lines also give no problem: Damascus/Syria, cut off/send to exile, Biqat-aven/Beth-eden. However, I will break/to Kir is not so clear. Both spans represent punishment, to be sure, but that was already reflected by b in the exploded text. There seems to be nothing more they have in common except for structural position. They complete the pyramid. They occupy corresponding places in it. That is the meaning of the notation x/y. It means that no claim is made for a semantic recursion on this level, but that these spans form part of the pattern just the same. The tie is purely structural.

Most of the work on discourse structure reflected in this Appendix is related in one way or another to recursion patterns. However, some sections are also analyzed for their logical relationships, with spans marked CONDITION/CONSEQUENCE, MEANS/RESULT,[7] etc. At other times, spans have been categorized thematically as with Threat/Warning or place names (Figure 9).

A table of notation conventions is included at the end of the Appendix for ease of reference.

3. Passages referred to in the text

Each passage where the discourse structure has a bearing on the recommendations to translators will now be discussed. The passages will be taken up in biblical order, except where two or more passages are discussed together for purposes of comparison.

3.1 Israel's crimes and punishment (2.6b-16)

Understanding the organization of this passage helps a great deal to see what its message is and how to translate it. (See also the discussion of the text under 2.9-13 and the restructuring in Translating Amos, Section 2.3.) In its organization it identifies social crimes with sin against the Lord and indicates that these are examples of Israel's breaking the special relationship which she had with him. The organization also throws light on the nature of the punishment. Whereas Israel with the Lord was strong, Israel without the Lord will be weak.

The main features of the organization can be seen in Figure 11. Two main structures are woven together. One is the listing of Israel's crimes of two types: social crimes and religious crimes. The list begins with two social crimes and ends with two religious crimes, and in the middle they are interrelated.

The other structure is an inverted recursion pattern ABCDC'B'A'. A reminds Israel of the salvation of its ancestors from Egypt and the conquering of Canaan. The Lord did this, and Israel is reminded that her strength comes from him as a result of the special relationship between him and his people. A' promises punishment, in a form which is just the opposite of the strength described in A. Israel has broken her part of the special relationship and will not have the Lord with her. This will leave her weak.

[199]

Crime 1		Selling people to slavery for trivial debts	2.6b
Crime 2		Oppressing the poor	2.7a
Crime 3		Abuse of women, sex	2.7b
Crime 3a		Abuse of God (result of Crime 3)	2.7c
Crime 4a		Abuse of sacred places (location of Crime 4)	2.8a
Crime 4		Exploiting the system of loans to the poor	2.8b
Crime 5a		Abuse of house of God (location of Crime 5)	2.8c
Crime 5		Exploiting the system of fines	2.8d
	A	Salvation: Israel plus the Lord is strong	2.9-10
	B	Prophets chosen by the Lord	2.11a
	C	Nazirites chosen by the Lord	2.11b
	D	Isn't that so?...says the Lord	2.11c
Crime 6a	C'	Nazirites made to fail by Israel	2.12a
Crime 7a	B'	Prophets made to fail by Israel	2.12b
	A'	Punishment: Israel without the Lord is weak	2.13-16

Figure 11. Crimes 1, 2, etc., are social injustices; Crimes 3a, 4a, etc., are crimes against God.

Israel's silencing of the prophets (B') is balanced against God's choosing the prophets (B); Israel's corrupting the Nazirites (C') is balanced against God's choosing the Nazirites (C). Here the structure made up of crimes is linked with the inverted recursion, tying together the whole catalogue of Israel's sin with the breaking of the special relationship.

Then, in climactic position, at the center of the balanced pattern, comes a very personal expression pressing the point home: "Isn't that right, Israel? The Lord is saying this."

3.2 Amos 3.1-2 as the conclusion to 1.2--3.2

In earlier sections of this Appendix (1.21 and 1.22) we pointed out that hear this word introduces a concluding section. In this section we show how that conclusion ties in with what has gone before. Spans in 3.1-2 match, in reverse order, different length spans in 1.2--2.16, sometimes using the same wording. This is shown in Figure 12.

The pattern is shown, as usual, by the capital letters. The E/E' in the middle could be equally well called A/A'. The center and the ends of the pattern have the same theme, and it is that of the Lord's accusation and punishment.

A	Word spoken against you	"The Lord roars...	1.2
B	Families of the earth	Damascus	1.3-5
		Gaza	1.6-8
		Tyre	1.9-10
		Edom	1.11-12
		Ammon	1.13-15
		Moab	2.1-3
C	Family brought up from Egypt	Judah	2.4-5
		Broke covenant	2.4
		Israel	2.6-16
		"brought...Egypt"	2.9-11a
D	Oh sons of Israel	"Oh sons of Israel"	2.11b
A E	Word spoken against you	Account of crimes and punishment	2.12-16
A' E'	Word spoken against you	"Hear this word that the Lord has spoken against you	3.1a
D'	Oh sons of Israel	Oh sons of Israel,	3.1b
C'	Family brought up from Egypt	against the whole family which I brought up out of the land of Egypt,	3.1c
		'You only have I known	3.2a
B'	Families of the earth	of all the families of the earth;	3.2b
A'	Word spoken against you	therefore I will punish you for all your iniquities.'"	3.2c

Figure 12

"Word spoken against you" is the wording of 3.1a. The other cases which balance it and each other are all related to the idea of the Lord speaking against Israel.

"Oh sons of Israel" has the same wording in both cases, and "I brought up out of the land of Egypt" is almost the same. Judah is specifically included in the grouping of families brought up from Egypt because its sin is specifically breaking its relationship with the Lord (2.4), as is emphasized for Israel in more detail (see Appendix, Section 3.1).

"All the families of the earth" (3.2b) is balanced by the messages to the non-Jewish nations.

Argument	Relationship	Text (RSV)	
A	Harmony. Man's rel. to man shown by agreement	Do two walk together unless they have an appointment?	3.3
B	Disaster. Lion's rel. to animal shown by roaring	Does a lion roar in the forest when he has no prey?	3.4a
		Does a young lion cry out from his den, if he has taken nothing?	3.4b
C	Disaster. Superior's rel. to inferior shown by trapping	Does a bird fall in a snare on the earth, when there is no trap for it?	3.5a
		Does a snare spring up from the ground, when it has taken nothing?	3.5b
D	Disaster. Man's rel. to man shown by trumpet sound	Is a trumpet blown in a city, and the people are not afraid?	3.6b

General premise:
1. Nothing happens without a reason; 2. nothing happens without a sign

Figure 13 - continued

Figure 13 - continued

Argument	Relationship	Text (RSV)	
Specific premise: 1. Disaster happens because God acts; 2. Prophecy is the sign of God's action	C' Disaster. Superior's [=God's] rel. to inferior shown by disaster/revelation to the prophets	Does evil befall a city, unless the Lord has done it?	3.6b
		Surely the Lord God does nothing, without revealing his secret to his servants the prophets.	3.7
Conclusion: 1. When God brings disaster people fear; 2. when God speaks, people must prophesy	B' Disaster. Lion's [=God's] rel. to man shown by roaring [=warning]	The Lion has roared; who will not fear?	3.8a
	A' Harmony. God's rel. to the prophet shown by the prophet's obedience	The Lord God has spoken; who can but prophesy?	3.8b

Figure 13

From the standpoint of Figures 3 and 5 the structure of this conclusion includes a little too much because it seems to have 3.2c balanced against 1.2, which we feel on other grounds is in a separate main section. It could, of course, be taken as the conclusion to the conclusion, not balanced against 1.2.

But that is not particularly important. What is important is to see that the message to Israel has a frame around it and that such a frame helps to spell out its theological implications. Preceding the message to Israel is the one to Judah, where the sin is specifically that of breaking the special relationship to the Lord. Following the message to Israel comes this conclusion which emphasizes Israel's special guilt because of its special relationship to the Lord; it is because of that relationship that Israel will be particularly punished for its sin.

3.3 The prophetic role (3.3-8)

In the discussion of the text under 3.3-8, there is an indication of some of the problems in the organization of this section. We will not repeat those points here. Instead, Figure 13 shows how the ideas are organized on three levels.

At the right there is the translation of the text, with its series of nine questions and a statement. In the middle column are some of the themes and their organization into a recursion pattern in inverted order.

Then, in the first column is the logical relationship of the ideas. The first part is a series from natural life, and they illustrate the general premise that nothing happens without a reason, and nothing happens without a sign. Then this general idea is made more specific in the next grouping. It is not just that "nothing" happens; disaster happens. And it is not just that there is a reason; God acts. This does not mean that God is the reason for the disasters in the previous questions but that the argument is building up from a general illustration to a more specific illustration. Then comes the conclusion. God has brought disaster, so people should be afraid; at the same time, God has spoken, and his prophets must carry his message.

3.4 The laments (5.1-3, 5.16-17)

We present these two passages together (Figure 14) because they are short and they balance each other in the overall structure (Appendix, Figures 3, 5). There may be some question about the display of 3a-g in the first passage. "To-the-house-of Israel" (3g) is clearly a recursion of "Oh-house-of-Israel" (1d). "Will-have-left one-hundred" (3c) and "shall-have-left ten" (3f) we consider to be recursions of "she-has-fallen" (2a) and "she-has-been-abandoned on-her-land" (2d) as specific instances of a more general picture. That is, "fallen" and "abandoned" are general, while "all but one hundred will be killed" and "all but ten will be killed" are specific. x/y are not considered to be recursions except that they occupy similar places in the structure. x/x are recursions, of course, as are y/y. There is an implicit [to Israel] (3d),[8] as seen both from the meaning and from the overall pattern. So the organization of 3b-g is the reverse of 1d--2e.

The pattern of 5.16-17 should be clear.

```
    ┌  a  Hear () the-word this [which]              5.1a
    │     b  I am-lifting-up against-you                b
    └  a  [as] a-funeral-song,                          c
       ┌  b  oh-house-of Israel:                         d
       │     c  She-has-fallen;                          2a
       └     x  not she-shall-add to-rise,               b
       ┌  b  the-virgin-of Israel;                       c
       │     c  she-has-been-abandoned on-her-land,      d
       └     x  there-is-none-raising her-up.            e
    a  For thus says-the-Lord God:                      3a
       ┌     y  the-city, the one-sending-
       │                    forth a-thousand,            b
       │     c  it-will-have-left one-hundred            c
       └ [b  to Israel];                                 d
       ┌     y  the-one-sending-forth one-hundred        e
       │     c  shall-have-left ten                      f
       └  b  to-the-house-of Israel.                     g


              *  *  *  *  *  *  *  *  *


    ┌ a  Therefore, thus says-the-Lord,               5.16a
    │ a  the-God of hosts,                               b
    └ a  the-Lord:                                       c
      b  In all-of places                                d
         c  [there-is] wailing,                          e
      b  and-in-all-of the-streets                       f
         c  they-say "Alas, alas!"                       g
         d  and-they-call the-farmer                     h
         c  to mourning,                                 i
         c  and-wailing-to                               j
         d  the-knowers-of                               k
         c  lamentation;                                 l
      b  and-in-all-of vineyards                         17a
         c  [there-is] the-wailing,                      b
      b  for I-will-pass through-your-midst,             c
    a  says-the-Lord.                                    d
```

Figure 14

3.5 Seek...and live (5.4-6, 5.14-15)

We have already discussed For thus says the Lord to the house of
Israel (Appendix, Section 1.22) as the opening of Part 2. It does not fit
into any balanced pattern within 5.4-6 or between that passage and 5.14-
15 or anywhere within the book. Otherwise, the two passages under consideration, which balance each other in the overall structure of the book
(Appendix, Figures 3, 5) pattern as in Figure 15 on the level with which
we are working (for other ways of looking at part of 5.4-6, see Appendix,
Section 2). They are structurally somewhat different in spite of their
great similarity, and they complement each other in meaning, the first
being a negative statement (avoid destruction) and the second being
a positive statement (obtain mercy).

[205]

The recursions in these passages are so strong that they do not need justification except for a few details. The display of e and f is somewhat arbitrary. d$^+$ is in both occurrences a continuation of d, rather than a recursion in a strict sense.

Note that for 5.4-6 there is a recursion pattern which could not be seen when the shorter part of this passage was used for illustration in Appendix, Section 2. The words "house of God" form the place name Bethel. In the earlier discussion we emphasized the recursion of the place name. Now the wording "house of" takes on additional importance as well because of the recursion in house of Joseph in 6d. The meaning of Bethel also shifts. In the lines labeled b it means the place of worship; in those labeled b' it means the people of Israel.

We have included some of the logical relationships of these passages in the graphs at the left of the exploded text. These vary between the two passages in different ways from the variation in recursion pattern.

1   2   3   4

		P.	a	Seek-me and-live;	5.4
			b	and-not seek Bethel [=house-of-God],	5a
			c	and-Gilgal not shall-you-enter	b
				d and-Beersheba not shall-you-go-over-to,	c
			c	for Gilgal () shall-surely-go	
				into-exile,	d
			b	and-Bethel [=house-of-God] shall-be for-nothing.	e
		P.	a	Seek () the-Lord and-live,	6a
				e lest he advance	b
				f like-a-fire,	c
			b^1 oh-house-of Joseph [=people-of Israel],	d
				e and-it-consume,	e
				f and-there-is-none-extinguishing [it]	f
			b^1 for-Bethel [=house-of-God/people-of-Israel].	g

G Seek God, avoid destruction (neg.)

CONDITION — NEGATIVE

CONSEQUENCE — NEGATIVE

*   *   *   *   *   *   *   *   *

Figure 15 - continued

[206]

Figure 15 - continued

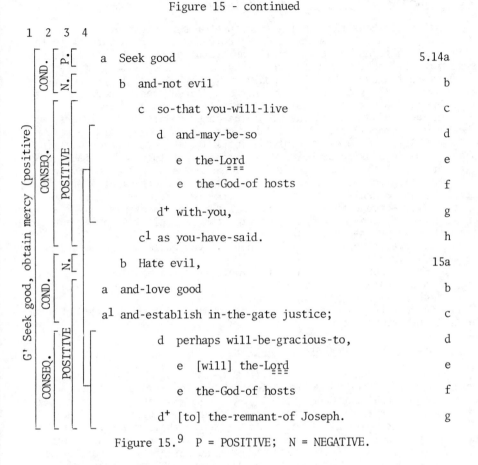

Figure 15.⁹ P = POSITIVE; N = NEGATIVE.

The first passage breaks neatly into two parts which could be re-stated as "If you seek God (CONDITION), he will not destroy you (NEGA-TIVE CONSEQUENCE)" (column 2). In the next column the CONDITION and the CONSEQUENCE each have an internal structure.

The second passage, on the other hand, breaks into CONDITION and CONSEQUENCE in a more complex way (again column 2), with two pairs of the sequence CONDITION/CONSEQUENCE. The internal structures are again different.

In addition to the recursion of seek...and live between the two passages, note the recursion of Joseph. In the first passage the house of Joseph [=people of Israel] is being consumed by fire. In the second, the Lord will be kind to what is left of it. This progression here in the center of the book is picked up again in the epilogue (Amos 9.8b and 11-15).

3.6 Warning to sinners and righteous (5.10-13)

Figure 16 shows the complex structure of this passage.

The top and bottom sections (verses 10 and 13) are a warning to the wise, the righteous who try to tell the truth in court. According to the structural balance, "the wise" who is warned to "keep silent" (verse 10) is "him who reproves" and who "speaks uprightly" (verse 13). The "evil time" (verse 13) is the time when they are "hated" and "abhorred" (verse 10). The reason for keeping silent (verse 13) is in verse 10.

Inside the warning to the righteous comes a warning to sinners, with the result in the middle (5.11g-n) between two statements of the reason.

So 5.10-13 has a very involved, intricate structure which gives the passage the impression of being very sloppily put together if it is read with the expectation that the flow of ideas moves smoothly and logically from one thing to the next in a straight line. The organization is not a straight-line organization. It is more like the circular ripples which appear after someone throws a stone in water, and as people read it they cross configurations of ripples, meeting the same circles coming out from the middle which they crossed going in to the middle.

There are three lines which do not fit very well in the recursion pattern displayed:

a	for I-know-[that] many-[are] your-transgressions	5.12a	
a	and great-[are] your sins		b
a	oh-afflictors-of		c

It may be that they are part of an additional structure we have not seen or that they simply do not fit.

3.7 False reliance on armies (6.12-14)

Figure 17 shows the nearly perfect symmetry of this whole passage taken together, which is evidence for considering it one section (see the discussion of the text under 6.12-14). Span 13d is not a recursion, but its presence contributes to the pattern. Spans 14d, e are out of normal place in the grammatical structure to emphasize their importance in the peak of the final pattern. Note that there are five recursion patterns in this series, each of them with the same number of ties (four) except the middle one (13a-c) which has two. The final pattern (verse 14) has some variations in keeping with its climactic character. It has two spans at the middle of the pattern and two at the end.

3.8 Nobody can escape (9.1-4)

In Figure 18 the pattern of the major structural divisions can be seen in the graph, with a balanced pattern of directions and judgments the center of which is between verses 2 and 3.

3.9 Power of God to punish and create (9.5-6)

In Figure 19 the meaning of the segment labeled "Punish" (9.6g-m) is debatable. It is identical to a segment in 5.8, which is there interpreted as part of God's creative activity (Figures 3, 5). In 5.8 it was considered to mean his creation of water, the oceans, etc., because of the

Warning to sinners and righteous

To sinners

To righteous

To right

```
1 2 3        a  They-hate in-the-gate                        5.10a
             b    the-reprover,                                  b
             b    and a-speaker blameless                        c
             a  they-abhor.                                      d
               c  Therefore,                                    11a
             a  because-of your-trampling                        b
        x    b1 upon the-poor                                    c
        y    x  and a-tax-of grain                               d
             a  you-take                                         e
             b1 from-him,                                        f
                   d  houses-of-hewn-stones                      g
                   e  you-built                                  h
                   e1 but-not dwell                              i
                   d  in-them,                                   j
                   d  vineyards-of beauty                        k
                   e  you-planted                                l
                   e1 but-not you-drink                          m
                   d  their-wine;                                n
             a  for I-know-[that] many-[are] your-
                                   transgressions,             12a
             a  and great-[are] your-sins,                      b
             a  oh-afflictors-of                                c
             b1 the-righteous                                   d
             a  oh-takers-of a-bribe,                           e
        x    b1 and-the-needy                                    f
        y    x  in-the-gate                                      g
             a  they-[=you]-turn-aside                          h
               c  Therefore                                    13a
             b    the-wise-one                                  b
             a1 in-the-time that                                c
             b    will-keep-silent                              d
             a1 for a-time evil it [is].                        e
```

Figure 16. a = sin; a1 = time of sin; b = the wise
condemner of the sin; b1 = the victim of the sin;
c = "therefore"; d = valued product; e = work which
created valued product; e1 = deprivation of valued
product; x = semantically unrelated number of a
pair.

placement of The Lord is his name, which seems to divide God's creative
activity from his activity in punishment. Here, in 9.6, it seems to
balance the punishment by earthquake in 9.5 and therefore seems to refer
to flood. It is, of course, possible that either or both interpretations
could be wrong. However, it is not at all impossible that the same imagery
and wording would change significance in a different context.

```
a   Do-[they]-run                                               6.12a
  b   on-rocks                                                     b
    c   horses?                                                    c
á       d  Or does-one-plow                                        d
    c  with-an-ox                                                  e
  b   the-sea?                                                     f
a¹ But you-have-turned [have managed to turn]                      g
  b¹ to-poison                                                     h
    c¹ justice                                                     i
        e  and-the-fruit-of                                        j
    c¹ righteousness                                               k
  b¹ to-wormwood.                                                  l
a² Oh-those-rejoicing                                            13a
  f  in-Lodebar, [=nothing]                                        b
a² those-saying                                                    c
    x  "Is-it-not                                                  d
      g  by-our-strength                                           e
        h  we-have-taken                                           f
      g  for-ourselves                                             g
  f  Karnaim?" [=two-horns=power]                                  h
a³ But behold-I am-raising-up                                    14a
      ḡ  against-you,                                              b
        i  O-house-of Israel,                                      c
          j  says the-Lord                                         d
          j  the-God-of hosts,                                     e
        i_ a-nation                                                f
      ḡ  and-they-will-oppress you                                 g
  f  from-the-entrance-of Hamath                                   h
a⁴ f̶  to-the-brook-of Arabah.                                     i
```

Figure 17

[210]

```
        a  I-saw the-Lord standing beside the-altar,
                                    and-he said        9.1a
                 b¹  "Smite                             b
          Judgment   c   the-capitals,                  c
 A               b¹  so-they-shake                      d
                     c   [do] the-thresholds            e
                 b¹  and-break-them                     f
                     c   on-the-heads-of                g
                         d   all-of-them;               h
    Sword                 d   and-the-rest-of-them      i
 B               c¹  with-the-sword                     j
                 b¹  I-will-slay.                       k
                 b¹  Not he-will-flee                   l
                     c   to-them                        m
    Away         b   a-fugitive [=one of the fugitives] n
 C               b¹  and-not he-will-escape             o
                     c   to-them                        p
                 b   an-escaper [=one of those who escape]. q
                 b²  If they-dig                        2a
    Down         c²  into-Sheol,                        b
 D               c²  from-there                         c
                 b¹  my-hand will-take-them.            d
                 b²  Or-if they-go-up                   e
    Up           c²  to-heaven,                         f
 E               c²  from-there                         g
                 b¹  I-will-bring-them-down.            h
                 b²  Or-if they-hide                    3a
    Up           c²  on-top-of Carmel,                  b
 E'              c²  from-there                         c
                 b¹  I-will-search,                     d
                 b¹  and-I-will-take-them.              e
                 b²  Or-if they-are-hidden              f
                     c²  from-before my-eyes            g
    Down              d   on-the-floor-of the-sea,      h
                     c²  from-there                     i
 D'              b¹  I-will-command                     j
                 c¹  the-serpent,                       k
                 c¹  and-it                             l
                 b¹  will-bite-them.                    m
```

Figure 18 - continued

Figure 18 - continued

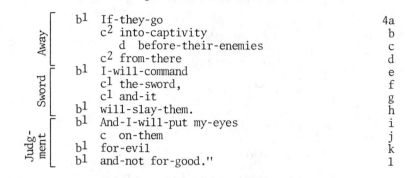

		b¹	If-they-go	4a
C'	Away	c²	into-captivity	b
			d before-their-enemies	c
		c²	from-there	d
	Sword	b¹	I-will-command	e
B'		c¹	the-sword,	f
		c¹	and-it	g
		b¹	will-slay-them.	h
	Judg-ment	b¹	And-I-will-put my-eyes	i
A'			c on-them	j
		b¹	for-evil	k
		b¹	and-not for-good."	l

Figure 18. b = event; c = affected by punishment;
c¹ = instrument of punishment; c² = range of
punishment; d = additional components.10

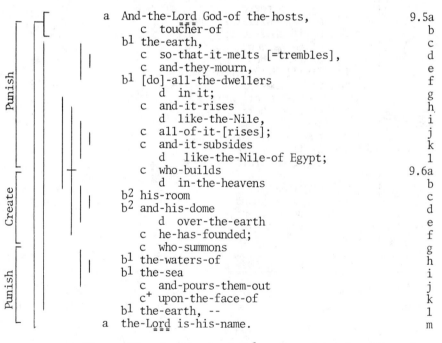

		a	And-the-Lord God-of the-hosts,	9.5a
			c toucher-of	b
		b¹	the-earth,	c
			c so-that-it-melts [=trembles],	d
Punish			c and-they-mourn,	e
		b¹	[do]-all-the-dwellers	f
			d in-it;	g
			c and-it-rises	h
			d like-the-Nile,	i
			c all-of-it-[rises];	j
			c and-it-subsides	k
			d like-the-Nile-of Egypt;	l
Create			c who-builds	9.6a
			d in-the-heavens	b
		b²	his-room	c
		b²	and-his-dome	d
			d over-the-earth	e
			c he-has-founded;	f
			c who-summons	g
		b¹	the-waters-of	h
Punish		b¹	the-sea	i
			c and-pours-them-out	j
			c⁺ upon-the-face-of	k
		b¹	the-earth, --	l
		a	the-Lord is-his-name.	m

Figure 19. a = the Lord; b¹ = that which is affected
by God's action; b² = that which is created by God's
action; c = event; c⁺ = non-recursive continuation
of the event; d = other categories.11

[212]

Table of Notational Conventions (See Appendix, Section 2)

Display format

```
 1  2  3
┌─┐
│ │CONSEQ.│ │        a  Does-it-fall,              3.5a
│ │       │ │ │      b  a-bird,                       b
│ │       │ │ │         c  into a-trap-on             c
│ │       │ │ │         c  the-ground,                d
│ │       │ │        b¹ and-bait                      e
│ │COND   │ │        a  there-is-not to-it?           f
└─┘
```

| (graph) | (exploded text) | (reference and line number) |

Conventions in exploded text

-	combines English words which correspond in meaning to one word in Hebrew
( )	indicates untranslated Hebrew function word
[ ]	indicates implicit meaning
a/a, b/b	recursion of some feature
$\bar{a}$	the negative or opposite of a
a^1, a^2	other kinds of a
a'	a second occurrence of a, so marked for ease of reference
a^+	semantic continuation of a previous a
$\not{a}$ b	semantically a, but structurally b

Conventions in graph

┌   a span, usually longer than a single line of
│
└   exploded text (which is itself a span)

│ │   │ │   recursion ties

┼┼   multiple patterned recursion ties

A A
B B   recursion ties in alternative notations
B A
A B

[213]

Conventions in graph - continued

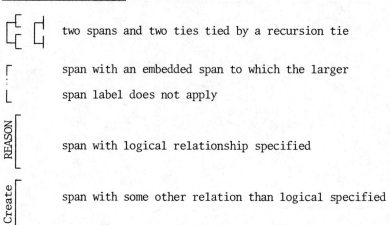

two spans and two ties tied by a recursion tie

span with an embedded span to which the larger
span label does not apply

span with logical relationship specified

span with some other relation than logical specified

TRANSLATING AMOS

1. For discussion of dates and difficulties of dating which are not relevant for the translator, see the commentaries. The earthquake in the days of Uzziah, king of Judah, is mentioned in Zech 14.5. This does not necessarily mean that the memory of this particular earthquake was still alive in Zechariah's days, as this may be a literary allusion. On the other hand, Flavius Josephus (Antiquitates IX, 10,4) connects the earthquake with the events in 2 Chr 26.16-20. The excavations of Hazor revealed destructions in stratum VI which were due to a violent earthquake dated by all excavators around 760. See Y. Yadin, Y. Aharoni, R. Amiran, T. Dothan, I. Dunayevsky, J. Perrot, Hazor II, An Account of the Second Season of Excavations 1956, 1960, pp. 24ff.; 36f.

2. There have been several articles on the translation of Biblical poetry in TBT over the past few years: Aleksander Bierwisch and Paul Ellingworth, "Psalms in Serbian Popular Verse," TBT 24.2 (April 1973): 234-240; Keith R. Crim, "Translating the Poetry of the Bible," TBT 23.1 (January 1972):102-109; Wesley Culshaw, "Translating Biblical Poetry," TBT 19.1 (January 1968):1-6; Howard A. Hatton, "Translation of Poetry: A Thai Example," TBT 25.1 (January 1974):131-139. See also Jan de Waard, "Biblical Metaphors and Their Translation," TBT 25.1 (January 1974):107-116; William A. Smalley, "Restructuring Translations of the Psalms as Poetry," in On Language, Culture and Religion: In Honor of Eugene A. Nida, edited by Matthew Black and William A. Smalley. The Hague: Mouton, 1974: 337-371.

3. Parallelism in Hebrew poetry can become extremely complicated, as may be seen by some of the patterns shown in the Appendix.

1.1 INTRODUCTION: THE PROPHET

1. So K. Budde, Zu Text und Auslegung des Buches Amos, JBL 43, 1924, pp. 46-131; 44, 1925, pp. 63-122; E. Sellin, Das Zwölfprophetenbuch übersetzt und erklärt, Leipzig, 1929-30; A. Weiser, Die Prophetie des Amos, ZAW Beih. 53, 1929; idem, Das Buch der zwölf kleinen Propheten I, ATD 24, Göttingen, 1956; K. Cramer, Amos. Versuch einer theologischen Interpretation, BWANT 51, 1930; C. van Gelderen, Het Boek Amos, Kampen, 1933. The same preference is to be found in W. Baumgartner, Hebräisches und Aramäisches Lexicon zum Alten Testament I, Leiden, 1967 s.v. ḥazah, and in the translations of Mft, Dhorme, and BJ. See also J. de Waard, "Selected Translation Problems from the Prophets with Particular Reference to Bamiléké," TBT 22 (1971):146-154, especially pp. 146-147.

2. Modern research shows that the book of Amos is made up of a collection of oracles together with a collection of reports concerning visions.

3. The most important arguments for such a reading are to be found in C. F. Keil, Biblischer Commentar über die zwölf kleinen Propheten, Leipzig, 1888; A. van Hoonacker, Les douze petits prophètes, Paris, 1908; J. Touzard, Le livre d'Amos, Paris, 1909; S. Amsler, Amos, in Commentaire de l'Ancien Testament XIa, Neuchâtel, 1965; R. S. Cripps, A Critical and Exegetical Commentary on the Book of Amos, London, 1969; H. W. Wolff,

Amos, in Biblischer Kommentar Altes Testament XIV/2: Dodekapropheton 2: Joel und Amos, Neukirchen, 1969. The arguments are that (1) in comparable titles of prophetic books of the Old Testament the verb for 'to see' is never used without a grammatical object and 'words' is the only available object, and (2) this is the way the text has been read by ancient translators. (So all known LXX manuscripts [see J. Ziegler, Duodecim prophetae, in Septuaginta, Vetus Testamentum Graecum auctoritate academiae litterarum Göttingensis editum XIII, Göttingen, 1967] and Vulgate.)

The expression "to see a word" occurs also elsewhere in the Old Testament (Isa 2.1 and Micah 1.1; compare also Isa 13.1 and Hab 1.1), but the remarkable statement that "Amos saw the words of Amos" is without parallel in the Old Testament. It is, of course, true that much of the harshness of the expression is due to the hand of the final redactor who tried to combine the two sources of the book in the title. Though we are able to reconstruct with some degree of certainty the work of a "school of Amos" as well as that of later interpreters and redactors, we are not primarily concerned with such a reconstruction in the field of translation. Our concern is to translate the book of Amos as it has been transmitted, not to give a translation of its sources. This means that in a dynamic translation harsh expressions or constructions of the source text which betray the work of a redactor, disappear.

More recent translations in English, such as NEB and NAB, have tried to smooth out this particular difficulty by translating idomatically: "The words of Amos...which he received in vision(s)." But such a translation is not obligatory. At quite an early time the word for 'vision' was already used in the more general sense of 'revelation,' and this general use gave rise to the more specific meaning 'word revelation,' 'oracle.' In the same way the verb for 'to see' could be used for the reception of revelation generally and for the reception of divine oracles in particular. (See Koehler-Baumgartner, s.v. ḥazah; L. Koehler, Theologie des Alten Testaments, 1966, par. 36; H. Wildberger, Jesaja, in Biblischer Kommentar Altes Testament X/1, Neukirchen, 1965, p.5.)

4. The meaning of the name is obscure. It can be compared with the name Amasiah (2 Chr 17.16) which in Hebrew sounds like "Yahweh bears." Amos may even be a shorter form of the same name. (Compare M. Noth, Die israelitischen Personennamen, 1928, p. 178. See also Wolff ad loc. for Aramaic parallels and Cripps in the introduction to his commentary [p. 10] who defends a passive meaning "borne [by God].")

5. L. Köhler (Amos in Schweiz. Theol. Zeitschrift 34, 1917, pp. 10-21; 68-79; 145-157; 190-208) thinks that the absence of the father's name may lead to the conclusion that Amos was the son of poor people.

6. The perfect tense of the verb 'to be' in Hebrew clearly indicates the past. (See P. Joüon, Grammaire de l'hébreu biblique, Rome, 1947, par. 154m.)

7. See the Ugaritic texts 62,55 and 113,71.

8. So Targum: "marey geytin," "masters (i.e. owners) of the flock."

9. On the basis of the related root in Arabic, these might be sheep of a particular breed with short legs and producing good wool.

10. Tekoa is a village of Judah, 17 kilometers south of Jerusalem built upon a hill 825 meters above sea level. (Compare G. E. Wright, F. V. Filson, W. F. Albright, The Westminster Historical Atlas to the Bible, London, 1957, Plate IX.) The precise location of ancient Tekoa was

probably on the east side of modern ḫirbet tekuꜥ. The rabbinic and mediaeval thesis that Tekoa was located in the northern kingdom or more particularly in the tribe of Asher (so Kimhi) lacks convincing arguments.

Because Tekoa was a border place it was fortified by King Rehoboam, according to 2 Chr 11.6. In 2 Sam 14 a story is told about an important role played by a "wise woman of Tekoa."

1.2 THE POWER OF GOD TO PUNISH

1. For the similarities and differences with regard to the so-called theophanic hymns see especially Wolff, op. cit., p. 147f. and the literature cited there.

2. This is shown in Hebrew by the change from imperfect to (consecutive) perfect tense. See G. Beer, R. Meyer, Hebräische Grammatik, Berlin, 1952-55, par. 101/6.a. Compare also Joüon, par. 119 cij.

3. Whereas Hebrew sha'aq applies only to lions, its Arabic cognate can be used of several animals. The only time Hebrew sha'aq is used with regard to a person in particular condition (Psa 38.9), it is equivalent to 'groan' and it translates the anguished cries of a sufferer (see A. A. Anderson, The Book of Psalms, Vol. I, in the New Century Bible, London, 1972, ad loc.). The LXX in marking the speaking of the Lord as a loud one uses a Greek verb phtheggomai which can refer to human beings, animals, thunder and other inanimate things. Aquila and Symmachus, on the other hand, use a Greek verb bruchaomai, an onomatope properly used of lions and other animals. It should, however, be noted that when used of persons their particular condition is dying or a painful experience!

4. This is a possibility which has been defended by several scholars. So J. Wellhausen, Die kleinen Propheten übersetzt und erklärt, 1963, ad loc.; Sellin and Cripps ad loc. The first line of 1.2 reoccurs in Joel 4.16. The whole question who uses the text of whom is not relevant for translation purposes. Compare also M. Weiss, "In the Footsteps of One Biblical Metaphor," Tarbiz 34, 1964-65, pp. 107-128.

5. For Koehler-Baumgartner we have to do with a homophonous Hebrew verb ʾabal, cognate of Accadian abālu meaning 'vertrocknen.' See also V. Maag, Text, Wortschatz und Begriffswelt des Buches Amos, Leiden, 1951 ad loc. On the other hand, E. Kutsch ('Trauerbräuche' und 'Selbstminderungsriten' im AT, Theol. Studien 78, 1965, p. 35f.) is of the opinion that both specific meanings 'dry up' and 'mourn' stem from one and the same root with the generic meaning 'diminish.'

6. The word also occurred as a common noun standing for farmland and garden-land (see Isa 16.10; Jer 2.7; 2 Kgs 19.23).

1.3--3.2 ISRAEL'S SPECIAL GUILT AMONG THE NATIONS

1. It seems better, therefore, not to place the title of 1.3--2.16 before verse 1, as has been done in some translations (NAB, Zür).

2. See especially Keith R. Crim, "Translating the Poetry of the Bible," TBT 23 (1972), pp. 102-110.

3. In contrast with the present tense (tade legei kurios) in the introductory formulae of the following oracles, LXX has here the reading kai eipe kurios. A translation of the past tense has been defended by

Weiser, Wolff, and Amsler and is to be found in the translation of Dhorme.

4. See especially the important 'Exkurs' on pesha^c in Wolff, pp. 185-186.

5. See Translator's Handbook on Mark on 1.4 and Translator's Handbook on Luke on 1.77.

6. Compare W. R. Harper, A Critical and Exegetical Commentary on Amos and Hosea, Edinburgh, 1960, ad loc.; and M. Delcor in Les petits prophètes, Tome VIII, 1 of L. Pirot and A. Clamer, La Sainte Bible, Paris, 1961, ad loc.

7. A number followed by the next higher number is frequent in Hebrew literature. One and two (Psa 62.11; Job 40.5), two and three (Sirach 26.28), three and four (Prov 30.15,18,21,29; Sirach 26.5) and nine and ten (Sirach 25.7-11). The sequence three and four is the most frequent. See especially W. M. W. Roth, The Numerical Sequence x/x + 1 in the Old Testament, VT 12 (1962), pp. 300-311; idem, Numerical Sayings in the Old Testament, VT (Suppl. 13), 1965. Compare also J. de Waard, art. cit., pp. 148-149.

8. The Translator's Translation (stage 4) e.g. reads: "because the people of...have committed many crimes." Compare also Robinson's observation in Th. H. Robinson and F. Horst, Die zwölf Kleinen Propheten, HAT 1.14, Tübingen, 1954, ad loc: "Ausdruck zur Bezeichnung einer unbestimmten, aber nicht grossen Zahl."

9. Keil, Touzard, Wellhausen, Cripps, van Gelderen, Amsler are all in favor of a reference to 'punishment.' Wolff, on the other hand, sees a reference to the 'word of God.' Compare, however, van Hoonacker who sees already rightly that the discussion is irrelevant to a certain extent: "l'objet signifié par le suffixe et que Jahvé ne retirera point, c'est sa parole, savoir l'arrêt de condamnation, ou la proclamation de la peine: je ne retirerai point la chose; le contexte donne à l'idée sa détermination précise." In the LXX, the majority of manuscripts have the reading auton which refers to the word of God, only the Lucianic recension followed by the Bohairic translation and the Syrohexaplar reads auten which should refer to 'punishment.'

10. So Targum: yat yatbhey'ara^c gila^cd. It should, however, be noted that the more specific LXX reading (tas) en gastri echousas tōn en Galaad (the pregnant women of Gilead) presupposes a Hebrew original harot hagila^cd which has now been found back in 5Q4 1. According to Wolff, this specific reading (also found in Vetus Latina) has been introduced from 1.13. But there are arguments for regarding this reading as original.

11. See J. Benzinger, Hebräische Archäologie, 1907, pp. 209-210; K. Galling, Biblisches Reallexikon, 1937, pp. 137-139; G. Dalman, Arbeit und Sitte in Palästina, III, Gütersloh, 1933, p. 83, 88f.

12. As already proposed by van Hoonacker, op. cit., ad loc.

13. None of the existing Greek translations seem to have made this component explicit. LXX renders 'armenot consistently with themelia which means either "foundations (of buildings)" or "building-sites"; tas aulas in Theodotion stands for any dwelling and bareis in Aquila and Symmachus may focus on the dimensions of the buildings. Even if the meaning 'tower' is presented in bareis, it is the dimension aspect which is important, not its being a fortified place. It is possible that themelia reflects a relationship with the Hebrew root rmh I and bareis with the Hebrew root rwm.

[218]

14. So Budde and Wolff and Moffatt. The same interpretation is found in W. Gesenius and F. Buhl, Hebräisches und Aramäisches Handwörterbuch über das Alte Testament, 1949, s.v. yashab. Van Gelderen argues that in case of a strict parallel we should expect the reading yosheb kisse', but it can be said that such an explicit reading is unnecessary because of the parallelism! On the other hand, though the use of a collective sg. noun yosheb for 'population' is possible, one could also argue that in case of a meaning 'inhabitants' we should expect a plural. Semantically, the parallelism remains the strongest argument for the interpretation. Interestingly, even the LXX translates according to the parallelism. Though it has the reading katoikountas (inhabitants), it reads in the next half line phulēn for "him that holds the scepter"!

15. Of the versions, none seems to apply a consistent translation method. They all seem to translate the first part of the first compound noun (pediou), but whereas Aquila and Symmachus translate the second part as a symbolic designation in reading respectively anōphelous (valley of the useless) and adikias (valley of injustice), LXX and Theodotion give a transcription according to a different vocalization of the Hebrew: ōn. For the many hypotheses to which this geographical identification has given rise, see the commentaries. Similarly, Symmachus and Theodotion translate the first part of the second compound noun (oikou and oikōi), but whereas Theodotion translates also the second part: truphēs (house of daintiness), Symmachus gives a transcription of the Hebrew: eden. As to method, the same applies to LXX, only that eks andrōn should be traced back to Hebrew bene (compare Bohairic translation) and that the particular reading charran should be considered as 'Sonderüberlieferung' (see Wolff, ad loc.).

16. Compare Van Hoonacker, ad loc. and Brockelmann, Syntax, par. 92a.

17. See A. R. Johnson, The Vitality of the Individual in the Thought of Ancient Israel, 1964, p. 56.

18. It is true that the reading of MT is confirmed by the "standard text" Mur 88 III 25 (see Discoveries in the Judaean Desert of Jordan II: Les grottes de Murabbaʿât, 186) as well as by the Targum and Vulgate, but the absence of the variant text in the LXX tradition (with the exception of C and mss. 68 and 613) almost certainly means that this text was not yet known to the LXX translators. The more so as 'adonai has frequently been added by later hands to the original Amos text elsewhere.

19. So Keil, Touzard, van Gelderen ad loc.

20. So a.o. S. R. Driver, The Books of Joel and Amos (The Cambridge Bible, 1897), revised by H. C. O. Lanchester, 1915, ad loc.; W. Nowack, Die kleinen Propheten, HK, 1922, ad loc.; Wellhausen and van Hoonacker, ad loc.

21. The proposal of Robinson, Budde, Sellin, Maag and Amsler to read la'aram for le'edom (even retained as a possibility by K. Elliger in BHS (Biblia Hebraica Stuttgartensia 10: Liber XII prophetarum, Stuttgart, 1970) has to be rejected as such a reading lacks versional support and obscures the relationship between verses 9 and 6b. So rightly Wolff, ad loc.

22. See especially W. Schotroff: 'Gedenken' im Alten Testament, WMANT 15, 1967, p. 202. See also B. S. Childs, Memory and Tradition in Israel, Stud. in Bibl. Theol. 37, 1962, p43f. and for other componential meanings of the same verb P.A.H. de Boer, Gedenken und Gedächtnis in der Welt des AT, 1962.

23. Weiser's statement ad loc: "ferner lässt sich nicht sagen, was mit dem Bruderbund...gemeint ist" is fully correct.

24. Compare also 1 Kgs 9.13 where Hiram calls Solomon my brother! Understanding the passage this way, of course, would mean that the captives of verse 9 were Israelites.

25. Those who think verse 9a speaks about Phoenicians being raided by their fellow people of Tyre see in the 'covenant of brothers' the "ties of kinship" and the obligations "brothers' of the same tribe have toward each other. However, the lack of historical evidence for this has already been mentioned.

Finally, some see in the 'covenant of brothers' the blood relationship between Edom and Israel (Essau and Jacob!). But this relationship is nowhere called a 'covenant,' and it is difficult to see how Tyre can be reproached for not having respected such a relationship existing between two other nations.

26. See Brown-Driver-Briggs s.v. rahamim and shahat; W. Robertson Smith, Kinship and Marriage in Early Arabia, 1885, p. 28. Compare also NEB: "stifling their natural affections," and Sellin, ad loc.

27. Reading with the Syriac and the Vulgate wayyittor instead of wayyitroph and with LXX, Symmachus, Theodotion, Syriac, Vulgate and Targum shamar lanetsah instead of shemara netsah. This reading has been first proposed by J. Olshausen (Die Psalmen, 1853, p. 397 ad Psa 103.9) and it has been taken over by most scholars (the last to be mentioned is K. Elliger in BHS) with slight differences as to the interpretation of the subject of both verbs. Olshausen himself, in the traces of LXX, Syriac version and Vulgate, took both verbs as transitive and Edom as subject and he is followed in this by a. o. Sellin, Touzard, Amsler, Cripps, Weiser, Moffatt, NAB. On the other hand, van Hoonacker takes both verbs as intransitive so that 'anger' and 'wrath' are the respective subjects. Compare also NEB. Semantically and translationally, however, these differences are of little importance. For the reading of NAB see also Textual Notes on the New American Bible, Textual Notes on Old Testament Readings, a separate booklet accompanying the St. Anthony's Guild edition.

28. The Hebrew text runs literally: 'his anger tore perpetually and his wrath kept forever.' In order to make sense out of this text one has to postulate (a) an implicit simile in the first half line such as "like a wild beast its prey" as well as an implicit object "the Israelites" and (b) an implicit object such as "prey" in the second half line. Evidence for an implicit simile can be found in the parallel construction in Job 16.9: "His wrath has torn me" (compare TEV: In anger, God tears me limb from limb). Restructured and explicitly stated, the Hebrew text has then the following meaning: "In anger, Edom tore the Israelites perpetually as a wild beast its prey and in fury they watched continually over their prey." For a defense of MT see especially Wolff ad loc. Compare also A. Neher, Amos, 1950, p. 49. Wolff takes the verb taraph in the sense of 'to plunder' (a meaning supported by LXX) and he thinks that Jerusalem is the implicit object in the first half line.

29. "Upon the walls" is lacking (compare verse 10). This has been taken as evidence that a region rather than a town called Teman was intended. (So already Wellhausen, ad loc.)

30. For the vocalization of the infinitive biqᶜam see Jouon, par. 70d and H. Bauer and P. Leander, Historische Grammatik der hebräischen Sprache, 1922, par. 343b.

31. There are many biblical and extra-biblical examples of this particular atrocity. See for the first one 2 Kgs 8.12 and 15.16, for the second one the appraisal of Tiglatpileser I: "Er zerfetzte der Schwangeren Bäuche/durchbohrte der Schwachen Leib" (cited by H. Schmökel, Ur, Assur und Babylon, 1955, p. 114). Compare also Homer, Ilias VI, 57f.

Because of the peculiar relationship between the two sentences, changes in the text have sometimes been proposed (one of these has recently been followed by NEB). J. J. P. Valeton, Amos en Hosea. Een hoofdstuk uit de geschiedenis van Israëls Godsdienst, Nijmegen, 1894 ad loc. thinks that harot is a scribal error for betsurot, "fortified cities," and he is followed in this by Budde. Both authors point out that the same verb baqaᶜ is also used for making a breach in the walls of a city. Sellin ad loc. wants to read har (mountain area) instead of harot and this reading must have inspired NEB: "they invaded the ploughlands of Gilead." More recently, an approach from the side of comparative philology has been made. Reider (VT 6, 1954, p. 279) compares Arabic harrat and translates "stony tracts." There is, however, no support and no reason for such a change.

32. For Wolff one even has to read the conventional formula, as the unusual wehitstsatti should come from Jer 49.27 and be due to a copyist.

33. In the versions much evidence can be found for early translation technical operations, but there is no reason to follow their evidence. Most LXX mss. read "her kings" (a 'correction' of the possessive has only taken place in 130 and 407ᵗˣᵗ) connecting thus 'kings' with 'Rabbah,' a much nearer antecedent in the text! There is no reason whatsoever to presuppose the existence of a different Hebrew Vorlage (against Wolff).

The Lucianic main group, Aquila, Symmachus, Syriac and Vulgate vocalize mlkm as milkom (melchom) and think thus of the god of Ammon. Accordingly LXX and Syriac read "their (his) priests and their (his) leaders." This does not mean that they read kohanayw instead of huʾ (against Wolff), but that they divided the officers into two specific groups of religious and non-religious officials.

34. Compare the inscription found on the tomb of Eshmunazar, king of Sidon (3rd century B.C.): "I adjure every prince and every man that they open not this resting-place...nor take away the coffin of my resting-place, nor carry me from this resting-place (and lay me) on a second resting-place...For every prince and every man who shall open this resting-place ...may they have no resting-place with the Shades, nor be buried in a grave" (Corpus Inscriptionum Semiticarum 1.3 in the translation of G. A. Cooke, A Text-Book of North-semitic Inscriptions, Oxford, 1903, p. 31). See also M. J. Lagrange, Etudes sur les religions sémitiques, Paris, 1905, pp. 314-341.

35. This is the way it was understood by at least one ancient translation. The Vulgate focuses on the completeness of the burning: eo quod incenderit ossa regis Idumeae usque ad cinerem.

36. So Targum: wesadinun baggiraʾ bebeyteyh. Wolff (op. cit., p. 162) gives a free translation which rightly renders the meaning: "es hat daraus Kalkverputz für sein Haus gemacht."

37. So LXX: themelia tōn poleōn autēs.

38. The town is mentioned in line 12f of the Mesha stone (see the edition by Cooke) according to which Kerioth was an important center of worship of the national god Chemosh. According to K. H. Bernhardt (Zur Identifizierung moabitischer Ortslagen, Zeitschrift des Deutschen Palästina

Vereins 76, 1960, pp. 136-158), Kerioth should be identical with the modern ḳurēyāt ʿalēyān.

39. For this and for literature on the subject see V. Maag, op. cit., p. 207, note 664.

40. See also A Translator's Handbook on Ruth on 1.1. A literal translation has been given in NAB.

41. No doubt torah and ḥuqqim have to be interpreted according to the meaning these terms had in the vocabulary of the deuteronomistic school from which they are taken.

42. Compare also E. A. Nida, Bible Translating, London, 1961, p. 197f.

43. So Keil, op. cit., ad loc. For the LXX translator, they are "worthless human products": ta mataia;...ha epoiēsan."

44. Most commentators understand the word righteous to mean 'the innocent party in a lawsuit' and so they see the judges as the ones who for silver or "for money" have been taking bribes from the guilty party. (For the definite use of keseph see Brockelmann, Syntax, par. 21c. be after the use of a verb of selling can only be interpreted as be pretii.) Sell, then, would be picture language. (So Keil, Sellin, Robinson, Cripps, van Gelderen, Amsler, Wellhausen, Driver.) In fact, the first half line in the Hebrew seems to have been understood in that way by at least some ancient translators. In one of the Lucianic subgroups (62, 147), the setting has been made explicit: en krisei (in trial).

However, if and the needy for a pair of shoes expresses the same thought, judges should also be the ones who are doing the selling; sell would be picture language for 'to condemn,' and a pair of shoes would express the insignificance of the bribe which the judges were willing to take. But few commentators want to understand it this way. Only Wellhausen and Sellin interpret the text consequently according to the parallelism. Under reference to 1 Sam 12.3 LXX, Wellhausen observes: "Ein Paar Schuh ist ein sprichwörtlich geringfügiger Preis" (op. cit., ad loc.).

Instead, many of them want to see creditors as the ones doing the selling here, and a meaning 'to sell into slavery.' It is the debt which is insignificant. So a.o. Driver, Cripps (though conscious of the awkwardness of the change of subject) and van Gelderen (who sees no conflict, as for him the subject is of a more generic character, judges and rich people being taken together as members of the same corrupt upper class and judged according to the same conduct).

45. Some commentators, at least, rightly defend this last interpretation. So a.o. van Hoonacker, Weiser, Wolff.

46. The discussion whether be and baʿabur are equivalents or whether baʿabur naʿalayim should rather mean "for the sake of a pair of sandals" (stolen, borrowed and lost?) is translationally not very relevant.

47. For the Hebrew dual form see Joüon, op. cit., par. 91c.

48. So Budde and Maag. For both ʾerets is epexegetical. The same interpretation is also to be found in Valeton, op. cit., ad loc. and in F. Hitzig, Die zwölf kleinen Propheten erklärt, Vierte Auflage, besorgt von H. Steiner, Leipzig, 1881, ad loc.

49. So Keil, C. von Orelli, Die zwölf kleinen Propheten, Dritte Auflage, München, 1908, ad loc. and C. van Gelderen. This interpretation is typical of the older exegesis and is defended by Gesenius, Ewald, Maurer, Schmoller and others.

50. So M. A. Beek, The Religious Background of Amos 2.6-8, Oudtestamentische Studien 5, 1948, p. 135. Beek translates bero'sh with "at the expense of" referring to the parallel text 1 Chr 12.19. 'aphar must then be deleted as a gloss.

51. This interpretation has also been given in one ancient translation, the Targum.

52. It has especially been argued that all ancient translations favor (2), but this argument is not as impressive as it seems to be at first sight. The LXX in reading ta patounta epi ton choun tēs gēs kai ekondulizon eis kephalas ptōchōn presents a doublet and translates the Hebrew text twice. This means that the Hebrew Vorlage was corrupt and Maag (op. cit., p. 199) gives a very convincing reconstruction of the original text and the way in which it became corrupted. The Vulgate text qui conterunt super pulverem terrae capita pauperum may have been influenced by LXX in its interpretation of the verb, so that only the Targum remains.
No interpretation can simply be dismissed as "nonsense" (Wellhausen's qualification of 1a). One cannot get rid of the impression that it has often been the "logic" of the western mind which dictated the choice.

53. So Cripps, Wolff, Maag. For Maag see especially p. 228ff.

54. So rightly Koehler-Baumgartner and Brown-Driver-Briggs s.v. halak; Wolff, op. cit., p. 202 (referring also to Hos 3.3).

55. Some defenders of this interpretation have proposed making such a change (so Budde and Weiser). There is, however, absolutely no textual support for such a transposition.

56. See especially Maag, op. cit., p. 174ff. Remarkable is Norman H. Snaith's treatment of the passage. First he defines na'arah as "a young girl, under the age of puberty" (The Book of Amos, Part Two: Translation and Notes, London, 1946, p. 82), but then equates na'arah with qedeshah (temple prostitute) (ibidem, p. 43).

57. LXX: paidiskē; Vulgate: puella; Syh: neanis.

58. For this particular consecutive use of lema'an see Joüon, par. 169g.

59. Not taking the hiphil of the verb natah intransitively (so a.o. Brown-Driver-Briggs s.v.), but transitively with ellipsis of 'body' (so a.o. Maag, p. 88).

60. A very plausible reconstruction of a possible chain of events with regard to (a) has been given by Maag (op. cit., p. 235, note 22). According to him, temple officers could have brought sacrifices for poor people who were not able to pay the price of an animal. As a security for debts they took then the clothes of the poor. The series of events implicit in (b) has been made explicit by commentators in several ways. So it has been said that they lie down to sleep on these clothes which would have been an additional sin against the law which prescribed that a cloak taken during the day as a pledge should be returned before nightfall (Exo 22.26; Deut 24.12f.). Others think that they lie down on these clothes for their feasts or even their sacred prostitution (Jerome in his explanation of the paraphrase of the LXX).

61. So T. H. Robinson, The Book of Amos, in National Adult School series of translations into colloquial speech, 1921, and N. H. Snaith, op. cit., p. 45.

62. So J. Halévy, Recherches bibliques. Le livre d'Amos, Revue Sémitique 11, 12, 1903/04, ad loc.

63. See also A Translator's Handbook on Mark on 2.22, and A Translator's Handbook on Luke on 1.15.

64. The Hebrew word translated cedar trees probably indicates one particular species of the genus 'conifer,' a tree which could reach a height of ten to twenty-five meters. Such a modern scientific description is, however, not very useful for translation purposes, especially if the particular tree, and sometimes even the family to which it belongs, is completely unknown in the receptor culture.
According to Koehler (ʾerez, Zeitschrift für die Alttestamentliche Wissenschaft 55, 1937, p. 163ff.) only three species can be taken into consideration: Juniperus excelsior (5-20 m.), Pinus Pinea (10-20 m.), Abies Cilicia Kotschy (10-25 m., rarely 50 m.). As the height is the ground of the comparison, the last one is perhaps meant here (as well as in Isa 2.13). See also Fauna and Flora of the Bible,Helps for Translators, Volume XI, London, 1972 s.v. cedar.

65. The meaning of the word rendered by oaks is not so certain. The Hebrew word was originally used for any big tree and later more specifically for oaks, but there seems to be no unanimity among modern botanists as to which of the six species of oak found in Palestine the Hebrew word refers. For ʾallon in the sense of "big tree" see especially Hess, Beduinisches im Alten Testament, Zeitschrift für die Alttestamentliche Wissenschaft 35, 1915, p. 124f. Fauna and Flora of the Bible s.v. oak tree, thinks of the species quercus aegilops (15 m. high) which has a heavy trunk and may well symbolize strength. A parallel development in referential meaning can be noted for the Greek drus (LXX).

66. See Isa 37.31 (=2 Kgs 19.30) and the inscription quoted in note 34 in which the following sentence occurs: "may he have no root beneath, or fruit above, or any beauty among the living under the sun."

67. It is only because he disregards this character of idiom that Neher (op. cit., ad loc.) can explain the meaning of the individual words 'fruits' and 'roots' as referring to 'young' and 'old.' Compare also H. L. Ginsberg, "Roots Below and Fruit Above" and Related Matters, in Hebrew and Semitic Studies, presented to G. R. Driver, D. W. Thomas and W. D. McHardy (eds.), 1963, pp. 59-71.

68. See Koehler-Baumgartner, s.v. halak, and especially Sellin: "ʾolek = ich erhielt euch am Leben." So also Ehrlich, Cramer, van Gelderen. The component of guidance is strongly expressed in one LXX ms (233) which reads hōdēgēsa.

69. See Notes on the Book of Amos (Old Testament Translators' Translation), ad loc. and A Translator's Handbook on Mark on 1.3.

70. So rightly Brown-Driver-Briggs s.v. qum. Compare also Wolff ad loc.: "qum hi. bezeichnet...die Amtseinsetzung der Propheten..."

71. Compare Maag, note 528: "qum": aufstellen = (durch Berufung) erstehen lassen."

72. See a.o. Maag, op. cit., note 377: "Für Amos heisst nabiʾ somit ein berufsmässiger Künder des göttlichen Wortes."

73. Compare also A Translator's Handbook on Mark on 1.2. See now also Barclay M. Newman and Eugene A. Nida, A Translator's Handbook on the Acts of the Apostles, London, 1972, on 2.16.

74. Some scholars believe that this second line should be transposed after verse 12 (so Baumann, Budde and Sellin), but textually and stylistically there seems to be no decisive argument for such a transposition.

75. It may possibly refer to parents who consecrated their children as Nazirites and who, in a period in which they were responsible for the keeping of that vow, made these children drink wine. (So Maag, op. cit., note 390. Compare also Beek, art. cit., p. 138.)

76. In Hebrew, 2.13 has a rhyme and style similar to 2.9a, with which it is balanced, but it continues the direct statement with the pronoun you which began in verse 10. However, in the remaining verses the Hebrew is no longer direct but changes to them again, so even the place of the switch in pronouns balances.

77. The first one through comparison with an Aramaic verb, the others through comparison with Arabic verbs.

78. So Targum, Jewish tradition generally, Ewald, G. A. Smith, Driver, Snaith, Gesenius, Keil, Brown-Driver-Briggs s.v. In this case ʿuq is considered to be an Aramaism for Hebrew tsuq.

79. Through comparison with Arabic ʿaqa (groan, creak). So already Aquila: trizēsō hupokatō humōn katha trizei hē hamaksa; Vulgate: ecce ego stridebo super vos sicut stridet plaustrum onustum faeno. This interpretation has been followed by Hoffmann, Marti, Weiser, van Gelderen and Touzard. NEB makes the subject as acted upon instead of acting: "I groan under the burden of you as a wagon creaks under a full load."

80. Through comparison with post-biblical Hebrew ʿuqah (excavation), Arabic ʿaqqa and Ugaritic ʿqq (split). So H. Gese, Kleine Beiträge zum Verständnis des Amos-buches, Vetus Testamentum 12, 1962, pp. 417-424; Wolff, op. cit., ad loc.

81. Through comparison with Arabic ʿaqa (stop, hinder). Such a reading is presupposed by LXX A: kōluō. It has first been defended by J. G. Wetzstein, (Briefliche Bemerkungen von Consul Dr. J. G. Wetzstein, mitgetheilt von E. Riehm, Zeitschrift für die Alttestamentliche Wissenschaft 3, 1883, pp. 273-279) and followed by Harper, Budde, van Hoonacker, Amsler.

82. Through comparison with Arabic ʿaqa and ʿauq. So L. Koehler and W. Baumgartner, Lexicon in Veteris Testamenti Libros, Leiden, 1958, s.v. and Maag.

83. Through comparison with Arabic ʿuj (withdraw, flee away). So Hitzig's later view.

84. (1) and (3) are closest to the use of related Aramaic or post-biblical Hebrew vocabulary. Both (1) and (2) have important support from ancient versions.

85. The weight is expressed through the verb (whatever its interpretation may be) and through a secondary device. lah can best be taken as dativus incommodi.

86. Even in passages where the reference does not seem to be to the Day of the Lord, day has ominous associations in Amos: day of battle, day of the whirlwind (1.14); darkens the day into night (5.8); darken the earth in broad daylight (8.9); a bitter day (8.10).

87. See Brockelmann, Syntax, par. 71a and par. 77f.

88. So Maag, op. cit., note 479, Snaith and Cripps. For a comparable meaning of the Greek gumnos see Herodotus 2.141. See also Horatius, Carmina I, 22.

89. According to some scholars, section 3.1-2 is the final paragraph of a larger discourse unit: 1.3--3.2. Such a division has first been proposed by Budde and it has been defended again by Maag. One possible link seems to be a situational one in that 3.1-2 may have found its origin in a discussion in which the people of Israel reacted against the preceding message by calling upon their special status and particular privileges. (So Weiser, op. cit., ad loc.: "Der kurze Spruch ist aus der Diskussion entstanden.") Such an appeal is then characterized as an illusion (so Sellin, op. cit., ad loc.).

90. (a) eliminates the difference between the speech of the prophet and the speech of the Lord; (b) introduces into the direct speech of the Lord a clearly secondary--and according to some scholars, even contradictory--element. Even if one does not want to combine in the actual text 3.1 and 9.7 as J. Morgenstern (Amos Studies, Part Four, in Hebrew Union College Annual, 32, 1961, p. 309) does (compare also Sellin ad loc.), it cannot be denied that both texts belong closely together. And 9.7 makes abundantly clear that the exodus tradition provides no ground for the certainty of election.

Verse 1b has been regarded as a gloss so as more clearly to cover Judah. So Meinhold, Marti, Weiser, Hölscher, T. H. Robinson, Snaith, Wolff (who gives five important arguments on p. 212). Though there are insufficient textual arguments to omit verse 1b, its explanatory and thus secondary character can leave no doubt.

91. The comparative sense of min has wrongly been defended e.g. by Th. C. Vriezen (Die Erwählung Israels nach dem Alten Testament, in Abhandlungen zur Theologie des Alten und Neuen Testaments 24, 1953, p. 37) and it is wrongly reflected in NAB: "You alone have I favored, more than all the families of the earth." For the negative force of min see Brockelmann, Syntax, par. 111c,f.

92. For the degree of overlapping of both the verbs yada⁻ and baḥar see especially Wolff, op. cit., ad loc., and W. Schotroff in Theologisches Handwörterbuch zum Alten Testament s.v. yada⁻, col. 692.

93. R. Smend (Das Nein des Amos, Evangelische Theologie, 23, 1963, p. 409) has made the interesting suggestion that the secondary discourse element 1b gives in fact an exegesis of yada⁻.

94. So Maag, op. cit., p. 187. Compare also R. Knierim, Die Hauptbegriffe für Sünde im Alten Testament, 1965, pp. 236-242.

3.3--4.3 THE PROPHET'S ROLE AND COMMISSION

1. Some scholars cannot see how verse 3 belongs to this section because of its peaceful picture, where so many of the other pictures have to do with disaster. (So Marti, Gese (art. cit., p. 425) and W. H. Schmidt, Die deuteronomistische Redaktion des Amosbuches, Zeitschrift für die Alttestamentliche Wissenschaft, 77, 1965, pp. 168-193.) Others insist that 3.3-6 and 3.7-8 are two different sections and that they should have different section headings, such as "Disaster Comes from the Lord" (3-6) and "The Prophet Has to Speak" (7-8). H. Gressmann (Die Schriften des Alten Testamentes, 1921, p. 339f.) has been the first to give such an analysis of the discourse which is already found in the first edition of his book (1910).

2. But exactly these features make verse 7 a secondary element, and
if one considers this verse as a later literary composition the unity of
3.3-8 becomes rather clear. So rightly Marti, Duhm, Nowack, Sellin, Weiser,
Gese, Schmidt, Wolff and S. Lehming (Erwägungen zu Amos, Zeitschrift für
Theologie und Kirche, 55, 1958, pp. 145-169).

3. See Carl Brockelmann, Grundriss der vergleichenden Grammatik...,
II, p. 197f.

4. Compare H. Lausberg, Elemente der literarischen Rhetorik, 1967,
p. 145: "Die 'rhetorische Frage' peitscht die Affekte durch die Evidenz
der Unnötigkeit der fragenden Formulierung auf."

5. See a.o. E. A. Nida, Toward a Science of Translating, Leiden,
1964, p. 229f. and E. A. Nida and C. R. Taber, The Theory and Practice of
Translation, Leiden, 1969, p. 30.

6. At least one of the ancient versions made use of the first of
these meanings ('to arrange') and many modern English translations have
done the same: "by agreement" (TT), "they have agreed" (NAB, NEB), "they
have planned" (Mft). This is the reading of Aquila (suntaksōntai). It is
difficult to evaluate the reading of the LXX gnōrisōsin heautous: "They
become acquainted with each other." It is generally held that the LXX
translator read nodaʿu instead of noʿadu with interchange of ʿayin and
daleth. He would then have been the victim of a simple metathesis substi-
tuting the well-known verb yadaʿ for the less known verb yaʿad. The
occurrence of the verb yadaʿ in the preceding verse might have contributed
to this behavior.

Though this explanation is possible, it can nevertheless be questioned for several reasons:

(a) the niphal of the verb yadaʿ is rarely rendered by gnōrizein in
the LXX; in fact, there are only two occurrences: Exo 21.36 and Ruth 3.3;
3.3;

(b) the verb yadaʿ is never rendered by gnōrizein in the LXX of Amos;

(c) in none of the existing Greek manuscripts of Amos has an attempt
been made to 'correct' the apparently 'wrong' reading;

(d) "to become acquainted with each other" and "to meet each other"
belong to the same semantic domain, the first term being more specific,
the latter more generic. It should also be noted that greetings and such
questions as "where do you come from?" and "where do you go?" accompany
the event of the meeting so that gnōrizein can very well translate the
second component of yaʿad;

(e) that it is the verb yaʿad which has been rendered seems to be
confirmed by the variant reading which is especially found in the
Lucianic recension: gnōrisōsin heautois: "they make (it) known to each
other." In this reading the first component of yaʿad has been made
explicit.

D. W. Thomas (Note on noʿadu in Amos III.3 Journal of Theological
Studies, New Series, 7, 1956, pp. 69-70) makes a comparison with the
Arabic root wdʿ and proposes a translation "to reconcile one with another,"
"to make peace." Note that this sense would come nearly back to that which
has been proposed by several scholars "to be agreed," "be in harmony" (so
a. o. Harper and van Gelderen). However, such a meaning lacks any foundation in the Hebrew itself.

On the other hand, the second meaning, 'to meet,' was used in another
of the ancient translations, as well as in many more recent ones. This is

the reading of Theodotion (sunelthōsin allēlois), of the Dutch "Staten Vertaling" and "Leidsche Vertaling," the variant reading of BJ, and the private translation of many commentators such as Sellin, Wellhausen, Weiser, and Wolff.

7. The decision as to which component should be made explicit in the translation has often been taken on the basis of false arguments. One cannot say that component (a) cannot be rendered because two men can also meet by accident (so rightly Erling Hammershaimb, The Book of Amos, A Commentary, New York, 1970 (translation from the third Danish edition Amos Fortolket published in 1967 by Nyt Nordisk Forlag, Copenhagen; English translation by John Sturdy, p. 58), or that component (b) cannot be translated because two men can also live in the same house so that they do not need to meet! It is not justified to press the consequence-condition relationship that way.

A decision has also sometimes been influenced by rich allegorical interpretation of this verse. So for some the two men represent the Lord and Israel, for others the Lord and the prophet. However, the sentence should simply be taken as an example from daily life. It is possible that there is some hint of the Lord and his prophet (the other possibility has to be excluded because of the structure of the discourse), and that this verse provides a hidden answer to the skeptical question (raised by enemies) of what Amos would have to do with the Lord. Such a possibility exists, in which case there would be a direct relationship between themes A and A' as indicated in Figure 13 of the Appendix. However, one cannot be sure, since no evidence is available.

8. See Fauna and Flora of the Bible, s.v. lion.

9. Compare G. Dalman, Arbeit und Sitte in Palästina, VI, p. 338; J. G. Wilkinson, The Manners and Customs of the Ancient Egyptians, London, 1878, Vol. 2, p. 103, 109f.; W. Corswant, Dictionnaire d'archéologie biblique, Neuchâtel-Paris, 1956, p. 149.

10. The copyist could have made a visual error because of the occurrence of exactly the same word after almost the same consonants in the second line (so Cripps, Touzard, Sellin, Snaith, Wolff). For Maag and also for Amsler paḥ is an exegetical gloss to moqesh since the meaning of the last word was already unknown to the LXX translator. An additional argument for the deletion of paḥ would be that the word disturbs the meter 3+2.

11. This seems to be the interpretation of the Targum. The LXX in reading aneu ikseutou "without a fowler" probably read a participle of the verb yaqash (meyaqqish?). This reading has been taken over by the Vulgate (absque aucupe) and by Luther (Vogler). The meaning bait is given in Brown-Driver-Briggs s.v. and has been defended by a.o. Wellhausen, van Hoonacker, van Gelderen, Harper, Touzard, Snaith and Amsler.

12. According to Gesenius s.v. this is the first possible meaning: Stellholz. So also Weiser, whereas Wellhausen and Harper consider this sense as a second possibility. A shift of meaning from bait to the fatal instrument to which it was attached is, of course, very well imaginable. It is also possible that moqesh indicated both the instrument and the bait.

13. Gesenius s.v. gives this as a second possible meaning. It has been defended by many scholars such as Budde, Marti, Gressmann, Sellin, Maag, M. A. Canney (Amos in Peak's Commentary, 1920), and most recently again by Wolff. Archeological evidence underlines the frequent use of throwing-

sticks in the Middle East, especially in connection with fowling. See e.g. pictures 9b and 17b in M. von Oppenheim, Der Tell Halaf, 1931, and picture 18 in A. Moortgat, Die bildende Kunst des Alten Orients und die Bergvölker, 1932.

14. So Cripps. Compare the reading of the Syrohexaplar (in margin): aneu diktuou: "without a net."

15. Both questions start with the same Hebrew question particle and they have the same local setting in a city. They both have to do with city people, after the hunters of the earlier questions.

16. Even the lion of verse 8 is a picture of God in that context.

17. So rightly W. Zimmerli, article pais, Theologisches Wörterbuch zum Neuen Testament, Band V, p. 663f.

18. Compare A Translator's Handbook on Luke on 12.37.

19. In Hebrew the condition-consequence relation is expressed through the initial sentence position of the first subject and through the verbal tenses, since the perfect tense indicates the independent event and the imperfect tense the dependent one. See D. Michel, Tempora und Satzstellung in den Psalmen, Abhandlungen zur Evangelischen Theologie 1, 1960, p. 128ff.

20. The last question may also very well refer back to the first one (verse 3), in which case the two who walk together are the Lord and his prophet. For some scholars this is an absolute certainty. So Morgenstern, who maintains: "No other interpretation of this passage is justifiable" (Amos Studies I, HUCA XI, 1936, p. 32). The discourse structure is, of course, in favor of this interpretation. Moreover, if this is the main thesis of this argument it becomes clear that verse 3 is more the statement of the thesis than an illustration to enforce the argument and so it is clear why this verse is not put in parallelism.

21. Some translations (see TEV section heading) take verses 13-15 to refer to Samaria in spite of the mention of Bethel, and others emphasize Bethel as a separate place. So BJ, which emphasizes Bethel and for that reason has to introduce three different section headings for three different sections.

22. Only the LXX has the reading en Assuriois; the other Greek translations follow the Hebrew text (en azoto) and the same is true for Targum and Vulgate. It would be very difficult, if not impossible, to explain Ashdod as secondary reading.

23. So LXX: epi to oros. Joüon (par. 136j) speaks in this connection about a possible "pluriel de généralisation."

24. So Gesenius-Kautzsch, par. 124e.

25. So rightly Wolff. Ancient translators often seem to make explicit what is not implicit in the Hebrew word! See for this Symmachus: achortasias (famine), LXX: thaumasta (remarkable things) and Vulgate: insanias.

26. Reading yeşobeb with Targum (tqphh), Syriac version (nhdrjh) and Vulgate (circuietur) and taking tsar not as 'distress' but as 'enemy,' a meaning which seems to be required by the larger context. Enemy should remain indefinite (NAB, NEB, TT, TEV) and should not be personalized (Mft, S-G).

27. Several scholars have proposed restricting this unit to verse 12a, b, and c, concluding it with the clause "so the Israelites will be saved" and taking the clauses of verse 12d with the following paragraph, verses 13-15. (So, among others, H. Gressmann, A. Weiser, F. Nötscher,

V. Maag, and S. Amsler.) In doing so, the next paragraph is provided with
a clear addressee (the people of Israel who dwell in Samaria) which is
otherwise lacking. None of the existing translations consulted ever made
such a division of the text, since the arguments against it are rather
strong. This is especially true for Wolff's argument against the use of
a participle construction as opening phrase of a new paragraph (op. cit.,
p. 235).

Such a division also seems to go against the linguistic structure of
verse 12 in which both parts of the comparison are neatly balanced so
that the sentences starting respectively with 'as' and 'so' are of about
equal length.

28. A. R. Hulst (Old Testament Translation Problems, Leiden, 1960,
p. 239) has coded this particular verse 'C,' which means according to
the introduction (p. viii) that "more than one legitimate translation of
the Masoretic text is possible."

29. So rightly Henry R. Moeller, "Ambiguity at Amos 3:12," TBT 15,
1964, pp. 31-34.

30. The same reading is found in the version put forth by the Jewish
Publication Society of America.

31. Among commentators this interpretation has been defended by van
Gelderen and Morgenstern (Amos Studies, Part Four, ad loc.).

32. The same view is expressed by van Hoonacker and A. Neher, Amos,
Contribution à l'étude du prophétisme, Paris, 1950.

33. See Exo 22.9-12; Gen 31.39; 1 Sam 17.34f. and par. 266 of the
Code of Hammurabi.

34. A. Weiser (in Die Prophetie des Amos, p. 144ff.) has pointed out
the irony of the 'rescue' and though some later commentators do recog-
nize this they do not always draw the semantic conclusions from this important statement.

35. Isaac Rabinowitz's proposal (The Crux at Amos III 12, Vetus
Testamentum 11, 1961, pp. 228-231) to read ūbad mishshōq is followed
here. The conviction that d-m-sh-q represented an erroneous fusion of
two words is already very old. Early Jewish commentators like Ibn Ezra
and Kimhi suggested already that the last word be read as shoq: 'leg,'
'support,' and this suggestion was taken over by Joseph Reider (DMSQ in
Amos 3:12, Journal of Biblical Literature 67, 1948, pp. 245-248) and
according to Rabinowitz by M. L. Margolis. On the other hand, the reading
bad for the first word has already been proposed by H. J. Elhorst, De
Profetie van Amos, Leiden, 1900, ad loc. Against this solution Wolff has
argued that shoq is never used in Hebrew with this figurative meaning.
Although figurative extensions of shoq are not lacking in Old Testament
Hebrew, it is true that this particular non-literal meaning of the word
does not occur. However, one should take into account that here one has
to do with a very specialized vocabulary and that this figurative meaning did already exist in Aramaic (see M. Jastrow, Dictionary of Talmud
Babli, Yerushalmi, Midrashic Literature and Targumim, New York, 1950,
s.v. shaqaʾ).

36. This is Moeller's translation, art. cit., p. 34.

37. See J. P. Pritchard, The Ancient Near East in Pictures, Princeton,
1954: 451, 658, and 660.

38. For other cultural equivalences, see especially A Translator's
Handbook on Luke on 8.16.

39. See E. Jenni, article on bayit in Theologisches Handwörterbuch zum Alten Testament edited by Ernst Jenni and Claus Westermann, München-Zürich, 1971, col. 311. The expression house of Jacob occurs again in 9.8 in what seems to be a secondary text, but Jacob alone is mentioned in 6.8; 7.2,5; 8.7. The use of tribal names is a frequent feature in Amos. There is, apart from house of Jacob, house of Joseph in 5.6 and house of Isaac in 7.16.

40. That the wrong choice of participants has some bearing upon the text is clear from Sellin's argument. For him the participants can only be Israelites, but then they cannot warn the house of Jacob. So 'house of Jacob' must be a scribal error for 'house of Jeroboam.' Again, this can only be stated because 9.8b is not considered to be a genuine Amos text. Interestingly, one LXX manuscript (86) has the marginal reading israēl for iakōb. In the Bohairic translation, this reading even came into the text, giving rise to a conflate reading: "Israel, the house of Jacob."

41. One proposed solution is to give a transliteration of the Hebrew word, such as "God (of) Sabaoth" (so TT and BJ), since in the course of time this expression came to be used as a personal name. But this is certainly not true for this Amos text in which one finds the earliest attested form with the definite article. Moreover, in many languages such a personal name would not be understood and could be given a very different meaning (a choice term for black magic!).

42. Such a translation already has ancient support. Compare the frequent translation of tseba'oth by pantokratōr in the LXX.

43. In fact, it has been proposed to take 'Bethel' here as the god Bethel, known from the Elephantine texts and, according to some, from Old Testament texts such as Jer 48.13, so that the reference here would be to the altars of this god either in Samaria or in the whole Northern Kingdom. See O. Eissfeldt, Der Gott Bethel, Archiv für Religionswissenschaft 28, 1930, pp. 1-30, and J. P. Hyatt, The Deity Bethel and the Old Testament, Journal of the American Oriental Society 59, 1939, pp. 81-98. For further references see also Koehler-Baumgartner, Lexikon, s.v. In this context, it seems, however, far more natural to think of the famous cultic center Bethel in the Northern Kingdom.

44. It is debated whether winter houses and summer houses are separate buildings or part of one and the same building. Several scholars take the latter view, that the winter house was on the ground floor and the summer house was simply the upper story which was built on the roof of the house (compare Judges 3.20 and Jer 36.22; so G. Dalman, Arbeit und Sitte I,2, p. 473; VII, p. 79; Harper and others [see literature mentioned in Harper ad loc.]).

However, the only Oriental inscription from the time of Amos which has been discovered up till now and which makes mention of a winter and a summer house clearly means two separate buildings. It is the famous Barrekub inscription found at Zenjirli in North Syria. For the text see H. Donner and W. Röllig, Kanaanäische und Aramäische Inschriften I, Wiesbaden, 1971, Nr. 216, p. 40, and for the translation, idem, II, Wiesbaden, 1968, pp. 233-234. The German translation of the last part of the inscription (16-19) runs as follows: "Und ein schönes Haus hatten meine Väter, die Könige von Sam'al, nicht; es war das Haus des Kilamuwa, das ihnen gehörte, und das war Winterhaus für sie und Sommerhaus. So habe ich dieses Haus gebaut." The editors rightly comment (p. 234): "Das

Gebäude, dessen Errichtung Gegenstand der Inschrift ist, sollte offenbar dem Ubelstande abhelfen, dass die Könige vom Sam'al nur einen einzigen Palast als Winter--und Sommerquartier besassen."

45. It does not seem probable that information is added since the phraseology would be anticlimactic. For that reason Marti proposed that batim rabim was a misreading of bate habhenim "houses of ebony" or "houses decorated with ebony," a proposal accepted by Robinson, Maag, Osty, and Amsler. However, the information need not be taken as added, and text-critical grounds for the emendation are completely lacking.

46. Moreover, it is the interpretation found in the ancient versions. So LXX: oikoi heteroi polloi and Vulgate: aedes multae.

47. RSV, unlike TEV, NEB, JB, NAB, S-G, has God speaking throughout the passage.

48. This in spite of earlier attempts to see in the leading men the implicit object of the comparison. Such an interpretation has been favored by the masculine form of the plural imperative shimᶜu and by the presence of several masculine genders in this paragraph. However, feminine forms of the second person plural are rarely used and often replaced by masculine forms (so Joüon, par. 150a), and the use of other masculine genders in this paragraph can partly be explained by the desire to be grammatically in concord with the opening imperative. No artificial conflict should be built up between a wrong interpretation of grammatical meaning and the meaning of the total discourse.

49. This is the implicit ground selected by A. Weiser who speaks of "adliges Vollblut" (Profetie, p. 156) and "edelste Rasse" (Zwölf kleinen Propheten, p. 150.)

50. Compare Psa 22.12. According to Dalman (op. cit., VI, p. 176) the asking for drinks may allude to the fact that these cows "von ihren Hirten verlangten, das Trinkwasser an sie heranzubringen."

51. See S. Speier, Bemerkungen zu Amos (IV 1a), Vetus Testamentum 3, 1953, p. 306f.: "ein üppig gebautes Mädchen." His arguments are based upon comparative philology, more particularly on usages in modern Arabic.

52. It is remarkable to see that though none of the ancient versions made the implicit object of the comparison explicit, at least some of them felt the need to make the implicit ground of the comparison (namely 'fat-ness') explicit in rendering the Hebrew expression by "fat cows." (So Symmachus: hai boes eutrophoi "healthy [in the sense of 'well-nourished'] cows"; Syro-hexaplaric text, translated saginatae "fat" (the Göttingen Septuagint apparatus); Vulgate: vaccae pinques "fat cows.") It is like-wise remarkable that no modern English translator--with the exception of the translators of TEV--seems to have shared this feeling, although it is clear that a literal translation of the source metaphor makes little, and perhaps even wrong, sense.

53. See James Lauriault, "On Handling Meanings in the Vernacular," TBT 9, 1958, pp. 145-151.

54. So Vulgate: dominis vestris. It is, of course, not true that the Vulgate text presupposes a different Hebrew form (against Wolff, op. cit., p. 241.) The variant reading has a translational character. The use of third person plural possessive in the Hebrew text, which conflicts with the direct discourse, can easily be explained syntactically as caused by the chain of appositional participles.

55. The Hebrew does not use one of the two common terms for husband, but an extremely rare one typical of patriarchal society in which the husband is the 'master' (compare Gen 18.12.)

56. This is what has happened in the LXX: epidote hēmin. Compare also Vulgate afferte and Syriac version. The explicit object wine (oinon) is found in a late correction of codex W and in the Sahidic and Armenian translations.

57. See A Translator's Handbook on Acts 3.14; A Translator's Handbook on Romans 1.2, 3b-4; 6.19; 7.12.

58. For ki see Joüon, par. 165b, e; for hinneh see Joüon, par. 164a.

59. As to the setting, J. Touzard (op. cit., ad loc.) thinks of the particular circumstances in which the Assyrians deported their captives: a ring with a cord attached to it was put through the lower lip of the captives. Sometimes the commentary on this passage reveals false presuppositions: (a) that the text should be understood literally (so especially Budde, op. cit., ad loc.), or (b) that the metaphorical image of cows is still presupposed, so that the instruments mentioned in the source text should be understood as suitable for the violent transport of cattle. William L. Holladay (A Concise Hebrew and Aramaic Lexicon of the Old Testament, Leiden, 1971, s.v., tsen) still adds a question mark to the proposed meaning "butcher's hook"; for others like Sellin, Procksch, Maag and Amsler, dughah simply is a misleading gloss since cows cannot be treated with fish-hooks. But it does not seem to be a sound principle to violate the source text in order to satisfy false presuppositions! It is noteworthy that Sellin, who convincingly refutes an exegesis which is on a "false track," becomes himself the victim of a false exegesis. On the other hand, to say that the second instrument is a fishing tool, but that the extraordinary circumstances require the exceptional use of an extraordinary instrument to push cattle, such as a harpoon (so Wolff; compare BJ), seems a rather desperate attempt to serve different interpretations at once, and as such, it is more desperate than convincing.

60. So a.o. Gesenius-Buhl, s.v. tsen; Brown-Driver-Briggs, s.v. tsinnah; RSV, S-G, NAB.

61. From the Hebrew homonym tsinnah, a large rectangular shield. This homonym has been read by the Targum: tereysa', by Aquila: thureois, and it is probably presupposed by most of the other ancient versions which remain in the semantic domain of weapons and which read either a generic term for 'arms' (Symmachus and LXX: hoplois) or specific words for certain arms (Vulgate: contus "pike" and Theodotion: dorasin "spears.") This particular homonym has also been selected as text reading by NEB and TT, and it has been defended by Snaith and others.

62. So Wolff, who refers to Accadian sinnitu, "snares" (see The Assyrian Dictionary of the Oriental Institute of the University of Chicago, 1956, 16.201.) Compare also S. J. Schwantes, Note on Amos 4.2b, Zeitschrift für die Alttestamentliche Wissenschaft 79, 1967, p. 82f).

63. So a.o. Gesenius-Buhl and Brown-Driver-Briggs, RSV, S-G, Mft, NAB.

64. From the Hebrew homonym sir 'pot,' which has been read by Aquila and Jerome (in lebetibus pisciculōrum), LXX (lebētas 'pots'; in view of the following hupokaiomenous it is possible that the Hebrew hapax dughah has been read as dalgah, a reading which has been taken over by the Vulgate in ollis ferventibus) and by some modern English translations such as NEB and TT.

65. For the accusative of direction see Brockelmann, Syntax, par. 89, and Gesenius' Hebrew Grammar as edited and enlarged by the late E. Kautzsch, 2nd revised edition translated by A. E. Cowley, Oxford, 1910, par. 118d ff.

66. The LXX reading eksenechthēsesthe does not necessarily presuppose a hophal vocalization of the Hebrew verbal form, as it may simply be a translational transformation.

67. So LXX aporriphēsesthe and Jerome proiiciemini. The hiphil vocalization of the MT depends upon a certain interpretation of the following object noun. Compare Keil (op. cit., ad loc.) who makes the following interesting suggestion: "Der masoretischen Vocalisation liegt vermutlich die Ansicht zu Grunde, dass harmonah dem talmudischen harmana' entsprechend, königliche Macht oder Herrschaft bedeute." In this connection he quotes Rashi's comments: abjicietis auctoritatem i.e. paene regiam.

68. The Vulgate transliterates Armon. The LXX read a combination of a common noun and a proper name hahar harimmon (the mountain Rimmon with dittography) and gives a transliteration of the proper name. For all the orthographical variants, see the edition of Ziegler.

69. It is unnecessary to give a detailed list of all the conjectural readings which have been proposed, but one should be mentioned in particular, since it has unfortunately been followed in several modern English translations. It is the proposal to change the unintelligible Hebrew word rather dramatically so as to get another rare Hebrew word with the meaning 'dung-heap' (reading hammadmenah, a word only found in Isa 25.10.) This conjectural reading was first proposed by Duhm (see Zeitschrift für die alttestamentliche Wissenschaft 31, 6) and it is followed by Robinson and Snaith. So S-G has "and you will be cast upon the refuse heap," NEB: "and pitched on a dunghill," NAB: "and you shall be cast into the mire." In spite of this astonishing unanimity--without parallel in translations in other major languages!--and in spite of the footnote in the NEB saying that this is the probable reading, such a reading has rightly been rejected by the majority of scholars, and consequently it should not be adopted in translations.

70. So Elhorst, van Hoonacker, Sellin, Weiser, Maag, Amsler, and Wolff.

71. The emendation is supported in part by the reading hermōna found in the hexaplaric recension, the catena group, and, according to Eusebius (Onomasticon, p. 146), in Aquila. It is possible that the reading armenian found in 407, Symmachus, the Syro-hexaplaric text, and in the Onomasticon of Eusebius (without source indication), as well as the Targum reading hurmini, refer to a province of Armenia. The paraphrase of the Targum could perhaps be translated as "far beyond the mountains of Armenia." Whether this reading presupposes a vocalization har minni (Hammershaimb, op. cit., ad loc.) is uncertain. Although the possibility of an emendation of this type should be kept in mind, it is less advisable to introduce it in translation as TT proposes: "and be thrown on the mountains of Armenia."

4.4-12   ISRAEL DOESN'T LEARN GOD'S LESSONS

1. An additional difficulty is that this time the transition is rather strange and the meaning of verse 12 is far from clear, as will be shown in the detailed treatment below.

2. So S-G uses a title "The Sacrilege of Sacrifice" for the first message and "Repeated Chastisements Are Futile" for the rest. On the other hand, BJ covers the messages with a rather long title and uses "Doxology" for the hymn.

3. Three lines have a meter 3+3 and one has a meter 2+2.

4. So J. Begrich, Die priesterliche Tora, in Gesammelte Studien zum Alten Testament, Theologische Bücherei 21, 1964, pp. 232-260.

5. See F. M. Abel, Géographie de la Palestine, Tome II, Paris, 1967, p. 270f., 336f.

6. That is what a few exegetes, mainly older ones (so Keil, Harper, Touzard, Cripps), pretend to be the case. However, even ironically it would be impossible to make such an exaggeration. Moreover, such an interpretation rests upon a false understanding of Deut 14.28 (namely that tithes should only be brought every third year) and upon a highly improbable reading of the Hebrew text. "Every morning" is normally expressed in Hebrew by the preposition le and the plural form of the noun: labbeqarim. For lishloshet yamim in the sense of "the third day" see Brockelmann, Vergleichende Grammatik, I, p. 485.

7. See among others Elhorst, Wellhausen, Sellin, van Gelderen, Weiser, Maag, Wolff, Amsler, Hammershaimb.

8. See A Translator's Handbook on Luke, 2.24.

9. Johs. Pedersen, Israel, Its Life and Culture, III-IV, London-Copenhagen, 1947, p. 338.

10. Compare E. A. Nida, Bible Translating, p. 234.

11. See especially Pedersen, op. cit., pp. 307-313.

12. The introductory infinitive absolute qatter, surrounded by imperatives, has the function of an imperative. See Gesenius' Hebrew Grammar, par. 113bb, and Joüon, par. 123x. There is no necessity to change the vowels of MT.

13. See Holladay, Lexicon, s.v.

14. The preposition min has to be taken in a partitive sense (Brockelmann, Syntax, par. 111a) and not in a privative sense as has wrongly been done in NEB ("without leaven") and TT ("what is unleavened.")

15. See especially Pedersen, op. cit., p. 323ff.

16. Each paragraph begins in Hebrew with a first person singular form of the verb in the past tense.

17. LXX reads kai oud' hōs 'even not in this way' in all the other occurrences of the refrain. Also the variant reading kai oud'houtōs is found, in verse 8 mainly in manuscripts of the Alexandrian group, in verses 9, 10, and 11 mainly in other manuscripts. For details see the edition of Ziegler.

18. For the literary interrelationships see Wolff, op. cit., pp. 251-253.

19. Compare V. Maag, op. cit., p. 21: "Der Parallelismus membrorum ist stellenweise straff, stellenweise locker oder in auffallend langen Perioden durchgeführt, oder er verschwindet so zu sagen ganz. Man kann sich daher fragen, ob nicht eher gehobene Prosa vorliegt."

20. It may even be that the Hebrew particle does not connect verse 6 with the preceding passage but stresses the information which follows.

21. More precisely, a "complex metaphor." See especially M. B. Dagut, A Linguistic Analysis of Some Semantic Problems of Hebrew-English Translation, Doctoral Thesis (mimeographed), Jerusalem, 1971, pp. 96-146.

[235]

22. In fact, some of the ancient versions show clearly that the idiom--in spite of the illuminating parallel information--was already misunderstood at a quite early time. So e.g. LXX which reads gomphiasmon odontōn 'toothache!' Targum ʾaqhayut, Syriac qahyut, Vulgate stuporem dentium 'bluntness.' It is highly improbable that these versions read a Hebrew noun qehayon (so Harper, Wolff, Hammershaimb) since such a noun is not attested in the Hebrew of any period! Apart from possible cross-influences, it is more likely that the familiar figure of 'teeth be-coming blunt' (proverbial in Jer 31.29f.) simply replaces the figure that was not understood, whereby some morphological resemblances with the root qhh may have played a less significant part. One should not follow P. de Lagarde (Bildung der Nomina, 201) and Brown-Driver-Briggs (s.v.) and "correct" the Hebrew text by reading qehayon. After all, Symmachus and Theodotion have the "right" (i.e. literal) understanding of the MT (katharismon.)

23. Compare A Translator's Handbook on Ruth, 1.1.

24. This does not imply that originally this paragraph may have pre-ceded verse 6 (so Harper, op. cit., ad loc.). It only means that the original text deals with these plagues distinctly, with hunger first, according to the classical schema, and therefore does not make these semantic relationships fully explicit in its surface structure.

25. See R. B. Y. Scott, Meteorological Phenomena and Terminology, Zeitschrift für die alttestamentliche Wissenschaft 64, 1952, p. 23. Compare also Dalman, Arbeit und Sitte III, pp. 4-6.

26. See A Translator's Handbook on Ruth, 1.22.

27. One ancient version thought about such human diseases as fever and jaundice! So LXX: epataksa humas en purōsei kai en ikterōi.

28. So Dalman, op. cit. I/2, p. 326: "Blasswerden der Spitzen des grünen Getreides infolge Würmerbildung."

29. Some translators understand the Hebrew as meaning 'the multitude of your gardens and vineyards' (RSV footnote, NAB, TEV.) This meaning is supported by several ancient versions. So Targum saqyut, Symmachus and Theodotion to plēthos and Vulgate multitudinem. But to understand the Hebrew sentence structure in this way is very hard, if not impossible. This particular use of the infinitive construct in Hebrew would be with-out analogy.

30. Reading heherabti. This emendation was first proposed by Wellhausen. It should also be noted that the structure of the other paragraphs of this section makes the original presence of such a verbal form very probable.

31. Consulting commentaries and recent translations on this particu-lar verse may be rather discouraging and confusing because of the almost wild abundance of interpretations which can be found. However, most of these differences are due to proposals for drastic or minor changes in the Hebrew text for which there is no particular need, and which can therefore be passed over in silence.

32. Other modern English translations like Mft ("flower of your steeds,") NEB ("your troops of horses,") and TT ("your squadrons of horses") go back to a different reading or a different understanding of the Hebrew word for "taking captive." Mft follows the proposal first made by H. Zeydner (in: Bijdragen tot de tekstcritiek op het Oude Testa-ment, Theologische Studien, 1886, pp. 196-207, and 1888, pp. 247-264;

for this text see especially TS 1888, p. 249ff.) to read sebi (=tsebi)
'glory.' This proposal has been accepted by Elhorst, Richter
(Erläuterungen zu dunklen Stellen in den kleinen Propheten, 1914), Sellin,
Budde, Maag, Amsler and Wolff. On the other hand, NEB and TT seem to
understand the Hebrew word differently on the base of a cognate Arabic
word. Apart from the fact that it is unlikely that the horses were killed
(see above), there is no urgent need to change the Hebrew text or to
understand it in a different way.

33. For the explanatory use of the waw see Gesenius-Kautzsch, (German
edition), par. 154a. It is not necessary to delete the waw. The whole discussion about this particle is translationally without interest.

34. It is certainly not necessary to follow the same versional evidence partly based upon a different vocalization of the Hebrew text as
has been suggested in some commentaries. LXX reads kai anēgagon en puri
tas parembolas humōn en tēi orgēi humōn (many mss. mou) "I have made go
up your camps with fire in your (my) anger," thus vocalizing Hebrew
b'sh as be'esh (with fire) and reading, at least in many manuscripts,
be'api (in my anger). Several scholars like Elhorst, Sellin, van Hoonacker,
van Gelderen considered the Hebrew text presupposed by the LXX as original, and especially the last two scholars give interesting arguments as
to how the MT became "corrupted." It should, however, be noted that all
the other versions support MT and that in view of the total discourse of
this paragraph the reading of MT alone makes a good connection with the
result of pestilence. The LXX reading is not followed by any modern translation.

35. So among others Wellhausen, Sellin, Budde, Weiser, van Gelderen,
Cripps, van Hoonacker, Touzard, Morgenstern, Hammershaimb. See, however,
especially Wolff's important arguments against this opinion, his own
interpretation and rather convincing reconstruction of the setting of
this paragraph (op. cit., p. 261f.).

36. It has been suggested that a concrete punishment like the one
mentioned in 3.14b originally stood here but was omitted through scribal
changes (so, among others, van Hoonacker and Sellin). Or this may be a
replacing formula, that is, a scribe replaced an original, terrible
threat by a euphemistic this (so H. Gressmann, op. cit., p. 344). Or this
euphemistic this may have been intended in the sense of the oath-formula,
"Thus will God do to me and thus will he add." (This is the opinion of
Harper and Cripps. For the oath-formula, compare A Translator's Handbook
on Ruth, p. 18.) However, there is no evidence for anything of this kind.

Closely related to the replacement theory is the idea of some other
scholars that an original this is intended to heighten the suspense (so
van Gelderen and Robinson, op. cit., p. 87). However, a connection with
the standard oath-formula cannot easily be made, and such psychological
arguments seem to be rather modern and sophisticated, and so all these
explanations sound unlikely.

37. Wolff thinks of a later preacher in the time of Josia who referred to the ruins of the Bethel sanctuary (2 Kgs 23.15ff.). The imperfect tense of the Hebrew verbs would then refer to a unique present act,
which is grammatically possible (see Brockelmann, Syntax, par. 42f.).

4.13   THE POWER OF GOD TO CREATE

    1. See especially F. Horst, Die Doxologien im Amosbuch, Zeitschrift für die alttestamentliche Wissenschaft 47, 1929, pp. 45-54. With this closing section the total discourse unit 6-13 shows a pattern consisting of plague--theme of return--doxology. Such a pattern also occurs in 1 Kgs 8.33ff.
    2. The first four half lines of the Hebrew poem have three stressed syllables each, the last line has four.
    3. The second Hebrew verb, usually rendered "create," had not yet undergone the spiritualization so typical of this verb in e.g. Gen 1.1. So rightly Maag, op. cit., p. 134. Compare also P. Humbert, Emploi et portée du verbe bârâ..., Theologische Zeitschrift 3, 1947, p. 401ff.
    4. Seemingly, none of these problems exist for the translators of NEB. For them God "forges the thunder," in which they follow the LXX, whose reading is certainly not based on the original Hebrew and has no other support. "Showers abundant rain on the earth," is based on a conjecture which NEB calls "probable reading."
    5. Only very rarely will the translator be able to maintain something of the original ambiguity in the translation. One of the ancient versions succeeded in doing so because the same double meaning existed in the receptor language. So LXX: kai ktizōn pneuma.
    6. So most of the older commentators and more recently Hammershaimb.
    7. So Wolff. The ancient versions normally took it that way. So Aquila tis homilia autou; Symmachus to phōnēma autou; Theodotion ton logon autou. In all these cases, autou can only refer to God and not to the plural anthrōpous. In the case of the Vulgate eloquium suum it is the noun eloquium which reveals that the reference is to God. Some deviating readings in some of the ancient versions are due to a misunderstanding of the hapax legomenon sheho. So LXX in reading ton christon autou 'his Messiah' substituted meshīho for mah-sheho, and the Syriac in reading mana' hi 'eshbuhteh 'how great is his glory' probably substituted mah shebeho for the same. (See Mark Sebōk, Die Syrische Uebersetzung der zwölf kleinen Propheten und ihr Verhältnis zu dem massoretischen Text und zu den älteren Uebersetzungen, namentlich den LXX und dem Targum, 1887.) The Targum reading mah ʿobadohiy may go back to a substitution maʿasehu, and there is no reason to make this substitution with Sellin.
    8. Versional evidence is divided. LXX presuppose weʿeyphah: orthron kai homichlēn; the Vulgate, on the other hand, the MT faciens matutinam nebulam.

5.1-3   CONCLUSION: LAMENT FOR ISRAEL

    1. On the surface level, the unity seems to be guaranteed by the use of the Hebrew particle meaning 'for' which introduces verse 3 and thus relates it to the foregoing verse. However, it is well known that such a particle is often due to an editor who uses it as a literary device to connect completely independent statements.
    2. The lack of clarity in the Hebrew here led to a wrong identification in one of the ancient versions. With the exception of most manuscripts of the Lucianic main group, LXX reads akousate ton logon kuriou touton 'hear this word of the Lord.' One cannot say that LXX substitutes

yhwh for hzh as has been defended in the past (so Vater, Amos übersetzt und erläutert mit Beifügung des Hebräischen Textes und des Griechischen der Septuaginta nebst Anmerkungen zu letzterem, 1810, ad loc.) since hzh has been rendered by touton. It seems also hardly justified to describe the intention of the translators in the following way: "LXX kann nicht früh genug herausstellen, dass Amos 'Jahwes Wort' verkündet" (Wolff, ad loc.) On the contrary, the translators felt the need to identify the message, but they made information explicit which was not implicit in the particular discourse.

3. On this see especially H. Jahnow, Das hebräische Leichenlied im Rahmen der Völkerdichtung, Zeitschrift für die alttestamentliche Wissenschaft, Beihefte 36, 1923, p. 101.

4. In Hebrew the funeral song consists of two lines, each one divided into two halves. In both cases the first half is longer than the second one. The lines of the first half have three beats each, whereas the lines of the second half have only two. As a result each line has a meter 3+2.

5. The Hebrew genitive construction has an underlying semantic structure of the type A=B in which both terms are equated. (See chapter 3 in E. A. Nida and C. R. Taber, The Theory and Practice of Translation.) It is important to note this since in one of the ancient versions this underlying semantic structure has been wrongly taken to be of the type A is part of B, which in turn has given rise to a complete semantic distortion of the whole poem. (So the Targum: bnt' hd' khnsht' dyshr'l, "one of the daughters of the community of Israel.") However, even a right translation such as the virgin Israel, in which the semantic relations are clearly stated, does not always solve the translational problem.

6. For this see J. de Waard, "Biblical Metaphors and Their Translation," The Bible Translator 25, 1974, pp. 107-116.

7. So James Luther Mays, Amos, A Commentary, The Westminster Press, Philadelphia, 1969, p. 85.

8. It seems also to be more in accordance with the stereotyped formula to read simply "the Lord" instead of the Lord God. Such an operation is not simply arbitrary, so as to assure a 3+2 meter which would otherwise be lacking, but also it has internal evidence, as can be seen from the literal counterpart in the opening formula to verse 4.

9. See Gesenius' Hebrew Grammar, par. 117z.

10. That some adaptation to the receptor language is necessary was already felt by ancient translators. Compare the words eks hēs in the LXX and the same translational solution found in the Targum, the Vulgate, and in the Syriac version.

11. This does not mean that weha'ir has to be added to the Hebrew text as has been proposed by Gressmann, Maag, Morgenstern and--as a possibility--by Elliger in Biblia Hebraica Stuttgartensia (BHS). One has simply to do with information which is implicit in the source text and which often has to be made explicit in translation.

12. For the organization of armed forces in Israel, see especially R. de Vaux, Les institutions de l'ancien testament, II, Paris, les éditions du cerf, 1967, pp. 25-30.

1. It is true that verse 4 shows some formal relationships with the preceding paragraph: the opening formula in verse 4a is identical with the reconstructed opening formula of verse 3, and verses 3 and 4 are related in Hebrew by a particle usually rendered 'for.' Nevertheless, verse 4 can better be considered as the opening verse of a new paragraph for several reasons: (a) the connecting particle in the beginning is also often found as introducing independent sayings; (b) the setting changes from a war scene to that of sanctuaries and exile; (c) the call to life contrasts with the funeral song of the preceding paragraph; (d) the connection of verse 4 with the following verses is clearly shown by the fact that verse 4b gives an exhortation which is followed by a warning in verse 5a, which warning in its turn is motivated in verse 5b; and (e) the overall structure of Amos (Appendix, Section 1).

2. For the interesting exegetical implications of the use of the Hebrew verb darash, see especially Arvid S. Kapelrud, Central Ideas in Amos, 2. reprint, Universitetsforlaget Oslo, 1971, pp. 35-37; and C. Westermann, Die Begriffe für Fragen und Suchen im Alten Testament, Kerygma und Dogma 6, 1960, pp. 2-30. However, the interesting scholarly discussions have no direct bearing upon translation.

3. See Gesenius' Hebrew Grammar, par. 110f.; Joüon, par. 168a; K. Beyer, Semitische Syntax im Neuen Testament, 1968, p. 243.

4. Other examples are "Gilgal shall taste the gall of exile" (George Adam Smith); "Gilgal wird Galle weinen" (Ewald); "Gilgal giltig entgilt es" (Baur); "Die Rollstadt rollt von dannen" (Orelli). Unfortunately, most of the examples lack naturalness of expression.

5. In fact, this is already explicit in Hebrew, since the Hebrew uses a masculine gender in the verbal forms to indicate that it is the population of the town which is concerned. Place names are feminine when the place itself is concerned and often masculine when the focus is on its population. See Joüon, par. 134g. So it is not true that the third person masculine of the verbs "must refer to the respective sanctuaries rather than to the cities in which they were located" (so Morgenstern, op. cit., ad loc). Moreover, it is semantically impossible for a sanctuary to undergo the event described by the verb.

6. This is S. Mowinckel's translation in Det Gamle Testamente oversatt av Michelet, Mowinckel og Messel, vol. 3, Oslo, 1944.

7. Because of this, scholars have proposed changes in the Hebrew text, but none of these changes is necessary. For all the changes proposed, ranging from reasonable to rather wild, see the commentaries. It is true that the transitive use of the verb tsalah remains strange, but such a use is not without parallel (compare 2 Sam 19.17), and it is also possible to consider beyt yoseph as an accusative of direction (so van Gelderen). It is likewise true that it is strange that the image of the comparison in the second half line (the fire) becomes the grammatical subject of the third half line, but one should not go so far as to say that this is linguistically impossible (so Wellhausen, Amsler).

It is not impossible to give a different translation of the existing Hebrew text on the surface level. Compare the translation of the LXX: hopōs mē analampsēy hōs pur ho oikos Iōsēph ('that the house of Joseph not flame up like a fire'). Wolff seems to think that this is a good dynamic rendering of the Hebrew, but he does not explain why. Anyway, his own translation is not half so dynamic and the only agreement with the LXX is the grammatical subject position of 'the house of Joseph.' The LXX translation analampsēy of the verb tsalaḥ remains puzzling. The often quoted example from Ecclesiasticus 8.10 is not really illuminating. It is true that a verb tsalah is found in the Hebrew text of Ecclesiasticus 8.10 (for this see Israel Lévi, The Hebrew Text of the Book of Eccle-siasticus, Leiden, E. J. Brill, 1951) with the meaning 'to kindle,' and some modern English translations like S-G, Mft, and TT want to read the same meaning in Amos 5.6. However, there is no evidence of the use of such a verb or such an Accadic loan verb (so H. Zimmern, Akkadische Fremdwörter als Beweis für babylonischen Kultureinfluss, Leipzig, 1914, and Sellin and Weiser) in the time of Amos, and, moreover, such a read-ing presupposes a change of the Hebrew text (ba'esh for ka'esh). In the case of Ecclesiasticus, the LXX uses the transitive verb ekkaiō (see J. Ziegler, Sapientia Iesu Filii Sirach, Septuaginta XII/2, Göttingen, 1965), though it should be recognized that a verb like analampō could not be used since its transitive meaning seems to be exclusively metaphorical. Did, then, the LXX translator of Amos presuppose the use of a same Hebrew verb as in Ecclesiasticus and did he--rightly or wrongly--think it to have both a transitive and intransitive meaning? Though the LXX rendering is very dynamic, its equivalence is still questionable.

8. See Eugene A. Nida and Charles R. Taber, The Theory and Practice of Translation, Leiden: E. J. Brill.

9. Bethel, which gives the necessary connection with verse 5, has rightly been maintained and not eliminated as in some modern English translations, or replaced by "(the house of) Israel" (NAB, NEB, Mft) as in LXX, which gives the generic information tōi oikōi Israel, thus harmo-nizing the overall information of the text. However, the Targum, Aquila, Symmachus, Theodotion, and the Vulgate support the MT.

10. Since G. A. Smith (in The Expositors Bible, 1896) up to the present time (see recently Wolff, op. cit., ad loc.) it has been taken that an original hoy preceding the participle form has been skipped. According to Mays (op. cit., ad loc.) restoration of a hoy is not neces-sary since the definite plural participle used alone may have the effect of a woe-pronouncement. It would be a typical feature of Amos' style to characterize the receptors by means of this device. See also E. Gersten-berger, "The Woe Oracles of the Prophets," Journal of Biblical Literature 81, 1962, pp. 252, 254.

11. NEB "that turn justice upside down" seems to follow Budde and Maag's proposal to read hophekhim lema'alah, the last word being the supposed reading of the LXX. Wolff (op. cit., p. 269f.) has clearly shown that such a reading is highly improbable.

12. This plant belongs to the genus artemisia and is therefore called artemisia absinthium or, with regard to the Palestinian variety, artemisia judaica. See Fauna and Flora of the Bible, p. 198, and M. Zohary, Plant Life of Palestine: Chronica Botanica, New Series of Plant Science Books 33, 1962, p. 134.

13. There are sufficient arguments to consider His name is the Lord as the final verse of the strophe, in which case one is left with the puzzle of verse 9. It is hard, if not impossible, to say what verse 9 is:

perhaps an isolated fragment of another hymn, perhaps the beginning of
the next strophe, perhaps something else. On the other hand, one has to
translate the traditional Hebrew text, and it cannot be denied that in
that text verse 9 belongs to verse 8. To say, as some commentators do,
that verse 9 belongs to verse 8 but that its connection with the context
cannot be determined, is not very helpful. If there is a relationship
between verses 9 and 8, such a relationship has to be determined.

Some modern English translations like NEB and TT give a completely
different translation of verse 9 in that they read the names of stars in
verse 9. Though such a translation should be rejected on the base of
arguments given below, it at least has the advantage of making a clear
link between verse 9 and the opening line of verse 8. Because of this
relationship, NEB restructures the text in such a way that it transposes
the line "his name is the Lord" from the end of verse 8 to the end of
verse 9.

It should be observed that NAB makes exactly the same transposition,
but that its translation of verse 9 is the traditional one. This seems to
be a much more acceptable solution. But in that case some relationship
must exist between the theme of destruction in verse 9 and the theme of
the last lines of verse 8: He calls for the waters of the sea/and pours
them out on the earth.

14. This is also true of the first line of verse 8, since for the
original reader this line certainly alluded to a myth or legend of which
we do not know the details.

15. Even the Hebrew vocabulary is not technical, and the reference
to stars is only indirect, so the ancient translators sometimes missed
the meaning. So LXX: poiōn panta kai metaskeuazōn, "who makes everything
and changes it." Is panta a translation of the etymological meaning of
kimah? K. Vollers (Das Dodekapropheton der Alexandriner, Zeitschrift für
die alttestamentliche Wissenschaft 3, 1883, pp. 219-272, and 4, 1884, pp.
1-20) proposed a Hebrew Vorlage kol uyeseb which is, however, extremely
doubtful. LXX may have missed the meaning because of the isolated reference to stars within the total context and the lack of parallelism. So
this line became rather a topic, and a good one!

16. So G. Fohrer, Hiob, Kommentar zum Alten Testament XVI, 1963,
p. 206. Compare also Friedrich Horst, Hiob, Biblischer Kommentar XVI/1,
1968, p. 146. See also S. Mowinckel, Die Sternnamen im Alten Testament,
Supplement to Norsk Teologisk Tidskrift, 29, Oslo, 1928.

17. In all these cases it is a question of restructuring and not
a text-critical operation of transferring this line to the beginning of
verse 8 because of the supposed loss of some initial words (so Harper).

18. Numerous changes of the Hebrew text have been proposed, but they
are either completely unnecessary or translationally irrelevant. Most of
these changes are proposed on the basis of the LXX. Some of these dis-
regard any translational activity on the side of the LXX translator. A
repetition of the same Hebrew word in parallelism may be strange, but it
cannot be stated with Ewald, Nowack, Sellin, Robinson, Budde, Maag,
Amsler and others that the Hebrew text read originally sheber instead of
the first shod, because of the LXX translation suntrimmon. In the first
place, the LXX translation of sheber is not concordant; in the second
place, who wants to deny translators the right to use stylistic variants?
Van Hoonacker rightly stresses this particular point. One may have to

change yabo' into yabi', but this is a minor operation without relevance
for a dynamic translation. To do this on the basis of the LXX is nevertheless doubtful, since here too the translator may have used some transformation. The verb blg poses most problems, but even there MT is not
impossible (see Koehler-Baumgartner, s.v.). Moreover, this verb is presupposed by Aquila and Symmachus.

NEB offers the following peculiar translation: "who makes Taurus
rise after Capella and Taurus set hard on the rising of the Vintager,"
which is essentially the reading of TT (although the latter uses more
common language). Such a reading has to be rejected on the following
grounds: (a) it presupposes minor changes of the Hebrew text; (b) its
information is uninteresting and makes no sense after the information of
verse 8 (so rightly Wellhausen, ad loc.). G. Hoffmann [Versuche zu Amos,
Zeitschrift für die alttestamentliche Wissenschaft 3, 1883, p. 107ff.]
was the first to read here the names of three constellations. He has been
followed by others, especially more recently by G. R. Driver ["Two Astro-
nomical Passages in the Old Testament," Journal of Theological Studies
(Oxford), 4, 1953, pp. 208-212], whose influence on NEB is undeniable. The
versions never understood and could perhaps never have understood the
text in such a way. (c) its information in such terms would be incomprehensible, not only for many readers of the present day but also for many,
if not all, readers of the source.

19. The final literary composition presents several layers of the
tradition which are artificially connected with each other. This particular division has marked disadvantages, since it obscures other existing
relationships. Verse 12 presents the reason for the punishment announced
in verses 16-17, so that these verses belong together. In the light of
this relationship one could envisage a division into two paragraphs,
respectively verses 7+10-11 and verses 12-17. But then the particular
character of verses 14-15 and also to a certain extent that of verse 13
will be left unmarked, so that the relationships within the paragraph
12-17 remain rather obscure.

As a way to solve this problem, Mft tries to save the relationship
between verses 12 and 16 by putting verse 13 between round brackets and
by putting verses 14-15 at the end of the chapter between double square
brackets. However, this implies a surgery of the text which does not belong to the task of the translator. Moreover, it cannot be denied that
certain relationships exist between verse 4b, verses 7+10-12 on the one
hand and verses 14-15 on the other, and these are relationships within
the same section, so that it seems to be unjustified to remove verses
14-15 from this section. Thus it may be concluded that although no paragraph division is completely satisfactory, the one we propose structures
the material more clearly and reflects the overall structure of the book.

20. Another unifying feature is that all these words are spoken by
Amos, even verse 12. Verse 13 presents particular problems which will be
dealt with below. However, it is clear that there is a ground-implication
relationship between verses 12 and 13. Verse 12 not only provides the
ground for the Lord's punishment in verses 16-17, but also for a certain
human attitude which is described in verse 13. For that reason, verse 13
belongs to this particular paragraph.

21. See the discussion in A Translator's Handbook on Ruth, 4.1. It
should be noted that in Tell en-Nasbeh an area has been found with long

stone benches outside the gate. See C. C. McCown, Tell en-Nasbeh I, Berkeley and New Haven, 1947, p. 196.

22. Compare W. R. Harper, op. cit., ad loc.: "'Abhor' is a synonym of 'hate,' but stronger." Unfortunately, it can never be known what the connotative meaning of these verbs exactly was.

23. The two Hebrew participles present semantically both an object and an event. For some scholars the focus here is upon the object and consequently they think of two officials, respectively the judge and the advocate of the innocent. (For the first, see, among others, Wolff, op. cit., ad loc.; for the second, see especially Maag, op. cit., p. 30: "den Anwalt des Unschuldigen.")

However, apart from the fact that such distinctions are rather modern, the Hebrew evidence for the second case is not very strong. So it seems much better to focus upon the event expressed by both participles. With regard to the first participle, it would still be possible to think of such a specific activity as presenting someone's case before the court (so NEB: "You that hate a man who brings the wrongdoer to court").

24. Such a restructuring may seem particularly necessary in the case of verse 11b, since the Hebrew construction (a first clause stating an activity and a second one stating its futility) has the very peculiar form of what has been called futility curses. See especially D. R. Hillers, "Treaty Curses and the Old Testament Prophets," Biblica et Orientalia 16, 1964, p. 28f. Other biblical examples of this particular form can be found in Hos 4.10; Micah 6.14f.; Lev 26.26b; Deut 28.30; 38-41. A non-biblical example is the Sfire text given in Donner-Röllig, op. cit., nr. 222A, 22-24.

25. NEB in reading "you levy taxes on the poor" is the only modern English translation which follows the reading beshaskhem proposed by H. Torczyner (in Journal of the Palestine Oriental Society 16, 1936, p. 6f.) on the basis of Accadian šabāsu šibsa ("to levy taxes"). This reading has been accepted by Maag, Amsler, Wolff and Mays. See also Koehler-Baumgartner, Lexikon s.v. bshṣ. The other translations still follow Wellhausen's proposal to read buskhem. Both readings imply, of course, a change of the Hebrew text. The traditional proposal has, however, the advantage of being based on the Hebrew itself and of offering a very simple explanation of how the actual Hebrew form came into being. Moreover, it is in agreement with the LXX: katekondulizete "you oppressed" (this metaphorical meaning of the Greek verb is certainly to be preferred to the literal meaning "strike with the fist," which Wolff proposes). Torczyner's proposal has the disadvantage of having to depend on arguments from comparative philology and to presuppose in addition a metathesis. Its only advantage is that the obtained meaning gives a good parallel to the next half line. Semantically, the difference between the two readings is simply that of generic and specific information, since "levy taxes" is certainly an "oppression." The reverse is not true, and so the traditional reading should be preferred in translation, since it includes the other.

26. See Wolff, op. cit., p. 292: the poor are "von ihrem Recht abgedrängt." Compare also Mft: "defrauding the poor of justice."

27. Questions have been asked as to the identity of the speaker. Is Amos speaking here or one of his pupils? Or does this sentence only contain an observation made by a reader? Also, the identity of the "wise man"

has been questioned. If Amos is speaking here, does he allude to his own wisdom, or does he refer to the wise in general? As to the statement itself, does it include some form of evaluation or is it a strictly neutral one? Why are the wise keeping quiet, because of the injustices in court or because of the judgment of God? All these questions are no doubt valid, but it will be hard to provide a fully satisfactory and objective answer to them, as can be seen from the very different opinions expressed by commentators. Fortunately, the answers to these questions do not seem to have any direct bearing upon translation.

Commentators are usually silent about the verb 'to be silent.' It can be questioned whether 'to be silent' is really the meaning of the Hebrew verb, although recent investigations have shown that this is most probably the correct translation. See especially E. Y. Kutscher, Mittelhebräisch und Jüdisch-Aramäisch im neuen Köhler-Baumgartner, in Hebräische Wortforschung, Festschrift zum 80, Geburtstag von Walter Baumgartner, Leiden, 1967, pp. 158-175. Kutscher discusses the possibility that the Hebrew root dmm might have the meaning 'to complain,' but he finally accepts the meaning 'to be silent' on the base of Lieberman's argument that in the printed editions of the Tosephta the root dmm, present in the manuscripts, has often been changed into the current root shtq (art. cit., p. 167).

28. See especially F. Hesse, Amos 5.4-6, 14f., Zeitschrift für die alttestamentliche Wissenschaft 68, 1956, pp. 1-17.

29. So rightly Mays, op. cit., p. 100; Wolff, op. cit., ad loc. ("bedacht sein auf," "besorgt sein um"), and C. Westermann, Kerygma und Dogma 6, 1960, p. 15.

5.16-17   LAMENT FOR ISRAEL

1. All attempts to maintain the construction of the MT and to get reasonable sense out of it are rather far-fetched. The best solution remains Wellhausen's proposal to move the second ʾel and put it in front of the preceding noun. It is not true that there is no text-critical ground for such a change (against van Gelderen), since such a reading is presupposed by the Vulgate: et vocabunt agricolam ad luctum et ad planctum eos qui sciunt plangere. It may be true that the LXX already presupposes the MT, but it should be noted that the main group of Lucian, the subgroup 62-147 and the margin of 86 read eis kopeton and that the Lucianic subgroup 46-86(!)-711 reads kai eidotas thrēnon. Compare also the Syriac version.

2. So H. Gese, Kleine Beiträge zum Verständnis des Amosbuches, Vetus Testamentum 12, 1962, pp. 417-438, especially p. 432f., and Koehler-Baumgartner, s.v. ʾikar.

3. Mays (op. cit., ad loc.) follows Gese's proposal (art. cit., p. 434) to read koremim "vineyard workers." However, Wolff is certainly right in stating that the parallel locatives in verse 16 make such a reading improbable.

4. According to Sellin (op. cit., ad loc.) this would also be true of Hebrew culture ("in den Weinbergen findet keine Totenklage statt") and that is one of the reasons why he considers verse 17a as a gloss.

[245]

1. This text furnishes the earliest datable reference to the day of the Lord and scholars have engaged in long discussions about the origin of this idea and its meaning to Amos' contemporaries. See the commentaries and the literature on the different hypotheses (mythical, liturgical, and historical) provided there. However, these discussions have no direct bearing on translation.

2. See Gesenius-Kautzsch, Grammar, par. 136c.

3. So Elhorst, van Hoonacker, Touzard, Sellin, Cripps, van Gelderen, Robinson-Horst, Maag, Amsler, Wolff. The only clear exceptions are Harper and Mays.

4. The Hebrew has only one subject and uses a chain of consecutive perfect tenses expressing a continuation of the story. So rightly Joüon, par. 119q.

5. Such a reading is justified by the explanatory character of the second 'and' in the Hebrew text. However, in view of its last word (lo), the second Hebrew half line could also be considered as an independent nominal clause which provides an affirmative answer to the question in the first half line.

6. The text has been rendered in this way by the LXX and by some modern translations such as BJ.

7. Those who think that the day of the Lord originally means the day of the Lord's manifestation during the New Year festival certainly see a close connection between the two sections 18-20 and 21-27.

8. See Brockelmann, Syntax, par. 133b, and idem, Grundriss, par. 294.

9. See D. B. Long, "Further Comments on the Chokwe Translation," The Bible Translator 5, 1954, pp. 87-96.

10. The Hebrew for the beginning of this verse has some problems, but most translations follow the solution shown in the RSV and TEV. "For though you present burnt offerings to me..." disturbs the regular parallelism of the context. This dependent clause has sometimes been considered as a gloss and not been translated (Mft) or has been transposed after verse 23 and connected with the independent clause verse 24 (so NAB). Neither of these solutions seems to be satisfactory. It would be better to say that of the original sentence the conditional clause is left while the concluding clause is missing. So several scholars reconstructed the original concluding clause, but the different results clearly demonstrate that no certain conclusion is possible. Budde reconstructed the apodosis as lo' 'esmah (I will not rejoice), Sellin as lo' 'ennahem (I will not change my mind), and Morgenstern as lo' 'eqahinah miyyadekhem (I will not accept them from your hands).

On the other hand, it is also possible to find the concluding clause in the next Hebrew line. This solution lies behind some of the ancient versions (LXX: dioti ean enegkēte moi holokautōmata kai thusias humōn ou prosdexomai and Vulgate: quod si adtuleritis mihi holocaustomata et munera vestra non suscipiam), and also behind most modern English translations including TEV. It should be noted that semantically there is almost no difference between the last two approaches.

11. Compare E. A. Nida, Bible Translating, p. 234.

12. So Koehler-Baumgartner, Lexicon, s.v. shlm. It is true that this is the only place in the Old Testament where the singular shelem occurs.

However, a "correction" into a plural form is unnecessary. In a Punic inscription (in the offer-tariff from Marseille) from the fourth century the singular is found: shlm kll (for the text see Corpus Inscriptionum Semiticarum I, 165). According to R. Dussaud (Les origines cananéennes du sacrifice israélite, Paris, 1921, p. 142ff.) this would mean 'holocaust' and this meaning has been accepted as probable by Charles F. Jean and Jacob Hoftijzer (Dictionnaire des inscriptions sémitiques de l'ouest, Leiden, 1965, s.v. kll$_2$). On the other hand, Cooke, (op. cit., p. 118) does not consider Punic shlm as a specific kind of offering. He thinks shlm kll to be a subordinate kind of kll which seems to correspond with Koehler's conception of Hebrew shelem.

13. In the light of this primary emphasis it does not seem to be necessary to name the particular kind of offering in the translation (cf. Mft) and thus create a secondary focus, which was probably never intended by the author. So Maag, op. cit., p. 203: "Die vorexilischen Propheten scheinen sich im allgemeinen um die besonderen Abstufungen innerhalb der Gattung zbḥ nicht weiter gekümmert zu haben, Amos aber will hier gerade eine möglichst vollständige Aufzählung des kultischen Vielerlei bieten." Of course, the connective nominal phrase "offerings of your fatted beasts" must be restructured so that the focus is expressed.

14. This was the Assyrian style. For pictures see J. P. Pritchard, op. cit., 200; H. Gressmann, Altorientalische Bilder zum Alten Testament, 1927, 151, and C. H. Kraeling, "Music in the Bible," New Oxford History of Music I (Ancient and Oriental Music, edited by E. Wellesz), 1959, Plate VIIIa.

15. Some commentators do not interpret the verbal form as a jussive one, but as a future, and they understand the divine justice and righteousness with which the Lord will either judge or save Israel. But such an interpretation seems to be linguistically impossible. The interpretation of judgment is especially to be found in van Hoonacker and Weiser; the interpretation of salvation has again been given recently by J. Ph. Hyatt, "The Translation and Meaning of Amos 5.23-24," Zeitschrift für die alttestamentliche Wissenschaft 68, 1956, pp. 17-24. However, if the Lord's justice and righteousness were intended, the use of explicit first person possessive suffixes "my justice" and "my righteousness" would have been obligatory (so rightly Amsler). There are limits to the implicitness of information in the communication process! Moreover, the discourse structure of the paragraph makes such an interpretation impossible. It is significant that Weiser has to rearrange the discourse for his interpretation.

16. Semantically, it seems to be without interest to discuss at length whether ʾeythan means here "strong-flowing" or "ever-flowing." The first meaning has especially been defended by R. Smend in his discussion of the Hebrew text of Sirach 40.13 (Die Weisheit des Jesus Sirach erklärt, Berlin, 1906, ad loc.), it has been considered by Hammershaimb (op. cit., ad loc.), and it is given in some private translations (so Morgenstern: "a mighty stream"). Even if "strong-flowing" should be the primary meaning, it certainly includes the meaning "ever-flowing."

17. So clearly the Syriac version. The only thing one can say with certainty about the LXX and Vulgate is that they opt for the past tense. In all the printed editions of the LXX, the question mark appears at the end of verse 25.

18. It is only defended by older commentators, especially Calvin and Keil.

19. One of the exceptions is the Dutch New Version. This interpretation came up especially in the last century with Ewald, and since then it has been followed by such scholars as Graf, Valeton, Elhorst, van Hoonacker, Touzard, Cripps, Robinson-Horst, Weiser, Morgenstern, and Mays. Compare, however, already CD 7.14, 15 (edition C. Rabin, The Zadokite Documents, Oxford, 1958, ad loc.).

20. So Guthe, Marti, Sellin, Maag, E. Würthwein (Amos 5.21-27, Theologische Literaturzeitung 72, 1947, pp. 144-152; see also his article "Kultpolemik oder Kultbescheid?" in Festschrift A. Weiser, 1963, pp. 115-131), van Gelderen, L. H. K. Bleeker (De kleine profeten I, Hosea, Amos, Groningen, 1932, ad loc.), Amsler, Wolff.

21. Especially R. G. Bratcher (ed.), Old Testament Quotations in the New Testament (Helps for Translators 3), New York, 1967, and Barclay M. Newman and Eugene A. Nida, A Translator's Handbook on the Acts of the Apostles (Helps for Translators 12), London, 1972.

22. Even rather literal English translations restructure the text by reversing the order of "your images" and "the star of your god," following the LXX. Such a restructuring does not, of course, imply that the order of the LXX is the original one! In addition, they render "the star of your god" with "your star-god" (RSV, Mft, NAB), and although such a rendering may not be defensible on the grammatical level, it certainly is acceptable on the level of semantics!

23. NEB interprets this verse in a completely different way, one which is improbable according to the Hebrew and is based upon cuts made in the transmitted text.

24. See also the treatment of the quotation of this verse in Acts 7.43 in B. M. Newman and E. A. Nida, A Translator's Handbook on the Acts of the Apostles, London, 1972, ad loc. For the textual relationships between Hebrew texts, versions, and the New Testament, see J. de Waard, A Comparative Study of the Old Testament Text in the Dead Sea Scrolls and in the New Testament, Leiden, 1966, pp. 41-47.

25. Compare Jean Clavaud, "Problems Encountered in Translating the New Testament into Modern Cambodian," The Bible Translator 24, 1973, pp. 419-422.

26. Compare O. Eissfeldt, Lade und Stierbild, Zeitschrift für die alttestamentliche Wissenschaft 58, 1940/41, pp. 190-215. For archeological evidence, see also J. P. Pritchard, op. cit., 535.

27. This may originally have been the case here, too. It has been observed that the sentence "says the Lord, the God of hosts" at the end of verse 8a is clearly redundant (the reason why it is rarely translated). It may have been placed there by scribal error, having stood originally at the end of verse 7. Therefore, some modern English translations like S-G and Mft put this sentence at the end of verse 7 and thus characterize this verse as a word of the Lord. The translator may very well follow this example. Even if he does not want to reconstruct the text, he may nevertheless translate in this way, since the verdict is normally given by the Lord.

28. The Hebrew text cannot be changed one way or another, as unfortunately Mft has done.

29. See E. A. Nida, "Difficult Words and Phrases," The Bible Translator 1, 1950, pp. 25-29, and Newberry Cox, "Translation Problems in
Conob," The Bible Translator 1, 1950, pp. 91-96.
30. Because of these obscurities, several scholars consider the text
corrupt and propose changes. Some of these have been taken over by Mft
and TT. Mft reads "who are like gods in Israel," following S. Oettli's
proposal (Amos und Hosea, 1901, p. 72) to read the text as wekhe²lohym
(hemmah) bebheyt yisra²el. This proposal has become extremely popular,
and it has been adopted by many recent scholars (Robinson, Weiser, Maag,
Morgenstern). It still figures as a probable (!) reading in Elliger's
edition in Biblia Hebraica Stuttgartensia, in spite of the fact that the
Hebrew consonantal text has to be changed in at least four different
places and no ancient version can be quoted in support of such changes.
The reading of TT: "you people of Israel, go from one important nation to
another and visit them" reflects Torrey's proposal (Journal of Biblical
Literature 13, p. 62f.) to read nqphw for nqbhy and to connect this sentence with the following verse. However, even apart from a necessary
change of text, the connection with verse 2 is impossible on the ground
of the discourse structure.
A new solution has been proposed very recently by W. L. Holladay
(Amos VI 1 Bβ: A Suggested Solution, Vetus Testamentum 22, 1972, pp. 107-
110). He reads the sentence in the following way: tebhu²ath leḥem beyt
yisra'el, and together with the understanding of re²shit as "first fruits"
he obtained the following reading of the Hebrew line: "the pick of the
first (fruits) of the nations,/the harvest of bread (food) of the house
of Israel."
However, the proposed solutions are very diverse and unconvincing,
and they lack textual support. So the translator is encouraged to stay
with the Hebrew text and try to make some sense out of it.
31. Such an interpretation requires a change of text: one will have
to read "are you better" instead of "are they better" and "is your territory greater than theirs" instead of "is their territory greater than
yours" (so Mft, NAB, NEB). But such a change has no textual support and,
moreover, it goes against the facts. More than that, the territory of
these city-states is smaller than that of Israel! Also, this interpretation presupposes a destruction of these towns, something which had not
yet taken place, so that whoever wants to maintain this interpretation
has to consider it as a later insertion. So only the other interpretation
in the text can be retained (with Sellin, van Gelderen, Maag, Amsler,
Mays).
32. As a matter of fact, TEV follows neither the first nor the second
interpretation and its text is incomprehensible. The use of past tenses
were and was seems to imply that those cities no longer exist although
nothing is explicitly said about their destruction. But the possessive
suffixes are not interchanged so that the implied negative answer to the
questions becomes fully meaningless. The text of TEV could be used if the
past were changed into a present: "are they...," "is their...," but even
then it is not very helpful for languages in which rhetorical questions
do not exist.
33. See The Westminster Historical Atlas to the Bible, Plate XI A,
and F. M. Abel, Géographie de la Palestine, Tome II, Paris, 1967, p. 101.

34. So Sellin and Maag. See especially Maag's excursus pp. 170-172.
He translates the Hebrew verb with "wegbeschwören."

35. As proposed by Wellhausen. Most recent commentators like Wolff,
Hammershaimb, and Mays have returned to Wellhausen's interpretation. It
has at least the advantage of being supported by the Vulgate: solio
iniquitatis.

36. Such a necessary restructuring in which 'reign' becomes implicit
in the expression "time of violence" and in which the time component becomes
explicit, has, of course, nothing to do with the adaptation of the emendation shenath hamas (year of violence), first proposed by Gressmann and
later by Maag, Amsler, Elliger (Biblia Hebraica Stuttgartensia), and
Koehler-Baumgartner (Hebräisches und Aramäisches Lexikon zum Alten Testament, Lieferung II, Leiden, 1974, s.v. yshbh). It only shows that in the
deep structure, emendations are sometimes not very different from the
transmitted text, in spite of their very different surface form.

37. Brown-Driver-Briggs (s.v. srh) rightly speak of a "contemptuous
hyperbole."

38. So the explicit translation of the Targum: ʿal ʿarṣan dimkhabeshan
beshen. See Alexander Sperber, The Bible in Aramaic, Vol. III: The Latter
Prophets according to Targum Jonathan, Leiden, 1962, ad loc.

39. See Jean Clavaud, art. cit., p. 420.

40. So van Hoonacker, van Gelderen, Robinson, Wolff.

41. So Oort, Elhorst, Harper, Wellhausen, Nowack, Sellin, Bleeker,
Maag, Amsler, Morgenstern, Mays.

42. It has been understood (a) in the general sense of 'to sing'
(S-G; so Vulgate: qui canitis ad vocem psalterii, and J. A. Montgomery
[Journal of Biblical Literature, 1906, p. 51] on the basis of Samaritan
evidence), or 'to play' (so the Targum according to the first and second
Rabbinic Bible of Bamberg, which uses a verb ngn: 'make music,' 'play'),
(b) in the specific meanings of 'shout' (BJ; so Wellhausen, Sellin, van
Gelderen, Bleeker, Maag, Wolff. Compare Arabic phurūt), 'croon' (Mft,
Dhorme), or 'play short notes' (so Morgenstern: "to split," "to break into fine pieces." Compare Hebrew peret, Lev 19.10); (c) in the sense of
'improvise' (NAB,TT: "you make up songs"; so Touzard, Hammershaimb, Mays,
Köhler comparing Arabic phārit [improvisator]); and (d) in the sense of
'to pluck' (NEB: "you who pluck the strings of the lute"). Also in comparison with Hebrew peret, Lev 19.10. Compare also LXX epikrotountes which
can mean 'rattle on, over,' 'strike with a rattling sound' or 'snap.'
However, the Greek verb is normally followed by an accusative or instru-
mental dative. The use of the preposition pros in the LXX implies probably
that the verb is used in the sense of 'to clap.' So van Hoonacker, Amsler:
"s'agiter," "battre des mains." NEB's rendering "strings of the lute" is
hardly possible and this in turn makes the interpretation 'to pluck' highly improbable.

43. For archeological evidence of the vessel concerned, see A. M.
Honeyman, "The Pottery Vessels of the Old Testament," Palestine Explora-
tion Quarterly, 1939, p. 83f., and Plate XIX, Figure 6. See also J. P.
Pritchard, Die Archäologie und das Alte Testament, Wiesbaden (without
date), p. 48 and Plate 14.

44. On the other hand, the LXX has the quality of the wine in mind:
ton diulismenon oinon "wine filtered thoroughly," and it is followed in
this by the Syriac version. Although this reading makes excellent sense

in a context in which everywhere quality is stressed (furniture, meat, oil), it nevertheless presupposes a slightly different Hebrew reading: bimzuqqeqey yayin, which is hardly original. The Vulgate supports the MT: bibentes in fialis vinum, and even the Targum does so indirectly, though in its text it is neither the quantity nor the quality which is stressed but rather the quality of the bowls, which were made of silver.

However, because of the overall use of typical religious terminology in this verse, some scholars think that the reproach is directed against the use of sacrificial bowls, from which it was not permissible to drink. In making such information explicit, TT renders: "you drink wine from sacred bowls." But the total discourse, verses 4-6a, makes such an interpretation highly improbable. Moreover, none of the ancient versions understood the text this way. Even if the vocabulary of this verse were to contain allusions to certain religious practices, the stress remains on the luxurious life of the leaders. So the meaning given in NEB and TEV should be taken as the correct one.

45. Even when taken in a temporal sense, it belongs to the introductory 'therefore' and not to the following statement, so that an explicit translation would be: "therefore it is now valid that..."

46. It occurs only here and in Jer 16.5, although in the latter text it is associated with mourning. It is, however, very well attested in Punic, Phoenician, and other inscriptions, where it has the certainly not unrelated two meanings of "(religious) association or brotherhood" and "(religious) feast (with symposium)." See H. Donner-W. Röllig, op. cit., nr. 60, line 1, and nr. 69, line 16; Charles F. Jean-Jacob Hoftijzer, Dictionnaire..., s.v., mrzh; J. Cantineau, Le Nabateen, Vol. II, Paris, 1932, p. 118: "sorte d'association religieuse avec festin annuel" and H. Gressmann, hē koinōnia tōn daimoniōn, Zeitschrift für die neutestament-liche Wissenschaft 20, 1921, pp. 224-230. For the relationship of the two meanings in Ugaritic, see the observation in Donner-Röllig, Vol. II, p. 73: "In Ugarit scheint das Wort eine Art religiöse Gemeinschaft zu bezeichnen, vielleicht die Gemeinde, die zusammen den mrzh begeht."

In accordance with this usage, some of the ancient versions prefer to take the Hebrew word in the sense of 'association' (so Symmachus: kai periairethēsetai hetairia truphētōn, and Vulgate: auferetur factio lascivientium), and they are followed in this by such modern translations as Mft ("that dissolute crew shall disappear") and Dhorme.

47. Such a translation does not, of course, imply that Symmachus' reading truphētōn (of those who live luxuriously) is followed! It only shows that languages can independently make the same kind of transformation.

48. It is possible that the Hebrew formula reflects an ancient rite of touching the throat during oath-taking, and that later on the word for 'throat' became a dead metaphor equivalent to the reflexive pronoun. See the examples from Mari quoted by Wolff (op. cit., p. 326) and the literature quoted there. One wonders how the same author (ibidem, p. 324) knows that a translation 'himself' is an undertranslation because it does not communicate "dass in nphsh immer noch das mitschwingt, worauf jemand als Person begehrend und verlangend aus ist." There are certainly parallels for this in other languages in which one, for example, swears literally by "the head of the body," which means, nothing more than "one's very self."

49. So Maag: "Wohntürme." See especially p. 125f.

50. NEB translates: "city and all in it I will abandon to their fate." Such a translation sounds, however, rather anachronistic.

51. The proposal, made by Matthes, Elhorst, Hoffman and Morgenstern to vocalize umillo'ah and to read "and its fortress" is more ingenious than convincing.

52. Does the Lord continue to speak in verse 9 and almost to the end of verse 10, and does the prophet after the final hush give a kind of theological commentary in the last sentence of verse 10 and in verse 11? Or is the prophet speaking throughout this paragraph? Whether it is partly or wholly the prophet who is speaking or one of his pupils is fully secondary in this respect.

53. In many parts of the world it is not unusual for ten people to live in one or two rooms.

54. The LXX has the following extra: kai hupoleiphthesontai hoi kataloipoi (and the rest will remain). It cannot be said with certainty where this supplementary information comes from. LXX could be based upon a different Hebrew Vorlage reading, nish'ar she'ar, but such a Vorlage is unattested up till now. Dependent upon such a presupposed Vorlage or independent from it, the reading could also present a kind of commentary mitigating the hard punishment (see Wolff). More probably, however, it is an explicit statement of some implicit information which explains the entrance of the new participants in verse 10.

55. Because of the difficulties presented by this first Hebrew sentence, many changes in the Hebrew text have been proposed, some of which are reflected in modern English translations like Mft and NAB. But there are no objective bases for such changes.

56. Some translations even changed the Hebrew text in such a way that they make a woman out of the survivor (so Mft)! Such a procedure should not be followed.

57. So especially Harper and Duhm.

58. So G. R. Driver (A Hebrew Burial Custom, Zeitschrift für die alttestamentliche Wissenschaft 66, 1954, pp. 314-315) who postulates a general Semitic root ṣrph with the meaning 'embalm.'

59. For the meaning 'maternal uncle' see especially B. Felsenthal, Zur Erklärung von Amos 6.10, in Semitic Studies in Memory of Rev. Dr. Alexander Kohut, Berlin, 1897, pp. 133-137. For the generic meaning 'relative' see Ibn Caspi's observation quoted by Gruenberg in Jahrbuch der jüdischen literarischen Gesellschaft, Berlin, 1928, p. 284f.

60. The Vulgate thinks of the first meaning (et tollet eum propinquus suus et conburet eum), the Syriac version of the second. It cannot be excluded that both meanings were originally related. For an impressive defense of this, see especially Maag, op. cit., pp. 164-167.

61. The concise form of the expression is partly due to the fact that in Hebrew (as well as in Semitic languages in general) one can combine a command and its carrying out. Instead of saying, "he tells him to smite, and he smites," one can say "he tells him, and he smites."

62. This is the truth in Duhm's and Sellin's arguments. Only, it should not be stated that such information was explicitly to be found in the original Hebrew text!

63. Such a transformation does not mean, of course, that one changes the active Hebrew verb wehikkah into a passive one wehukkah, as has been

proposed by Weiser and Maag.

64. LXX succeeded in translating with a similar assonance: thlasmasi and ragmasin.

65. The style of this verse is typical of the technique of folk wisdom which makes its point through leading questions and comparisons (cf. 3.3-8). See also R. B. Y. Scott, "Folk Proverbs of the Ancient East," Transactions of the Royal Society of Canada 55, 1961, pp. 52f. In particular the second rhetorical question of Amos 6.12 seems to reflect a more widely spread folk wisdom as is shown by the Latin parallels in Ovid: Non profecturis litora bubus aras (Heroides V, 116) and Nec sinet ille, tuos litus arare boves (Tristia V, 48). The exceptional absence of a concluding announcement of punishment does not mean that this verse is only a fragment. It has a unity in itself.

66. For the impersonal use of the third person singular, see Joüon, par. 155e.

67. This division bbqr ym was first proposed by J. D. Michaelis in Deutsche Ubersetzung des Alten Testaments I, 1772(!).

68. See I. Löw, Die Flora der Juden, I, Vienna, 1928, p. 387, and Fauna and Flora of the Bible, p. 167f.

69. So Targum: "you have turned judgment into the poison of evil serpents."

70. Targum: lo'midda'am (nothing) and nikhsyn (possessions, herds); LXX: oudeni logōi and kerata; Symmachus: alogos and ∅; Vulgate: in nihili and cornua. Only the Syriac version reads in verse 13b qerita' (town).

71. The formula may originally have stood at the end of the saying, or it may be a secondary addition.

72. The first name has been translated as "the entrance of Hamath" (RSV, S-G); "the approach to Hamath" (TT), "Labo of Hamath" (NAB), "Lebo-hamath" (NEB), "the pass of Hamath" (Mft, TEV). The second name has been translated as "the brook of the Arabah" (RSV, TEV, S-G), "the gorge of the Arabah" and "the Wadi (of the) Arabah" (TT, NAB, Mft). With regard to the first geographical name, all of these are possible, but none is certain.

7.1-9 THE PROPHET'S EXPERIENCES

1. Of modern translations, NEB proposes quite a different reading: "a swarm of locusts hatched out," which may go back to versional evidence, but there is no reason to abandon the Hebrew text or its vocalization. NEB may render as an event the LXX interpretation (epigonē) of a differently vocalized Hebrew y ts r (yetser) or interpret in a specific way the emendation yotse' proposed by Gressmann and Maag. Who knows? Also, the Targum and the Syriac version are based on a reading yetser, but the Vulgate supports MT: fictor locustae. There is no reason to abandon the Hebrew text or its vocalization.

2. See especially John A. Thompson, "Translation of the Words for Locust " The Bible Translator 25, 1974, pp. 405-411.

3. So Syriac leqshā. See C. Brockelmann, Lexicon Syriacum, 1928, s.v.

4. See G. Dalman, Arbeit und Sitte I, p. 409f.; J. Pedersen, op. cit., III-IV, p. 70: "A chance allusion in Amos shows us that the first mowings of the grass were reserved for the king, of course for his horses and his mules, which were indispensable especially for the army"; R. de Vaux, op. cit., I, p. 217: "Le roi paraît encore avoir eu un droit sur la première

coupe des herbages, Am 7 1, peut-être comparable au droit de pacage qu'exerçait le souverain d'Ugarit." On the other hand, Power (Note to Amos 7.1, Biblica 8, 1927, p. 87ff.) thinks only corn can be meant since according to Palestinian culture only corn was cut.

5. So W. R. Smith, Religion of the Semites, London, 1927, p. 246.

6. According to Sellin, op. cit., ad loc.

7. So van Gelderen, op. cit., ad loc. The interpretation of the sentence as an anacoluthon has already been defended by Studer in 1888 and by W. Riedel in 1902 (Alttestamentliche Untersuchungen I, pp. 19-36: Bemerkungen zum Buche Amos) according to the references in Budde, op. cit., ad loc.

8. Following C. C. Torrey's proposal (in Journal of Biblical Literature 13, 1894, p. 63) to read: wayehi hu' mekalleh. For wehayah as scribal mistake for wayehi, see Joüon, par. 119z.

9. See E. A. Nida, "Difficult Words and Phrases," The Bible Translator 1, 1950, pp. 25-29; L. and E. Twyman, "Suki Translation," The Bible Translator 4, 1953, pp. 91-95.

10. More literally even: "as who can Jacob stand?" For mi as accusative of circumstance, see Gesenius' Hebrew Grammar, par. 118m ff. Compare also A Translator's Handbook on Ruth, 3.16.

11. See W. Eichrodt, Theology of the Old Testament I, 1961, pp. 216f. Many modern English translations have used the verb "to relent" (S-G, Mft, NEB, TT), which apart from the primary meaning of "abandon harsh intention" has an additional meaning of "compassion." However, observe that (a) the particular emotive component of the English verb is absent from the Hebrew verb, since no forgiveness is implied, and that (b) such a typical English verb may not help the translator in other languages.

12. It may be rendered either "He was calling to punish by fire" or "He was calling the fire to punish." Commentators usually propose changing the Hebrew text, but the translator should be careful about following such changes, since the ancient versions presupposed the transmitted Hebrew text. The only change of text which can be taken into consideration consists, like in verse 2, of a redistribution of the consonants of the Hebrew text. The result will then be: "he was summoning a rain of fire," reading lerabib 'esh. This reading has first been proposed by M. Krenkel, Zur Kritik und Exegese der kleinen Propheten, Zeitschrift für wissenschaftliche Theologie 14, 1886, p. 271, and it has been taken over again recently by D. R. Hillers, "Amos 7.4 and Ancient Parallels," Catholic Biblical Quarterly 26, 1964, pp. 221-225. This reading has been skillfully defended by Wolff. It remains therefore strange that Elliger (in Biblia Hebraica Stuttgartensia) does not mention this reading at all, but gives instead Elhorst's proposal to read lahebeth 'esh. Cf. Mft: "showed me himself calling down fire." However, the metaphor "rain of fire" can rarely be translated literally, the necessary restructuring of this reading will partly correspond with that of the traditional reading, and "punishment" certainly remains the implicit aim.

13. It has a meter 3+3, 4, and verse 9a shows a synonymous parallelism with crosswise arrangement of subject and predicate.

14. In agreement with the introductory formulae of the preceding vision-reports, many scholars want to supply the subject of the second sentence, "the Lord" in the Hebrew text, here. In fact, LXX (houtōs edeikse moy kurios kai idou hestēkōs...) may reflect a Hebrew text in

which the position of wehinneh and 'adonay (or yhwh!) was inverted. One should, however, be careful not to jump to conclusions, since LXX may simply be translational. This is what has happened in some of the Vulgate manuscripts. Although all manuscripts read the second sentence as et ecce Dominus stans, some manuscripts read the first sentence as haec ostendit mihi dominus (A M) and others as haec ostendit mihi dominus deus (C), and so they make the implicit object explicit.

As far as translation is concerned, it is not very relevant at this point whether one wants to make such a textual transposition or not since it will be necessary in translation to make the subject of "standing" explicit, regardless of how the text is read. If such a transposition is made, the subject of the participle "standing" remains implicit as in the first vision-report. For this the same reason could be quoted as in verse 1: the focus is not on the person but, in this case, on the object which is shown. However, translators will then have to state explicitly the subject of "standing." Since the implicit subject is most probably "the Lord," the translation will not be different from that of the transmitted text.

15. NEB makes another subject explicit by reading: "there was a man standing," and it is likewise true that such a reading has some support from the ancient versions, but nevertheless it cannot be recommended. For the Greek manuscripts reading anēr hestēkōs see Ziegler, op. cit., ad loc. Such a reading presents new information and raises questions as to the identification of the participant. The phrase is therefore automatically in focus and contrasts with the intention of the reconstructed source text.

16. So among others Oort, Elhorst, Wellhausen, Cripps, Amsler, Hammershaimb, Wolff. Such a dittography existed already in the Vorlage of the ancient versions because they presuppose the reading of the MT. However, none of them took the Hebrew word to mean 'plumb line' (see below). It cannot be excluded that homath 'anak is an erroneous reading of an original homath 'eben (so Sellin and Maag), but such a reading would result in exactly the same translation.

17. The Hebrew word does not occur anywhere else in the Old Testament, so one must depend heavily upon information from cognate languages.

18. Van Hoonacker (op. cit., ad loc.) proposes to read hammat 'anak (de plomb brûlant), which reminds one of the death penalties described in the Mishnah (Sanhedrin 7.2): "...they set him in dung up to his knees and put a towel of coarse stuff within one of soft stuff and wrapt it around his neck; one witness pulled one end towards him and the other pulled one end towards him until he opened his mouth; a strip of lead (so Gemara 52a) was kindled and thrown into his mouth, and it went down to his stomach and burnt his entrails" (translation of Herbert Danby, The Mishnah, Oxford, 1954). See especially H. Junker, Zu Amos 7, 7-9, Biblica 17, 1936, pp. 359-364. The versions are of little help. LXX reads adamas (steel), Aquila ganōsis (varnishing), Theodotion tēkomenon (melted), Vulgate trulla cementarii (trowel of a bricklayer).

19. This is rightly felt by such scholars as Budde, Sellin, Robinson, and Maag. Only their proposal to read beqiroth (walls) instead of beqerebh (in the midst) has no textual support.

20. It is possible that the Hebrew expression setting a plumb line in the midst of my people Israel was an existing idiom for judgment or re-

minded one of a related idiom in which one of the terms belonging to the same semantic domain as "plumb line" was used. But evidence for this is completely lacking.

21. Weiser (op. cit., p. 185, note 1) observes: "Die mehrfach vertretene Deutung auf eine Prüfung des Volkes durch Jahwe mit dem Ergebnis, dass Israel nicht 'lotrecht' sei und deshalb keine Vergebung zu erwarten habe, trägt die entscheidende Gedankenverbindung in den Text ein und verwischt durch solche rationale Begründung den ursprünglichen Charakter des Wortes und der dahinterstehenden Offenbarung." First of all, what is implicit in the text is never "eingetragen," and second, Weiser never envisaged a translation of this text in an African language!

22. See W. F. Albright, The High Place in Ancient Palestine, Volume du congrès Strasbourg 1956, Supplements to Vetus Testamentum IV, Leiden, 1957, pp. 242-258.

23. The high places of Isaac may particularly refer to the sanctuary of Beersheba (see 5.5).

24. See Efrain Alphonse, "The Translator's Struggles," The Bible Translator 2, 1951, pp. 106-112, and D. B. Long, art. cit., p. 92.

25. Compare Ernest L. Richert, "How the Guhu-Samane Cult of 'Poro' Affects Translation," The Bible Translator 16, 1965, pp. 81-87.

7.10-17   THE PROPHET'S ROLE AND COMMISSION

1. So the narrative does not have the form of a biography but that of an "apophthegm" in which certain biographical data are used to prepare a prophetic saying.

2. This has been done in one of the ancient translations. So Targum: rabba'.

3. For a strong negative connotation, see especially P. Humbert (Un héros de la justice, Amos, Lausanne, 1918, p. 11): "Visionnaire, lui crie-t-on, le taxant ainsi d'halluciné dont la raison a sombré dans l'enthousiasme extatique et ne donne le jour qu'aux vaticinations les plus échevelées." Without going to such an extreme, many commentators basically agree with such a statement. One should compare Koehler-Baumgartner's interpretation (s.v. hoze: "abschätzig gebraucht"--no other texts than Amos 7.12!) with Maag's statement (op. cit., p. 147): "Ursprünglich aramäische Synonym zum genuin-hebräischen ra'ah wurde hazah zum Terminus für visionäres Schauen, für das eine verfeinerte Religiosität das alltägliche ra'ah nicht mehr anzuwenden liebte."

4. For the dativus commodi which cannot be reproduced on the word level of translation, see Joüon, par. 133d.

5. Adding to this confusion the translator may also observe that some translations have a present tense in the text and a past one as alternative reading (NEB) or a past tense in the text and a present one in a note (TT).

6. Among more recent researchers the present tense has been defended by, among others, Nötscher, Maag, Neher, E. Baumann (Eine Einzelheit, Zeitschrift für die alttestamentliche Wissenschaft 64, 1952, p. 62), Deden, Fosbroke, R. Hentschke (Die Stellung der vorexilischen Schriftpropheten zum Kultus, Beihefte Zeitschrift für die alttestamentliche Wissenschaft 75, 1957, pp. 149-152), S. Lehming, (Erwägungen zu Amos, Zeitschrift für Theologie und Kirche 55, 1958, pp. 145-169), R. Smend

(Das Nein des Amos, Evangelische Theologie 23, 1963, pp. 416-418), Wolff, Hammershaimb. On the other hand, the past tense has been defended by, among others, H. H. Rowley (Was Amos a Nabi?, Festschrift O. Eissfeldt, 1947, pp. 194ff.), Cripps, Würthwein, Osty, R. E. Clements (Prophecy and Covenant, 1965, p. 36f.), H. Graf Reventlow (Das Amt des Propheten bei Amos, Forschungen zur Religion und Literatur des Alten und Neuen Testaments 80, 1962, pp. 14-24), Mays.

7. Three things make a present tense more likely: (a) verse 14 is an answer to what Amaziah is saying in verses 12-13, that Amos is a typical professional prophet; (b) verse 14 is a strong independent statement, not only an introductory sentence to verse 15; (c) the past tense in verse 15 is a flashback which serves to determine the present.

8. The translation herdsman presupposes a generic meaning of the corresponding Hebrew word, which is probably correct. In the case of a hapax like boqer, however, it is hard to be sure. In view of its derivation from baqar one thinks first of all of a specific meaning 'cowherd' (so Aquila, Symmachus, Theodotion and Quinta: boukolos). But the information in verse 15 deals with sheep and goats (tso'n). So LXX adapts boqer to this information and renders it with aipolos (goatherd). It seems easier, however, to presuppose a more general meaning for boqer in verse 14. To take boqer as a corruption of noqed (see 1.1) with Marti, Duhm, Sellin, Maag, Amsler, Hammershaimb, and to render "shepherd" (compare S-G, NAB) lacks any textual foundation. The fact that the Targum has the same rendering in 1.1 and 7.14 does not mean that it had noqed in its Vorlage of 7.14.

9. Compare Symmachus' reading echōn sukomorous.

10. It is possible that the Hebrew verb implies a technical treatment of making the fruits edible by nipping them with a nail or with iron. It is such a treatment which has been rendered in the LXX: knizōn sukamina (who makes incisions in sycamore figs). Compare also Theodotion: charassōn sukaminous. Another example of explicit information can be quoted from the Targum which underlines the fact that the trees in question only grew in the plains (ly bshphyl'). It is, however, doubtful whether the translator should make all this information explicit in his translation since it is certainly not foregrounded in this particular text.

11. Compare the Targum: "Prophesy not against Israel, and teach not against the house of Isaac."

12. For cultural information on the contemporary Middle East, see A. Musil, Arabia Petraea III, 1908, p. 293.

8.1-3   THE PROPHET'S EXPERIENCES (FOURTH VISION)

1. It is probably right to speak of a specific type of vision, since examples can be adduced from elsewhere. So S. E. Loewenstamm (klwb qyts, A Remark on the Typology of the Prophetic Vision, Tarbiz 34, 1964/65, pp. 319-322) quotes the example of Alexander the Great, who, during the siege of Tyre, had a vision of a dancing satyr and got the following explanation: sē Turos (Tyre is yours).

2. One of the English translations (Mft) removes verse 3 from its actual context to insert it into verse 10. This is no doubt done because of the thematic link between both verses mentioned above. But in this way verse 3 looses its transitional function and the parallel character with

7.9 (not removed in the same translation!). Such a procedure should not be followed.

3. The word occurs only twice in the Old Testament (here in the sense of 'basket' and in Jer 5.27 with the meaning of 'cage').

4. So rightly Harper, op. cit., ad loc. For the etymology, see especially W. Baumgartner, Die Etymologie von hebräisch Kelub Korb, Theologische Zeitschrift 7, 1951, p. 77f. One has probably to think of a derivation from a root klb with the meaning 'to bind,' 'to plait.' Compare Ethiopian karabō (basket) and Tigre karba (fasten). For the latter, see E. Littmann and M. Höfner, Wörterbuch der Tigre Sprache, Wiesbaden, 1962, 399b.

5. For the arguments see Wolff, op. cit., ad loc.

6. This was done in many of the ancient versions. Both participants have been made explicit (although syntactically in different ways) in the Lucian recension (main group + first subgroup), the Syriac, Achmimic, Sahidic, and part of the Ethiopic translations, as well as in the Latin codex Constantiensis. Only the speaker has been made explicit in the marginal reading of 86 and only the addressee in the second Lucianic subgroup and the Arabic translation. Lack of consideration of translation techniques can lead to such a wrong statement as that the Syriac version adds both participants according to the analogy of 7.8! (Against Wolff, op. cit., p. 366).

7. The sound-play was not necessarily the same in Amos' days. Both words may have been homonyms. See B. D. Rahtjen, "A Critical Note on Amos 8.1-2," Journal of Biblical Literature 83, 1964, pp. 416-417, and Donner-Röllig, op. cit., nr. 182.

8. For the impossibility of the traditional translation see the commentaries, especially Maag, op. cit., p. 154f. Van Gelderen (op. cit., p. 224f.) gives an impressive defense of part of the traditional reading, namely, shiroth, but remains completely unable to explain the semotactic context of the verb yalal. Unfortunately, the ancient versions are of no help in this matter.

8.4--9.4   GOD WILL PUNISH ISRAEL

1. This vision does not have the parallels of wording which the previous visions have and occupies a very different structural position in the book of Amos.

2. Quoting people's own testimony against themselves is one of Amos' favorite devices (4.1; 6.2,13).

3. The Hebrew text of this verse presents a number of textual difficulties, but except for a slight change of vocalization of the first verbal form (vocalizing hasha'phim with LXX [ektribontes]) it seems quite unnecessary to make any alterations. All modern English translations, with the exception of NEB, present the same understanding of the text. As so often in NEB, readings which are presented as probable (like 'plunder' here) are in fact most improbable. For a defense of the construction welashbith, see Jouon, par. 124p, and Gesenius-Kautzsch, par. 114p. The great majority of emendations which have been proposed are semantically without interest and do not influence the translation.

4. A number of commentators take the view that the quotation is only contained in the first line of the Hebrew text of verse 5 and that start-

ing from the second line of the Hebrew text the prophet speaks again (so recently again E. Hammershaimb). Also, two English translations (S-G and Mft) are in favor of such a view. However, syntactically such a position can hardly be defended. Moreover, it would destroy to a large extent the device of a self-incriminating testimony, which Amos is using here.

5. Such a translation should not be taken to imply that "sabbath" is derived from the Hebrew verb šbt ("to rest"). On the contrary, the verb is derived from the noun, which, in turn, comes from a Babylonian word whose precise meaning is not certain.

6. With Elhorst, Duhm, Robinson, Weiser, and Wolff.

7. For the ephah, see the discussion in A Translator's Handbook on Ruth, pp. 39-40. See also R. B. Y. Scott, "Weights and Measures of the Bible," The Biblical Archaeologist 22, 1959, pp. 22-40.

8. Some scholars take the expression the pride of Jacob in the sense it had in 6.8 ("arrogance"). Yahweh would then be swearing "sarcastically by the unchangeable fact" of Jacob's pride (Wellhausen, op. cit., p. 93). If "pride" is understood positively ("majesty"), then Yahweh would be swearing seriously (see van Gelderen, op. cit., pp. 233-236). Some of the ancient versions take the pride of Jacob in the unfavorable sense of 6.8, but then they let the Lord swear against it (so LXX omnuei kurios kath' huperēphanias Iakōb and Vulgate iuravit Dominus in superbia Iacob). However, the Hebrew preposition cannot have that meaning.

9. This solution is rightly defended by several commentators (so, among others, Marti [op. cit., p. 217: "So wahr ich der Stolz Jakobs bin, vergesse ich nie eure Thaten"], Weiser, Amsler, Hammershaimb, Mays). It is also found in the Syriac, which reads: "The Lord, the Mighty One of Jacob, has sworn."

10. Some English translations keep the Hebrew form, rendering verse 8 either as one continuous rhetorical question (RSV, NAB) or as two separate ones (Mft). Others render the first half of the verse as one (TT) or two (NEB) rhetorical question(s), but they formulate the second half as a positive statement. Probably this is done not for translational reasons but on the (wrong) textual assumption that only the first line of the Hebrew text is a rhetorical question.

11. The explanation of the difficulty is probably that verse 8 was originally a separate saying, which has been added secondarily to its present context.

12. Reading, as universally accepted, kaye'or for MT kha'or ("like light").

13. In accordance with the qere.

14. wenigreshah is missing in the parallel text 9.5 and in the LXX (kai anabēsetai hōs potamos sunteleia kai katabēsetai hōs potamos Aiguptou; compare, on the other hand, the translation of wenigreshah in Symmachus and Theodotion: kai eksōsthēsetai). Metrically, it does not match the regular meter 3+3, and its character as a gloss can easily be explained by the necessity to correct the preceding corrupt reading kha'or.

15. It has been calculated that eclipses of the sun took place on February 9th, 784 B.C. and on June 15th, 763 B.C. The former was a complete eclipse. The eclipse of 763 B.C. is mentioned in an Assyrian text. See R. W. Rogers, Cuneiform Parallels to the Old Testament, New York, 1912, p. 233.

16. See especially Jahnow, op. cit., p. 22, and E. Kutsch,
"Trauerbräuche" und "Selbstminderungsriten" im Alten Testament,
Theologische Studien 78, 1965, pp. 25-42. The shaving of the head is mentioned in the Old Testament in relation to Moabites (Isa 15.2), Phoenicians (Ezek 27.31) and Philistines (Jer 47.5). With regard to the wearing
of sackcloth: on the Ahiram sarcophagus there are women who have sackcloth
on their loins and are naked to their waists. See H. Gressmann, Bilder...,
illustration 665, and J. B. Pritchard, Pictures..., 459.

17. See J. de Waard, "The Translation of Some Figures of Speech from
Psalms in Bamiléké and Bamoun, "The Bible Translator 20, 1969, p. 145f.

18. See Gesenius' Hebrew Grammar, par. 122g.

19. It is rare in the Old Testament, occurring only five times: Exo
8.17; Lev 26.22; 2 Kgs 15.37; Ezek 14.13.

20. This translational necessity does not imply that one has to
'correct' with Maag the Hebrew text into debhary and to explain the MT by
a mistake of a copyist who took the original suffix y for an abbreviation
of the name of God.

21. See C. H. Doke, "The Points of the Compass in Bantu Languages,"
The Bible Translator 7, 1956, pp. 104-113, and A Translator's Handbook on
Luke, on Luke 13.29.

22. The Targum understands the phrase to refer to the nation as a
whole, which is compared with pretty girls: "In that day the assembly of
Israel (knysht' dysr'l) shall wander about, who are like pretty girls...
and they will be smitten and prostrated with thirst."

23. This has nothing to do with the unacceptable emendation
ha'ammitsim proposed by Sellin, Maag, and Morgenstern ("The Loss of Words
at the Ends of Lines in Manuscripts of Biblical Poetry," Hebrew Union
College Annual 25, 1954, pp. 41-63).

24. So wrongly van Hoonacker and Mays.

25. In one English translation (Mft) the last Hebrew line has been
transferred to the beginning and combined with the preceding verse in
the following way: "On that day they shall faint, faint, fall, and never
rise again, the maidens fair and stalwart youths, who swear..." It is no
doubt true that syntactically the Hebrew participle "who swear" is in
apposition to the grammatical subjects of verse 13. However, the mention
of girls and young men is a stylistic device, and it would be ridiculous
to suppose that what is said in verse 14 is restricted to young people.
Moreover, although the last Hebrew line of verse 14 is a kind of conclusion of verses 13 and 14, it should not be forgotten that verse 14 is a
clearly structured unit in itself: the first part gives the reason for
punishment, and the second part announces the punishment.

26. Doughty (Travels in Arabia Deserta, London, 1930, I, p. 269) has
pointed out that the nomadic population applies the oath-formula wahjâth
to inanimate objects such as coffee!

27. So Peshitta and Vulgate.

28. dodeka for derek. So, among others, Sellin, Zimmerli (Geschichte
und Tradition von Beerseba, 1932, p. 3), Galling, Maag, Deden, Hammershaimb.

29. (a) as a proper name of a god ("your God": S-G, TT); (b) as a
word meaning "love" ("By the life of your love": NAB), and (c) as a word
meaning "tutelary deity" ("As your Patron lives": Mft). None of these
meanings is absolutely certain. See Donner-Röllig's commentary on dwdh on
the Mesha stone (op. cit., II, p. 175) and M. Leahy, "The Popular Idea of

God in Amos," Irish Theological Quarterly 22, 1955, pp. 68-73. Finally, there may be a reference to Ugaritic drkt, which would lead to a meaning "power," (Ed. Jacob, Ras Shamra et l'Ancien Testament, 1963, p. 65f.; S. Bartina, "Vivit Potentia Beer-šeba!", Verbum Domini 34, 1956, pp. 202-210; Koehler-Baumgartner, Lexicon).

30. So LXX: kai zēy ho theos sou Bērsabee. The rather uniform LXX tradition certainly does not favor the tendency of some modern commentators like Budde, van Gelderen, and Wolff to do away with the LXX reading.

31. This time it is not the Lord who shows something to Amos, but it is Amos who sees the Lord (verse 1). The visual element is not elaborated, and there is no dialogue between God and the prophet. The vision only sets the stage for the saying of the Lord, which gets all the emphasis. Through these formal differences and especially through the particular focus on the divine word some kind of climax is reached. The content of the saying also completes the information of the preceding reports. In the fourth vision-report it was only said that the end had come; the fifth one portrays in what inevitable way it comes.

32. According to the transmitted Hebrew text, the content of the vision ends with the first sentence.

33. It has been suggested that the implicit addressee might have been a supernatural being such as an angel, an impersonal power of nature, or Amos himself. None of these suggestions is really satisfactory. A supernatural being or an impersonal power of nature would be a case of new information, and one would therefore expect an explicit statement in the source text. On the other hand, one can hardly imagine that the prophet would be capable of destroying a temple building. For that reason many commentators have proposed changing the Hebrew text in such a way that the Lord himself becomes the agent of the actions expressed in the following sentences. In order to make such a reading possible, the verbal phrase 'and he said' has to be placed at the end of the first Hebrew line, the first imperative has to be changed into 'he struck' (so that this event becomes part of the vision), and the second imperative (following now the verbal phrase 'and he said') has to be changed into a first person singular verbal form: 'I will break' (so essentially P. Volz [in Theologische Literaturzeitung 25, 1900, p. 291], Marti, Robinson, Weiser, Maag, Amsler, Wolff).

Unfortunately, sufficient textual support for such drastic changes is lacking. The only text which makes the Lord the agent of the destructive actions is the LXX manuscript 410: pataksō...kai diakopsō. The place of the corresponding verbal phrase kai eipe remains unchanged in this manuscript. So the translator should follow the modern English translations (with the exception of NEB, which has a strange mixture of imperative and first person singular which adds to the confusion) by maintaining the imperatives and by introducing them with the verbal phrase and he said or he gave the command, without making the addressee explicit.

34. Is this the reason why the addressee has been made explicit through the personal pronoun "me" in the Latin codex Constantiensis and in the Ethiopic version?

35. The translation "ceiling" probably goes back to a change of text, sippun being read for sippim.

36. The Vulgate clearly thought of the latter: superliminaria; the LXX understands the entrance in general (ta propula), whereas the Syriac

equivalent (from the Accadian <u>askuppatu</u>) has a more generic meaning, including that of "threshold."

37. For that reason many "improvements" of the text have been proposed in the commentaries, but many of these so-called "improvements" are even more obscure than the transmitted text. So the translator had better follow the traditional reading, which is found in all modern English translations with the exception of NEB. The <u>them</u> can refer to the last noun if that is taken to mean "lintels" or "<u>ceiling</u>," but it must refer to columns if the last noun is rendered with <u>thresholds</u> or <u>foundation</u>, which can hardly be broken off on the heads of <u>people</u>. Some <u>English</u> translations can be taken either way, but the translator should make sure that the meaning is clear.

38. See especially J. Pederson, <u>op. cit.</u>, I-II, pp. 460-462.

39. A rendering such as "if they <u>hide</u>" may be based on translational grounds, quite apart from the view that <u>minneged ʿeynay</u> is a later addition to the text (see especially Maag and <u>Wolff</u>).

40. The Hebrew word rendered <u>bottom</u> has this meaning only here; in other contexts it means the 'ground <u>floor</u>' (of a building).

9.5-6 THE POWER OF GOD TO PUNISH AND CREATE

1. For the translators of NAB, this episode has a syntactic relationship with verse 4b. So they take the information of verse 5a as a concluding sentence of the second half of the preceding verse: "I, the Lord God of hosts," and the participles throughout this episode as appositions to the first person. The result is that the Lord continues to be the speaker in this episode and remains in fact the speaker throughout the whole section. Although such a solution is not completely impossible and although it may be preferred in certain translational situations, there are nevertheless sufficient formal arguments to consider verses 5-6 as a distinct episode.

In the <u>Textual Notes on the New American Bible</u> it is said (p. 446) that the <u>waw</u> before ʾadonay has been omitted. The translation would, however, not necessarily change if the <u>waw</u> were maintained. One could see here the poetic use of an emphatic <u>waw</u>. Compare Joüon, par. 177n. However, many of the possessive suffixes have to be changed.

This does not mean, of course, that there is no thematic link with the preceding episode. Verses 5-6 underline again and in a different way the thought of verse 4b. Therefore that verse has the double function of recapitulating the information of the first episode and of introducing that of the second.

2. See Koehler-Baumgartner, <u>Lexikon</u>, ("wanken"), and especially P. Joüon, Notes de lexicographie hébraique, Biblica 7, 1926, pp. 165-168.

3. According to NAB there are two things which God does ("I melt the earth with my touch") which causes one single effect ("so that all who dwell on it mourn"), and this is also the conception of LXX: <u>ho ephaptomenos tēs gēs kai saleuōn autēn</u>.

4. The first Hebrew verb does not have the form of a participle and it interrupts formally the chain of participles with which each new line of verses 5-6 starts. For that reason, it has sometimes been thought that this particular line is a later edition, presumably taken from 8.8.

5. Others take the moving of the earth as happening at the same time

as the mourning: people mourn while the earth rises and falls like the Nile River. This kind of connection has been made in translations such as Mft, NAB, and TT.

6. Some of the English translations have "stair" (NEB) or "stairway" (TT); others have upper chambers or simply "chambers" (S-G, Mft) in the plural; others speak of "upper chamber" (NAB) in the singular. In fact, these various translations are to be found in ancient translations as well. The meaning "stair" is found in LXX (anabasis), Vulgate (ascensio), and Peshitta; the meaning "upper rooms" in Symmachus (ta huperōa autou). In MT there is a difference between the kethibh, which has the singular form, and the qere, which has the plural. LXX and Vulgate are in agreement with the kethibh; Peshitta and Symmachus agree with the qere.

7. In order to obtain this meaning, it may be necessary to change the Hebrew text into ʿaliyyathō. Apart from the usual confusion of yod and waw, MT can easily be explained by a dittography of the mem. But the dittography of the mem must then be very old, since the form of MT is confirmed by many of the versions and recently also by the fragments from Murabbaʾat. So P. Benoit, J. T. Milik and R. de Vaux, Les grottes de Murabbaʾāt, Discoveries in the Judaean Desert II, Oxford, 1961, 183. Perhaps the noun of MT could be considered as a nomen loci, in which case a change becomes semantically superfluous.

9.7-15   EPILOGUE: PUNISHMENT AND RE-CREATION OF ISRAEL

1. Those modern English translations which have section divisions and accordingly, use section headings normally make a division either after verse 8a (NAB, NEB) or after verse 8 (S-G). The first division is probably inspired by the fact that verse 8b contains a promise that the house of Jacob will not completely be destroyed, and this promise is taken as an introduction of the theme of restoration. However, in view of the content of verses 9 and 10 such a division can hardly stand. Even at a rather superficial reading it will be clear that the major division will have to be made after verse 10. Then verses 1-10 form one section, which gives an exposition of one central theme: the judgments of the Lord. Verses 11-15 form a second section, which deals with the theme of the future restoration of Israel (so rightly TEV; compare also BJ).

2. In verses 7-10 there are several themes which are connected with each other. In verse 7 the exodus is ranged along with migrations of other peoples; verse 8 combines in a curious way the themes of surveillance, destruction, and salvation; verses 9 and 10 take up again the theme of destruction, but verse 9 introduces a pictorial comparison drawn from agricultural life. Such a combination of different themes and styles in the actual composition makes it probable that these verses are a literary reflection of a discussion about the last vision. The opening verse clearly functions as a disputation saying.

3. LXX (huioi Aithiopōn) and Vulgate (filii Aethiopum) translate using the Hebraism "sons of."

4. This in spite of the identification of Caphtor with Kappadokia in the LXX, Symmachus, and Vulgate. Compare also the Targum: Kappotekaia. For this, see especially G. A. Wainwright, Caphtor-Cappadocia, Vetus Testamentum 6, 1956, pp. 199-210.

5. This does not imply, of course, that one has to change the Hebrew text into ʿeynay as suggested by Oort, Sellin, Robinson, Maag, and Amsler.

6. It would be possible to render the last sentence in the following way: "I will not at all destroy the house of Jacob." (For the unusual position of the negation before the infinitive absolute, see Joüon, par. 123o and Gesenius-Kautzsch, par. 113v.) However, the context is more in favor of the other possible translation: "I will not completely destroy the house of Jacob."

7. Much has been written about the identification of the sinful kingdom and the house of Jacob, and though these discussions are exegetically important, they are not relevant for translation.

8. There are no doubt a number of problems of interpretation, mainly due to the fact that the particular Hebrew word for sieve occurs only here, whereas the meaning of the Hebrew word normally rendered with 'pebble' remains a guess, although the guess is most probably right. So already Aquila: psēphion (small pebble), Vulgate: lapillus, and Targum: ʾbn.

9. "Grain" has been made explicit in a number of Vulgate manuscripts: sicut concutitur triticum in cribro. Sellin, Maag, and Osty think primarily of "sand."

10. Following some of the ancient versions (for example, LXX and Vulgate), most modern English versions (RSV, S-G, Mft, NAB) change the Hebrew text of the citation slightly, mainly but not exclusively with regard to vocalization, in order to obtain the reading "Disaster shall not reach or overtake us." NEB reproduces the transmitted Hebrew text by translating "Thou wilt not let disaster come near us or overtake us," and it is followed in this by TT and basically also by TEV. Although the proposed changes of text have the overwhelming support of the great majority of scholars, there seems to be no necessity to alter the transmitted source text. One could even say that the change of text leads to the loss of the disputation character of the saying, a loss which is translationally certainly significant. It also destroys the theme which began in 9.7, that Israel is wrong in counting on special treatment.

11. Within each of these two groups of sayings there are some important differences. Verse 11 is in poetic form, whereas verse 12 is in prose. Also, the third person plural subject of the verb in verse 12 has no antecedent in the preceding verse. The second group of sayings has been written as poetry, but here also there are certain tensions. Verses 14 and 15 elaborate the introductory theme (I will restore the fortunes of my people Israel), and the restoration is seen as a reversal of God's judgment. Such a view is absent from (or only implicit in) verse 13.

12. Therefore it seems utterly wrong to look for another basis for comparison such as 'shelter' (compare the modern English metaphor "umbrella"). (So Mays, op. cit., p. 164). If one does so, one has to say that the expressions used in the rest of the verse do not fit a 'hut.' However, at least in the restored Hebrew text, the image is consistent. The arguments to read feminine singular suffixes in verse 11b in agreement with LXX and Vulgate are most convincing.

13. Both a new verb and the nota accusativi before all the nations are lacking.

14. See especially K. Galling, "Die Ausrufung des Namens als Rechtsakt in Israel," Theologische Literaturzeitung 81, 1956, pp. 65-70.

15. So Driver, Gunkel, Mitchell, Keil, Nowack, Marti, Harper, von Orelli, Hammershaimb, and others.

16. So, among others, Gressmann, Duhm, Cripps, van Gelderen.

17. See E. Preuschen, Die Bedeutung von shwb shbwt im Alten Testamente, Zeitschrift für die Alttestamentliche Wissenschaft, 1895, pp. 1-74; E. L. Dietrich, Die endzeitliche Wiederherstellung bei den Propheten, Beihefte Zeitschrift für die Alttestamentliche Wissenschaft 40, 1925; E. Baumann, shwb shbwt, eine exegetische Untersuchung, Zeitschrift für die alttestamentliche Wissenschaft 47, 1929, pp. 17-44; M. A. Dupont-Sommer, Les inscriptions araméennes de Sfiré, 1958, p. 128.

18. Older English translations took the Hebrew noun to be of another root and they translated literally "to turn again the captivity," which seems less likely. This interpretation is still reflected in Mft: "when I bring back the exiles of my people Israel." Semantically the difference is not too important, since the latter meaning is included in the former.

NOTES TO APPENDIX

1. N. A. Mundhenk first called to our attention the balanced structure of this part of Amos and led us to investigate other similar aspects of the structure of the book.

2. The latter part of I could also be taken as ambiguous: the creation of water, or destruction through a flood. See also Appendix, Section 3.9.

3. There is an attempt to catalogue all of the published claims for chiastic structures in the Old Testament by Angelico di Marco, "Der Chiasmus in der Bibel" (in two parts), Linguistica Biblica 36 and 37, 1975 and 1976.

4. Wellhausen, op. cit., p. 75.

5. This was called to our attention by Hendrikus Boers.

6. This example of chiastic structure was reported by Nils Wilhelm Lund, "The Presence of Chiasmus in the Old Testament," American Journal of Semitic Languages 46, 1929/30, p. 108.

7. We have followed John Beekman and John Callow, Translating the Word of God, Grand Rapids, Michigan: Zondervan Publishing House, 1974, as a handy guide in determining these.

8. We are not saying that anything should be added to the text, but that implicitly the semantic content and ordering are as described.

9. The pattern in 5.4-6a was noted in Lund, op. cit. That of 5.14-15b was noted in Kenneth E. Bailey, A Study of Some Lucan Parables in the Light of Oriental Life and Poetic Style, St. Louis, Missouri: Concordia Seminary Doctoral Thesis, 1972, p. 68.

10. The graph is after Bailey, op. cit., p. 71, and Lund, op. cit., pp. 125-126.

11. N. A. Mundhenk made some helpful criticisms of an earlier attempt to analyze the structures in this display.

GLOSSARY

This glossary contains terms which are technical from an exegetical or a linguistic viewpoint. Other terms not defined here may be referred to in a Bible dictionary.

adjective is a word which limits, describes, or qualifies a noun. In English, "red," "tall," "beautiful," "important," etc., are adjectives.

borrowing is the process of using a foreign word in another language. See loan word.

climactic position is the place in a story or speech, etc., which is the most important or the turning point or the point of decision. See climax.

climax is the point in a story or speech, etc., which is the most important or the turning point or the point of decision.

condition is that which shows the circumstance under which something may be true. In English, a conditional phrase or clause is usually introduced by "if."

consequence is that which shows the result of a condition or event.

consonants were originally the only spoken sounds recorded in the Hebrew system of writing; vowels were added later as marks associated with the consonants.

construction. See structure.

context is that which precedes and/or follows any part of a discourse. For example, the context of a word or phrase in Scripture would be the other words and phrases associated with it in the sentence, paragraph, section, and even the entire book in which it occurs. The context of a term often affects its meaning, so that it does not mean exactly the same thing in one context as it does in another.

culture is the sum total of the ways of living built up by the people living in a certain geographic area. A culture is passed on from one generation to another, but undergoes development or gradual change.

cultural translation is that kind of translation in which certain details from the culture of the source language are changed because they have no meaning or may even carry a wrong meaning for speakers of the receptor language. Cultural translation should be used only when absolutely necessary for conveying the intended meaning, and it may be important to add an explanatory note.

[266]

discourse is the connected and continuous communication of thought by means of language, whether spoken or written. The way in which the elements of a discourse are arranged is called discourse structure. (In this Handbook, direct or indirect discourse is described as direct or indirect quotation.)

explicit refers to information which is expressed in the words of a discourse. This is in contrast to implicit information. See implicit.

generic has reference to all the members of a particular class or kind of objects. It is the contrary of specific. For example, the term "animal" is generic, while "dog" is specific. However, "dog" is generic in relation to "poodle."

idiom is a combination of terms whose meanings cannot be derived by adding up the meanings of the parts. "To hang one's head," "to have a green thumb," and "behind the eightball" are American idioms. Idioms almost always lose their meaning completely when translated from one language to another.

implicit refers to information that is not formally represented in a discourse, since it is assumed that it is already known to the receptor. This is in contrast to explicit information, which is expressed in the words of a discourse. See explicit.

irony is a sarcastic or humorous manner of discourse in which what is said is intended to express its opposite; for example, "That was a wise thing to do!" is intended to convey the meaning "That was a stupid thing to do."

kernel is a sentence pattern which is basic to the structure of a language. Kernels may also be called "basic sentence patterns," out of which more elaborate sentence structures may be formed.

level refers to the degree of difficulty characteristic of language usage by different constituencies or in different settings. A translation may, for example, be prepared for the level of elementary school children, for university students, for teen-agers, or for rural rather than urban people. Differences of level also are involved as to whether a particular discourse is formal, informal, casual, or intimate in nature.

loan word is a foreign word that is used in another language. See borrowing.

meter, in Hebrew poetry, refers to the measured number of accented words in a line. In most Hebrew poetry, a regular pattern is formed.

overlapping is the way in which part of the meanings of two words cover the same general area of meaning, although the remainder of the meanings covered by the two words is not the same. For example, "love" and "like" overlap in referring to affection.

[267]

parallelism is a form of style in which essentially the same message is repeated, using the same or a similar construction, but using different words that have similar or related meanings. The words that correspond to each other in the two statements are said to be parallel.

particle is a small word whose grammatical form does not change. In English the most common particles are prepositions and conjunctions.

passage is the text of Scripture in a specific location. It is usually thought of as comprising more than one verse, but it can be a single verse or part of a verse.

phrase is a grammatical construction of two or more words, but less than a complete clause or a sentence. A phrase is usually given a name according to its function in a sentence, such as "noun phrase," "verb phrase," "descriptive phrase," etc.

play on words in a discourse is the use of the similarity in the sounds of two words to produce a special effect. See pun.

premise is the logical basis for an idea or an action.

pronouns are words which are used in place of nouns, such as "he," "him," "his," "she," "we," "them," "who," "which," "this," "these," etc.

prose is the ordinary form of spoken or written language, without the special forms and structure of meter and rhythm which are characteristic of poetry.

pun is the use of similar sounds of two words to produce a special effect; usually humor is intended. See play on words.

quotation is the reporting of one person's speech by another person. Direct quotation is the reproduction of the actual words of one person embedded in the discourse of another person. For example, "He declared, 'I will have nothing to do with this man.'" Indirect quotation is the reporting of the words of one person in the discourse of another person in an altered grammatical form. For example, "He said he would have nothing to do with that man."

receptor is the person(s) receiving a message. The receptor language is the language into which a translation is made. The receptor culture is the culture of the people for whom a translation is made, especially when it differs radically from the culture of the people for whom the original message was written. See source language.

restructure is to reconstruct or rearrange. See structure.

rhythm is the periodic pattern of accented syllables in a line of poetry.

Semitic refers to a family of languages which includes Hebrew, Aramaic, and Arabic.

sentence is a grammatical construction composed of one or more clauses and capable of standing alone.

source language is the language in which the original message was produced. For the Old Testament it is the Hebrew language spoken at that time.

structure is the systematic arrangement of the form of language, including the ways in which words combine into phrases, phrases into clauses, and clauses into sentences. Because this process may be compared to the building of a house or a bridge, such words as structure and construction are used in reference to it. To separate and rearrange the various components of a sentence or other unit of discourse in the translation process is to restructure it.

style is a particular or characteristic manner in discourse. Each language has certain distinctive stylistic features which cannot be reproduced literally in another language. Within any language, certain groups of speakers may have their characteristic discourse styles, and among individual speakers and writers, each has his own style.

tense is a grammatically marked identifier of time, generally relative.

theme is the subject of a discourse.

tone is the spirit, character, or emotional effect of a passage or discourse.

transition in discourse involves passing from one thought-section or group of related thought-sections to another. Transitional words, phrases, or longer passages mark the connections between two such sets of related sections and help the hearer to understand the connection.

translation is the reproduction in a receptor language of the closest natural equivalent of a message in the source language, first, in terms of meaning, and second, in terms of style.

undertranslation is a translation that falls short of reproducing in the receptor language an equivalent of the message in the source language.

verbs are a grammatical class of words which express existence, action, or occurrence, as "be," "become," "run," "think," etc.

viewpoint is the place or situation or circumstance from which a speaker or writer presents a message. If, for example, the viewpoint place is the top of a hill, movement in the area will be described differently from the way one would describe it from the bottom of a hill. If the viewpoint person is a priest, he will speak of the temple in a way that differs from that of a common person.

[269]

vowels were not originally included in the Hebrew system of writing; they were added later as marks associated with the consonants.

INDEX

This index includes concepts, key words, and terms for which the Handbook contains a discussion useful for translators.

land 146,151,156-157,168
  heathen land 156-157
  unclean land 156-157
law(s) of the Lord 43-44
leaven 84
legs 71-73
Leviathan 175
light 116-117
lime 42
line, measuring line 156-157
lion 26,63-64,67,117
lo 93,142,182
locusts 89,143
Lodebar 136,138-139
Lord, the LORD 27,173
  Lord God 66
  Lord of hosts 74
  Lord's name 135
  Sovereign Lord 66

maiden 49
make (create) 93-94
mansions 132-133
melt 177,187
merchants 162-164
mercy 39,111
Mesha, king of Moab 22-23
message of the Lord 34,35,57-59
  authority of the message 30
mildew 88
Moab 28,33,41-42
mountains of Samaria 69
mourn, mourning 113,130,160,167,
  177-178
music 129-130

name 94,135,185
nation 139
Nazirite 46,52-53
new moon 163
noon 166

oak 51-52
oath 78,132,165,170-171
ocean (under the earth) 145-146
offerings 84,119-120,123
  burnt offerings, cereal offerings, grain offerings, peace
  offerings 119-120
officers 41
oil 130

olive tree 89
oppress, oppression 69-70,139
Orion 105
oxen 137

palace 33,160
pastures 27
pestilence 89-90
Philistia, Philistines 35-37
Phoenicians 37
plague 89-90
play on words 102,158-159
pledge 49
Pleiades 105
plot,plotting 151
plumb line 147-148
poetry, Hebrew poetry 10-15,26
poor 1,162,164
preach 156
pride of Jacob 165
priest 22,151
profane 49
prophesy 1-2,53-54,153,156
prophet 1-2,22,52-54,152-153
  prophet's son 154
pun 102,158-159
punishment 1-2,31-32,36-40,43-45,
  55-56,84,91-92,145,161,165

questions (rhetorical) 62-63,117,
  122,137,165
quotation
  indirect quotation 69,156
  quotations within quotations 76,
  151-152,183

Rabbah 40-41
Rahab 175
rave 156
rebel, rebellion 82-83
remnant 36,111
repent 144
restore the fortunes 187
reveal 23
righteous, righteousness 47,104,121
river 121
roar 26,63-64
rocks 137

sabbath 163
sackcloth 167